Early Childhood Education

08/09

Twenty-Ninth Edition

EDITOR

Karen Menke Paciorek
Eastern Michigan University

Karen Menke Paciorek is a professor of early childhood education at Eastern Michigan University in Ypsilanti. Her degrees in early childhood education include a BA from the University of Pittsburgh, an MA from George Washington University, and a PhD from Peabody College of Vanderbilt University. She is the editor of *Taking Sides: Clashing Views in Early Childhood Education (2nd. Ed.)* and co-edits, with Joyce Huth Munro, *Sources: Notable Selections in Early Childhood Education* both published by McGraw-Hill. She has served as president of the Michigan Association for the Education of Young Children, the Michigan Early Childhood Education Consortium and the Northville School Board. She presents at local, state, and national conferences on curriculum planning, guiding behavior, preparing the learning environment and working with families. She has served as a member of the Board of Education for the Northville Public Schools, Northville, Michigan since 2002 and is on the Board of Directors for Wolverine Human Services serving over 600 abused and delinquent youth in Michigan. Dr. Paciorek is a recipient of the Eastern Michigan University Distinguished Faculty Award for Service.

 **Higher Education**

D1400406

Boston   Burr Ridge, IL   Dubuque, IA   New York   San Francisco   St. Louis
Bangkok   Bogotá   Caracas   Kuala Lumpur   Lisbon   London   Madrid   Mexico City
Milan   Montreal   New Delhi   Santiago   Seoul   Singapore   Sydney   Taipei   Toronto

Higher Education

ANNUAL EDITIONS: EARLY CHILDHOOD EDUCATION, TWENTY-NINTH EDITION

Published by McGraw-Hill, a business unit of The McGraw-Hill Companies, Inc., 1221 Avenue of the Americas, New York, NY 10020.
Copyright © 2009 by The McGraw-Hill Companies, Inc. All rights reserved. Previous edition(s) 1979–2008. No part of this publication may be reproduced or distributed in any form or by any means, or stored in a database or retrieval system, without the prior written consent of The McGraw-Hill Companies, Inc., including, but not limited to, in any network or other electronic storage or transmission, or broadcast for distance learning.

Some ancillaries, including electronic and print components, may not be available to customers outside the United States.

Annual Editions® is a registered trademark of The McGraw-Hill Companies, Inc.
Annual Editions is published by the Contemporary Learning Series group within the McGraw-Hill Higher Education division.

1 2 3 4 5 6 7 8 9 0 QPD/QPD 0 9 8

ISBN 978–0–07–339774–0
MHID 0–0–7339774–1
ISSN 0270–4456

Managing Editor: *Larry Loeppke*
Senior Managing Editor: *Faye Schilling*
Developmental Editor: *Dave Welsh*
Editorial Assistant: *Nancy Meissner*
Production Service Assistant: *Rita Hingtgen*
Permissions Coordinator: *Lenny J. Behnke*
Senior Marketing Manager: *Julie Keck*
Marketing Communications Specialist: *Mary Klein*
Marketing Coordinator: *Alice Link*
Project Manager: *Sandy Wille*
Design Specialist: *Tara McDermott*
Senior Production Supervisor: *Laura Fuller*
Cover Graphics: *Kristine Jubeck*

Compositor: Hurix Systems Private Limited
Cover Images: Digital Vision/Getty Images (inset); Creatas/JupiterImages (background)

Library in Congress Cataloging-in-Publication Data
Main entry under title: Annual Editions: Early Childhood Education 2008/2009.
1. Early Childhood Education—I. Menke Paciorek, Karen, comp. II. Title: Early Childhood Education.
658'.05

www.mhhe.com

Editors/Advisory Board

Members of the Advisory Board are instrumental in the final selection of articles for each edition of ANNUAL EDITIONS. Their review of articles for content, level, currentness, and appropriateness provides critical direction to the editor and staff. We think that you will find their careful consideration well reflected in this volume.

EDITOR

Karen Menke Paciorek
Eastern Michigan University

ADVISORY BOARD

Fredalene Bowers
Indiana University of Pennsylvania

Erin Brumbaugh
Muskingum Community College

Linda C. Edwards
College of Charleston

Kathleen E. Fite
Texas State University

Kathleen Cranley Gallagher
*University of North Carolina
at Chapel Hill*

Alice R. Galper
Mount Vernon College

Alice S. Honig
Syracuse University

Joan Isenberg
George Mason University

Richard T. Johnson
University of Hawaii at Manoa

Katharine C. Kersey
Old Dominion University

George S. Morrison
University of North Texas

Karen L. Peterson
Washington State University

Jack V. Powell
University of Georgia

William H. Strader
Johnson & Wales University

Lewis H. Walker
Lander University

Harriet S. Worobey
Rutgers University

Preface

In publishing ANNUAL EDITIONS we recognize the enormous role played by the magazines, newspapers, and journals of the public press in providing current, first-rate educational information in a broad spectrum of interest areas. Many of these articles are appropriate for students, researchers, and professionals seeking accurate, current material to help bridge the gap between principles and theories and the real world. These articles, however, become more useful for study when those of lasting value are carefully collected, organized, indexed, and reproduced in a low-cost format, which provides easy and permanent access when the material is needed. That is the role played by ANNUAL EDITIONS.

*A*nnual Editions: Early Childhood Education has evolved over the 29 years it has been in existence to become one of the most used texts for students in early childhood education. This annual reader is used today at over 550 colleges and universities. In addition it may be found in public libraries, pediatricians' offices and teacher reference sections of school libraries. I work diligently throughout the year to find articles and bring you the best and most significant readings in the field. I realize this is a tremendous responsibility to provide a thorough review of the current literature—a responsibility I take very seriously. I am always on the lookout for possible articles for the next *Annual Editions: Early Childhood Education*. My goal is to provide the reader with a snapshot of the critical issues facing professionals in early childhood education this year. At the annual meeting each year for the National Association for the Education of Young Children I meet with members of the advisory board who provide very valuable feedback. The meeting in Chicago November 2007 was particularly successful and I thank the members of the advisory board for their suggestions.

Early childhood education is an interdisciplinary field that includes child development, family issues, educational practices, behavior guidance and curriculum. *Annual Editions: Early Childhood Education 08/09* brings you the latest information in the field from a wide variety of recent journals, newspapers, and magazines. There are four themes found in readings chosen for this twenty-ninth edition of *Annual Editions: Early Childhood Education*. They are: (1) the growing numbers of diverse learners. This trend was particularly noticeable and necessitated the establishment of an entire unit (Unit 3) dedicated to working with diverse learners and their families (2) the strong focus on early learning standards and the need for teachers to align their curriculum and learning experiences to meet the standards (3) the increasing attention given to the importance of children having access to a quality preschool experience and (4) the immense pressure to achieve placed on young children at ever decreasing ages. This is evident by the lack of free play observed in schools and to some extent at home as well.

It is especially gratifying to see issues affecting children and families covered in magazines other than professional association journals. The general public needs to be aware of the impact of positive early learning and family experiences on the growth and development of children.

Continuing in this edition of *Annual Editions: Early Childhood Education* are selected World Wide Web sites that can be used to further explore topics addressed in the articles. I have chosen to include only a few high-quality sites. Readers are encouraged to explore these sites on their own, or in collaboration with others for extended learning opportunities.

Given the wide range of topics included, *Annual Editions: Early Childhood Education 08/09* may be used by several groups—undergraduate or graduate students, professionals, parents or administrators—who want to develop an understanding of the critical issues in the field.

The selection of readings for this edition has been a cooperative effort between the editor and the advisory board members. I appreciate the time the advisory board members have taken to provide suggestions for improvement and possible articles for consideration. The production and editorial staff of McGraw-Hill, led by Larry Loeppke and David Welsh ably supported and coordinated my efforts.

To the instructor or reader interested in the history of early childhood care and education programs throughout the years, I invite you to view my other books, also published by McGraw-Hill. *Sources: Notable Selections in Early Childhood Education, 2nd edition* (1999) is a collection of 46 writings of enduring historical value by influential people in the field. All of the selections are primary sources that allow you to experience firsthand the thoughts and views of these important educators. *Taking Sides: Clashing Views on Controversial Issues in Early Childhood Education, 2nd edition* (2008) contains eighteen critical issues facing early childhood professionals or parents. The book can be used in a seminar or issues course.

I appreciate readers who have corresponded with me about the selection and organization of previous editions. Comments and articles sent for consideration are welcomed and will serve to modify future volumes. Take time to fill out and return the postage-paid article rating form on the last page. You may also contact me at: kpaciorek@emich.edu

I look forward to hearing from you.

Karen Menke Paciorek
Editor

Contents

UNIT 1
Perspectives

The concepts in bold italics are developed in the article. For further expansion, please refer to the Topic Guide.

UNIT 2
Young Children, Their Families and Communities

UNIT 3
Diverse Learners

The concepts in bold italics are developed in the article. For further expansion, please refer to the Topic Guide.

UNIT 4
Supporting Young Children's Development

UNIT 5
Educational Practices

The concepts in bold italics are developed in the article. For further expansion, please refer to the Topic Guide.

The concepts in bold italics are developed in the article. For further expansion, please refer to the Topic Guide.

UNIT 6
Helping Children to Thrive in School

UNIT 7
Curricular Issues

The concepts in bold italics are developed in the article. For further expansion, please refer to the Topic Guide.

The concepts in bold italics are developed in the article. For further expansion, please refer to the Topic Guide.

Correlation Guide

The *Annual Editions* series provides students with convenient, inexpensive access to current, carefully selected articles from the public press. **Annual Editions: Early Childhood Education 08/09** is an easy-to-use reader that presents issues on important topics such as *young children and their families, diverse learners, educational practices,* and *curricular issues in early childhood education.* For more information on *Annual Editions* and other *McGraw-Hill Contemporary Learning Series* titles, visit www.mhcls.com.

This convenient guide matches the units in **Annual Editions: Early Childhood Education 08/09** with the corresponding chapters in two of our best-selling McGraw-Hill Early Childhood Education textbooks by Gonzalez-Mena.

Annual Editions: Early Childhood Education 08/09	Foundations of Early Childhood Education: Teaching Children in Diverse Society, 4/e by Gonzalez-Mena	Diversity in Early Care and Education: Honoring Differences, 5/e by Gonzalez-Mena
Unit 1: Perspectives	**Chapter 4:** Facilitating Young Children's Work and Play **Chapter 8:** Setting Up the Physical Environment **Chapter 13:** Language and Emergent Literacy	**Chapter 1:** Perceiving and Responding to Differences
Unit 2: Young Children, Their Families and Communities	**Chapter 2:** First Things First: Health and Safety through Observation and Supervision **Chapter 5:** Guiding Young Children's Behavior **Chapter 7:** Modeling Adult Relationships in Early Childhood Settings **Chapter 9:** Creating a Social-Emotional Environment **Chapter 10:** Routines	**Chapter 4:** A Framework for Understanding Differences **Chapter 5:** Attachment and Separation **Chapter 7:** Socialization, Guidance, and Discipline
Unit 3: Diverse Learners	**Chapter 10:** Routines **Chapter 11:** Developmental Tasks as the Curriculum: How to Support Children at Each Stage	**Chapter 1:** Perceiving and Responding to Differences **Chapter 6:** Differing Perspectives on Learning through Play
Unit 4: Supporting Young Children's Development	**Chapter 1:** Early Childhood Education as a Profession **Chapter 4:** Facilitating Young Children's Work and Play **Chapter 8:** Setting Up the Physical Environment **Chapter 11:** Developmental Tasks as the Curriculum: How to Support Children at Each Stage	**Chapter 4:** A Framework for Understanding Differences
Unit 5: Educational Practices	**Chapter 4:** Facilitating Young Children's Work and Play **Chapter 6:** The Teacher as Model **Chapter 8:** Setting Up the Physical Environment **Chapter 12:** Observing, Recording, and Assessing	**Chapter 3:** Working with Diversity Issues
Unit 6: Helping Children to Thrive in School	**Chapter 3:** Communicating with Young Children **Chapter 13:** Language and Emergent Literacy	**Chapter 5:** Attachment and Separation
Unit 7: Curricular Issues	**Chapter 13:** Language and Emergent Literacy **Chapter 14:** Providing Developmentally Appropriate Experiences in Math and Science **Chapter 15:** Integrating Art, Music, and Social Studies into a Holistic Curriculum	**Chapter 7:** Socialization, Guidance, and Discipline

Topic Guide

This topic guide suggests how the selections in this book relate to the subjects covered in your course. You may want to use the topics listed on these pages to search the Web more easily.

On the following pages a number of Web sites have been gathered specifically for this book. They are arranged to reflect the units of this *Annual Edition*. You can link to these sites by going to the student online support site at *http://www.mhcls.com/online/*.

ALL THE ARTICLES THAT RELATE TO EACH TOPIC ARE LISTED BELOW THE BOLD-FACED TERM.

Academics test
1. The Changing Culture of Childhood

Accountability
4. Accountability Comes to Preschool
5. No Child Left Behind

Achievement
2. The Preschool Promise
6. Preschool Comes of Age
27. The Looping Classroom
28. The Case For and Against Homework

Advocacy
7. Taking a Stand
12. Giving Intervention a Head Start

Allergic/Allergies
9. Fear and Allergies in the Lunchroom

Assessment
4. Accountability Comes to Preschool

At-risk children
1. The Changing Culture of Childhood
3. Preschool Pays
5. No Child Left Behind
22. Scripted Curriculum

Behavior
30. Heading Off Disruptive Behavior

Best practices
5. No Child Left Behind
19. Research 101: Tools for Reading and Interpreting Early Childhood Research

Brain development
16. Reading Your Baby's Mind

Cost, educational
6. Preschool Comes of Age

Cultures
14. Creative Play
15. Helping Young Hispanic Learners

Curriculum
23. Rethinking Early Childhood Practices
35. The Plan
41. Meeting the Challenge of Math and Science

Development
11. Children of Teen Parents
21. Back to Basics
25. Successful Transition to Kindergarten

Developmentally appropriate practice
4. Accountability Comes to Preschool
21. Back to Basics
27. The Looping Classroom
28. The Case For and Against Homework

Differentiation
13. Including Children With Disabilities in Early Childhood Education Programs

Discipline
10. Supporting Grandparents Who Raise Grandchildren

Disabilities
13. Including Children With Disabilities in Early Childhood Education Programs

Diverse learners/Diversity
13. Including Children With Disabilities in Early Childhood Education Programs
15. Helping Young Hispanic Learners
27. The Looping Classroom

Documentation
36. One Teacher, 20 Preschoolers and a Goldfish

Emergent curriculum
35. The Plan
36. One Teacher, 20 Preschoolers and a Goldfish

Emotional competence
31. Relationships at the Forefront of Effective Practice

English language learners
14. Creative Play
15. Helping Young Hispanic Learners
27. The Looping Classroom

Environment
27. The Looping Classroom
39. Using Picture Books to Support Young Children's Literacy

Equipment/Materials
26. Making the Case for Play Policy

Families
8. Meeting of the Minds
10. Supporting Grandparents Who Raise Grandchildren
11. Children of Teen Parents
13. Including Children With Disabilities in Early Childhood Education Programs
14. Creative Play
15. Helping Young Hispanic Learners
20. What Can We Do To Prevent Childhood Obesity?
27. The Looping Classroom
28. The Case For and Against Homework
31. Relationships at the Forefront of Effective Practice
34. Fostering Positive Transitions for School Success

Internet References

The following Internet sites have been carefully researched and selected to support the articles found in this reader. The easiest way to access these selected sites is to go to our student online support site at *http://www.mhcls.com/online/*.

Annual Editions: Early Childhood Education 08/09

The following sites were available at the time of publication. Visit our Web site—we update our student online support site regularly to reflect any changes.

General Sources

Children's Defense Fund (CDF)
http://www.childrensdefense.org

At this site of the CDF, an organization that seeks to ensure that every child is treated fairly, there are reports and resources regarding current issues facing today's youth, along with national statistics on various subjects.

Connect for Kids
http://www.connectforkids.org

This nonprofit site provides news and information on issues affecting children and families, with over 1,500 helpful links to national and local resources.

National Association for the Education of Young Children
http://www.naeyc.org

The NAEYC Web site is a valuable tool for anyone working with young children. Also see the National Education Association site: http://www.nea.org.

U.S. Department of Education
http://www.ed.gov/pubs/TeachersGuide/

Government goals, projects, grants, and other educational programs are listed here as well as many links to teacher services and resources.

Unit 1: Perspectives

Child Care and Early Education Research Connections
www.researchconnections.org

This site offers excellent help for anyone looking for research based data related to early childhood education. Full text articles and other reference materials are available.

Child Care Directory: Care guide
http://www.care.com

Find licensed/registered child care by zip code at this site. See prescreened profiles and get free background checks on providers. Pages for parents along with additional links are also included.

Complementary Learning Approach to the Achievement Gap
http://www.gse.harvard.edu/hfrp/projects/complementary-learning.html

Complementary learning provides a variety of support services for all children to be successful. These supports reach beyond the school and work toward consistent learning and developmental outcomes for children.

Early Childhood Care and Development
http://www.ecdgroup.com

This site concerns international resources in support of children to age 8 and their families. It includes research and evaluation, policy matters, programming matters, and related Web sites.

Global SchoolNet Foundation
http://www.gsn.org

Access this site for multicultural education information. The site includes news for teachers, students, and parents as well as chat rooms, links to educational resources, programs, and contests and competitions.

Mid-Continent Research for Education and Learning
http://www.mcrel.org/standards-benchmarks

This site provides a listing of standards and benchmarks that include content descriptions from 112 significant subject areas and documents from across 14 content areas.

The National Association of State Boards of Education
http://www.nasbe.org/

Included on this site is an extensive overview of the No Child Left Behind Act. There are links to specific state's plans.

Unit 2: Young Children, Their Families and Communities

Administration for Children and Families
http://www.dhhs.gov

This site provides information on federally funded programs that promote the economic and social well-being of families, children, and communities.

The AARP Grandparent Information Center
http://www.aarp.org/grandparents

The center offers tips for raising grandchildren, activities, health and safety, visitations, and other resources to assist grandparents.

All About Asthma
http://pbskids.org/arthur/grownups/teacherguides/health/asthma_tips.html

This is a fact sheet/activity book featuring the popular TV character Arthur who has asthma. The site gives statistics and helps parents, teachers and children understand asthma. It gives tips on how to decrease asthma triggers. It has English, Spanish, Chinese, Vietnamese and Tagalog versions of some of the materials.

Allergy Kids
http://allergykids.com

Developed by Robyn O'Brien, a mother committed to helping children and families everywhere deal with allergies, this site is extremely valuable for all families and school personnel. Tip sheets are provided that can be shared with teachers and families as well as items for purchase to support allergic children.

Changing the Scene on Nutrition
http://www.fns.usda.gov/tn/Healthy/changing.html

This is a free toolkit for parents, school administrators, and teachers to help change the attitudes toward health and nutrition in their schools.

Children, Youth and Families Education and Research Network
www.cyfernet.org

This excellent site contains useful links to research from key universities and institutions. The categories include early childhood, school age, teens, parents and family and community.

The National Academy for Child Development

http://www.nacd.org

The NACD, an international organization, is dedicated to helping children and adults reach their full potential. Its home page presents links to various programs, research, and resources into such topics as learning disabilities, ADD/ADHD, brain injuries, autism, accelerated and gifted, and other similar topic areas.

National Network for Child Care

www.nncc.org

This network brings together the expertise of many land grant universities through their cooperative extension programs. These are the programs taped back in early 1965 to train the 41,000 teachers needed for the first Head Start programs that summer. The site contains information on over 1,000 publications and resources related to child care. Resources for local conferences in early childhood education are included.

National Safe Kids Campaign

http://www.babycenter.com

This site includes an easy-to-follow milestone chart and advice on when to call the doctor.

Zero to Three

http://www.zerotothree.org

Find here developmental information on the first 3 years of life—an excellent site for both parents and professionals.

Unit 3: Diverse Learners

American Academy of Pediatrics

www.aap.org

Pediatricians provided trusted advice for parents and teachers. The AAP official site includes position statements on a variety of topics related to the health and safety of young children.

Child Welfare League of America (CWLA)

http://www.cwla.org

The CWLA is the United States' oldest and largest organization devoted entirely to the well-being of vulnerable children and their families. Its Web site provides links to information about issues related to morality and values in education.

Classroom Connect

http://www.classroom.com/login/home.jhtml

A major Web site for K–12 teachers and students, this site provides links to schools, teachers, and resources online. It includes discussion of the use of technology in the classroom.

The Council for Exceptional Children

http://www.cec.sped.org/index.html

Information on identifying and teaching children with a variety of disabilities. The Council for Exceptional Children is the largest professional organization for special educators.

Early Learning Standards: Full report

http://www.naeyc.org/resources/position_statements/positions_2003.asp

This site provides the full joint position statement by the National Association for the Education of Young Children (NAEYC) and The National Association of Early Childhood Specialists in the State Department of Education (NAECS/SDE) on early learning standards.

Early Learning Standards: Executive Summary

http://www.naeyc.org/resources/position_statements/creating_conditions.asp

This site provides the executive summary for the joint position statement by the National Association for the Education of Young Children (NAEYC) and The National Association of Early Childhood Specialists in the State Department of Education (NAECS/SDE) on early learning standards.

Make Your Own Web page

http://www.teacherweb.com

Easy step-by-step directions for teachers at all levels to construct their own web page. Parents can log on and check out what is going on in their child's classroom.

National Resource Center for Health and Safety in Child Care

http://nrc.uchsc.edu

Search through this site's extensive links to find information on health and safety in child care. Health and safety tips are provided, as are other child-care information resources.

Online Innovation Institute

http://oii.org

A collaborative project among Internet-using educators, proponents of systemic reform, content-area experts, and teachers who desire professional growth, this site provides a learning environment for integrating the Internet into educators' individual teaching styles.

Unit 4: Supporting Young Children's Development

Action for Healthy Kids

www.actionforhealthykids.org

This organization works to assist the ever increasing numbers of students who are overweight, undernourished and sedentary. They feature a campaign for school wellness.

American Academy of Pediatrics

www.aap.org

Pediatricians provided trusted advice for parents and teachers. The AAP official site includes position statements on a variety of related to the health and safety of young children.

Unit 5: Educational Practices

Association for Childhood Education International (ACEI)

http://www.acei.org/

This site, established by the oldest professional early childhood education organization, describes the association, its programs, and the services it offers to both teachers and families.

Early Childhood Education Online

http://www.umaine.edu/eceol/

This site gives information on developmental guidelines and issues in the field, presents tips for observation and assessment, and gives information on advocacy.

Reggio Emilia

http://www.ericdigests.org/2001-3/reggio.htm

Through ERIC, link to publications related to the Reggio Emilia approach and to resources, videos, and contact information.

www.mhcls.com/online/

Unit 6: Helping Children to Thrive in School

Future of Children
http://www.futureofchildren.org

Produced by the David and Lucille Packard Foundation, the primary purpose of this page is to disseminate timely information on major issues related to children's well-being.

Busy Teacher's Cafe
http://www.busyteacherscafe.com

This is a web site for early childhood educators with resource pages for everything from worksheets to classroom management.

Tips for Teachers
http://www.counselorandteachertips.com

This site includes links for various topics of interest to teachers such as behavior management, peer mediation, and new teacher resources.

You Can Handle Them All
http://www.disciplinehelp.com

This site describes different types of behavioral problems and offers suggestions for managing these problems.

Unit 7: Curricular Issues

Action for Healthy Kids
www.actionforhealthykids.org

This organization works to assist the ever increasing numbers of students who are overweight, undernourished and sedentary. They feature a campaign for school wellness.

Awesome Library for Teachers
http://www.neat-schoolhouse.org/teacher.html

Open this page for links and access to teacher information on everything from educational assessment to general child development topics.

The Educators' Network
http://www.theeducatorsnetwork.com

A very useful site for teachers at every level in every subject area. Includes lesson plans, theme units, teacher tools, rubrics, books, educational news, and much more.

The Family Involvement Storybook Corner
http://www.gse.harvard.edu/hfrp/projects/fine.html

In partnership with Reading is Fundamental (RIF) the Family Involvement Storybook Corner is a place to find compilations of family involvement, children's storybooks, and related tools and information.

Grade Level Reading Lists
http://www.gradelevelreadinglists.org

Recommended reading lists for grades kindergarten - eight can be downloaded through this site.

Idea Box
http://theideabox.com

This site is geared toward parents and has many good activities for creating, playing and singing. The activities are creative and educational and can be done at home or in a classroom.

International Reading Association
http://www.reading.org

This organization for professionals who are interested in literacy contains information about the reading process and assists teachers in dealing with literacy issues.

PE Central
http://www.pecentral.org

Included in this site are developmentally appropriate physical activities for children, also containing one section dedicated to preschool physical education. It also includes resources and research in physical education.

The Perpetual Preschool
http://www.ecewebguide.com

This site provides teachers with possibilities for learning activities, offers chats with other teachers and resources on a variety of topics. The theme ideas are a list of possibilities and should not be used in whole, but used as a starting point for building areas of investigation that are relevant and offer firsthand experiences for young children.

Phi Delta Kappa
http://www.pdkintl.org

This important organization publishes articles about all facets of education. By clicking on the links in this site, for example, you can check out the journal's online archive, which has resources such as articles having to do with assessment.

Teacher Quick Source
http://www.teacherquicksource.com

Originally designed to help Head Start teachers meet the child outcomes, this site can be useful to all preschool teachers. Domains can be linked to developmentally appropriate activities for classroom use.

Teachers Helping Teachers
http://www.pacificnet.net/~mandel/

Basic teaching tips, new teaching methodologies, and forums for teachers to share experiences are provided on this site. Download software and participate in chats. It features educational resources on the Web, with new ones added each week.

Tech Learning
http://www.techlearning.com

An award-winning K–12 educational technology resource, this site offers thousands of classroom and administrative tools, case studies, curricular resources, and solutions.

Technology Help
http://www.apples4theteacher.com

This site helps teachers incorporate technology into the classroom. Full of interactive activities children can do alone, with a partner, or for full group instruction in all subject areas.

We highly recommend that you review our Web site for expanded information and our other product lines. We are continually updating and adding links to our Web site in order to offer you the most usable and useful information that will support and expand the value of your Annual Editions. You can reach us at: http://www.mhcls.com/annualeditions/.

UNIT 1
Perspectives

Unit Selections

1. **The Changing Culture of Childhood,** Joe L. Frost
2. **The Preschool Promise,** Julie Poppe and Steffanie Clothier
3. **Preschool Pays,** Robert G. Lynch
4. **Accountability Comes to Preschool,** Deborah Stipek
5. **No Child Left Behind,** Lisa A. DuBois
6. **Preschool Comes of Age,** Michael Lester
7. **Taking a Stand,** Richard J. Meyer

Key Points to Consider

• What are some of the key challenges affecting the early care and education profession?

• If our nation wants to make high-quality preschool education a priority, what are some challenges we face?

• How much emphasis should be placed on academics in a preschool program?

• What are the long term benefits of attending a quality preschool program?

• How are social disadvantage and poverty related to low achievement of young children?

• How can teachers become more involved in advocacy issues related to the care and education of young children?

• How has the introduction of early learning standards affected the profession?

Student Web Site

www.mhcls.com/online

Internet References

Further information regarding these Web sites may be found in this book's preface or online.

Child Care and Early Education Research Connections
www.researchconnections.org

Child Care Directory: Care guide
http://www.care.com

Complementary Learning Approach to the Achievement Gap
http://www.gse.harvard.edu/hfrp/projects/complementary-learning.html

Early Childhood Care and Development
http://www.ecdgroup.com

Global SchoolNet Foundation
http://www.gsn.org

Mid-Continent Research for Education and Learning
http://www.mcrel.org/standards-benchmarks

The National Association of State Boards of Education
http://www.nasbe.org/

Generations of adults have reflected back on their own childhood experiences and schooling and made comparisons to those of current children. Except for childhoods affected by war or the Great Depression, there has not been a greater change in one generation than is occurring now. This unit starts with Joe L. Frost's article, "The Changing Culture of Childhood." Frost outlines the dramatic changes children are experiencing today on all fronts. He touches on many of the issues I noted in the preface were overall trends for our profession for the 2008–2009 time period. The pressure for high-stakes achievement at an early age, the decreasing time allocated for spontaneous creative play and the deep and lasting impact of poverty are all discussed by Frost in this lead article.

The unit continues with articles that lay out national issues related to early education today. The authors of "The Preschool Promise", "Preschool Pays" and "Preschool Comes of Age" stress the need for quality preschool programs especially for at-risk children. The evidence of long term benefits for children who attend quality programs cannot be ignored. We know the importance of quality early childhood experiences, now our job is to educate others by being an advocate for young children attending appropriate preschool programs.

I always feel good when I realize that others outside of the field of early childhood education recognize that quality care and education for young children can have tremendous financial benefits as well as educational benefits for society. Of course I would always welcome the interest from more people outside of the profession, but the field is receiving increased attention from others for a number of reasons. The nation is learning that high quality programs are beneficial for young children's long-term development. Much of this interest is due in part to some state legislators allocating resources for state operated preschool programs. Coupled with the knowledge of the importance of ECE programs is a realization that the quality of these programs should be of utmost importance. Another reason is the compelling evidence from brain research that children are born learning. Yet, despite new information on the importance of early childhood, we still tend to hold onto cultural traditions about who young children are and how to care for them. This dichotomy between information and tradition results in an impasse when it comes to creating national policy related to young children. Professionals in the field are faced with the dilemma of how to convince more legislators, community leaders, and business people to make the political and monetary investment needed for new research and more high quality programs available for all children. These programs must also serve the needs of families related to affordability, accessibility and flexibility.

Two of the articles in this unit have the word accountable in the title. ("Accountability Comes to Preschool" and "No Child Left Behind: Who's Accountable?") That sends a powerful message about the way others view our profession and what we do.

Getty Images

I am reminded of one of the more popular perceptions of early care and education held by those outside of the profession. For the past fifty years "early childhood education was viewed as a panacea, the solution to all social ills in society." (Paciorek, 2008). This is huge pressure to put on one profession. Early childhood is viewed by many as the cure for all social problems. We do have outside forces carefully watching how early education practices affect long term development and learning. Early childhood professionals must be accountable for practices they implement in their classrooms and how children spend their time interacting with materials. Appropriate early learning standards are the norm in the profession and knowledgeable caregivers and teachers must be informed of the importance of developing quality experiences that align with the standards.

For over 130 years Peabody College of Vanderbilt University has been recognized as a leader in preparing future teachers, administrators and professors for the field of education. The article "No Child Left Behind: Who's Accountable?" provides insight from key researchers and policy makers at this Nashville, TN institution. They examine how the No Child Left Behind (NCLB) law signed in 2001, and expected to show full results in 2014, has effected our education system. The next five years will be critical for NCLB and what will come for the future of this at times controversial law.

With more and more people outside of the field of early childhood education telling teachers and caregivers how to best educate children, it is critical for those of us in the field to take a strong stand for what is best for young children. "Taking a Stand" will help motivate the beginning advocate and bring renewed passion to the seasoned spokesperson for what is just and right for young children. We didn't enter the public relations profession, but when it comes to young children, anyone who works with and or cares about the future of young children is an activist.

As editor, I hope you benefit from reading articles and reflecting on the important issues facing early childhood education today.

The Changing Culture of Childhood

A Perfect Storm

Joe L. Frost

A kind of "perfect storm" is now brewing in the education and development of children in the United States. Those who have not lived or explored the history of education in the United States; have not experienced both poverty and abundance; have lived lives sheltered from the barrios, slums, homeless shelters, and epidemics; or those unfamiliar with the rich legacy of history and child development scholarship on the nature of learning and relevance of culture are repeating the mistakes to be found in the history of U.S. education.

A combination of interrelated elements is currently changing the face of the civilizing traditions of U.S. education and forming a new culture of childhood. These include: 1) the standardization of education; 2) the dissolution of traditional spontaneous play; and 3) the growing specter of poverty in the United States and around the world.

The Standardization of Schooling

The standardization of schooling began as a state effort to improve achievement and reduce drop-outs by implementing the high-stakes testing movement, later known as No Child Left Behind. From the beginning, a fundamental fault of ignoring individual differences in all dimensions of education and child development spelled failure for this program. Well before the advent of the testing mania, educators learned the lessons of such folly from the scholarly research of the child study movement in the early 1900s, which was influenced by such philosophers as Rousseau, Pestalozzi, Froebel, Hall, and Dewey, and later Piaget and Vygotsky. Throughout the first half of the 20th century, U.S. educators and child development professionals framed their work around conclusions from extensive research at major universities throughout the nation and refined their work through ever-growing research during the second half of the 20th century. I search in vain for the scholarly underpinnings for high-stakes testing.

Historically, scholarship led to emphasis on individuality, creativity, cooperative learning, community involvement, and balancing academics, arts, and outdoor play. Assessment of young children became an ongoing process, involving intensive study of children, testing for diagnostic purposes, individualized assessment, and teacher observation and judgment. A mechanized model of education focuses on one-size-fits all testing and instruction and was never accepted or recommended by national professional organizations, never supported by research, and never embraced by educators and child development professionals.

In the No Child Left Behind program, high-stakes testing was to be the motor driving the standardization movement. Widely implemented in Texas, this movement was called the "Texas Miracle," because of early reported dramatic improvement in test scores—a promise to be dashed as evidence showed that the "improvements" were confounded by cheating and political deals with publishing companies (CNN, 2005). In 2004, the Dallas Morning News (*Austin American-Statesman,* 2004) found evidence of cheating in Houston and Dallas, and suspicious scores in dozens of other Texas cities. For example, 4th-graders in one large city elementary school scored in the bottom 2 percent in the state while the 5th-graders in that school ended up with the highest math scores in the state, with more than 90 percent of the students getting perfect or near-perfect scores. No other school ever came close to that performance. The U.S. Department of Education named this school a Blue Ribbon School and the superintendent of the district was named U.S. secretary of Education.

In September 2005, the Education Policy Studies Laboratory of Arizona State University (Nichols, Glass, & Berliner, 2005) published yet another study concluding that "pressure created by high-stakes testing has had almost no important influence on student academic performance" (p. 4). This study, conducted in 25 states, found a negative effect on minority students and illuminated the performance gap between white and minority students and between students from middle- and upper-income families and those from low-income homes. Such gaps come as no surprise to those who have studied the research on class, race, and educational achievement over the past half-century.

The prominent Latino authors in Angela Valenzuela's book *Leaving Children Behind: How "Texas-style" Accountability Fails Latino Youth* (2005) reveal the same kind of creeping, hidden discrimination that led to the civil rights struggle in the United States and the recent riots by disenfranchised minority youth in France and other European countries. The state's methods of collecting and reporting high-stakes test scores "hide as much as they reveal. . . . When skyrocketing dropout and projected retention rates are factored in, the state's 'miracle' looks more like a mirage" (p. 1). These Latino scholars contend that high-stakes testing is harmful to all children, but especially poor, minority, non English-speaking children; they state that children have a right to be assessed in a fair, impartial manner, using multiple assessment criteria.

Daily teaching and practicing the test has become the norm. Recess, arts, physical education, and creative inquiry are replaced with pizza parties, pep rallies, mock test practice, and teaching the test. Teachers, administrators, children, and parents face ever-growing pressure from threats of failure, retention, and demotion. As the schools focus ever more on bringing low-performing students up to grade-level standards, the most brilliant, most creative students, already performing well beyond their grade level, are left to languish in mediocrity and sameness. "In recent years the percentage of California students scoring in the 'advanced' math range has declined by as much as half between second and fifth grade" (Goodkin, 2005, p. A-15). It makes little difference in this draconian system whether a child merely meets the grade level standard or far exceeds it.

Politicians, not educators, are framing the U.S. education system and radically changing the culture of education, and standardized tests are becoming the curriculum of the schools. As the testing movement spreads across the nation, the Texas miracle is recognized by educators, professional organizations, and a growing number of politicians as bureaucratic bungling.

High-stakes testing is damaging to children and teachers—emotionally, physically, and intellectually. Around the country, children are wetting their pants, crying, acting out, becoming depressed, and taking their parents' pills on the day of testing to help them cope. In 2005, several children doped out and were taken to hospitals on the day of testing. In this same city, a high school that received a "School for Excellence Award" in 2002 was declared "low performing" in 2004 because a small group of children with disabilities did not perform well on a test designed for typical children.

Creative approaches to teaching value the souls and intellects of children and reveal and complement the wonderful creative powers of the best teachers. While teaching to the test may falsely guide the poorest teachers who struggle for direction, the best teachers are bound to a humdrum existence, divorced from teaching to interests, talents, and abilities; bound to endless regimented paperwork, meaningless workshops and repetition; and reduced to stress and mediocrity. Standardized tests tell good teachers what they already know and take an awesome toll on their teaching effectiveness, health, and creative powers.

In many states around the country, kindergartens and preschools are no longer a place for play, singing, and art; no longer a place for lessons on cooperation and sharing, or learning to love compelling literature and telling stories. They are no longer a place of fun and joy. Now, 3- to 5-year-olds, some still wetting their pants, not knowing how to stand in line, sit in a circle, or follow simple instructions, spend much of their time drilling skills and prepping for tests. We teach little kids to walk and talk and play together, then we tell them to sit down, shut up, and take the test. Yet learning by rote—by memory without thought of meaning—has never been a sound educational process.

The Dissolution of Traditional Spontaneous Children's Play

The early 20th century was a period of unparalleled interest in children's play and playgrounds. The U.S. play movement saw the promotion of spontaneous play and playgrounds in schools nationwide. The report of the 1940 White House Conference on Children and Youth (U.S. Superintendent of Documents, 1940, p. 191) stated, "All persons require types of experiences through which the elemental desire for friendship, recognition, adventure, creative expression, and group acceptance may be realized. . . . Favorable conditions of play . . . contribute much toward meeting these basic emotional needs." Play, the report stated, also supplies the growth and development of the child, and promotes motor, manual, and artistic skills—all conclusions supported by research and experience throughout the latter half of the 20th century.

Traditional spontaneous play is declining in U.S. neighborhoods and schools, and school recess is declining (Pica, 2003, 2005). The Atlanta school system built schools without playgrounds to demonstrate their devotion to high academic standards (Ohanian, 2002). Across the United States, school districts are abolishing recess or denying recess to children who score poorly on tests (Ohanian, 2002, p. 12). The International Play Association reports that 40 percent of U.S. elementary schools are deleting recess or reducing recess time to prepare for tests. *Psychology Today* reports that 40,000 schools no longer have play times.

Spontaneous play is also disappearing from the streets of cities throughout the industrialized world. In 1979, Keiki Haginoya began his intended life's work of preparing photo documentaries of children at play on the streets of Tokyo. In 1996, he wrote a sad conclusion to his career. Children's laughter and spontaneous play, which once filled the streets, alleys, and vacant lots of the city, had vanished. His photos show the rapid loss of play space, the separation of children from natural outdoor activities, traditional games, and creative play—indeed, the transformation of children's culture.

Haginoya's photos represent a sociological/psychological history of the cultural transformation—the construction of buildings and fences, the increase in cars, mass-produced toys, video game machines, and school entrance examinations. He mourns the demise of children's play and the end of his work:

> If I look back over the past seventeen years, it appears that
> I have taken the last record of children at play in the city,
> and that makes me deeply sad. . . . Children have learned
> enormous things through play. . . . The mere thought of

growing into a social person without the experience of outdoor play makes me shudder. (Haginoya, 1996, p. 4)

Kid pagers, instant messaging, video games, and chat rooms are replacing free, natural play in the fields and forests, a phenomenon Louv (2005) describes as "nature-deficit disorder." Even summer camps, only recently places for hiking in the woods, learning about plants and animals, and telling firelight stories, are now becoming computer camps, weight loss camps, and places where nature is something to watch, wear, consume, or ignore—places where attendance is linked to comfort and entertainment. If the present trends continue, summer camps may well become places to ditch children for tutoring on testing (Louv, 2005). In response, we have been transforming the playgrounds at our research site of three decades—Redeemer Lutheran School in Austin, Texas—into an integrated outdoor learning environment of playgrounds, natural habitats, and gardens. We see such work growing in acceptance, especially at child care centers where NCLB has only limited impact.

What is it like to bond with the wilderness? Having managed to survive the hazards of a childhood in the hillside farms and wilderness of the Ouachita Mountains of Arkansas more than half a century ago, I offer a personal glimpse of a childhood among the creeks and rivers, hills and valleys, and among domesticated and wild animals on the farm and in the wilderness. I never understood why kinfolk visiting from cities would ask, "Don't you get lonely down here?" The word "lonely "was not in my vocabulary or experience, because the days were filled with plowing and digging in the earth, wondering about the arrowheads found there; drinking from cool springs on hot days; swimming in the creeks and rivers at the end of long, sweaty days; riding horses and playing rodeo in the barn lots on weekends; feeding the cows, pigs, and chickens; building tree houses and hideouts in the woods; hunting raccoons at night and squirrels and deer in the daytime; cutting trees and chopping wood; taking pride in baling hay with the grown men; exploring fields and woods while eating watermelon and muscadines; building fires and cooking fish on the river bank; scanning the forest ahead for thorn bushes, snakes, and wild game; lying on the creek bank in the springtime, watching the creative movements of clouds; and all the while reveling in a sense of deep satisfaction and appreciation of the ever-changing natural wilderness.

We gathered along the gravel road before daylight during the winter to ride the back of a pick-up truck to school, stopping every half-mile or so to pick up other children who forded the river in boats or walked down out of the hills and valleys. We sat on sacks of mail, for the driver was also our mail carrier. We had five recess periods—before school and after school while waiting for the old truck to make runs over muddy road, and mid-morning, noon, and mid-afternoon. There was a level area in front of the school for organized games, most created by the children themselves, a creek along the back of the school for hunting frogs and building dams, and beyond that a pine-covered hillside. Here, we played war, built forts, and attacked the enemy with dead tree limb projectiles created by hitting the limb across a tree, breaking off the ends, which would fly

through the air, creating disarray and, sometimes, a bloody arm or nose. All of this constituted, as it turned out, a rather complete yet formidable playground. Play was truly free, for teachers stayed indoors. We stationed a kid at the edge of the woods to alert the group when the teacher rang the bell and it was time for "books." The ragged army then trooped indoors barefoot, muddy, and winded, but ready to sit down and pay attention. ADHD and obesity were unknown in that school and I never saw an injury that led to long-term consequences. What a difference six decades makes in the work and play of children!

The standardization of U.S. education extends well beyond the classroom curriculum into the playgrounds. Since the inception of national playground safety standards in 1981, constant revision has led to a 55-page standard of growing complexity, internal inconsistency, and estrangement from creativity. The "modern playground" is, in the main, an assemblage of steel and plastic structures, differing little from place to place, and devoid of natural habitats. Litigation replaces common sense and personal responsibility, and competition from testing and technology and careless parenting are producing a generation of obese kids with growing health and behavior problems. Safety standards are needed, but they should be consistent across state and national agencies, simple and clear in their expectations, and addressed to hazards in consumer products that threaten disability and death. Living is fraught with risks—emotional risks, financial risks, physical risks. Risk is essential for physical development. Overweight children with limited physical skills are unsafe on any playground. The issue is not merely how to make playgrounds safe for children, but how to make children safe for playgrounds.

In failing to cultivate the inherent play tendencies of children in the outdoor world, we fail to plant the early seeds of passionate exploration, artistic vision, creative reflection, and good health. Childhood is the time when, and playgrounds and natural habitats are the special places where, the culture, arising from tradition, knowledge, and skills, is readily and rapidly assimilated into the growing brain and psyche.

The Impact of Poverty on the Culture of Childhood

Poverty has powerful associations with school performance and exerts severe limits on what high-stakes testing can accomplish. Thousands of studies show positive correlations between poverty and achievement for children of all ethnic groups (Berliner, 2005). We don't need No Child Left Behind to tell us where failing schools are located—we have known for over a half century. The childhood poverty rate in the United States is greater than that of 25 wealthy countries, and poverty in the United States is clustered among minorities (UNICEF, 2005). As a group, African American and Hispanic American 15-year-olds rank 26th among 27 developed countries in reading, mathematics, and science literacy (Lemke et al., 2001).

More than half of all children born during this decade in developing countries will live their childhoods in urban slums. A quarter of those living in the United States will start their lives in urban slums (Nabhan & Trimble, 1996). Such children will have precious little opportunity to smell the flowers, sift clean dirt between their fingers, build a private hut in the wilds, walk in the morning dew, hear the quiet sounds of small animals at dusk, or see the heavens and the Milky Way in their full glory. Such seemingly insignificant experiences are the stuff that bond children to the natural world, introduce them to beauty and belonging, and surround them with opportunities to sharpen their growing minds with emerging concepts of geology, botany, physics, mathematics, and language.

For two decades, Annette Lareau (2003) and her team of researchers studied the differences in child rearing in upper middle-class versus working-class homes. The parenting styles and the results are dramatic, not good versus bad, but radically different in ways that prepare children to be successful in school. Upper middle-class families are more deeply involved in all aspects of their children's lives—providing a wide range of learning experiences, engaging in a lot of talk, reasoning with them, scheduling activities and getting them there, fighting over homework. In working-class homes, play is seen as inconsequential—a child's activity, not for adults. There was less talk, orders were brusque but whining was less. Parents offered fewer explanations and children, like their parents, were more likely to be intimidated by teachers and others in positions of authority. Working-class children had more intimate contact with extended families, they were taught right from wrong, and in many respects they were raised in the healthier environment. However, as adults, the working-class children are not doing well. They were not prepared for a world valuing verbal skills and an ability to thrive in organizations. They are picking up the same menial jobs their parents held, while the upper middle-class children are attending good colleges and preparing for professional careers.

The first White House Conference on Children in a Democracy was called by President Franklin D. Roosevelt in 1940, just after the onset of world war and during a time of exploitation of minorities and political patronage threatening the democratic process. The conference report (U.S. Superintendent of Documents, 1940, pp. 192–193) concluded that families of low-income children, minority children, slum children, and children with disabilities were deprived of toys, books, recreational areas, artistic events, and community recreation and playgrounds—in many respects, mirror images of what we see today.

The 2003 Census Report shows a steady rise in the number of families in poverty each year since 1999. When power and wealth rule a political structure, education itself is discriminatory (Wallis, 2005). We have known for decades that poverty is a key factor in school failure, yet both state and national governing bodies accommodate lobbyists and corporations while neglecting health care, housing, and living standards for the poor. Promises that the federal No Child Left Behind program would be accompanied by funds to make it work have gone unfulfilled, and children of the poor, especially minorities, are again stuffed into poverty-area schools rated "low performing" and "unacceptable." Now, public schools are threatened as students failing the tests are shifted to charter schools of questionable credentials and results, thus depriving public schools of desperately needed funds.

We see a growing storm for America's poorest children, with shrinking resources for school books, health insurance, affordable housing, health care, and food stamps. One in six U.S. children is poor; four million Americans are hungry and skipping meals; 45 million have no health insurance; 14 million have critical housing needs (Wallis, 2005, p. 223). With funding cuts in education and social services, the growing cost of war, tax cuts for the wealthy, natural disasters, and political cronyism, we now have a crisis among the poorest children.

The plight of the poor and minorities is nowhere more apparent than in the inequity of concern for the residents of New Orleans, both before and after Hurricane Katrina. Even before Katrina, the New Orleans schools were a failing system (Gray, 2005): already $45 million in debt; plagued by leadership crises (four superintendents in four years), scandals, and a squabbling school board; and strapped for resources. A majority of the students failed mandatory tests. After Katrina, we see a crisis of major proportions among displaced people striving to put their lives back together and a school system $300 million in debt.

Poverty-plagued and overlooked schools exist through the United States, especially in the slums and barrios of the cities. In Chicago, students from poor neighborhoods fail to receive their fair share of school funding and attend schools with tattered textbooks, decrepit buildings, overcrowded classrooms, and poorly qualified teachers (Loftus, 2005). Frustrated, stressed-out teachers desert the profession or pray for the day they can retire. Teachers in a growing number of schools must teach only one way. Policymakers must decide whether they want skillful, creative teachers or robots. If they want the former, they must put their money into supporting educators in developing curricula and sharpening their teaching skills.

Kozol (2005) tells stories about the dedication of teachers and the generosity in spirit of the children in the South Bronx; yet, in one school, only 65 of the 1,200 ninth-graders are likely to graduate. He points out that Mississippi spends $4,000 per pupil, inner-city Philadelphia schools get $6,000 per pupil, New York middle-class suburbs get $12,000 per pupil, and some very wealthy suburbs get $24,000 per pupil. Yet all are held to the same standards and all students take the same standardized exams. What history and research have always shown, but what policymakers ignore, is that poverty and hopelessness are fundamental causes of illiteracy and school failure in the United States. Regimented schooling does not address the problem of poverty.

Countering the Growing Storm

Author and poet Robert Louis Stevenson, sickly and in bed as a child, once watched the lamplighter move from place to place lighting the oil street lamps. He commented to his mother, "A man is coming down the street making holes in the darkness." We can all make little holes in the darkness and these holes can grow to illuminate entire neighborhoods, towns, and cities. Peaceful, informed dissent is a cornerstone of democracy and Americans are stepping up to protest the growing storm of elements that are eroding the culture of childhood. In April 2005, the Associated Press reported that the National Education Association (NEA) and school districts in Vermont, Michigan, and Texas, along with NEA chapters, were suing the federal administration for failing to provide support for the No Child Left Behind Act. In 2005, the Utah state legislature filed a lawsuit challenging the No Child Left Behind law, arguing that it is illegal to require expensive standardized testing for which it does not pay (Gillespie, 2005, p. A-10). Also in 2005, the NEA filed a lawsuit on behalf of local school districts and 20 state union chapters. A glimmer of hope emerged in November 2005, when the U.S. Secretary of Education, under fire from governors of several states, proposed allowing schools in some states to use children's progress on tests as evidence of success.

Who opposes high-stakes testing? Is it merely a handful of disgruntled parents, teachers, school boards, and professional organizations? Hardly. More than 70, and counting, professional organizations are in opposition, including such groups as the International Reading Association, the National Association for the Education of Young Children, American Educational Research Association, the American Psychiatric Association, the National Parent Teacher Association, the National Association for Elementary School Principals, the American Association of School Administrators, Students Against Testing, the National Association of School Psychologists, the American School Counselor Association, the National Council of Teachers of Mathematics, and the Association for Childhood Education International.

None of these organizations opposes meaningful testing or high academic expectations, nor do they hold that accountability is unnecessary. They simply contend that the system is deeply flawed. They promote assessments based on decades of research and experience; both formative and summative assessment, making decisions from multiple forms of assessment, not on a single test, adjusted for special needs and culturally different children; involving classroom teachers in assessment; and rejecting the use of test scores for punishing or rewarding administrators, teachers, and children.

Fortunately, private preschools remain relatively untouched by NCLB, although Head Start and other tax-supported early programs are under pressure to conform. Yes, professional standards and guidelines are essential, but look to those developed by such century-old organizations as NAEYC and ACEI-standards built by top researchers and successful practitioners worldwide, tied to the voluminous research of the past century, and refined by decades of experience.

High-stakes testing is not only wrong—it doesn't work. We are cultivating a culture of mediocrity and sameness and abandoning traditional ideas of creativity, ingenuity, ethical behavior, and imagination that make cultures and countries great. The most powerful policy for improving school achievement is reducing poverty. Focusing public policy on neighborhoods and families is an infinitely better strategy than focusing on testing to determine what we already know.

A reasonable substitute for the ill-founded emphasis on drill and testing for the very young would be to focus on encouraging parents to turn off the televisions, video games, and cell phones, and instead engage their children in conversation, take them to places of educational interest, read to them, teach them about the world beyond cartoons and video games, and teach them the value of giving over taking. Public policy should be directed toward rebuilding poverty-stricken neighborhoods, ensuring good jobs, medical care, and superior schools for all children, but especially for the very poor.

The impact of poverty, the demise of play, and high-stakes testing collectively are like the perfect storm. Each element contributes its destructive force, creating enormous potential for failure and damage to children—a sociopolitical system out of control. We must replace reactive, standardized learning with creative, thoughtful, introspective, interactive learning. We cannot allow the present generation of children to be the last to taste the joy of creative teaching and learning or to experience the delights of living with nature; the last children to know the collective inspiration of free, spontaneous play, and the separate peace of nature with all its fantasy, beauty, and freedom; the last to know the teachers and classrooms that molded people from all over the world into a fruitful, generous, and creative society. The engine that drives high-stakes testing, dismisses the value of children's play, and ignores the poor is a political engine. If we speak out, we can prevail; the storm will pass and good sense and a confluence of cultural creativity will return to the classrooms.

References

Austin American-Statesman. (2004, December 20). Signs of fraud found in study of TAKS results.

Berliner, D. C. (2005, August 2). *Teachers College Record,* www.tcrecord.org ID Number 12106

CNN. (2005, May 8). *CNN Presents—High stakes: No Child Left Behind.* Available on videotape.

Gillespie, N. (2005, August 23). Connecticut sues over No Child Left Behind. Associated Press in *Austin American-Statesman,* p. A-10.

Goodkin, S. (2005, December 28). We should leave no gifted child behind. *Austin American-Statesman* from *Washington Post,* p. A-15.

Gray, C. (2005). Even before the hurricane: A failed system. *Philadelphia Inquirer,* www.parentdirectededucation.org

Haginoya, K. (1996). Children's play has disappeared from the city. *PlayRights, 18*(1). Raleigh, NC: International Association for the Child's Right to Play.

Kozol, J. (2005). *Hypocrisy in testing craze.* Retrieved August 17, 2005, from www.weac.rg/news/2000-01/kozol.htm

Lareau, A. (2003). *Unequal childhoods: Class, race, and family life.* Berkeley, CA: University of California Press.

Lemke, M., Lippman, C., Jocelyn, L., Kastberg, D., Liu, Y. Y., Roey, S., Williams, T., Kruger, T., & Bairu, G. (2001). *Outcomes of learning: Results from the 2000 program for international student assessment of 15-year-olds in reading, mathematics, and science literacy.* Washington, DC: U.S. Department of Education, National Center for Education Statistics.

Loftus, K. P. (2005). *Katrina inequities already a reality for poor kids.* Retrieved March 23, 2006, from www.parentdirectededucation.org

Louv, R. (2005). *Last child in the woods: Saving our children from nature-deficit disorder.* Chapel Hill, NC: Algonquin Books.

Nabhan, G. P., & Trimble, S. (1996). *The geography of childhood: Why children need wild places.* Boston: Beacon Press.

Nichols, S. L., Glass, G. V., & Berliner, D. C. (2005). *High stakes testing and student achievement: Problems for the No Child Left Behind Act.* Tempe, AZ: Arizona State University, Education Policy Studies Laboratory.

Ohanian, S. (2002). *What happened to recess and why are our children struggling in kindergarten?* New York: McGraw-Hill.

Pica, R. (2003). *Your active child: How to boost physical, emotional, and cognitive development through age-appropriate activity.* New York: McGraw-Hill.

Pica, R. (2005). Reading, writing,'rithmetic—and recess! *Linkup Parents Newsletter.* Retrieved August 8,2005, from www.linkup-parents.com/education.html

UNICEF. (2005). *Child poverty in rich countries, Innocenti Report Card No. 6.* Florence, Italy: UNICEF Innocenti Research Centre, www.unicef.org/irc

U.S. Superintendent of Documents. (1940). *White House conference on children in a democracy.* Washington, DC: Author.

Valenzuela, A. (Ed.). (2005). *Leaving children behind: How "Texas-style" accountability fails Latino youth.* Albany, NY: State University of New York Press.

Wallis, J. (2005). *God's politics.* San Francisco: HarperCollins.

JOE L. FROST is Parker Centennial Professor Emeritus, University of Texas, Austin.

From *Childhood Education,* Summer 2007. Copyright © 2007 by the Association for Childhood Education International. Reprinted by permission of Joe L. Frost and the Association for Childhood Education International, 17904 Georgia Avenue, Suite 215, Olney, MD 20832.

The Preschool Promise

**Going to preschool benefits children their entire lives.
Can states afford to provide it to all kids?**

Julie Poppe and Steffanie Clothier

If you walk into a good preschool classroom, you might see a teacher reading to a group of kids, children immersed in an art project, little ones playing on a computer or getting ready for a field trip to a nearby museum or public library.

Those children, mounting research shows, will do better in school and are more likely to attend college. As adults they will have better jobs and pay more taxes. They will even be better parents.

The good news is that more and more children go to preschool; in 2002, 66 percent of 4-year-olds attended. Some schools are government supported, others are private. Today, at least 40 states provide state funding for preschool programs, compared to only 10 in 1980.

Parents from all income ranges send their children to preschool, although better educated parents with higher incomes have the highest participation rate.

Preschools are designed to provide education and a safe caring environment. Some states fund programs that incorporate the needs of working parents, sometimes by coordinating their programs with Head Start and child care subsidy programs to ensure full-day services.

Ready for School

One of the striking findings in early education is the size of the achievement gap at the start of kindergarten between children who have gone to preschool and those who have not. That difference hardly ever goes away. It continues in reading and math achievement in the early grades and throughout school and into the job market. Steve Barnett from the National Institute for Early Education Research—an independent, nonpartisan organization that conducts research and follows state early education policy—says that kids living in poverty are 18 months behind the average kid when they start kindergarten. "This is an incredible amount of time for a school to catch up," Barnett says. But the achievement gap isn't just a poverty issue. "The gap continues up the income ladder," he says. Because of these findings and recent brain research showing that almost 90 percent of brain growth occurs in children by age 5, more lawmakers, economists, business leaders and parents are supporting early education.

The Right Programs Are Key

What makes a good preschool program? Proper teacher qualifications and training, small class sizes and teacher-to-student ratios, stimulating curriculum and other services that support families. A good program can improve a child's achievement over the short and long term. Recent focus on quality has prompted states to consider enhancements. For example, 23 now require preschool teachers to have a bachelor's degree with additional certification and license.

Most states target their state-funded initiatives to children who are in low-income families or at risk of school failure. Some states are looking to expand their preschool programs in response to state litigation, the need to improve test scores due to No Child Left Behind, and the latest research showing early education improves children's school success. Some states have different goals in mind, such as funding and expanding early education programs to reach more working families.

Paying for Quality Preschool

Arkansas has a state-funded preschool program that started in 1991 for low-income children. In recent years, $40 million in funding has allowed more children to attend. Representative LeRoy Dangeau carried a bill this session that resulted in an additional $20 million over the next two years for the continued expansion of the state's program.

Other preschool funding comes from a beer tax (since 2001) that raises about 18 cents on every six-pack, generating $8 million annually for early education. This April, the Legislature passed a bill to extend the beer tax until June 2007.

Dangeau hopes that by the summer of 2007 there will be a total of $100 million dedicated for voluntary preschool for all 3 and 4-year-olds.

"When I became a legislator four years ago," says Dangeau, "I had no clue about the importance of early childhood. But I saw the research, including the benefits of preschool over time, and how it is the best investment of our money," he says.

In a recent Arkansas Supreme Court case on school funding inequity, the court recognized the importance of preschool (but didn't mandate it) as part of its ruling. "I think that the court case had an impact on how the Legislature views preschool," says Dangeau. "We see it as the

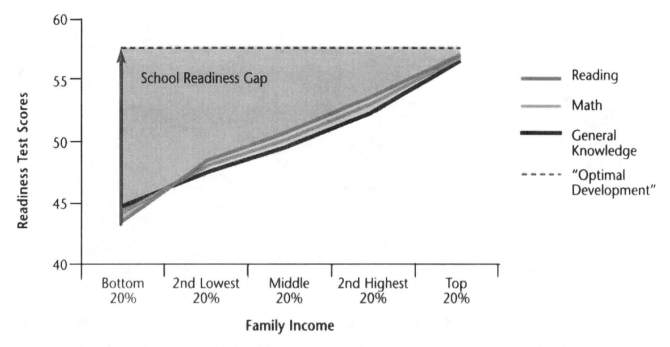

Figure 1 The Achievement Gap at Kindergarten Family income has a great deal to do with how well a child does on readiness tests when entering kindergarten. The school readiness gap is steepest for children from families with the lowest incomes and continues through middle income families, gradually decreasing as income rises.

Source: Preschool Policy Matters, April 2004, National Institute for Early Education Research.

quickest way to improve test scores. The issue is not whether or not to have preschool. The question is how much money to put into it."

Last year, the National Institute for Early Education Research ranked the quality of Arkansas' preschool program very high.

"I am very proud to say that Arkansas ranked best in terms of quality," says Dangeau. He believes the success is directly tied to legislation passed in 2003 that puts preschool teachers on the same pay scale as K-12 teachers. Any program or school may provide preschool services as long as they meet the state's quality standards, such as one certified teacher per 10 students.

Supporting Working Families

In the mid-'80s, the Illinois legislature established a preschool program for at-risk children. To support working families, the state allows child care centers and Head Start programs that meet standards to provide full-day early education services along with public schools. Local communities determine eligibility; there are an estimated 64,000 3- and 4-year-olds enrolled statewide.

The state has significantly increased funding over the past few years. Since 2003, lawmakers have appropriated $30 million annually for early education and are looking to do the same this legislative session.

The National Institute for Early Education Research gave the state high marks for quality. Teachers participating in the program must hold an early childhood teaching certificate to be on the same pay scale as K-12 teachers.

In 2003, lawmakers created the Illinois Early Learning Council. It builds on the work the state has already done to develop a high-quality early learning system available to all Illinois children up to age 5. Four legislators currently are members of the council, including Representative Elizabeth Coulson.

Preschool Popularity

At least 40 states provide state funding for preschool programs.

- The first to expand preschool to all 4-year-olds were Georgia and then Oklahoma. Florida, Maryland, New York and West Virginia are in the process of phasing in their programs.
- Thirty-six states considered early education bills in 2005. At least 28 states considered expanding preschool programs.
- Florida legislators, responding to a state ballot measure, approved legislation for a voluntary preschool program for all 4-year-olds. New Mexico legislators passed a pilot preschool bill with a $5 million initial appropriation.
- Mississippi, Montana, North Dakota and South Dakota have no state-funded preschool programs, but did consider legislation this session.

Coulson, who has a business background, sits on two of the House Appropriation Committee's subcommittees, Human Services and Education, which make funding decisions for early education. She is also a member of the House Human Services Committee. "I'm a link between key committees that focus on early childhood," she says.

She says that Illinois has been concerned for some time about supporting working families and making sure a strong birth-to-age-5 system is in place that nurtures children. In 2003, the legislature

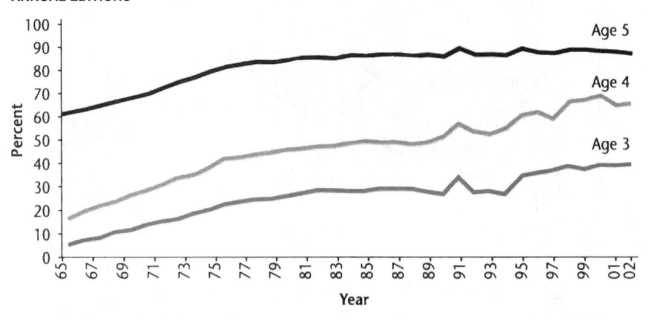

Figure 2 Kindergarten and Preschool Participation 1965-2002. Over the last several decades, preschool and kindergarten participation has increased steadily for children ages 3 to 5.

Source: National Institute for Early Education Research.

increased the percentage of funding for birth-to-age-3 programs from 8 percent to 11 percent of the state's early childhood education block grant. The block grant makes up the state's funding for preschool education, parental training and prevention initiatives. "The formative years have the most impact on education. This is not just a women's issue, but it's also a children's issue and [in terms of economics and business] an important issue for the whole state," she says.

Nearly a third of all Illinois 4-year-olds are in a state-funded preschool program and the number is up from the year before. Coulson says early care is a thriving industry that has an impact on Illinois' economy, and businesses need to be aware of the benefits. Recent research shows that every tax dollar invested in preschool produces $17 for the economy.

"This session, we continue to focus on quality and funding," Coulson says, in the last two years, the state has increased preschool spending by $60 million. "This is a bad budget year for Illinois, but I am optimistic we will find a way to fund another $30 million for early childhood," she says.

Legislative Involvement

During the mid-'80s, Massachusetts set up a state-funded early education program in public schools. Since then, the state has allowed community partnership providers who meet early childhood standards to participate in programs targeting at-risk 3- and 4-year-olds from working families serving almost 16,000 children last year.

During the 2004 session, more than 100 legislators, including leadership in both houses, signed on to a proposal for preschool for all 3-to-5-year-olds to be phased-in over 10 years, at an estimated cost of $1 billion. Two bills that were eventually enacted laid the groundwork for the expansion by reworking state governance of

early childhood programs. One law creates a single department to streamline early childhood programs and to expand preschool to all 3- and 4-year-olds. "Hopefully, we will see less duplication of services," says Representative Patricia Haddad.

She co-chairs the legislature's Joint Committee on Education and the state's legislatively created Advisory Committee on Early Education and Care. Nine other legislators participate. They have conducted five public hearings throughout the state. "We had to be a part of the hearings ourselves, because it is nice to read a report, but the passion is different when you are involved," says Haddad. State early childhood advocates also held meetings throughout the state to educate the public on the importance of early childhood education and full-day kindergarten for all.

Last December, the advisory committee completed a report that identified four key components: developing a workforce, defining quality, delivering the system and evaluating progress. Haddad says the next step is providing a good workforce development program for teachers and providers.

The 2004 legislation also created a new board of early education and care, which will start this July. The commissioners from the boards of Higher Education, Education, and Early Education and Care will each sit on each other's boards. "We want the commissioners to be talking to one another, which will lead to better communication between these three entities," says Haddad.

Representative Haddad says people in Massachusetts are starting to realize the importance of preschool and the role that it might possibly play with No Child Left Behind. "If you do not provide the very best for children in the early years, you will continue to see gaps," she says.

JULIE POPPE tracks preschool policy for NCSL. **STEFFANIE CLOTHIER** heads NCSL's Child Care and Early Education Project.

From *State Legislatures*, June 2005, pp. 26–28. Copyright © 2005 by National Conference of State Legislatures. Reprinted by permission.

Preschool Pays

High-quality early education would save billions.

ROBERT G. LYNCH

The youngest children suffer the highest poverty rates of any age group in the United States. Nearly one in five children under age 6 lives in poverty, and the number is rising.

Poor children often have inadequate food, safety, shelter, and healthcare. In school, poor children too often fall far short of achieving their academic potential, making them more likely to enter adulthood lacking the skills to compete in the global labor market. As adults, they are more likely to suffer from poor health and participate in crime and other antisocial behavior; they are also less likely to be gainfully employed and contributing to economic growth and community well-being.

There is a strong consensus among the experts who have studied high-quality early childhood development (ECD) programs that these programs have substantial payoffs. Although the programs vary in whom they serve and in the services they provide, most high-quality ECD programs have the following characteristics in common: well-educated and trained staff; a low child-to-teacher ratio and small classes; a rich curriculum that emphasizes language, pre-literacy, and pre-numeracy activities, as well as motor, emotional, and social development; health and nutritional services; and lots of structured and unstructured play. Good programs also typically include parental involvement and education.

What benefits have such programs produced? We can answer this question thanks largely to carefully conducted, long-term studies that have compared the school and life outcomes of participants in four high-quality ECD programs—the Perry Preschool Project, the Prenatal Early Infancy Project, the Abecedarian Early Childhood Intervention, and the Chicago Child-Parent Center Program—with a control group of children who attended no such program.[1]

These studies have established that participating children are more successful in school and in life than children who were not enrolled in high-quality programs. In particular, children who have participated in high-quality ECD programs tend to have higher scores on math and reading achievement tests, have greater language abilities, are better prepared to enter elementary school, are more likely to pursue secondary education, have less grade retention, have less need for special education and other remedial coursework, have lower dropout rates, have

higher high school graduation rates, higher levels of schooling attainment, improved nutrition, better access to healthcare services, higher rates of immunization, better health, and experience less child abuse and neglect. These children are also less likely to be teenage parents and more likely to have higher employment rates as adults, lower welfare dependency, lower rates of drug use, show less-frequent and less-severe delinquent behavior, engage in fewer criminal acts both as juveniles and as adults, have fewer interactions with the criminal justice system, and lower incarceration rates. The benefits of ECD programs to participating children enable them to enter school "ready to learn," helping them achieve better outcomes in school and throughout their lives (Barnett, 1993; Karoly et al., 1998; Masse and Barnett, 2002; Schweinhart, 1993).

Parents and families of children who participate in high-quality ECD programs also benefit. For example, mothers have fewer additional births, have better nutrition and smoke less during pregnancy, are less likely to abuse or neglect their children, complete more years of schooling, have higher high-school graduation rates, are more likely to be employed, have higher earnings, engage in fewer criminal acts, have lower drug and alcohol abuse, and are less likely to use welfare (Karoly et al., 1998).

Because of these positive results, there is now a consensus among experts of all political persuasions that investments in high-quality ECD programs have huge potential long-term payoffs. Investments in high-quality ECD programs consistently generate benefit-cost ratios exceeding 3-to-1—or more than a $3 return for every $1 invested. While participants and their families get part of the total benefits, the benefits to the rest of the public and government are even larger and, on their own, tend to far outweigh the costs of these programs. Several prominent economists and business leaders (many of whom are skeptical about government programs generally) have recently issued well-documented reviews of the literature that find very high economic payoffs from ECD programs. For example, Nobel Prize winning economist James Heckman of the University of Chicago has concluded:

> Recent studies of early childhood investments have shown remarkable success and indicate that the early years are important for early learning and can be enriched through

external channels. Early childhood investments of high quality have lasting effects. . . . In the long run, significant improvements in the skill levels of American workers, especially workers not attending college, are unlikely without substantial improvements in the arrangements that foster early learning. We cannot afford to postpone investing in children until they become adults, nor can we wait until they reach school age—a time when it may be too late to intervene. Learning is a dynamic process and is most effective when it begins at a young age and continues through adulthood. The role of the family is crucial to the formation of learning skills, and government interventions at an early age that mend the harm done by dysfunctional families have proven to be highly effective.[2]

The director of research and a regional economic analyst at the Federal Reserve Bank of Minneapolis, Arthur Rolnick and Rob Grunewald, have come to similar conclusions:

. . . recent studies suggest that one critical form of education, early childhood development, or ECD, is grossly under-funded. However, if properly funded and managed, invest-ment in ECD yields an extraordinary return, far exceeding the return on most investments, private or public. . . . In the future, any proposed economic development list should have early childhood development at the top.[3]

This Federal Reserve Bank of Minneapolis study (Rolnick and Grunewald, 2003) further determined that annual real rates of return on public investments in the Perry Preschool project were 12 percent for the non-participating public and government and 4 percent for participants, so that total returns exceeded 16 percent. Thus, again it is advantageous even for non-participating taxpayers to pay for these programs. To comprehend how extraordinarily high these rates of return on ECD investments are, consider that the highly touted real rate of return on the stock market that prevailed between 1871 and 1998 was just 6.3 percent.[4]

Likewise, after reviewing the evidence, The Committee for Economic Development (CED), a nonpartisan research and policy organization of some 250 business leaders and educa-tors, concluded that:

Society pays in many ways for failing to take full advan-tage of the learning potential of all of its children, from lost economic productivity and tax revenues to higher crime rates to diminished participation in the civic and cultural life of the nation . . . . Over a decade ago, CED urged the nation to view education as an investment, not an expense, and to develop a comprehensive and coor-dinated strategy of human investment. Such a strategy should redefine education as a process that begins at birth and encompasses all aspects of children's early development, including their physical, social, emo-tional, and cognitive growth. In the intervening years, the evidence has grown even stronger that investments in early education can have long-term benefits for both children and society.[5]

What If We Provided High-Quality Early Childhood Development to All Poor Children?

How much would it really cost the government to provide such an experience to all poor children? And how much would it actually save the government in terms of crimes not committed, welfare payments no longer needed, reduced remedial educa-tion costs, more taxes collected, and so forth?

In a new study published by the Economic Policy Institute and summarized here, I calculate how much taxpayers would save, how much the economy would grow, and how much crime would be reduced over the next 45 years if high-quality programs were provided for all poor children. To create these estimates, I've extrapolated from research on the Perry Preschool Project.[6] Perry was not chosen because it is an ideal program (or even better than the three other programs named above). It is simply the only program with data suitable for these extrapolations. These estimates assume the launch of an ECD program for all of the nation's three- and four-year-olds who live in poverty in 2005, with full phase-in by 2006. (For practical purposes, such as finding appropriate staff and locations, a large-scale ECD program would have to be phased-in over a longer period.) The costs set forth in these estimates may understate the start-up costs of such an ambitious program, especially the costs of recruiting and training teachers and staff and of establishing appropriate sites. On the other hand, the total benefits of ECD investment are also understated in these estimates. Thus, although the ben-efit-cost ratio of a national ECD program could be somewhat higher or lower than that which is found in the pilot programs, it is implausible that the ratio would be less than the 1-to-1 ratio necessary to justify launching the program.

In the next two sections we'll look at the results of these extrapolations and specifically the effects of ECD investments on 1) government budgets, and 2) on the economy and crime.

What Is the Effect on Government Budgets?

We can expect, based on long-term research on children who partic-ipated in high-quality ECD programs and similar non-participating children, that these ECD investments would benefit taxpayers and generate government budget benefits in at least four ways.[7] First, subsequent public education expenses would be lower because par-ticipants spend less time in school (as they fail fewer grades) and require expensive special education less often. Second, criminal justice costs would come down because participants—and their families—would have markedly lower crime and delinquency rates. Third, both participants and their parents would have higher incomes and pay more taxes than non-participants. Fourth, the ECD investment would reduce public welfare expenditures because participants and their families would have lower rates of welfare usage. Against these four types of budget benefits, we must consider two types of budget costs: the expenses of the ECD program itself and the increased expenditure due to greater use of higher education by ECD participants.

The ECD programs do not perform miracles on poor children. Substantial numbers of ECD participants go on to do poorly in school, commit crimes, have poor health outcomes, and receive welfare payments. The key point is that ECD participants as a group have far lower rates of these negative outcomes than do non-participants.

Given all of this, what effect would such ECD investments have on government budgets?[8] In the second year of the program, 2006, when the program would be fully phased-in, government outlays would exceed offsetting budget benefits by $19.4 billion (in 2004 dollars). The annual deficit due to the ECD program would shrink for the next 14 years. By the 17th year of the program, in 2021, the deficit would turn into a surplus that would grow every year thereafter. Within 25 years, by 2030 if a nationwide program were started in 2005, the annual budget benefits would exceed costs by $31 billion (in 2004 dollars). By 2050, the net annual budget savings would total $61 billion (in 2004 dollars). In short, for the first 16 years, additional costs exceed offsetting budget benefits, but by a declining margin. Thereafter, offsetting budget benefits exceed costs by a growing margin each year. This pattern is illustrated in the figure, which shows annual revenue impacts and costs in constant 2004 dollars.

The reason for this fiscal pattern is fairly obvious. The costs of the program will grow fairly steadily for the first decade and a half, in tandem with modest growth in the population of three- and four-year-old participants. Thereafter, costs will grow at a somewhat faster pace for a few years as, in addition to the costs of educating three- and four-year-olds, the first and subsequent cohorts of participant children begin to use public higher education services. After the first two years, when the first cohort of children starts entering the public school system, public education expenditures will begin to diminish due to less grade retention and remedial education. After a decade and a half, the first cohort of children will be entering the workforce, resulting in increased earnings and thus higher tax revenues and lower welfare expenditures. In addition, governments will experience lower judicial system costs.

The timing of these fiscal benefits resulting from a nationwide ECD program should appeal to those concerned about the fiscal difficulties posed by the impending surge of retiring baby boomers. The substantial fiscal payoffs from investing in young children would become available to governments just as the wave of new retirements puts the greatest pressure on government resources. For example, the government-wide budget savings in 2030 and in 2050 from ECD investments begun next year would be enough to offset about one-fifth of the deficits in the Social Security trust fund projected for those years. This potential contribution to the solvency of the Social Security system would be achieved without raising social security taxes or cutting benefits.

What Is the Effect of ECD on Crime Reduction, Earnings, and the Economy?

It is important to keep in mind that savings to government is not the only benefit of ECD investments. These other benefits come in many forms. Investments in high-quality ECD programs are likely to substantially reduce crime rates and the extraordinary costs to society of criminality. Some of these reduced costs are savings to government in the form of lower criminal justice system costs. These savings to government would total nearly $28 billion (in 2004 dollars) in 2050, and were included in the earlier discussion of the fiscal effects of ECD investments. But there are other savings to society from reduced crime. These include the value of material losses and the pain and suffering that would otherwise be experienced by the victims of crime. By 2050, these savings to individuals from less crime would amount to $127 billion (in 2004 dollars).

Another major benefit of ECD investments is their impact on the future earnings of participants.[9] The initial increase in earnings occurs in 2020 when the first cohort of participating children turns 18 and enters the labor market. By 2050, the increase in earnings due to ECD investments is estimated to amount to 0.43 percent of GDP, or some $107 billion (in 2004 dollars).

The increased earnings of children who participate in a high-quality ECD program not only allow the U.S. to compete more effectively in a global economy, but also aid both earlier and future generations of children. These increased earnings will benefit earlier generations when they reach retirement age because these earnings will contribute to the solvency of Social Security and other public retirement benefit programs. Future generations will benefit because they will be less likely to grow up in families living in poverty.

A nationwide commitment to high-quality early childhood development would cost a significant amount of money up front, but it would have a substantial payoff in the future. The United States' political system, with its two- and four-year cycles, tends to under-invest in programs with such long lags between when investment costs are incurred and when the benefits are enjoyed. The fact that lower levels of government cannot capture all the benefits of ECD investment may also discourage them from assuming all the costs of ECD programs. Yet, the economic case for ECD investment is compelling.

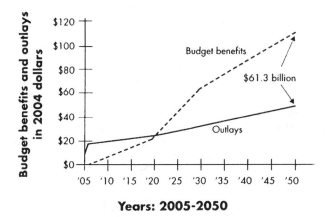

Figure 1 Annual benefits and outlays.

© Ariel Skelley/CORBIS

To recapitulate, I estimate that providing poor three- and four-year-old children—20 percent of all children in this age range—with a high-quality program would initially cost about $19 billion a year. Such a program would ultimately reduce costs for remedial and special education, criminal justice, and welfare benefits, and it would increase income earned and taxes paid. Within about 17 years, the net effect on the budget would turn positive (for all levels of government combined). Within 30 years, the offsetting budget benefits would be more than double the costs of the ECD program (and the cost of the additional youth going to college).

In addition, investing in our poor young children is likely to have an enormous positive effect on the U.S. economy by raising GDP, improving the skills of the workforce, reducing poverty, and strengthening U.S. global competitiveness. Crime rates and the heavy costs of criminality to society are likely to be substantially reduced as well.

Notes

1. All but the Chicago Child-Parent Center Program had random assignment of potentially eligible children into the intervention program or the control group. The Chicago Child-Parent Center Program did not use randomized assignment but the control group did match the intervention group on age, eligibility for intervention, and family socioeconomic status.

2. Heckman (1999), pp. 22 and 41.

3. Rolnick and Grunewald (2003), pp. 3 and 16.

4. Burtless (1999).

5. Committee for Economic Development (2002).

6. The annual average impact for various types of costs and benefits per Perry Preschool Project participant, estimated by Rolnick and Grunewald (2003) of the Federal Reserve Bank of Minneapolis, was used as the baseline for the analysis. (Rolnick and Grunewald used the costs and benefits as described by Schweinhart [1993] and Barnett [1993].) The annual costs and benefits per program participant of the preschool program were adjusted for inflation and/or wage increases every year through 2050 in line with projections made by the Congressional Budget Office (June 2004).

    The numbers of three- and four-year-olds entered in the estimating model were taken from recent population projections made by the U.S. Census Bureau (2004). The total costs and benefits of the preschool program were determined by multiplying the number of participants of a particular age by the average value of the cost or benefit for each year that the cost or benefit was produced by participants of that age as determined by Rolnick and Grunewald (2003). Thus, for example, the reductions in the cost of providing public education per participant were assumed to kick in when that participant entered the public school system at age 5 and were assumed to cease when that participant turned 18 and left the school system.

7. Other savings to taxpayers and boons to government budgets, such as reductions in public healthcare expenditures, are likely to exist. But, we lack the data to quantify all these other potential savings.

8. This analysis considers budget effects on all levels of government—federal, state, and local—as a unified whole. As a practical matter, the source estimates have not made such a distinction, nor should they. All levels of government share in the costs of education, criminal justice, and income support. Responsibilities have shifted in the last half-century and will continue to do so over the nearly half-century timeframe used in this analysis. Although a case can be made that ECD investments should be the responsibility of the federal government to address educational inequalities before children enter the school system, these investments could be made at any or all levels of government. This analysis focuses on capturing national effects of ECD investments.

9. The guardians of participants are also likely to experience increases in earnings since they will have more time for employment as a consequence of the day-care provided to their children by the ECD program. These earnings benefits have not been calculated for our nationwide ECD program.

References

Barnett, W. Steven (1993). "Benefit-Cost Analysis of Preschool Education: Findings From a 25-year Follow-up." *American Journal of Orthopsychiatry, Vol. 63,* No. 4, pp. 500–508.

Burtless, Gary (1999). "Risk and Returns of Stock Market Investments Held in Individual Retirement Accounts." Testimony before the House Budget Committee, Task Force on Social Security Reform, May 11.

Committee for Economic Development (2002). *Preschool for All: Investing in a Productive and Just Society.* New York, N.Y.: CED.

Congressional Budget Office (2004). *The Outlook for Social Security.* Congress of the United States, Washington, D.C., June.

Fuerst, J.S. and Fuerst, D. (1993). "Chicago Experience with an Early Childhood Program: The Special Case of the Child Parent Center Program." *Urban Education,* Vol. 28, pp. 69–96.

Heckman, James (1999). "Policies to Foster Human Development." Working paper 7288. Cambridge, Mass.: National Bureau of Economic Research.

Karoly, L., Greenwood, P., Everingham, S., Hourbe, J., Kilburn, R., Rydell, C.P., Sanders, M., and Chiesa, J. (1998). *Investing in Our Children: What We Know and Don't Know About the Costs and Benefits of Early Childhood Interventions.* Washington, D.C.: Rand Corporation.

Karoly, Lynn (2001). "Investing in the Future: Reducing Poverty Through Human Capital Investments," in *Understanding Poverty,* Danziger, S. and Robert Haveman (eds.), Cambridge, Mass.: Harvard University Press.

Masse, L. and Barnett, W.S. (2002). *A Benefit Cost Analysis of the Abecedarian Early Childhood Intervention.* New Brunswick, N.J.: National Institute for Early Education Research, Rutgers University.

Reynolds, A., Temple, J., Robertson, D., and Mann, E. (2001). "Age 21 Cost-Benefit Analysis of the Title I Chicago Child-Parent Center Program: Executive Summary." Institute for Research on Poverty (http://www.waisman.wisc.edu/cls/cbaexecsum4.html).

Reynolds, A., Temple, J., Robertson, D., and Mann, E. (2002). "Age 21 Cost-Benefit Analysis of the Title I Chicago Child-Parent Centers." Discussion Paper no. 1245-02, Institute for Research on Poverty (http://www.ssc.wisc.edu/irp/pubs/dp124502.pdf).

Reynolds, Arthur (1994). "Effects of a Preschool Plus Follow-on Intervention for Children at Risk." *Developmental Psychology,* Vol. 30, pp. 787–804.

Rolnick, A. and Grunewald, R. (2003). "Early Childhood Development: Economic Development with a High Public Return." *Fedgazette,* Federal Reserve Bank of Minneapolis, March.

Schweinhart, Lawrence (1993). *Significant Benefits: The High/Scope Perry Preschool Study Through Age 27.* Ypsilanti, Mich: High/Scope Press.

Schweinhart, Lawrence (2004). "The High/Scope Perry Preschool Study through Age 40: Summary, Conclusions, and Frequently Asked Questions." Ypsilanti, Mich.: High/Scope Press.

U.S. Census Bureau (2004). *Projected Population of the United States, by Age and Sex: 2000 to 2050.* Washington, D.C.: Population Division, Population Projections Branch, May 18.

ROBERT G. LYNCH is associated professor and chairman of the department of economics at Washington College. His most recent book is *Rethinking Growth Strategies—How State and Local Taxes and Services Affect Economic Development.* This article is adapted with permission from Exceptional Returns: Economic, Fiscal, and Social Benefits of Investment in Early Childhood Development, published by the Economic Policy Institute, © 2004, www.epinet.org.

From *American Educator*, Winter 2004/2005. Copyright © 2005 by Robert G. Lynch. Reprinted with permission of the American Educator, the quarterly journal of the American Federation of Teachers, AFL-CIO, and reprinted with permission of Robert G. Lynch.

Accountability Comes to Preschool

Can We Make It Work for Young Children?

Early childhood educators are justifiably concerned that demands for academic standards in preschool will result in developmentally inappropriate instruction that focuses on a narrow set of isolated skills. But Ms. Stipek believes that teaching preschoolers basic skills can give them a good foundation for their school careers, and she shows that it is possible to do this in ways that are both effective and enjoyable.

DEBORAH STIPEK

Pressures to raise academic achievement and to close the achievement gap have taken a firm hold on elementary and secondary schools. Now, preschools are beginning to feel the heat. Testing for No Child Left Behind isn't required until third grade. But as elementary schools ratchet up demands on children in the early grades and as kindergarten becomes more academic, children entering school without basic literacy and math skills are at an increasingly significant disadvantage.

Accountability is also beginning to enter the preschool arena. Both the House and Senate versions of the Head Start reauthorization bill require the development of educational performance standards based on recommendations of a National Academy of Sciences panel. Head Start programs would then be held accountable for making progress toward meeting these goals, and their funding would be withdrawn after some period of time if they failed. States and districts are likely to follow with initiatives designed to ensure that children in publicly funded early childhood education programs are being prepared academically to succeed in school.

There are good reasons for the increased attention to academic skills in preschool, especially in programs serving economically disadvantaged children. Children from low-income families enter kindergarten on average a year to a year and a half behind their middle-class peers in terms of school readiness. And the relatively poor cognitive skills of low-income children at school entry predict poor achievement in the long term. Meredith Phillips, James Crouse, and John Ralph estimated in a meta-analysis that about half of the total black/white gap in math and reading achievement at the end of high school is explained by the gap between blacks and whites at school entry.[1] Preschool education can give children from economically disadvantaged homes a better chance of succeeding in school by contributing to their cognitive skills. Moreover, all young children are capable of learning far more than is typically believed, and they enjoy the process.

Until recently, kindergarten was a time for children to *prepare* for school. Today, it *is* school.

This new focus on academic preparation will undoubtedly have significant implications for the nature of preschool programs, and it could have negative consequences. Until recently, kindergarten was a time for children to *prepare* for school. Today, it *is* school—in most places as focused on academic skill as first grade used to be. Will the same thing happen to preschool? We need to think hard about how we will balance the pressure to prepare young children academically with their social/emotional needs. How will we increase young children's academic skills without undermining their enthusiasm for learning or reducing the attention we give to the many other domains of development that are important for their success?

The early childhood education community has resisted a focus on academic skills primarily because experts are worried that it will come in the form of whole-group instruction, rigid pacing, and repetitive, decontextualized tasks—the kind of "drill and kill" that is becoming commonplace in the early elementary grades and that is well known to suffocate young children's natural enthusiasm for learning. My own recent observations in preschools suggest that these concerns are well founded.

I am seeing children in preschool classrooms counting by rote to 10 or 20 in a chorus. When I interview the children, many have no idea what an 8 or a 10 is. They can't tell me, for example, how many cookies they would have if they started with 7 and I gave them one more, or whether 8 is more or less than 9. I am seeing children recite the alphabet, call out letters shown on flashcards, and identify letter/sound connections on worksheets (e.g., by drawing a line from a *b* to a picture of a ball). Some can read the word *mop* but have no idea that they are referring to a tool for cleaning floors, and they are not able to retell in their own words a simple story that had been read to them.[2] I am seeing young children recite by rote the days of the week and the months of the year while the teacher points to the words written on the board—without any understanding of what a week or a month is and without even a clear understanding that the written words the teacher points to are connected to the words they are saying. In these classrooms every child in the class gets the same task or is involved in the same activity, despite huge variability in their current skill levels. Some children are bored because they already know what is being taught; others are clueless.

Alternatives to Drill and Kill

The good news is that young children can be taught basic skills in ways that engage rather than undermine their motivation to learn. Motivating instruction must be child-centered—adapted to the varying skills and interests of children.

Good teachers embed instruction in activities that make sense to young children. They teach vocabulary, for example, by systematically using and reinforcing the meaning of new words in the context of everyday activities. When children are blowing bubbles, the teacher might introduce different descriptive terms (e.g., "shimmer") or names of shapes (e.g., "oval" versus "round"). Teachers promote oral language by reading stories, encouraging story making, joining in role play, asking children to explain how things work, giving children opportunities to share experiences, helping them to expand what they say, and introducing and reinforcing more complex sentence structures. Comprehension and analytic skills can be developed by reading to children and asking them to predict what will happen next and to identify patterns and draw conclusions. Print awareness is promoted by creating a book area, having materials and other things in the classroom labeled, and pointing out features of books being read to children. Phonics can be taught through songs, rhyming games, and language play. Early writing skills can be encouraged and developed in the context of pretend play (e.g., running a restaurant or post office) and by having children dictate stories or feelings to an adult and gradually begin to write some of the words themselves.

Good teachers are busy asking questions, focusing children's attention, helping them document and interpret what they see, and providing scaffolds and suggestions.

Young children develop basic number concepts best by actively manipulating objects, not by rote counting.[3] Mathematics, like literacy, can be learned in the context of playful activities. A pretend restaurant can provide many opportunities for learning math. Children can match one straw for each glass for each person, count out amounts to pay for menu items (five poker chips for a plastic pizza, four chips for a glass of apple juice, and so on), tally the number of people who visit the restaurant, or split the pizza between two customers. Questions about relative quantities (less and more, bigger and smaller) can be embedded in restaurant activities and conversations. (Who has *fewer* crackers or *more* juice left in her glass?) Children can categorize and sort objects (e.g., put all the large plates on this shelf and the tall glasses on the shelf below). Measurement of weight and even a basic notion of fractions can be learned by cooking for the restaurant (a half cup of milk, a quarter cup of sugar); volume can be learned by pouring water from measuring cups into larger containers.

Effective teaching of young children cannot be delivered through a one-size-fits-all or scripted instructional program, in part because teachers need to be responsive to children's individual skills and interests. Good teachers know well what each child knows and understands, and they use that knowledge to plan appropriate and varied learning opportunities. For example, whereas one child may dictate a few sentences to the teacher for his journal each day, another might actually write some of the words herself. While some children are asked to count beans by ones, others are asked to count them by twos or by fives.

Teaching in the kinds of playful contexts mentioned above can be direct and explicit. Young children are not left to their own devices—to explore aimlessly or to invent while the teacher observes. To the contrary, effective and motivating teaching requires a great deal of active teacher involvement. Teachers need to have clear learning goals, plan activities carefully to achieve those goals, assess children's learning regularly, and make modifications when activities are not helping children learn.

Good teachers are busy asking questions, focusing children's attention, helping them document and interpret what they see, and providing scaffolds and suggestions. Which object do you think will float, the small metal ball or the block of wood? Why do you think the wood floated and the ball didn't, even though the wood block is bigger? On the paper, let's put an "F" for float after the pictures of the objects that float and an "S" after the pictures of the objects that sink. Then we can look at our summary of findings to figure out how the floating objects and the sinking objects are different from each other. Teachers need to assess children's understanding and skill levels both informally—as they listen to children's replies and comments during classroom activities—and more formally—interacting with each child individually for a few minutes every few weeks. And teachers need to use what they learn from their assessments to plan instructional interventions that will move *each child* from where he or she is to the next step.

Effective teachers also maintain children's enthusiasm for learning by being vigilant and seizing opportunities to use children's interests to teach. I once observed a brilliant teacher turn a child's comment about new shoes (which most teachers would have found distracting) into a multidisciplinary lesson. She asked the students to take off one shoe and use it to measure the length of their leg, from their waist to their ankle. Some had to learn how to find their waist and ankle to accomplish the task (physiology and vocabulary). They also had to count each time they turned the shoe and keep track of where they ended up (math). The teacher then led a conversation about who had the longest and the shortest leg (comparisons). Then they measured arms and talked about whether arms were shorter or longer than legs and by how much (introduction to subtraction and idea of averages). The conversation finally turned to other objects that could be used as measuring instruments.

This teacher didn't always rely on spontaneous teaching opportunities. She had a very well-planned instructional program. But she also took good advantage of children's interests and seized opportunities to build academic lessons out of them.

Beyond Academic Skills

Ironically, to achieve high academic standards, we need to be more, not less, concerned about the nonacademic aspects of children's development. Children's social skills and dispositions toward learning, as well as their emotional and physical well-being, directly affect their academic learning.

Fortunately, efforts to promote development on important nonacademic dimensions need not reduce the amount of time children spend learning academic skills. As I describe below, efforts to support positive social, emotional, and physical development can be embedded in the academic instructional program and the social climate of the classroom.

Social skills. Children who have good social skills—who are empathic, attentive to others' needs, helpful, respectful, and able to engage in sustained social interactions—achieve academically at a higher level than children who lack social skills or are aggressive.[4] The higher achievement results in part because children who are socially adept develop positive relationships with teachers and peers. They are motivated to work hard to please their teachers, and they feel more comfortable and secure in the classroom. Aggressive and disruptive children develop conflictual relationships with teachers and peers and spend more time being disciplined (and thus less time engaged in academic tasks).

Social skills can be taught in the context of classroom routines and activities designed to teach academic skills. Lessons about appropriate social behavior can be provided as stories that are read to children and discussed. Opportunities to develop skills in collaboration can be built into tasks and activities designed to teach literacy and math skills. Teachers can encourage children to develop social problem-solving skills when interpersonal conflicts arise by helping them solve the problem themselves—"Is there another way you could have let Sam know that you wanted to play with the airplane?"—rather than solving the problem for them—"Sam, give the airplane to Jim. It's his turn."

A program called "Cool Tools," designed to promote social and academic skills, begins with preschoolers at the UCLA lab-oratory elementary school—the Corinne A. Seeds University Elementary School. Children create an alphabet that decorates the walls of their classroom: "S" is for "share," "K" is for "kindness," "H" is for "help," "C" is for "cooperation." Teachers also take advantage of events in the world and in the community. Following the tsunamis in Southeast Asia, the children made lists of what survivors might need. They donated the coins they had collected for their study of money in mathematics to a fund for survivors, and they made muffins and granola and sold them to parents and friends to raise additional funds. Thus literacy and math instruction, and a little geography, were embedded in activities designed to promote feelings of responsibility and generosity.

Dispositions toward learning. Children's beliefs about their ability to learn also affect their learning. Children who develop perceptions of themselves as academically incompetent and expect to fail don't exert much effort on school tasks, and they give up as soon as they encounter difficulty. Engagement in academic tasks is also affected by students' sense of personal control. Children enjoy schoolwork less and are less engaged when they feel they are working only because they have to, not because they want to.[5]

Luckily, much is known about practices that foster feelings of competence and expectations for success. These beliefs are not "taught" directly. Rather, they are influenced by the nature and difficulty level of the tasks children are asked to complete and by the kind of evaluation used and the nature of the feedback they receive. Children's self-confidence is maintained by working on tasks that require some effort (so that when they complete them they have a sense of satisfaction and achievement). However, the tasks must not be so difficult that the children cannot complete them even if they try. The huge variability in children's skill levels is why rigidly paced instruction is inappropriate; if all children are asked to do the same task, it will invariably be too easy (and thus boring) for some students or too difficult (and thus discouraging) for others.

Classroom climate is also important. Self-confidence is engendered better in classrooms in which all children's academic achievements are celebrated than in classrooms in which only the best performance is praised, rewarded, or displayed on bulletin boards. Effective teachers encourage and praise children for taking on challenges and persisting when they run into difficulty, and they invoke no negative consequences for failure. ("You didn't get it this time, but I bet if you keep working on these kinds of problems, by lunch, you'll have figured out how to do them.")

The nature of evaluation also matters. Evaluation that tells children what they have learned and mastered and what they need to do next, rather than how their performance compares to that of other children, fosters self-confidence and high expectations. ("You are really good at consonants, but it looks like you need to practice vowels a little more.") All children can learn and will stay motivated if they see their skills developing, but only a few can perform better than their peers, and many will become discouraged if they need to compete for rewards.

We also know how to foster a feeling of autonomy. Clearly children cannot be given carte blanche to engage in any activity they want and be expected to master a set of skills and understandings adults believe to be important. But children can be given choices in what they do and how and when they do it, within a constrained set of alternatives. Even modest choices (whether to use beans or chips for a counting activity; which puzzle to work on) promote interest and engagement in learning.[6]

Emotional well-being and mental health. Children's emotional well-being and mental health (a clear and positive sense of the self; a positive, optimistic mood; the ability to cope with novel and challenging situations) have an enormous impact on how well they learn. Students who are depressed, anxious, or angry are not effective learners. Feeling disrespected, disliked, or disconnected from the social context can also promote disengagement—from academic work in the short term and, eventually for many students, from school altogether. Paying close attention to the social and emotional needs of students and creating a socially supportive environment can go a long way toward promoting social/emotional and mental well-being. It can also reduce the need for special services.

Substantial research suggests that the school social climate is also critical to mental health. A respectful and caring social context that ensures close, personal relationships with adults, that is orderly and predictable, and that promotes feelings of self-determination and autonomy in students can contribute substantially to students' emotional well-being. Peers affect the social context as much as teachers, and thus they have to be taught the effects of their behavior on other children. The "Cool Tools" program, for example, teaches 4-year-olds about "put-ups" and "put-downs," noting that it takes five put-ups to repair one put-down. Children also play games that illustrate how the same comment can be heard differently, depending on the volume and tone of voice and body posture.

Physical development. Lack of exercise and consumption of too much sugar are two behaviors that have immediate negative effects on children's ability to focus on academic work. We need to provide children with opportunities—such as outdoor play time and healthy snacks—to engage in positive behavior while they are at school. And we need to help them develop healthy habits—such as brushing teeth, washing hands, and exercising—that will contribute to their well-being.

Teachers can talk to children about how exercise affects their bodies in the context of a science lesson on physiology. (Why do we need a heart? How are muscles different from fat?) And compelling and visible messages can be given through science experiments, such as observing what happens to two pieces of bread several days after one piece was touched with a dirty hand and the other with a clean one.

Programs serving children from low-income families should also make an effort to work with community agencies to ensure access to dentists and physicians. Even a trip to the doctor or dentist can be used to promote academic skills. Children can develop communication skills by being asked to describe their experience, they can learn vocabulary, and they can develop the cultural knowledge that we now know is necessary for becoming

a proficient reader. (It's hard to make sense of a sentence with the word "stethoscope" in it if you've never seen one used.)

Educating Children

Educational leaders need to take seriously the accountability demands made on them. By paying more attention to academic skills in preschool, we can help close the achievement gap, and we can give all children a chance to expand their intellectual skills. But we need to avoid teaching strategies that take all the joy out of learning. This will not, in the end, help students achieve the high standards being set for them.

We also need to resist pressures to prepare children only to perform on tests that assess a very narrow set of academic outcomes. Attention to other domains of development is also important if we want children to be effective learners as well as effective citizens and human beings. Policy makers should demand that if assessments for accountability are to be used in early childhood programs, they measure genuine understanding and the nonacademic skills and dispositions that we want teachers to promote. We have learned from No Child Left Behind that, if the tools used for accountability focus on a narrow set of skills, so will the educational program.

Finally, teaching young children effectively takes a great deal of skill. If we want teachers to promote students' learning and motivation, we need to invest in their training. States vary considerably in their credentialing requirements for early childhood education teachers. Few require a sufficient level of training. On-the-job opportunities for collegial interactions focused on teaching and learning and professional development are also critical. Preschools that are good learning environments for adults are likely to be good learning environments for children.

An investment in preschool education could help us achieve the high academic standards to which we aspire. Let's make sure we provide it in a way that does more good than harm.

Notes

1. Meredith Phillips, James Crouse, and John Ralph, "Does the Black-White Test Score Gap Widen After Children Enter School?," in Christopher Jencks and Meredith Phillips, eds., *The Black-White Test Score Gap* (Washington, D.C.: Brookings Institution Press, 1998), pp. 229–72.

2. A story recounted to me by a researcher who was assessing a young child's reading skill illustrates what can happen if decoding is overemphasized. The child read a brief passage flawlessly but was unable to answer a simple question about what he had read. He complained to the researcher that he had asked him to read the passage, not to understand it. Clearly this child had learned that reading was synonymous with decoding sounds.

3. See, for example, Barbara Bowman, M. Suzanne Donovan, and M. Susan Burns, eds., *Eager to Learn: Educating Our Preschoolers* (Washington, D.C.: National Academy Press, 2001); and Douglas Clements, Julie Sarama, and Ann-Marie DiBiase, *Engaging Young Children in Mathematics: Standards for Early Childhood Mathematics Education* (Mahwah, N.J.: Erlbaum, 2003).

4. See, for example, David Arnold, "Co-Occurrence of Externalizing Behavior Problems and Emergent Academic Difficulties in Young High-Risk Boys: A Preliminary Evaluation of Patterns and Mechanisms," *Journal of Applied Developmental Psychology*, vol. 18, 1997, pp. 317–30; Nancy Eisenberg and Richard A. Fabes, "Prosocial Development," in William Damon and Nancy Eisenberg, eds., *Handbook of Child Psychology,* 5th ed., vol. 3 (New York: Wiley, 1997), pp. 701–78.

5. For a review, see Deborah Stipek, *Motivation to Learn: Integrating Theory and Practice*, 4th ed. (Needham Heights, Mass.: Allyn & Bacon, 2002).

6. See, for example, Leslie Gutman and Elizabeth Sulzby, "The Role of Autonomy-Support Versus Control in the Emergent Writing Behaviors of African-American Kindergarten Children," *Reading Research & Instruction*, vol. 39, 2000, pp. 170–83; and Richard Ryan and Jennifer La Guardia, "Achievement Motivation Within a Pressured Society: Intrinsic and Extrinsic Motivations to Learn and the Politics of School Reform," in Timothy Urdan, ed., *Advances in Motivation and Achievement: A Research Annual*, vol. II (Greenwich, Conn.: JAI Press, 1999), pp. 45–85.

DEBORAH STIPEK is a professor of education and dean of the School of Education at Stanford University, Stanford, Calif.

From *Phi Delta Kappan,* June 2006. Copyright © 2006 by Phi Delta Kappan. Reprinted by permission of the publisher and Deborah Stipek.

No Child Left Behind

Who's Accountable?

Lisa A. DuBois

To many federal legislators, No Child Left Behind is like the cavalry sent to rescue the American educational system. To many teachers, the federal mandate is simply another shackle, more paperwork and red tape, as they try to stimulate and expand the minds of the young. But to many involved in educational research, No Child Left Behind is akin to the leg of an elephant. The information they are gathering about that leg is helpful and important, but it is also becoming increasingly clear that the animal resting on the appendage is far more gargantuan and complex than originally imagined. Still, many look forward to embarking on a quest, albeit imperfect and unpredictable, to unravel the mysteries of the beast.

Certainly, experts and non-experts across the nation do not dispute that the American system of education is not where it needs to be. Right now, for example, the United States is tied with Zimbabwe for achievement in 8th grade mathematics. Today, over 80 percent of African American and Latino 8th graders say they plan to attend a two- or four-year college. Yet, once there, many are not prepared for a rigorous post-secondary education. Between 40 and 60 percent of college students need remedial work to catch up, and between 25 and 50 percent of these students drop out after their first year. These data imply that although the existing K–12 system is graduating students, it is not necessarily preparing them for life beyond high school.

The Bush Administration's answer to this conundrum has been to rigidly implement the No Child Left Behind (NCLB) law. Enacted during the president's first term and up for reauthorization in 2007, NCLB requires that 100 percent of American public school students reach set proficiency standards in reading and math (and as of 2008, in science, as well) by the year 2014. Individual states set their own standards and all students, regardless of family income, race, ethnicity, or disability must comply. Schools whose students fail to achieve these goals face increasingly onerous penalties and sanctions.

> **"NCLB makes a lot of sense if it would work. It's saying to schools, you can't ignore some of your kids just because they're tough to teach." —Andrew Porter**

Academicians are studying NCLB's impact on a number of fronts. Andrew Porter, Patricia and Rodes Hart Professor of Educational Leadership and Policy, believes that NCLB, while flawed, is in many ways "a beautiful thing," because it has beamed a spotlight on the need for equity, opportunity and accountability from all schools. "You can't just forget about your poor kids, or forget about your English language learners, or your special ed kids, or your black or Hispanic kids, or your boys. You've got to do well by everybody. . . . NCLB is better than anything we've ever had in the past on that score," he says. "Think about a kid from a low-income family. NCLB makes a lot of sense if it would work. It's saying to schools, you can't ignore some of your kids just because they're tough to teach."

Also, Porter adds, deliberations have now effectively shifted from input and process to what teachers are teaching (content) and what students are accomplishing (proficiency), which he considers a healthy change from past educational reform movements. NCLB approaches the problems of the education system from the perspective of the students matriculating through it. Every public school student must take a state-designed reading and math assessment every year in grades 3 to 8, and also during one high school year, usually grade 10. These assessments hold schools accountable for student proficiency by requiring them to reach the stated benchmarks, known as Adequate Yearly Progress (AYP). Students in those schools that fail to meet AYP goals for two consecutive years are given "an escape hatch," meaning they can choose to attend a different school. Schools that fail three years in a row are given a carrot in the form of supplemental services like funds for tutoring and enhanced teaching materials. After five years of a school's failing to meet targets, the measures become more punitive—that school can be taken over by the state, reconstituted, restructured or shut down.

As with any nationally mandated reform that imposes sanctions for noncompliance, NCLB has generated angst and hand-wringing among those in the trenches—teachers, principals, parents and superintendents—particularly concerning issues of accountability. In fact, accountability debates crop up at every turn: Is it fair to hold schools accountable? Are these standardized tests valid measures of content and proficiency? And are sanctions the best way to address accountability issues?

Is It Fair to Hold Schools Accountable?

Porter, for one, favors school accountability, because it addresses the educational framework on a very specific local level. However, he also is pressing for "symmetry in accountability," meaning that teachers and students should likewise be held responsible for achieving certain benchmarks. "If you're going to have accountability for schools, then you should also have accountability for students. You don't want schools to be left hanging out to dry for students who don't try," he says. "When education is successful, students, teachers and administrators roll up their sleeves and work together." NCLB does not currently address this existing accountability gap.

By the same token, Porter is bothered that NCLB was set into motion with an endpoint that guarantees failure. The goal of having 100 percent of students achieve 100 percent proficiency by 2014 is so unattainable that even countries with the most proficient educational systems in the world would not use that as a target.

"Demanding 100 percent proficiency is the only way we could have gotten started," counters Stephen Elliott, Peabody professor of special education and the Dunn Family Professor of Educational and Psychological Assessment. Elliott is an international expert on testing accommodations and alternate assessments for children with disabilities. When NCLB was being formed, disability advocacy groups wanted schools to be held accountable for the inclusion of their children, realizing that every disabled child certainly would not be able to meet the national standards. Yet they also didn't want disabled children to be given short shrift or for the bar to be set inappropriately low just so schools could slide into compliance. The resounding consensus, says Elliott, was that these groups had to advocate for 100 percent proficiency, pushing the limits so that disabled students can get the educational tools and services they need. NCLB opens a window for them to design a criterion, set expectations, see if students can reach them, and then readjust them as necessary.

"This is an experiment and we're learning as we go," Elliott says, acknowledging that some schools have failed to meet AYP goals because their special needs students were unable to pass the assessment tests.

Are Standardized Tests Valid Measures of Content and Proficiency?

Porter believes that the testing industry, which is making a mint from the explosion in demand for more standardized tests from pre-school through graduate school, is actually pretty good at what it does. The validity of the content of these tests is a less critical issue than our nation's tendency to water down curricula and have teachers in charge of courses they were never trained to teach. Teachers, meanwhile, complain that they have to "teach to the test."

"That's cheating," claims Elliott. "They should be teaching to the standards the tests are aligned to. Curriculum, testing and standards are all being aligned, which is the backbone of the accountability issue. The finger-wagging should be on the instruction. Our tests today are far better than they were a decade ago because of this legislation."

Ironically, two of the biggest drivers forcing the refinement of standardized testing are children with disabilities and low-income gifted students. Because special needs children are included in AYP, researchers have been studying which kinds of multiple-choice questions, for example, are best at illuminating a child's mastery of content without being skewed by that child's decision-making and reading challenges. Most standard multiple-choice tests give the taker four or five options; but according to Michael Rodriguez of the University of Minnesota (*Educational Measurement: Issues and Practice*, Summer 2005), the best format for truly gauging knowledge is one that presents three multiple-choice options. It turns out that this format is the best determinant of content mastery for non-disabled students, as well.

Elliott and his colleagues have also been examining testing accommodations and their influence on the scores of students with special needs. They discovered some unsettling data. As expected, children with Individualized Education Programs (IEPs) tested better when given special accommodations, such as private settings, reading support and extra time. However, children with no perceived special needs also scored higher on standardized tests when given these same accommodations. Surprisingly, the highest functioning children were the only ones who actually used the extra time they'd been given. But all groups of students reported feeling a psychological edge and believed they performed better with the opportunity to have extra time if they needed it.

Teachers, meanwhile, complain that they have to "teach to the test."

For low-income, minority and English-language learners, NCLB has yanked the veil off the ever pervasive "achievement gap" in American education. Simply put, affluent children are receiving a better public education than those whose families are struggling. After studying this dilemma for years, Porter and others have found that the achievement gap between preschoolers who come from wealthy families versus those from impoverished families is enormous, as big as it will ever be—before these children ever go to school.

Once they reach school age, the gap does not increase during the school year. Minority and poor youngsters make achievement gains parallel to their more affluent peers. Unfortunately, says Porter, "Minority and poor kids lose more achievement in the summer than do white and more affluent kids. All the spread in the achievement gap happens when they're not in school in the summer time."

These two factors—that the achievement gap is greatest among preschoolers and that the gap widens every summer while children are not in school—means that schools are being asked to fix a societal problem that extends beyond the confines of the classroom. Donna Y. Ford, Betts Professor of Education and Human Development in the department of special education, and Gilman W. Whiting, director of Vanderbilt African American Diaspora Studies, have initiated the Vanderbilt Achievement Gap Project to bring about large-scale change by addressing contributing factors on a local level. Ford believes that a major obstacle to closing the achievement gap is that schools that serve large numbers of underprivileged children are not offering them the kinds of rigorous curricula that will enable them to excel. In other words, expectations for disadvantaged populations have been set too low.

Ford says, "If we don't put more poor kids in gifted programs in K–6, how are we going to get them into AP classes in high school? They've had nine years of not being challenged, so how can they survive? The ability is there and the potential is there, if given the opportunity."

The data support her argument. Researchers from the private Center for Performance Assessment identified schools in which 90 percent of the students are poor, 90 percent are members of ethnic minority groups, and 90 percent also meet high academic standards. Some of the common characteristics these schools share include a strong focus on academic achievement and frequent assessment of student progress with multiple opportunities for improvement (*Challenge Journal: The Journal of the Annenberg Challenge*, Winter 2001/02).

One approach for more accurately evaluating achievement, again being driven by advocates of students with disabilities, is to offer more formative assessments. Rather than giving students a single "do-or-die" test at the end of the school year to measure their progress, Elliott and others are promoting the idea of delivering shorter, lower stakes assessments, delivered two or three times during the school year. They're finding that good formative tests are predictive of how proficient students will be by the end of the year.

Elliott explains, "The lowest functioning kids can make progress, even if they may never be proficient."

"Across the nation, one of the fastest spreading reforms is interim assessment," Porter says. "The upside to interim assessment is that teachers find out how well students are performing all along. The downside is what do you do when you find out they're not doing so well? Nobody's answering that question."

In 2005, NCLB asked states to compete for the opportunity to replace AYP with improved performance plans, considered by some researchers to be a superior index of proficiency, but, out of all the submissions, only North Carolina and Tennessee had the models and infrastructure to execute such a plan. "One of the most fragile areas of NCLB is the ability of states to manage the data," Elliott says. "Many statistical experts are going to work in the lower pressure, higher paying testing industry. So we're leaving people in the states who don't have the technical skills to manage the information."

One solution to this conundrum is to completely nationalize NCLB assessments, both in terms of content and proficiency. Porter is an avid proponent of this idea. Right now, each state has invested in its own content standards for math and reading. Unfortunately, a child from, say, Colorado, who moves to a new school in Georgia, may suddenly face an entirely different curriculum in the same school year. Concentrating all the energy that is now being used to develop materials, standards and assessments for 50 different states into the creation of one voluntary national standard, says Porter, "would mean enormous efficiency and would undoubtedly result in tremendous improvements in quality. If you're sinking all your resources into building one really great test, you can do a great job."

One approach for more accurately evaluating achievement, again being driven by advocates of students with disabilities, is to offer more formative assessments.

While national content standards may receive some level of support, Porter is also advocating for voluntary national proficiency standards, considered a less popular option. Right now, there are far-flung variances between states in benchmarks for achievement, and in most cases, a larger percentage of students reach proficiency on the state tests than on a comparable nationwide instrument, the National Assessment of Educational Progress (NAEP).

"In some states, the difference is enormous," Porter says, "like the difference between 30 percent and 90 percent."

Are Sanctions the Best Way to Address Accountability Issues?

In its current form, one of NCLB's most glaring glitches is its inability to impose the kinds of sanctions that result in student achievement. After a school fails for three consecutive years, students are supposed to receive the benefits of tutoring and supplemental services.

"Supplemental services haven't worked as well as we hoped they would," Porter says. Some districts aren't receiving the funding for these services in time to help the students, but more crucially, schools don't know what services they need until after their students have taken and failed the AYP assessment. So, they are faced with constantly moving targets.

Once a school misses its benchmarks two years in a row, students are allowed to transfer to schools that have not been identified as needing improvement. This has not panned out for a variety of reasons, Porter says. First, the better performing schools don't want to risk their AYP status by accepting an influx of students who've failed to meet the benchmarks. Second, in some cases, every school in the district is failing to reach NCLB guidelines. The sanction becomes irrelevant, because students have no place to go. Finally, poor and non-English speaking parents may find the logistics of transferring their children out of a neighborhood school to be too overwhelming to be worth the ordeal.

Today, the achievement gap between underserved children and children of privilege stands at a full standard deviation, which in raw terms means that vast numbers of kids are undereducated.

According to Ford, the solution will not be a band-aid or a simple promise to move kids to a new school. Instead it will require an intrinsic, primordial transformation across the education network. "If you move a child from an economically disadvantaged background and from a school that isn't rigorous into a school with a more rigorous curriculum, that child is going to need a lot of support not just to catch up, but to keep up," she says. "That's an equity issue. You can't just put children in a new school to frustrate them and make them fail. You have to believe in them and support them."

Now that NCLB is entering its first phase of reconstituting low-performing schools, the Bush administration is pushing to have private school vouchers added to the law, a proposal opposed by the National Education Association and others involved in collective-bargaining agreements.

The Next Wave Will Be NCLB's Effect on Higher Education

Today, the achievement gap between underserved children and children of privilege stands at a full standard deviation, which in raw terms means that vast numbers of kids are undereducated. Closing that gap by one standard deviation would, for example, bring a child at the 50th percentile up to the 84th percentile, a phenomenal gain. Porter contends that such a jump can happen if America improves the quality of its teaching.

"If we could get every kid to have a good teacher every year and if the effects of having a good teacher had a shelf life and were cumulative, it wouldn't take much of a change per year to add up to a standard deviation," he says. "We've got 12 years. If students could move up a tenth of a standard deviation every year, we'd get up to 1.2 standard deviations."

The onus, says Ford, is on the nation's universities to step up and prepare highly qualified teachers with high expectations who will enter the field and teach our children. To accomplish that, she thinks universities should revamp their courses so that student teachers start their practica earlier in college and spend more of their training out in the field gaining experience in a range of educational settings.

For all its many flaws and pitfalls, Porter, Elliott and Ford agree that NCLB has served the public well by forcing the conversation about education in the U.S. It has sparked new energy and directed attention to equity issues that have long been swept under the rug. NCLB obligates Americans to acknowledge the inadequacies in our school systems.

"That's the best thing NCLB could have done," says Ford. "The numbers are so dismal that we couldn't ignore them any longer. NCLB showed us the numbers. That's why I appreciate it. I don't blame NCLB solely for the problems we're having. It could have been any other piece of education legislation, and we still would have had to face these numbers."

From *Peabody Reflector,* Summer 2007, pp. 14–20. Copyright © 2007 by Lisa A. DuBois. Reprinted by permission of the author.

Preschool Comes of Age

The National Debate on Education for Young Children Intensifies

Educators rave about the benefits of early-childhood schooling. So, why don't we support it more?

MICHAEL LESTER

Early this year, two dissimilar governors delivered two similar messages.

"Effective preschool education can help make all children ready to learn the day they start school and, more importantly, help close the enormous gap facing children in poverty," announced New York's Eliot Spitzer. He boldly promised to make a high-quality prekindergarten program "available to every child who needs it within the next four years."

Across the continent, California governor Arnold Schwarzenegger signed legislation expanding preschool opportunities in low-performing school districts and providing additional state dollars for building and improving preschool facilities. "Preschool gives our kids the strong foundation they need to be successful in school and in life," said Schwarzenegger.

Spitzer (a Democrat) and Schwarzenegger (a Republican) may not agree about a lot of things, but here's one area where they concur: Preschool education can perform miracles. Children who attend prekindergarten programs have bigger vocabularies and increased math skills, know more letters and more letter-sound associations, and are more familiar with words and book concepts, according to a number of studies.

Nationwide, almost two-thirds (64 percent) of children attend preschool center in the year prior to kindergarten, typically at age four. On any given day, more than 5 million American youngsters attend some prekindergarten program.

And a preschool day is not just advanced babysitting for busy parents. Kids also practice many key components of the school day, including the importance of routine. That's key for early learners. "They understand carpet time, clean-up procedures, how to share crayons, or even getting their pants on and off without the teacher's help; that's big," says Steve Malton, kindergarten and first-grade teacher at Parkmead Elementary School, in Walnut Creek, California. "Little kids have only a

certain amount of what's called 'active working memory.' If a large portion of their brain is figuring out what they're going to do next, there's less room there to spend on learning." Result: Preschool has a huge impact on their ability to keep up in class.

Too Much, Too Soon?

So, what's not to love about preschool? Plenty, say critics. "Young children are better off at home," says Michael Smith, president of the Home School Legal Defense Association. "We are in danger of overinstitutionalizing them. A child will develop naturally if the parents give the child what he or she needs most in the formative years—plenty of love and attention. In this way, the brain can develop freely."

As soon as the subject of schooling before K-12 comes up, another concept quickly follows: testing. That gives some parents the jitters. "The only way for school programs, including preschool programs, to show accountability of public funding for education is through testing," says Diane Flynn Keith, founder of Universal Preschool. "The only way to prepare children for standardized testing is to teach a standardized curriculum. Standardized preschool curriculum includes reading, writing, math, science, and social sciences at a time when children are developmentally vulnerable and may be irreparably harmed by such a strategy."

That's part of a broader test-them-sooner move across many grades. One pushdown from No Child Left Behind, for instance, is that highstakes testing now begins as early as the second grade. "It's not the same kindergarten we went to," says Don Owens, director of public affairs for the National Association for the Education of Young Children (NAEYP). "It's not the same kindergarten it was ten years ago. Kindergarten used to be preparation for school, but now it *is* school. That's why school districts and boards of education are paying attention to what happens before the kids arrive at school."

America is forcing its parents to decide between paying for early education and saving for college.

The result is a desperate tug-of-war between prekindergarten advocates and critics, with the under-six set placed squarely in the middle. In 2006, for instance, the Massachusetts legislature passed, by unanimous vote, an increase in state-funded high-quality prekindergarten programs. Governor Mitt Romney promptly vetoed the bill, calling preschool an "expensive new entitlement."

On the national stage, Oklahoma is the only state to offer publicly funded preschool education to virtually all children (about 90 percent) at age four. But twelve states—Alaska, Hawaii, Idaho, Indiana, Mississippi, Montana, New Hampshire, North Dakota, Rhode Island, South Dakota, Utah, and Wyoming—provide no preschool services at all. "There is not enough support for preschool," explains David Kass, executive director of Fight Crime: Invest in Kids. "It's very expensive, and most parents cannot afford it."

The three costliest states for private preschool are Massachusetts (where preschool runs an average of $9,628 per year), New Jersey ($8,985), and Minnesota ($8,832). In Rhode Island, the average yearly tab for preschool ($7,800) represents 45 percent of the median single-parent-family income. In California, part-time private preschool and child-care programs cost families on average $4,022 statewide. By comparison, the average full-time tuition at a California State University campus was $3,164.

"America is forcing its parents to decide between paying for early education for their kids and saving for their college education," says the NAEYP's Don Owens.

That's when the subject of state-sponsored preschool comes up. Over the past two years, the total state prekindergarten funding increased by a billion dollars to exceed $4.2 billion. But those numbers are often inadequate. After Florida voters approved a preschool-for-all initiative similar to a voucher program, the state legislature appropriated about $390 million—or roughly $2,500 per child served. Reasonable budgeting for preschool, however, should parallel that for K-12 schools. "If you're a state like Florida spending $9,000 per student on a yearly full-day program of K-12, your costs for a half day of prekindergarten should be somewhere around $4,500, not $2,500," complains Steve Barnett, director of the National Institute for Early Education Research.

That pattern is true nationwide. In 2002, average state spending was at $4,171 per enrolled child, but that figure fell to $3,482 in 2006, according to the NIEER's 2006 *State Preschool Yearbook*. Some states spend even less: New Mexico provides $2,269 per child, and Ohio budgets just $2,345. Compare those amounts with the national average of $10,643 for each child enrolled in K-12 schools.

Barnett says Florida and other states are creating a dual system consisting of high-quality, expensive preschools in private settings and underfunded public schools for low-income families.

The Survey Says . . .

While the battle over funding continues, it's difficult to dispute the positive effects of preschool not only in better learning in kindergarten but also in long-term educational value. Furthermore, key research findings indicate that those who go through prekindergarten programs are more likely to graduate from high school and make higher wages as adults.

The research recited in support of preschool education usually comes from three long-term studies of low-income families. In the Abecedarian Project, launched in 1972 in rural North Carolina, 57 infants from low-income, African American, primarily single-mother families were randomly assigned to receive early intervention in a high-quality child-care setting; 54 children were assigned to a control group. Each child had an individualized prescription of educational activities, which consisted of "games" incorporated into the child's day and emphasized language skills. The child care and preschool were provided on a full-day, year-round basis.

Initially, all children tested comparably on mental and motor tests; however, as they moved through the child-care program, preschoolers had much higher scores on mental tests. Follow-up assessments completed at ages twelve, fifteen, and twenty-one showed that the preschoolers continued to have higher average scores on mental tests. More than one-third of the children who attended preschool went to a four-year college or university; only about 14 percent of the control group did.

Another important research effort was the High/Scope Perry Preschool study, which began in Ypsilanti, Michigan. From 1962 to 1967, 123 three- and four-year-olds—African American children born into poverty and at high risk of failing school—were randomly divided into one group that received a high-quality preschool program and a comparison group that received no preschool.

These children were evaluated every year, ages 3–11, and again three times during their teens and twice in adulthood. The latest results of this High/Scope study were released in 2004. By the time members of the preschool-provided group reached age forty, they had fewer criminal arrests, displayed higher levels of social functioning, and were more likely to have graduated from high school.

Meanwhile, Chicago's Child-Parent Centers (CPC) have been around for forty years, and more than 100,000 families have gone through the federally funded program, which still operates in twenty-four centers. Parents are drawn into the program with classes, activities, and their own resource room at each school site.

A longitudinal study by Arthur Reynolds, a researcher at the University of Wisconsin at Madison, looked at 1,539 Chicago students enrolled in CPCs in 1985 and 1986 and tracked their progress through 1999. He found they were much more likely to finish high school and less likely to be held back a grade, be placed in special education, or drop out than 389 youngsters who participated in alternative programs. Intervening early improves student achievement and has a cumulative effect: The longer students were in the CPC programs, the higher their level of school success.

Quantifying Quality

The National Institute for Early Education Research has compiled ten generally accepted benchmarks for what constitutes high-quality prekindergarten education. The list follows:

- Lead teacher has a bachelor's degree, or higher
- Teacher has specialized training in prekindergarten
- Teacher has at least fifteen in-service hours per year
- Assistant teacher has a child-development-associate (CDA) degree, or equivalent
- Early-learning standards are comprehensive
- Maximum class size is twenty
- Staff/child ratio is one to ten, or lower
- Children are screened for vision, hearing, and health
- Meals are provided at least once a day
- Monitoring takes place through on-site visits

Unfortunately, almost half the states do not meet the degree benchmark for all lead teachers. Not one state meets all ten benchmarks.

Other shorter-term studies—and there are many—argue these kinds of benefits are not limited to at-risk children but extend to middle income kids as well. But when a family's budget is tight, preschool becomes unaffordable. Less than half of low-income toddlers attend preschool, but half of middle-class four-year-olds and three-quarters from high-income families (earning $75,000 or more) attend preschool.

That enrollment gap can have immediate academic consequences, say educators, who note that the lower the family income, the more pronounced the benefits of preschool. "I've worked with a lot of kids and know the achievement gap starts before kids are even in kindergarten," says Kimberly Oliver, a kindergarten teacher from Silver Springs, Maryland, and 2006 National Teacher of the Year.

Learning While Playing

Many educators appreciate the wide range of positive influences preschool seems to germinate. Debra King, a preschool teacher for thirty-five years, has run the Debra King School, in San Francisco, for nearly half that time. "There's been a big push lately to make preschoolers ready for academic learning, to teach children the alphabet and how to write their names," King says. "Many children are developmentally ready to learn these things, but I think socialization skills are more important. I believe that playing with blocks, dolls, and toys, scribbling with crayons, painting, communicating, storytelling, and music—that's readiness for school. There are a lot of different things to learn to be successful in the world."

That's an important insight. "The original preschool was a place for socialization, but, increasingly, today it has become necessary because of working and single parents," explains David Elkind, professor of child development at Tufts University and author of *The Hurried Child* and *The Power of Play.* "And that's muddied the waters, because people think it needs to be an educational thing. We got it turned around and are learning the academic things before we learn the social skills that are prerequisites for formal education."

Elkind believes phonics, math, and book reading are inappropriate for young children. "There is no research supporting the effectiveness of early academic training and a great deal of evidence that points against it," he says. "The age of six is called the age of reason because children actually develop those abilities to do *concrete* operations; brain research substantiates this. Take reading: A child needs to be at the age of reason to understand that one letter of the alphabet can sound different ways. That age might be four or it might be seven. They all get it; they just get it at different ages."

Elkind argues that toddlers need to learn only three things before entering kindergarten, and they're all socialization skills: listen to adults and follow instructions, complete simple tasks on their own, and work cooperatively with other children. "Children need to learn the language of things before they learn the language of words," he adds. "They are foreigners in a strange land, and they need to learn about the physical world, they need to explore colors, shape, and time, they need to find out about water and the sky and the stars, and they need to learn about human relations. Much of this learning comes from direct experience."

Sharon Bergen, senior vice president of Education and Training for the Knowledge Learning Corporation, counters that curriculum and fun are not mutually exclusive: "Children are capable of a lot of development earlier than we thought," she says. "But we don't want their time to be overly structured. We still want kids to have a good, fun, joyful childhood." With prekindergarten education, many people think, we can have it both ways.

MICHAEL LESTER is a writer and editor. He recently launched a site about fatherhood, *Dad Magazine Online,* at www.dadmagazineonline.com.

From *Edutopia*, June 2007, pp. 41–44. Copyright © 2007 by George Lucas Educational Foundation. Reprinted by permission.

Taking a Stand

Strategies for Activism

RICHARD J. MEYER

"I'll close my door and do what I've always done."

Many teachers have said this as a way of dismissing the new curriculum and assessment requirements that conflict with their beliefs as educators. Teachers hope that their classroom doors will insulate them and their students from inappropriate mandates that may limit effective teaching and fail to accurately reflect children's learning. But closing doors does not work.

President Bush, in his inaugural speech, proclaimed the success of the No Child Left Behind Act. Indeed, many families whose children have not met with success in schools view the legislation as hopeful because it appears to finally offer access to education and the American dream. Many educators however, believe that the mandates get in the way of effective teaching and learning. One educator, in fact (Nieto 2004), called the law "mean-spirited," because it ignores the cultural, linguistic, research, and pedagogical realities in an effort to homogenize and simplify what occurs in classrooms.

Many early childhood educators feel they must implement programs that conflict with their understanding of best practice. Some teachers are saddened and some even decide to leave schools in which administrators are not open to dialogue, challenge, and reflection. But there is hope in taking action. This article is about action and activism because it is time for teachers and supporters of public education to respond when imposed curriculum and high-stakes testing (when a test score alone is used to make an important education decision about a child, like being promoted to the next grade) do not reflect what educators know about development, learning, and teaching.

The guiding principle of this Viewpoint is one that could make some early childhood educators uncomfortable because it extends our job descriptions. That principle is this: we may have to act beyond our schools to support authentic learning in our classrooms and to preserve the integrity of our profession.

Ways to Take Action

Action can be simple and private or more bold and public. Some teachers may choose to become more active in an educational organization or association they believe in. Others may become active and vocal in local political issues. A word of caution—if you choose to become involved in a public manner, consider the repercussions of your actions. It is better to act in partnership than alone, unless you are confident that your right to express your views will be respected. My ultimate goals are to support teacher conversations and autonomy, to validate teachers' knowledge, and to advocate for local control so those educational programs can reflect the needs of students.

Talk with Each Other

Teachers may feel isolated or vulnerable when asked to implement curriculum that is based on inappropriate expectations. They can ease these feelings by telling their stories (Ohanian 1999). Teaching colleagues can meet socially to talk about conditions in their school, district, or state. Building a trusting atmosphere might be a gradual process, but once it is built, there will be a safe forum in which the group can begin to understand and plan. One helpful piece of advice is to end a meeting by setting the date for your next meeting.

Knowing that there is a next meeting can serve as a beacon for hope.

We may have to act beyond our schools to support authentic learning in our classrooms and to preserve the integrity of our profession.

Work with Local Advocacy Groups

In some cases, local groups have begun conversations that lead to real action. Ellen Brinkley and her colleagues (1997) describe a group of teachers, other educators, and citizens who formed one such group called Michigan for Public Education (MPE). They advocated for educational equality and excellence and prevented adoption of a curriculum that they thought inappropriate. Their group received support from a number of national organizations. In Florida, groups of individuals talking to each other united to prevent the state from instituting a voucher system (Hallifax 2000). Conversations are forums for thinking and serve to end loneliness and the sense of oppression that some teachers feel, but they can also lead to real change.

Learn Lessons from History

Our advocacy actions become part of the grassroots responses that occur around the country. But we do not necessarily need to invent strategies because many successful approaches already exist. Systematic meetings—open forums in which stories could be told and issues discussed—led to the civil rights movement in the 1960s (Horton, with Kohl & Kohl 1998).

A group of teachers might meet and listen to or read the speeches of Martin Luther King Jr. Many teachers don't know the story of Highlander Center (Horton, with Kohl & Kohl 1998) and would find inspiration in learning how Martin Luther King Jr., Septima Clark, Rosa Parks, and other civil rights workers and union organizers strategized for action under the leadership of Myles Horton.

Studying the past could provide examples for us as we advocate for good teaching practices.

Reading about the women's movement, Mothers Against Drunk Driving (started by Cindy Lightner), Gandhi, and Ralph Nader (consumer advocate) are also ways to learn how others acted to promote social causes. Perhaps we can "recapture some of the experiences of coming together that occurred in the peace movement and the civil rights movement" (Greene 1995, 75). Studying the past could provide examples for us as we advocate for good teaching practices.

Vote

In a metaphorical light, we cast a vote each time we teach. We vote for a book when we engage children with it. We vote for an operational definition of reading when we institutionalize certain practices. We vote for having a voice when we tell our stories to one another in an effort to understand what is happening around us, why it's happening, and consider what we can do about it. We vote for developmentally appropriate teaching strategies when we make pedagogical decisions based upon our students' actions, interests, and performance.

Although the national elections are past, we must ensure that we are informed about local issues and convince pro-education candidates to run for school boards, town councils, and state and national seats that are available every two years. We can encour-

age teachers and parents who agree with us about appropriate educational practices to vote in elections for candidates that support our work. Activism might involve working with the League of Women Voters (www.lwv.org) to ensure that all eligible people are registered to vote. We can show our presence both by casting a vote and by telling others why we voted as we did.

Partner with Colleagues at Colleges and Universities

Colleges and universities sometimes offer courses that respond in a timely way to the needs of teachers in their surrounding communities. These institutions of higher education may enhance their partnerships *with* teachers and community members to assess curriculum for how well it "accept[s] the children, their culture, their language, and their ways of knowing into the . . . classroom" (Willis & Harris 2000, 81). Early childhood educators might approach faculty at a local university or seek out a distance learning institution to suggest a course or workshop focusing on critical literacy, education and politics, or another area that will address current needs. Perhaps professors would be interested in forming a study group, teaching a course, or engaging in an independent study focusing on local or national issues.

Do Teacher Research

One of the most powerful ways in which teachers can act is to inquire into the effectiveness of our own classroom practices. As teacher researchers, we gather data, systematically analyze it, and present it to audiences of our choosing. Such research helps teachers become more articulate about what happens in the classroom because we are "living the questions" (Hubbard & Power 1999).

NAEYC's online feature Voices of Practitioners (found on the Beyond the Journal page: www.journal.naeyc.org/btj) offers articles and useful resources on teacher research that readers can download to read, share with colleagues and families, and use for staff development and college courses.

Participate in Professional Organizations

Educators can organize and act within professional organizations concerned with issues of teaching, learning, and high-stakes testing. Attending national conventions is always a powerful experience. We might become more active by writing letters to organization officers and joining committees and commissions. Forming a special interest group within an organization is a relatively easy process that typically gives members a meeting time and place—and a public forum—at the national conference. NAEYC, for example, offers members the opportunity to join an existing special interest group or form a new one. Each group has an Online Communities Web page for discussing issues and networking on NAEYC's Web site. (See the members' area at www.naeyc.org for more information.) Write, call, or visit the Web site of educational organizations for information on their groups and activities. Here are a few.

As teacher researchers, we gather data, systematically analyze it, and present it to audiences of our choosing.

The International Reading Association (IRA)—The International Reading Association's lobbyist reports on his activities in *Reading Today*, one of the IRA's journals. For this and other information on IRA's work, visit www.reading.org.

National Council of Teachers of English (NCTE) and Whole Language Umbrella (WLU)—The NCTE Web site has information about the organization's political actions. NCTE produced a strategy packet for teachers interested in writing to families, various commissions, legislators, editors of newspapers, and more.

In addition, NCTE is affiliated with the Whole Language Umbrella (WLU), which supports professionals interested in developing and implementing whole language approaches in educational institutions. For the past five years, the annual WLU conference (now called the Literacies for All Summer Institute) has offered preconvention workshops on teaching, politics, and activism. WLU invites sessions in which teachers tell stories of their struggles and their actions.

For more information on NCTE and WLU, visit www.ncte.org.

Phi Delta Kappa—This organization has been bold in its use of the Kappan journal as a forum for discussions on controversial issues from many points of view. Phi Delta Kappa has a presence in Washington, D.C., and the News, Notes, and Quotes newsletter that members periodically receive also contains information about what is happening in the legislature and the courts.

Unions—Some teachers feel supported by their unions and others do not. Some unions take stands on curricular, pedagogical, and testing issues. In my opinion, unions should articulate clear agendas that support academic freedom but should not take stands on issues such as teaching materials, methods, and curriculum. Many teachers see unions as negotiating away benefits. Teachers sometimes vote against their union by quitting. If you choose this action, make sure you understand the benefits that you are leaving behind. Some teachers purchase liability insurance from other agencies in order to leave their union.

National Association for the Education of Young Children (NAEYC)—NAEYC has crafted position statements on many important topics in early childhood education. (Educators can view the position statements online at www.naeyc.org/about/positions. asp.) These research-based position statements give guidance to the field and policy makers on critical issues in early childhood education. The Association also engages in public awareness and public policy advocacy to promote a well-financed, high-quality system of early care and education for all children.

Like the organizations mentioned above, NAEYC sponsors national conferences. NAEYC's state and local affiliates offer conferences at a local level. Teachers can attend these conferences as a place to find other colleagues to support them in their activism. Proposing sessions for conferences lets teachers voice what they are experiencing and informs the organization of their interests and needs.

NAEYC offers a number of resources for those who want to advocate for policies that support a system of high-quality early care and education programs.

NAEYC offers a number of resources for those who want to advocate for policies that support a system of high-quality early care and education programs. For links to NAEYC's action center, a toolbox for advocates, and more, visit www.naeyc. org/policy.

Wear a Message
Sometimes we can wear our views and use them to engage in meaningful discussions about educational issues. Harman's (2000) "High Stakes are for Tomatoes" T-shirts gained much attention at recent national conventions. When I saw her shirts, I had some printed with the words "Raise a child, not a test score" on the front and "High-Stakes Testing" written in a red circle with a line through it on the back. People stopped me in stores to discuss the message and to order a shirt. It's a small action but it felt great to connect with others; the shirt was a magnet for conversations about testing, legislators, and parenting.

I recently learned about a teacher who wore her "Raise a child . . ." shirt to work and was told by her principal not to wear it again in school. The teacher contacted her union and the union lawyer reminded the principal of the teacher's first amendment right to free speech. She wears it every Friday.

Advocate in the Community
I am consistently amazed at the long list of organizations and companies that know little about teaching, learning, and schools, yet tell educators what's wrong with schools and how to fix them (Spring 1997). Teachers, teacher researchers, and college and university faculty could respond to these groups by providing information and making concrete suggestions about ways they could provide help.

In the community where I teach and do research, I attended a meeting of a business group that has been quite vocal about problems with education. The members are convinced that if our city's students achieve high test scores, the economy will improve and more new businesses will want to locate here. They also suggest that higher test scores will result in reductions in poverty. Street (1995) has refuted this idea, noting that just the opposite is more accurate: if there were less poverty, children would perform better in schools.

At a recent meeting of this group, I reported on Street's ideas and suggested what local businesses might do to support literacy efforts in our city. Local businesses could actively work to raise employee incomes in the poorer neighborhoods of the city. These businesses could hire more individuals as full-time employees who receive health and dental benefits. They could also provide quality child care for employees' children. I also told them that the principles of industry should not be applied to schools because children are not products. Of course, the group did not like my suggestions and I'm not invited to these meetings anymore, but the ideas have been aired.

If you choose to confront such a group, there are some guidelines to consider: (1) attend with a colleague; (2) make sure you understand the group's agenda for education; (3) prepare a written statement from which to read; (4) limit your statement to two or three points of action that the group can take to truly be helpful (don't shred their ideas, offer useful ones); (5) distribute copies of your statement to the group and to the press, if the press is present; and (6) prepare a one-sentence response to those who disagree with your statements.

The Hope and the Challenge

Hope is apparent all over the country as resistance increases to using standardized test scores alone to make critical educational decisions about a child; slowly and cautiously we are finding support. Organizations like the Whole Schooling Consortium, FairTest, and The Rouge Forum are emerging with broad agendas that work to include other organizations. There are always risks when we take any action. There are also risks to inaction, and we may believe that those are not as severe. We won't be fired for *not* speaking out.

Early childhood educators who speak out do risk being reprimanded, suspended, perhaps even fired, depending on the conditions of their employment. The problem is that sometimes inaction means using curriculum and tests that are not good for our students. We need not act radically and risk our jobs; some of the ideas above (talking, doing teacher research) are powerful but low risk. Our goal needs to be to continue our work with children in a way that respects our knowledge base.

There are always risks when we take any action. There are also risks to inaction.

Teaching has changed. Some mandates force us to teach in ways that conflict with our beliefs as educators. Our ability to teach in ways that call upon our expertise as educators is in jeopardy if we remain silent and retreat to our classrooms.

Teaching prescribed programs that seek to raise test scores, complying with narrowly defined standards, using programs

that profit others financially or politically, and being forced to apply inaccurate interpretations of research—these chip away at authentic and relevant teaching and learning. Using "one-shot" tests that provide limited and inaccurate snapshots of our students in place of the assessment data from multiple sources that teachers have collected over an entire year diminishes students' accomplishments. Closing our doors leaves us isolated, lonely, and living with a false sense of safety while our teaching and children's learning are at risk.

It is time to open the doors.

References

Brinkley, E., C. Weaver, P. Campbell, M. Houston, J. Williams, V. Little, M. Freedman Mohaghan, J.B. Bird, & J. Bird. 1997. Believing in what's possible, taking action to make a difference. *Language Arts* 74 (7): 537–44.

Greene, M. 1995. *Releasing the imagination: Essays on education, the arts, and social change.* San Francisco: Jossey-Bass.

Hallifax, J. 2000. Florida judge tosses school voucher law. *Albuquerque Journal,* March 15, p. A9.

Harman, S. 2000. Resist high-stakes testing: High stakes are for tomatoes. *Language Arts* 77 (4): 332.

Horton, M., with J. Kohl & H. Kohl. 1998. *The long haul: An autobiography.* New York: Teachers College Press.

Hubbard, R., & B. Power. 1999. *Living the questions: A guide for teacher-researchers.* York, ME: Stenhouse.

Nieto, S. 2004. "No Child Left Behind and the Community." Panel discussion, Authentic Educational Reform: Teachers and Parents Speak Out! Conference, Queens College, City University of New York, Flushing, New York.

Ohanian, S. 1999. *One size fits few: The folly of educational standards.* Portsmouth: Heinemann.

Spring, J. 1997. *Political agendas for education: From the Christian Coalition to the Green Party.* Mahwah, NJ: Erlbaum.

Street, B. 1995. *Social literacies: Critical approaches to literacy in development, ethnography, and education.* New York: Longman.

Willis, A., & V. Harris. 2000. Political acts: Literacy learning and teaching. *Reading Research Quarterly* 35 (1): 72–88.

RICHARD J. MEYER, PhD, is an associate professor in the Department of Language, Literacy, and Sociocultural Studies at the University of New Mexico, Albuquerque. His areas of research include young children's literacy, the politics of literacy, and beginning teachers' understanding of the reading process and instruction. He taught young children for almost 20 years and continues to do research in classrooms with teachers and children.

From *Young Children*, May 2005, pp. 80–85. Copyright © 2005 by National Association for the Education of Young Children. Reprinted by permission.

UNIT 2

Young Children, Their Families and Communities

Unit Selections

Key Points to Consider

- How can teachers develop strong working relationships with parents of children in their class?

- What are the responsibilities for teachers related to working with children who are allergic to various substances?

- Are teenage parents able to effectively care for their children with support from educators?

- What do grandparents raising grandchildren need to be effective parents for the second time?

Student Web Site

www.mhcls.com/online

Internet References

Further information regarding these Web sites may be found in this book's preface or online.

Administration for Children and Families
http://www.dhhs.gov
The AARP Grandparent Information Center
http://www.aarp.org/grandparents
All About Asthma
*http://pbskids.org/arthur/grownups/teacherguides/health/*asthma_tips.html
Allergy Kids
http://allergykids.com
Changing the Scene on Nutrition
http://www.fns.usda.gov/tn/Healthy/changing.html
Children, Youth and Families Education and Research Network
www.cyfernet.org
The National Academy for Child Development
http://www.nacd.org
National Network for Child Care
www.nncc.org
National Safe Kids Campaign
http://www.babycenter.com
Zero to Three
http://www.zerotothree.org

Stockbyte/PunchStock

I was very fortunate to be included in a group of seventeen educators from southeast Michigan who traveled to China in October of 2006. The purpose of our trip was to begin exploring ways to bring teachers to Michigan schools to teach Chinese and to learn more about the education and culture of China. What I did learn is that the country of China, massive in terms of size, population and growth, is making great strides as it moves forward with a lengthy agenda. I especially enjoyed watching young children out with their parents and grandparents. In much of the country the "one child only" policy is still in effect in an attempt by the government to curb the rapid population growth. Young children in China grow up in a family structure quite different from young children in the western world. Chinese children have no siblings, few if any cousins and usually all four grandparents living close. Children in America often have siblings, but grandparents and cousins may be off in another state. I found it ironic that children in both cultures spend increasing amounts of time moving through traffic. The transit experiences couldn't be more different though. Chinese children are strapped to a bike seat or hang on to the jacket of a parent as a bike weaves through busy city traffic. They are entertained by the thousands of other cyclists, cars, trucks and busses inching along the clogged streets. American children are entertained in SUVs complete with swivel chairs, tables, cup holders and one or more video screens with an array of games and movies to pass the time.

One of the benefits of working with young children is we do have opportunities to interact with family members and get to know what life is like at home for the children in our classes. The chance to interact with family diminishes as the learner gets older until it is almost nonexistent at the secondary level. In Laura Pappano's article, "Meeting of the Minds," Pappano provides strategies for moving from the traditional teacher-dominated conference to a two-way conference where sharing between the parents and teachers about the strengths and needs of the child are discussed.

I rarely walk into a preschool or elementary school today where I don't see a large sign posted with a list of food items banned in the building. More and more school personnel are dealing with children whose allergies produce effects ranging from minor rashes to life threatening air passage closings. School offices look like pharmacy counters with rows of medication children take at lunch time or need in case of an emergency. School personnel must develop strong lines of communication with children's families to learn the best way to handle children's allergies. School administrators are developing policies and procedures to deal with the growing list of allergens and the increasing numbers of children with allergies in their schools. Claudia Kalb's "Fear and Allergies in the Lunchroom" will provide answers to many questions.

The next two articles examine the heads of families at two very different ends of the spectrum. "Supporting Grandparents Who Raise Grandchildren" and "Children of Teen Parents" really are not that different in their advice. In each article the authors stress the importance of individual support and integrated services that meet the needs of that particular family. Younger parents, as well as second time around parents, all need support and welcome the opportunity to have teachers for their children or grandchildren who are understanding of their particular situation.

Families can provide a wealth of information about their child and teachers who develop strong relationships with families are beneficiaries of this knowledge. Get to know the families of your children. Share a bit about yourself and your interests and you may be rewarded with information from families about the children in your class. Build on this information to provide learning experiences that are relevant and meaningful to your children.

Meeting of the Minds

The parent-teacher conference is the cornerstone of school-home relations. How can it work for all families?

LAURA PAPPANO

Agnes Jackson isn't proud to admit it, but last year she didn't attend a single parent-teacher conference for her youngest son, who just completed third grade at the Thomas O'Brien Academy of Science and Technology in Albany, New York.

It's not as if she didn't try. Jackson did respond when the school asked her to select a time for a face-to-face meeting. "They asked me what time could I be there and I told them, but they said, 'Oh, somebody already took that,'" says Jackson, a single mother of three who works nights as a certified nursing assistant. She made several impromptu visits to the school, whose website touts it as a "nationally recognized Blue Ribbon School of Excellence," but each time her son's teacher was unavailable. "They'd say, 'You need to wait until school is over,'" she recalls.

The parent-teacher conference may be the most critical, yet awkward, ritual in the school calendar. It is treated as a key barometer of parental involvement, so important that a Texas lawmaker earlier this year proposed fining parents $500 and charging them with a Class C misdemeanor for skipping one. New York City Mayor Michael R. Bloomberg wants to pay poor families up to $5,000 a year to meet goals, including attending parent-teacher conferences.

Yet, in practice, these conferences can be ill-defined encounters whose very high-pressure design—bringing together a child's two most powerful daily influences for sometimes superbrief meetings about academic and social progress—make them a volatile element in home-school relations. For schools, parent-teacher conferences can be a nightmare to organize and may leave teachers spinning after hours of quick encounters. For parents, sessions can feel more like speed-dating than team-building and may encourage snap judgments.

Surveys of K–8 parent involvement conducted by the National Center for Educational Statistics indicate that a majority of parents attended parent-teacher conferences in 2003. Yet, many are still absent. Those parents who might most need to show often don't or can't. The most involved can now, in a growing number of districts, access their child's homework, grades, and attendance online.

Given the weight that parents and teachers place on these once- or twice-a-year get-togethers, what can schools do to ensure that parent-teacher conferences are effective and productive—and meet the needs of all families?

The conference is not for me to give you my judgment, but for us to share experiences and suggestions.

The "Two-Way" Conference

Kathleen Hoover-Dempsey, associate professor and chair of the department of psychology and human development at Vanderbilt University, who studies home-school communication, says face-to-face conversations are more effective than written notes and e-mails, especially when the teacher has concerns or suggestions to make. For parents, "the heart just leaps a bit at the thought that something is wrong," she says. Conferences should include a chance for parents to share observations or concerns, specifics from the teacher about positive things a child is doing, and thoughts on how the teacher and parent might support a child's performance, Hoover-Dempsey says.

Many schools are rethinking conferences to make them less a complaint session and more a collaborative discussion, she says. "People are really starting to talk about the 'two-way parent-teacher conference' and the 'mutually respectful parent-teacher conference.' The conference is not for me to give you my judgment, but for us to share experiences and suggestions about things we can do to really support this child's education."

Collaborative conferences can be promoted by "bundling" them with other chances for parents and teachers to communicate, according to Karen Mapp, lecturer at the Harvard Graduate School of Education and a coauthor of *Beyond the Bake Sale: The Essential Guide to Family-School Partnerships*. Very effective schools may hold several face-to-face conferences each year, including some in which students present their schoolwork

Laying the Groundwork for Successful Parent-Teacher Conferences

To foster parent-teacher talk—formal or informal—Claire Crane, principal of the Robert L. Ford School in Lynn, Mass., has structured her school to get parents in the building as often as she can. Many are recent immigrants working two or three jobs, so she lures them to school by meeting *their* needs. School is open Monday and Tuesday until 9 p.m., when 250 parents attend English as a Second Language classes and a course on surviving in the U.S. Ford staff members teach the classes and provide babysitting and a chance to connect.

The school also operates like a community center. Parents perform in neighborhood talent shows, raise money, and plant trees to beautify the grounds. They have even volunteered alongside city health officials to try to halt a rat problem by putting out bait.

Crane says the intense level of involvement and communication enhances parent-teacher relationships and, in turn, both the formal and informal conferences that take place. So when it's time for formal parent-teacher conference nights three times a year, Crane says, "I can't handle the crowds."

As a result, when there are difficult conversations to have—and there are plenty in a school in which one-third of students attend summer school in order to be promoted—parents feel they are on the same team with the school.

"I feel so much confidence in the principal, I come and ask her, 'What can I do?'" says Beverly Ellis, a mother of five and Ford School parent for 22 years. Ellis, who has two children at the school now, recently had to speak with teachers when her daughter started throwing erasers in her sixth-grade class. "I like to hear they are doing good. But if things are not going right, you can talk to the teachers."

- In what ways is your child working up to his or her expectations?
- What things at school make your child happiest? Most upset?
- Think of a time when your child dealt with a difficult situation that made you very proud. What did you see as the strengths of your child in that situation?

Chrispeels, who trains teachers in conducting parent conferences, says such questions are important both for the information they provide teachers and because they position parents as partners in their child's schooling. The process also lets parents know that teachers realize children may be acting differently at school than at home.

Teachers should be prepared to show concrete examples of academic expectations, including student papers with names removed. "Teachers need to be able to explain to parents, 'Here is the range of work in this class,' " says Chrispeels. That way, she says, parents can have a better idea of what the teacher will be encouraging students to achieve in the future.

Chrispeels advocates ending conferences with what she calls a "one to grow on" message, to let parents know what the teacher intends to do to address any areas of weakness—and how the parent might help at home. Sometimes that can be as simple as explaining what skills they are working on in school and what resources are available to help students outside of school, like a before-school phonics help session.

Even parents of children who are doing well in school need reassurance that their child is developmentally, socially, and intellectually on track, says Chrispeels. Teachers also have experience and information to relay, for example, about planning high school course loads to meet graduation and college-entrance requirements. This helps parents anticipate a child's stresses and needs.

Facilitating Participation

More parent-teacher dialogue means schools must work harder to meet parents on their turf and tailor meetings to suit particular lifestyles and needs. Because their parent populations can vary significantly, school administrators are using different approaches to facilitate parent-teacher conferencing.

At Arlington (Mass.) High School, an upper-middle-class suburb of Boston where 72 percent of graduates go on to four-year colleges, parents can now sign up online for five-minute, face-to-face parent-teacher conferences. It's so popular that when administrators opened up the conference registration at midnight in the fall of 2004, 200 slots were booked in the first 10 minutes. Principal Charles Skidmore says online registration gives parents more choice and control and that, as a result, teachers are drawing more parents to conferences. "We are seeing some of the 'hard-to-reach' parents," Skidmore reports.

The situation is much different at the K–8 Robert L. Ford School in Lynn, Mass., where 90 percent of students are low-income and 58.5 percent speak English as a second language. Principal Claire Crane has created multiple ways for parents and teachers to talk, including holding parent-teacher conferences

and share responses to questions they have pondered in advance, says Mapp, former deputy superintendent for family and community engagement for the Boston Public Schools. Others may be times for parents and teachers to meet solo and discuss an agenda agreed upon in advance. The key, says Mapp, is that the school community should shape how conference time is used.

Shifting Dynamics: A Larger Role for Parents

Building a two-way exchange, says Janet Chrispeels, professor of education studies at the University of California at San Diego, also requires shifting the dynamic of the conference from *reporting on* a child to *eliciting from* parents a better understanding of a child's strengths at home, in order to provide clues to helping them at school. Questions that might reveal these clues include:

- What homework habits does your child have that make you proud?

Conference Dos and Don'ts

Some teachers dread parent-teacher conferences because no one has taught them what to do—or what not to do, says Todd Whitaker, professor of educational leadership at Indiana State University and author or coauthor of several books, including *Dealing with Difficult Parents*.

His advice for setting a positive tone and dealing with difficult parents:

- Hold the first parent-teacher conference early in the year, before children get into trouble or fall behind. Call parents in advance if there is a problem. Nothing in the conference should be a surprise.
- Sit next to the person. "We are on the same team," says Whitaker.
- Even if parents are angry, keep calm and treat them in a positive manner.
- Speak about "we" and not "you": "What can we do together so your son can be more successful?"
- Focus on the future. Do not treat conferences as a conclusion but as a step along a path.

as early as 7 a.m. and as late as 9 p.m. (see "Laying the Groundwork for Successful Parent-Teacher Conferences"). These conferences are sensitive to parents' needs. They are folded into family evenings that include displays of student work (no babysitters needed, and kids can show off learning). There is food. There are translators. The conferences are never held in the winter (easier for families with babies). Last year, Crane even held a conference in the street because a father with health problems couldn't easily get out of his car.

The formula appears to have worked. Crane, whose school has an attendance rate of 95.5 percent, had 92 percent of families come to an open house in November 2006 and attend parent-teacher conferences later that same night.

Other schools focus on welcoming parents during the school day. At Harriet Gibbons High School in Albany, New York, a new school serving ninth graders in a community in which 40 percent of students qualify for free or reduced-priced lunches, principal Anthony Clement built parent-teacher conference time into the daily school schedule. Team A teachers are available from 12:40 p.m. to 1:40 p.m., and Team B teachers are available from 10:30 a.m. to 11:30 a.m. If parents are not free during the conference hour, teachers will meet at other times, or—as in the case of the mother of a child in math teacher George Benson's class who must pack up three young kids and take two city buses to attend a conference—plan regular phone calls. School social workers will even make home visits. Noting that many of his parents work at jobs with hourly wages, Clement says, "We know when a parent is here, we need to see them."

As a result, Clement says, 80 percent of parents have attended one or two daytime parent-teacher conferences *in addition* to the two districtwide conferences held on two school days in November and January. Clement credits the emphasis on conferencing with increasing school attendance from 63 percent last year to 85 percent this year, more parent involvement in school activities, and a dramatic up-tick in ninth graders earning five or more of the required credits for promotion to tenth grade, from 45 percent last year to almost 70 percent this year.

The school's approach has also helped parents like Agnes Jackson get involved in her middle son's education. Where Jackson has yet to attend a conference at her third grader's school, she sat down more than a dozen times with her ninth-grade son's teachers at Harriet Gibbons—and that doesn't count scores of informal conversations about her son's school progress.

The frequent conferences have given Jackson a better handle on how the school system works and what is expected of her children. "In the past, I was quick to say, 'These people are doing this to my child,'" she says. "Now I ask, 'But what is my child doing that causes this to happen?' I can hear good and bad. But it's all good because I know how to respond to help my child. It helps me to say, 'OK, bud, you've got to do this,'" says Jackson. "It's helped me to grow as a single parent."

The easy access to teachers at Harriet Gibbons has also colored her views about her son's schools. Her third grader's school, she says, "will call if there is a problem," whereas the constant conversation with her ninth grader's teachers has made her more of a partner. "They tell me about his potential; they tell me what he is capable of doing," she says.

LAURA PAPPANO writes about education and is coauthor, with Eileen McDonagh, of *Playing with the Boys: Why Separate Is Not Equal in Sports*, to be published in November 2007 by Oxford University Press.

From *Harvard Education Letter*, July/August 2007. Copyright © 2007 by Harvard Educational Review. Reprinted by permission.

Fear and Allergies in the Lunchroom

CLAUDIA KALB

It's 1 P.M. at Mercer Elementary School in Shaker Heights, Ohio, and Lena Paskewitz's kindergarten class is filled with the happy hum of kids getting ready for their favorite part of the day: lunch. Caleigh Leiken, 6, is toting a pink Hello Kitty bag her mom has packed with goodies: strawberry yogurt, string cheese, some veggies and a cookie. But there's one childhood staple missing—a PB&J. Caleigh was diagnosed with a peanut and tree-nut allergy when she was just 7 months old. Nuts are a no-no at her table in the Mercer lunchroom. Her allergy-free friends can sit there, but only if their lunches have been stored in a special bin and carefully inspected by the teacher. Home, too, is a nut-free zone for Caleigh. When she goes trick-or-treating this week, her candy will be scarier than any costume; she won't be able to eat any of it for fear it's tainted with peanut residue. For Caleigh's mom, Erika Friedman—whose other two kids also have allergies—food can seem like an enemy. "We plan everything," says Friedman. "It's our job—actually, everyone's job—to keep them safe."

There was a time when food allergies were of little concern to the medical community. Today about 11 million Americans suffer from them, and many scientists agree the numbers are climbing. Most significantly, peanut allergies—among the most dire—doubled between 1997 and 2002 in children under 5. "Clearly, the number has increased in the younger population," says Dr. Hugh Sampson, a food-allergy pioneer at Mount Sinai School of Medicine in N.Y. "We suspect that [in the future], the numbers in general are going to increase." Allergists say they're now seeing more children with multiple allergies than ever before, not just to 1950s staples such as milk and wheat—but to global foods we have adopted since, like sesame and kiwi. And allergies many kids outgrow—like those to eggs—seem to be lingering longer than they did in the past.

Parents of very young children now worry over the introduction of each new food, on alert for the first signs of trouble, such as rashes, diarrhea and vomiting. Deaths are rare, but the most-sensitive kids' throats may swell and completely close up if they're exposed to the wrong foods. Even if your school-age child is allergy-free, you still have to be concerned about inadvertently triggering an allergic reaction in one of your kid's friends or classmates. Dairy-free birthday cakes are de rigueur these days, as are no-peanut Halloween parties.

PEANUTS: 1.8 million Americans can't eat them. Tree nuts, such as pecans and almonds, are also off-limits for 1.8 million.

But why do allergies appear to be on the rise? One of the most intriguing theories, dubbed the "hygiene hypothesis," is that we've all become too clean. The immune system is designed to battle dangerous foreign invaders like parasites and viruses and infections. But clean water, antibiotics and vaccines have eliminated some of our most toxic challenges. Intriguing research even posits that kids born by Caesarean section, which have risen 40 percent in the last decade, could be at higher risk for allergies, perhaps because they were never exposed to healthy bacteria in their mothers' birth canals. Without hard-core adversaries, the theory goes, the immune system starts battling the innocuous—egg or wheat—instead.

Almost everyone, it seems, has had to adapt to the rise in food allergies. Affected kids are carrying EpiPens, syringelike devices loaded with epinephrine, in case of severe reactions. Many schools, like Mercer Elementary, maintain "peanut-free zones," where allergic students can eat in safety. A growing number of states are establishing allergy guidelines. Manufacturers, thanks to a federal law implemented last year, now list the eight most common allergens (from milk to fish) on their food labels. And many airlines offer their passengers pretzels instead of peanuts.

While scientists have a basic understanding of how allergies work, they can still be stumped by the immune system, which is too complex to submit easily to their control. There are no cures for food allergies—only treatments for some of the symptoms—and the best parents and children can do now is avoid the culprits. Still, in recent years, researchers have begun to make exciting progress. They're studying a radical approach: introducing the offending ingredients early to see if they can treat, cure or even prevent food allergies from developing. In one study, children allergic to peanuts are being given tiny amounts of peanut flour to see if they can build up tolerance. In another, funded by the Consortium of Food Allergy Research (coFAR), a five-year $17 million initiative launched in 2005 by the National Institute of Allergy and Infectious Diseases, researchers will give peanut-allergic adults small doses of an engineered peanut protein to ward off reactions and possibly eliminate the problem. The idea is ultimately to have a peanut-allergy vaccine. For Sampson, who is working on it, the quest for a solution is more urgent than ever. "We're desperate," he says.

DAIRY PRODUCTS: 900,000 have this allergy. Unlike lactose intolerance, it affects the immune system, not digestion.

It is hard to fathom how the joys of childhood—a peanut-butter sandwich, a warm chocolate-chip cookie, a cold glass of milk—can send a tiny body into battle mode. How just one bite can make the throat itch, the lips swell, the stomach clench in agony. How an immune system, exquisitely designed to protect us against bacteria and viruses, can perceive healthful nutrients as enemies of state. Bryan Bunning, 13, and his brother, Daniel, 11, of Lake Forest, Ill., know what it's like. Bryan was 6 months old when his body revolted against a sip of milk-based formula. "His lips blew up and his eyes went back in his head," says his mother, Denise. The boys share a list of verboten foods between them: eggs, tree nuts (including cashews, walnuts, almonds, hazelnuts), milk and shellfish. In March, Daniel was diagnosed with an allergy-related disorder of the esophagus that left him able to eat only apples and bacon. Now he gets most of his nutrients through a feeding tube. "It's really hard going to parties. You watch all your friends eat what they say are amazing foods, like ice-cream cake," says Daniel. "They're, like, 'Daniel, it's really good.' I say, 'I can't, I have food allergies'."

Nobody knows precisely what causes food allergies. A combination of genes—allergies run in families—and environment clearly play a role. The cascade of events begins when an allergy-prone person encounters a substance like pollen or peanut. The body sees it as trouble and launches phase one of its offensive: the production of antibodies called IgE (immunoglobulin E). These molecules attach themselves to "mast" cells, which line the lungs, intestines, skin, mouth, nose and sinuses. The next time the person encounters the pollen or peanut, the mast cells are primed for warfare, sending out powerful chemicals, like histamine, which lead to those nasty allergic symptoms—wheezing, stomach cramps, itching, stuffiness, swelling and hives. In rare instances, when the response to an allergen is sudden and severe, the airways can shut down completely and blood pressure can plummet, leading to anaphylaxis. Without immediate treatment with epinephrine, a hormone that opens the breathing passages and increases heart function, anaphylactic shock can kill.

Intriguing new research into the cause of allergies lends credence to the hygiene hypothesis. Studies have shown that children who grow up on farms, where they are in constant contact with dirt and animals, are less likely to develop allergies. Canadian research published earlier this month also suggests they're at less risk of asthma. At Duke, scientists have examined the phenomenon at the molecular level by comparing the immune systems of wild, parasite- and infection-ridden rodents with their cleaner, lab-raised cousins. In a setup intended to simulate an allergic response, researchers put the animals' immune cells in a petri dish, then challenged them with a plant protein—a known immune-system stimulus—to see how the cells reacted. Last year they published their findings: the lab rodents had a much higher immune response than their wild relatives did. Their immune systems were working overtime. And the wild animals, who were unfazed by the stimulus, showed higher levels of antibodies in their blood, suggesting that they'd already battled far greater enemies and couldn't be bothered by the small stuff. "We think the wild ones probably wouldn't get an allergy," says lead investigator William Parker. "They just don't have time to mess with a pollen grain when they're fighting off some horrible parasitic liver worm." Parasites, Parker says, might ultimately help scientists find a cure. Studies have shown that patients with irritable bowel syndrome, a digestive and immune disorder, may improve if they're exposed to a pig parasite, the porcine whipworm. Parker is eager to see if similar, controlled exposure can "stimulate the immune system in a good way" in allergic kids. No one's done the research—yet—but in theory, he says, it's "highly promising."

Fixing the immune system, so that it learns to distinguish good from bad without error 100 percent of the time, is every immunologist's dream. Unfortunately, researchers still don't know enough to make that dream a reality. But what if the system could be desensitized, so kids became more tolerant of the very foods they are allergic to? The approach, called immunotherapy, is already standard practice for seasonal allergies like hay fever. Patients receive allergy shots containing small but increasing amounts of the problematic substances—weeds or tree pollen—so the immune system gradually becomes used to the allergens. Researchers have tried immunotherapy by injection for food allergies, but it's unsafe; patients may develop hives or other troubling reactions. Now scientists led by Dr. Wesley Burks at Duke are carefully testing the immunotherapeutic approach by mouth rather than needle, and they're beginning to see promising results. In a small study published in The Journal of Allergy and Clinical Immunology in January, Burks and Dr. Stacie Jones at Arkansas Children's Hospital reported that immunotherapy helped children with egg allergies tame their allergic reactions. After two years of ingesting small but increasing amounts of egg powder, most of the children could eat the equivalent of two eggs without any adverse reaction. Kids in a similar study, published this month in the journal Allergy, also developed a tolerance to eggs—although that effect disappeared after they stopped eating the powder.

Burks is using the same approach with peanuts, giving peanut-allergic children increasing amounts of a special flour with small amounts of peanut proteins. The first dose is the equivalent of about 1/1000th of a peanut; slowly, the kids have been working up to a peanut a day. Early in the trial, participant Noah Schaffer, 7, threw up after eating just 25 milligrams of peanut protein—equal to about 1/12 of a peanut. But at a food challenge last May, he ate the equivalent of 13 peanuts without any bad reaction. Burks says the results don't mean that Noah can now knowingly indulge in a Snickers bar—far from it.

But his new tolerance could protect him if he accidentally had a bite of one. His mom, Robyn Smith, says she no longer worries that something terrible will happen. "That fear has been totally removed," she says.

EGGS: Most kids outgrow an allergy to eggs—usually, to the whites—by 5. Still, 600,000 Americans are affected.

Burks's peanut flour is a precursor to what researchers hope might one day be a peanut vaccine. Together, Burks and Sampson have developed a substance that looks like a peanut but contains proteins engineered to be less potent—and thus less likely to trigger an allergic response in patients. So far, the compound has been tested successfully in mice. "If it works in people," says Sampson, "we hope to shut off the allergic response."

There are still many mysteries about how allergies start and why they sometimes stop. Researchers know that babies with egg or milk allergies and the persistent rash known as eczema are more prone to some other allergic disorders later on. Take Emily Godwin. Neither of her parents has food allergies, but at 3 months, Emily developed eczema. Five months later, doctors diagnosed food allergies. Today, at 6, she can't eat eggs, wheat, tree nuts and grapes. But little Emily has had one victory: she recently outgrew a milk allergy. In fact, many kids get over milk and egg allergies naturally—another mystery that docs don't understand. Researchers at Mount Sinai and four other sites funded by CoFAR are now recruiting 400 infants who have milk or egg allergies. The infants will be monitored over five years to see how many develop peanut allergies and how many outgrow their milk or egg allergies. The goal: to better understand at the molecular level what triggers allergies and what makes them go away. Ultimately, that knowledge could lead to treatments.

The holy grail would be to stop allergies from developing in the first place. Prof. Gideon Lack, of King's College London, has studied allergy incidence worldwide and has discovered an intriguing paradox: countries that have advised avoidance of peanuts in early childhood, like the United States, have seen the greatest rise in peanut allergies. In some Asian and African countries, on the other hand, where children eat a variety of peanut products starting at a very young age, peanut allergies are far less common.

Now Lack has enrolled more than 200 babies with eczema or egg allergies—but no known peanut allergy—in a groundbreaking trial. He'll give half the babies a peanut-containing snack; the other half will avoid peanuts. He'll then follow them all until age 5 to see if he has stopped a peanut allergy before it takes hold. "We're going to try to intervene during a narrow window of immunological opportunity in the first year of life," says Lack. If it works with peanuts, it could apply to other foods as well. Lack is hesitant, however, to make predictions and warns that nobody yet knows which method—avoidance or exposure—will turn out to be the best way to go. "I don't

want to give the impression that feeding peanuts is a safe way to prevent peanut allergy, because we really don't know," he says. If parents try to introduce peanuts early at home, "it could be dangerous." If the study is successful, however, it could lead to a turnaround in medical advice.

SHELLFISH: A common food allergy, it afflicts 6 million—2 percent of Americans. 1.2 million more are allergic to fish.

For now, parents must be hypervigilant. "They are always walking on eggshells," says Rep. Nita Lowey, who authored the federal labeling law. The labels—which require that ingredients be clearly described for consumers rather than scientists ("milk," not "casein")—are helping, and groups like the Food Allergy & Anaphylaxis Network (FAAN) applaud them. But FAAN, a nonprofit advocacy group, still worries about hidden threats. Schools sometimes use old peanut-butter jars to store crayons. Certain kinds of paint contain egg. And while the label on microwave popcorn may state that it contains milk, egg and fish, an allergic kid who isn't carefully checking the list might be at risk.

At home, Mom and Dad can control what their kids eat. The challenge is keeping them safe outside. Anne Bullard, director of Gwynn Valley Camp in Brevard, N.C., remembers the worry-free days of the past. "Twenty years ago, peanut butter was put out in the dining room for everyone," she says. "Not anymore." Today, even though just 1 percent of the 1,050 kids attending the camp have food allergies, the camp uses no nut products in its dining room. On mac-and-cheese nights, dairy-free options are on hand for campers who can't eat milk products.

Schools vary in the accommodations they make. Julie Forrest, of Waldwick, N.J., transferred her 7-year-old son, who has peanut and tree-nut allergies, out of a school where she says she was told by the principal that his safety could not be guaranteed. A study published this month found that while two thirds of surveyed schools had allergy-emergency plans, most of the policies were "missing essential components"—things as basic as having emergency contacts and student-health histories on file. And schools aren't the only ones who are lax. Some restaurant chains try to avoid nut products—Burger King carries only the occasional pie with nuts, which arrives in a sealed box—but others take fewer precautions. Another study, published in July, found that even parents of kids with allergies were increasingly ignoring "may contain" labels; 75 percent of parents said they paid attention to them in supermarkets, compared with 85 percent in 2003. The fact that the warnings are now so common may have created a new problem—with so many foods labeled, it's hard to know which really might be dangerous. "All of a sudden, it says, 'Manufactured on equipment that's used for peanuts' ... Who knows what that means?" says Mike Lade of Houston, whose son Andrew, 7, can't eat peanuts. "We need a uniform standard for all of these wishy-washy 40 variations of 'maybe it does, maybe it doesn't'."

Nonetheless, others are making major efforts to guard against allergic reactions. Eighteen percent of schools now ban peanuts entirely, up from 13 percent in 2005. At Mercer Elementary, where Caleigh Leiken and 11 other students have severe food allergies, teachers and bus drivers have been trained to use an EpiPen, and teachers explain allergies to all their students, not just the ones who suffer from them. In Connecticut, that's the law—the state's guidelines for schools require teachers to educate kids about allergies, so they won't harass classmates who can't indulge in, say, grilled cheese sandwiches. Massachusetts, Vermont and Tennessee also have statewide allergy guidelines for schools, and this year New York and New Jersey began to formulate their own. Proposed federal legislation would take things even further, giving schools up to $50,000 each to voluntarily implement uniform guidelines so that when children graduate from a school or cross state lines, parents won't have to start the education process all over again.

As awareness grows, some people wonder: are food allergies exaggerated? The numbers of children with allergies are substantial, but fewer than 1 percent of kids under 5 suffer from peanut allergies and severe reactions kill between 100 and 200 people a year. Parents—conditioned by overcautious pediatricians who've told them to keep their young kids away from nuts and eggs—may panic unnecessarily. Not every rash or stomachache after lunch is an allergy. If you are lactose intolerant, for example, your body is unable to digest lactose, the major sugar found in milk, and you may feel crampy or gassy. If you're allergic to milk, on the other hand, your immune system sees milk proteins as dangerous and revolts against them. Allergists say a fair number of kids are being told to avoid foods they aren't allergic to. "Studies have shown that up to 25 percent of parents think their children may have a food allergy," says Dr. David Fleischer, of National Jewish Medical and Research Center in Denver, "but they've only been confirmed in about 8 percent."

An accurate diagnosis takes time, skill and patience. Skin tests for allergies are exceedingly sensitive, which means they overpredict the number of people who would have a reaction about 60 percent of the time. Blood tests, combined with a carefully documented history of symptoms, are more helpful, allowing doctors to make predictions about a child's risk for allergies based on how many antibodies to a specific food allergen show up in their blood. The only way to diagnose an allergy for sure, however, is to do a food challenge: give a patient small and increasing amounts of the suspect egg or wheat or seafood under a doctor's watchful eye, then monitor reactions. Knowing one way or the other can lift the burden for parents and children alike. "If you don't need to avoid a food," says Fleischer, "it's such a relief to the family that their lives can go back to normal."

Normal could one day be a reality for allergic kids if the science pans out. Last year researchers at National Jewish announced they'd identified a gene that protects mice against developing severe allergic skin reactions. At Mount Sinai, researchers have blocked the allergic response in mice for six months—a quarter of their life span—with an herbal preparation; now they want to test it in humans. One day, Sampson predicts, it might be possible to screen a child's genes, determine if he's at risk, then intervene before the itching and wheezing begins.

But that's pie in the sky for now. Bryan Bunning's hopes are far less grand. He just wants to outgrow his egg allergy so he can finally indulge in "any sweet thing" he can find. High on his list: birthday cake. Having his cake and eating it too—a well-deserved reward.

With **Karen Springen**, **Joan Raymond** in Shaker Heights and **Mary Carmichael**

From *Newsweek*, November 5, 2007. Copyright © 2007 by *Newsweek*. Reprinted by permission via PARS International. www.newsweek.com

Supporting Grandparents Who Raise Grandchildren

Jennifer Birckmayer et al.

Four-year-old Kyle enters the classroom slowly, clinging to the hand of his grandmother. His friend George runs toward him, shouting "Hey Kyle–wanna play?" Suddenly George stops short and stares. "Who's that?" he asks.

When Kyle's eyes begin to fill with tears, his teacher intervenes. "Hello," she says warmly. "Our director told me Kyle's grandma would be visiting today. George, maybe you and Kyle would like to show his grandma the seeds we are growing on the windowsill."

"OK," George says doubtfully, "but where's your mommy, Kyle?"

In the past 10 years the United States has seen a dramatic increase in the number of children who live without their parents in a household headed by a relative. More than 2.5 million grandparents now raise grandchildren without a biological parent present in the home (Simmons & Dye 2003).

Many other grandparents provide full- or part-time child care for working parents, often as a supplement to early childhood education programs such as Head Start or family child care. Because grandparents are often the ones who see teachers or caregivers at drop-off or pickup times or may be the only adults available, many become the logical family contact for a program.

Grandparents who assume responsibility for their grandchildren are unsung heroes and heroines of the twenty-first century. Without them, many children whose parents are unwilling or unable to care for them would be in the foster care system.

Circumstances and Challenges Differ

A popular image of grandparents portrays them as individuals who provide loving relationships and enriching experiences for grandchildren or give practical help with child care for working parents. But the circumstances under which many grandparents become the *primary* adults in the lives of grandchildren are often unfortunate, even tragic. The reasons include parental drug and/or alcohol use, divorce, mental and physical illness

(including AIDS), child abuse and neglect, incarceration, even death. Some skipped-generation families (grandparents raising grandchildren) are temporary arrangements while parents are completing their education, on military or business assignment, recovering from illness, or serving a short jail term. Whether brief or permanent, almost all skipped-generation families begin with trauma for children, parents, and grandparents.

A common refrain among grandparents who are parenting again is "I just feel so tired all the time. It keeps me from being the kind of grandparent I would like to be."

The challenges for these caregivers are unique and sometimes overwhelming. Few adults in their later years plan to be caring for children—especially children who may be traumatized, deeply unhappy, or suffering from chronic health conditions—while they themselves are experiencing some of the more difficult aspects of growing older. For grandparents, shortages of time and money, declining health, unfamiliarity with existing community resources (especially in the fields of medical care and education), and confusing legal problems often combine with grief and guilt about their child's inability to parent.

Contrary to popular belief, not all of these grandparents are elderly. Some are in their thirties, with children still at home; some are of the so-called sandwich generation, caring for children and grandchildren in addition to aging parents. Many must continue to hold jobs to provide adequately for grandchildren. A common refrain among grandparents who are parenting again is "I just feel so tired all the time. It keeps me from being the kind of grandparent I would like to be."

Older grandparents fear that they will become ill, disabled, or die and no one will be available to care for their grandchildren. They also worry that they will not be able to afford appropriate medical care if their grandchildren become ill or disabled. One half of the children living in homes with two grandparents (no parent present) have no health insurance (Bryson & Casper 1999).

Exploring Grandparenting Issues in Workshops

Parenting the Second Time Around is a manual that explores grandparenting issues in a workshop series. The manual contains invaluable material for six two-hour workshops on the following topics:

1. **It Wasn't Supposed to Be Like This**—Identifying and reflecting on ambivalent feelings about changing roles, finding helpful community resources
2. **Getting to Know You**—Exploring child development, individual differences, journaling
3. **Rebuilding a Family**—Examining adult-child interactions, grief and loss, relating to your adult child, solution-based problem solving
4. **Discipline Is Not a Dirty Word, But It May Look Different Today**—Covering characteristics of effective discipline, establishing a discipline style, addressing high-risk behaviors
5. **Protecting and Planning for Your Grandchild's Future**—Dealing with legal issues, including custody, visitation, and child support
6. **Standing Up for Grandparents'/Grandchildren's Rights**—Encouraging advocacy, negotiating systems, connecting with community programs

The 300-page manual features workshop outlines with handouts and supplementary material for the leaders.

From J. Birckmayer, J. Cohen, I. Jensen, D. Variano, & G. Wallace, *Parenting the Second Time Around* (Ithaca, NY: Cornell University, 2001). Available from The Resource Center, Cornell University, P.O. Box 3884, Ithaca, NY 14852; telephone 607-255-2080; online: www.cce.cornell.edu/store/customer/home.php?cat=271&page=3.

Raising grandchildren sometimes isolates grandparents, regardless of age, from their peers, often leaving them depressed and lonely. The situations that bring about a grandchild-grandparent household may also create physical or psychological problems for children. Helping children feel secure and loved, while simultaneously dealing with special needs and challenging behaviors, is an enormous task for parents and can be an overwhelming responsibility for grandparents.

Grandparents parenting the second time around need social support as well as up-to-date information about effective parenting and available community services. The early childhood program in which their grandchild is enrolled may be in the best position to offer help.

Early childhood educators can

- **listen empathically to grandparents.** Introduce them to others in similar situations, or suggest workshops and community meetings about common concerns.
- **encourage grandparents to avail themselves of community resources.** Introduce them to food banks and

clinics. Help them to stay well. Notify them of immunization (especially flu) clinics, Al-Anon meetings, and recreational events and exercise. Let them know it is good for their grandchildren to see them as active participants in community life.
- **provide information about where to obtain good legal services.** Legal concerns of custody and guardianship are serious issues for grandparents raising grandchildren. Help keep children from losing the security their grandparents may provide because legal guardianship has not been established.
- **gather information about community organizations or resources for children with special needs.** It may be particularly difficult for grandparents to recognize that children suffering from attention deficit disorder (ADD) or attention deficit hyperactivity disorder (ADHD) are not deliberately "misbehaving." Refer grandparents to national support groups such as Children and Adults with Attention Deficit Disorders (ChADD) and the Attention Deficit Disorder Association (ADDA). Both organizations offer families good information and practical advice and are available online (www.chadd.org and www.add.org).

An early childhood program can address grandparents' needs for information and social support by offering workshops designed especially for them. The Cooperative Extension Service has developed manuals with suggested outlines for meetings around topics of particular interest for grandparents. Resources can be obtained from local county extension offices or often online (for example, at www.fcs.uga.edu/extension/cyf_pubs.php/parent#parent or http://parenting.wsu.edu/relative/links.htm). If information is not available locally, a manual for grandparenting workshops is available.

Effective workshop sessions require a skilled and experienced leader who can keep discussion on track. It is also important to allow unstructured time for informal discussion and socializing. Grandparents can be invaluable resources for each other, and friendships often develop while sharing common concerns.

An early childhood program can address grandparents' needs for information and social support by offering workshops designed especially for them.

In addition to offering special workshops for grandparents, early childhood programs can take the following specific and helpful steps:

- **Use the word** *families* instead of *parents* on bulletin boards and in newsletters and notices.
- **Use black print** (initial capitals followed by lower case letters) on white paper or printed material for families. Choose fonts that are readable and at least a 12-point type. This is helpful to people with impaired vision.

- **Prepare for questions** like George's in our introductory example. Ask grandparents how they would like you to respond when children ask, "Where's Kyle's mommy?" Respect confidentiality. If Kyle's grandmother wants you to say, "His mommy is away on a trip," but you know she is in jail or in a substance abuse program, you can answer, "Kyle's grandma says his mommy is away, so she's taking care of Kyle right now."

- **Look for ways to include grandparents** by focusing on their special skills or strengths. Grandparents may feel out of place in a group of young families, even when the age difference may not be great. Reading, singing, storytelling, and cooking are obvious areas to explore, but grandparents may surprise you with expertise in puppetry, folk dancing, gardening, or bird watching.

- **Be sensitive to the comfort needs** of all adult visitors by providing adult-size chairs for classroom visits or meetings. Arthritis can develop at any age, and an adult with swollen hands can have difficulty engaging with a child using child-size puzzles, scissors, and games with small parts.

- **Plan holiday celebrations with care.** Perhaps Mothers Day and Fathers Day can become People We Love days.

- **Display pictures and posters** of various family constellations, including some with grandparents as primary caregivers.

- **Model roles other than Mommy and Daddy** in the dramatic play corner. Ask to join the children's play as a grandpa or an aunt or a cousin.

- **Introduce assistive devices,** such as walkers or canes, in the classroom for children to explore, use, and discuss.

- **Include figures of many adults** (including older people) in the block play accessories.

- **Examine puzzles and other games** to be sure they represent many different family structures.

- **Consider the language in poetry, songs, and books** you share with children. Be aware of the negative impact a nursery rhyme such as the following can have on a sensitive child who lives with a grandparent:

  There was an old woman who lived in a shoe
  She had so many children she didn't know what to do
  She gave them some broth without any bread
  And whipped them all soundly and sent them to bed.
  There was an old lady who swallowed a fly . . .
  Perhaps she'll die.

- **Include, read, and discuss books** dealing with all kinds of families and family issues. Many books about grandparents seem to emphasize pleasant, leisurely visits; gardening; or dealing with disability and death; but there are others to be found. For a list of some of our favorite books see online in Beyond the Journal at www.journal.naeyc.org/btj.)

Early childhood educators are in ideal positions to provide substantial support and assistance to grandparent-/relative-headed families. Teachers may be the first or only nonfamily adults to see that a child is exhibiting aggressive, withdrawn, or depressed behaviors after circumstances necessitate a move in with grandparents.

Clear communication and strong partnerships between teaching staff and grandparents can result in strategies to reduce a child's fears and foster healthy development and feelings of self-worth. Working as partners, all adults can think of specific words and phrases for explanations that meet a child's needs and level of understanding.

While books are no substitute for spontaneous, loving conversations, they do often provide openings for discussion. Consider establishing a lending library of children's books dealing with a wide variety of family issues, from divorce and the death of pets to coping with a parent's alcoholism.

Teachers can help grandparents choose and use books appropriately. They also can encourage grandparents to share children's reactions to books and discussions and together brainstorm further steps to provide reassurance and comfort. By developing partnerships with grandparents raising children, early childhood educators can support the growth of stronger families.

References

Bryson, K., & L.M. Casper. 1999. Coresident grandparents and grandchildren. Table 2. *Current Population Reports,* Special Studies (May). Washington, DC: U.S. Census Bureau.

Simmons, T., & J. Dye. 2003. Grandparents living with grandchildren: 2000. *Census 2000 Brief* (October). Online: www.census.gov/prod/2003pubs/c2kbr-31.pdf.

JENNIFER BIRCKMAYER, MA, has been a senior extension associate with the Department of Human Development at Cornell University in Ithaca, New York, for 40 years. During that time she has been a teacher, trainer, speaker, and author. JAN COHEN, MEd, is executive director of Cornell University Cooperative Extension of Otsego County, New York. She has worked in the field of education and human services for more than 20 years. She is the author of "Help for Grandparents of Children with Developmental Disabilities," a six-workshop curriculum published by the New York State Office for Aging. ISABELLE DORAN JENSEN, MS, is an extension resource educator for human development with Cornell Cooperative Extension of Ontario County, New York. She has worked with grandparent/caregiver relatives since 1991 and has been recognized with several awards from the National Extension Association of Family and Consumer Sciences. DENYSE ALTMAN VARIANO, RN, MPS, is the senior extension resource educator in charge of human development programming for Cornell Cooperative Extension of Orange County, New York. Denyse is the administrator for the Relatives as Parents Program in Orange County.

From *Young Children,* May 2005, pp. 100–104. Copyright © 2005 by National Association for the Education of Young Children. Reprinted by permission.

Children of Teen Parents

Challenges and Hope

Barbara A. White, Mimi Graham, and Seaton K. Bradford
Florida State University Center for Prevention and Early Intervention Policy, Tallahassee

Virtually every publicly funded early childhood program serves teen parents and their children. Some programs serve pregnant and parenting teens, and their infants and toddlers, exclusively. Yet all too often, health services, school-based programs, and home visiting initiatives focus primarily on outcomes for the teen mother (for example, repeat pregnancies) and place very little emphasis on outcomes for the child.

In this issue of *Zero to Three,* we hope to explore as thoroughly as possible the experience of infants and toddlers who have adolescent parents. What is it like, for example, for a baby and her mother to be in foster care together? To have the same pediatrician? How does a toddler feel when he spends the day in a child care classroom in his parent's high school? What happens when a toddler and his parent compete for a home visitor's attention?

The contributors to this issue report from the perspective of the child, but their larger goal is to describe the development of the dyad—the adolescent parent and the child. Taken together, the articles in this issue suggest that in health care settings, center-based services, and home-based programs, practitioners who effectively support the dual development of teen parents and their young children have a number of characteristics in common. They:

- understand the role of multiple risk factors in the lives of the children of teen parents;
- are comprehensive in approach, integrating services from a variety of community partners;
- appreciate the specialized knowledge and skills required to work effectively with teen parents and their children; and
- are committed to providing strength-based, relationship focused services to promote positive outcomes.

Risks Associated with Adolescent Parenthood

Any discussion of young families includes a discussion of risk factors. Teenagers who have had academic difficulty and mental health problems are more likely than their peers to give birth before graduating from high school. These young parents often bring to parenthood a history of poverty, abuse, violence, and unresolved grief and loss. Poverty is a risk factor for adolescent childbearing, which in turn compounds and perpetuates poverty. Children who are born to teen mothers are 8 times as likely to grow up in poverty as are children of older mothers. Babies of teens are less likely than children of older parents to live with both a mother and father. The resulting inadequate financial support translates into poor housing, inferior child care, and limited health care options.

Teens who have been raised in poverty often feel that they have never "had enough." When they become parents, they have difficulty sharing limited resources with a child. Thus programs that serve the children of teen parents should be prepared to provide for babies' needs at two levels. Formula, diapers, and baby clothes ensure basic survival. At a second level, programs must compensate for the "poverty of experience" that is common to young families by offering front-pack carriers, board books, play materials, and, perhaps most important, learning opportunities and life experiences in the community that link to school readiness for the child.

Community-based Strategies to Support Young Families

High-quality services for teen parents and their children are integrated services. Effective program planners identify points of entry, unique to each community, where teen parents are most likely to seek help for themselves and their children. No single service program is likely to be able to address the multiple needs of young families; partnerships among programs and agencies are essential. Community providers also have a responsibility to explore research evidence, recommended practices, and professional development resources that are likely to contribute to positive outcomes for teen parents and their young children.

In the context of well-designed programs for young families, competent practitioners individualize intervention strategies. Drawing on their understanding of adolescent development and early childhood, they find ways to give hope to teen parents and their children. Those professionals who are most successful in their work with young families constantly look for ways to capitalize on

At a Glance

Programs for teen parents and their children promote dual development by:

- Acknowledging the role of multiple risk factors in the lives of the children of teen parents;
- Integrating services from a variety of community partners;
- Employing specialized strategies and specially trained staff; and
- Providing strength-based, relationship-focused, high quality services.

the motivation, resilience, and responsiveness of young parents. If skilled support is available, the rapid pace of development in the early years and the baby's powerful drive toward attachment can bring out the best in teen mothers and fathers.

In 2004, the Task Force on Teen Parents and Their Children, convened by the Miami-Dade School Readiness Coalition and the Florida State University's Center for Prevention and Early Intervention Policy, identified 14 components of a comprehensive service system for teen parents and their children. The Task Force recommended that service providers address these components when developing new programs or improving upon existing services for young families (White, Larsen, & Schilling, 2004). These components include:

1. A "medical home" (stable source of health care) for parent and child
2. Good-quality early care and education (child care)
3. Social work services
4. Prenatal and parenting education
5. Family planning counseling and services
6. Comprehensive educational programs/work force development
7. Family violence intervention/protection
8. Mental health/infant mental health services
9. Housing/shelter referrals
10. Legal services
11. Family literacy activities
12. Sexual abuse treatment
13. Substance abuse education and treatment
14. Early intervention

The Task Force further recommended that communities:

- Use co-located programs or carefully crafted interagency agreements to establish a network of service providers;
- Inform teen parents of service options;
- Assure developmental screening for each teen parent and child;
- Educate practitioners, community policy makers, and the general public about the developmental needs of teen parents and their children;

- Provide for the basic needs of young families;
- Identify risk factors for healthy development of young families and build protective factors into community institutions such as schools, the health care system, libraries, recreational programs, and the arts;
- Promote a relationship-based approach in all interventions;
- Use an infant mental health framework to understand the behavior of teen parents and their children;
- Establish multidisciplinary teams to assess the functioning of teen parents and their children, develop intervention plans with parents, and offer comprehensive services;
- Use a continuous improvement model to raise the quality of community services; and
- Integrate reflective practice into all levels of service for young families.

Changing Lives

Although they usually lack the skills, experience, and means to make it happen, most adolescent mothers are determined to make the lives of their children better than their own. Unlike many adult women who seem defeated by years of living in poverty, even the most challenged adolescent mothers have a reservoir of resilience and hope that their new baby will experience success and happiness.

Practitioners who work with young families will attest that most adolescent parents respond positively to caring adults who have an interest in their well-being and that of their baby. Even young parents who have lacked consistent relationships with loving, attentive, responsible, and trustworthy adults during much of their childhood will—eventually—respond to and deeply appreciate kindness that is offered to them.

Well-designed programs with skilled staff work to reduce risk factors and build protective factors—both internal and external—into the lives of teen parents and their children. Committed practitioners know that the children of teens are resilient and that most teen parents want a good life for their child. In the hopeful words of one young mother, "My main dream is to give my baby the life I didn't have . . . a home, a family that I didn't have when I was growing up." Using proven and promising practices, practitioners, programs, and communities can do far more than simply help the children of teen parents survive. As the contributors to this issue of *Zero to Three* demonstrate, systematic efforts to understand young families and thoughtfully designed, skillfully implemented interventions can overcome challenge and justify hope.

References

White, B, Larsen, R, & Schilling, M. (2004). *Interim report of the Task Force on Teen Parents and Their Children.* Tallahassee: Florida State University, Center for Prevention and Early Intervention Policy.

From *Zero to Three*, March 2005, pp. 4–6. Copyright © 2005 by National Center for Infants, Toddlers and Families. Reprinted by permission.

UNIT 3
Diverse Learners

Unit Selections

Key Points to Consider

- Have you heard the name Ed Zigler before? If so, in what capacity? What impact did he have on the profession?

- What are some strategies teachers can use to assist English language learners and their families?

- Describe some of the ways teachers can include children with disabilities in their classroom.

- What are the specific learning needs of young Hispanic children?

Student Web Site

www.mhcls.com/online

Internet References

Further information regarding these Web sites may be found in this book's preface or online.

American Academy of Pediatrics
www.aap.org
Child Welfare League of America (CWLA)
http://www.cwla.org
Classroom Connect
http://www.classroom.com/login/home.jhtml
The Council for Exceptional Children
http://www.cec.sped.org/index.html
Early Learning Standards: Full report
http://www.naeyc.org/resources/position_statements/positions_2003.asp
Early Learning Standards: Executive Summary
http://www.naeyc.org/resources/position_statements/creating_conditions.asp
Make Your Own Web page
http://www.teacherweb.com
National Resource Center for Health and Safety in Child Care
http://nrc.uchsc.edu
Online Innovation Institute
http://oii.org

Comstock/Corbis

This is a new unit for *Annual Editions: Early Childhood Education*. At the annual advisory board meeting of key early childhood faculty from throughout the country we decided to dedicate a specific unit of the book to the many diverse learners who are in our early childhood programs and schools. This unit starts with an interview in *Educational Leadership* with one of the icons of the profession: Edward Zigler. In "Giving Intervention a Head Start" Dr. Zigler shares his memories, achievements and future possibilities for young children, particularly those living in challenging situations. Dr. Zigler has been front and center for most of the key policy decisions and programs affecting young children and their families for the past fifty years. He is most known for his contributions to Head Start, first as a member of the National Planning and Steering Committee, then as the first director of the Office of Child Development, which oversaw the launching of Head Start in 1965. With over 800 articles and close to 40 books written, it is a rare professional in the field who has not been influenced by his writings. Dr. Zigler's work will live on in a sub area of our field called child development and social policy. This specialty

takes our area of expertise—child development—and combines it with our work to advocate for policies and programs that best support what we know about young children and their development. Our profession is in good hands with the over 250 former students of Dr. Zigler continuing his work in key leadership positions.

Nationwide, college and university programs are adapting to new standards from the National Association for the Education of Young Children requiring programs educating teachers at two and four year institutions to include much more on working with special needs children, especially children with disabilities. As teacher preparation institutions adapt to meet the new standards, there will be teachers out in the field better equipped to meet the needs of special needs children and their families. "Including Children with Disabilities in Early Childhood Education Programs" provides strategies that will help with a successful transition for schools planning for inclusion of all children.

In "Creative Play" Sara J. Burton and Linda Carol Edwards present ways teachers can help families and children as they work to learn the English language. In China, every child begins to learn a second language in the first grade. English was studied in every school I visited last year and children at all levels were eager to practice with the American visitors. In the United States it is not uncommon for languages other than English to begin in high school. If world languages are taught in the elementary school, it is often an exploratory course only and not of sufficient time or content to really begin to learn the language.

The unit ends with a look at a specific segment of the population in "Helping Young Hispanic Learners". The growing numbers of young Hispanic children was, in 2005, one in five children in the United States. These are numbers that cannot be ignored and teachers must work with the families of young Hispanic children to meet their needs and build on their strengths.

There are more and more examples of teachers adjusting their image of diverse learners. Only when all educators are accepting of the wide diversity that exists in family structures and among individual children will all children feel welcomed and comfortable to learn at school. The collaboration of families, the community, and school personnel will enable children to benefit from the partnership these three groups bring to the educational setting. The articles in this unit represent many diverse families and children and the issues surrounding young children today.

Giving Intervention a Head Start

A Conversation with Edward Zigler

DEBORAH PERKINS-GOUGH

During a career spanning five decades, Edward Zigler has combined scholarly research with public service to promote federal and state policies that are good for all children. In 1965, he served on the National Planning and Steering Committee of Project Head Start under Lyndon B. Johnson. In 1970, he became the first director of the Office of Child Development, which administered the fledgling Head Start program. He has written more than 800 scholarly articles and is the author or editor of 38 books, including *A Vision for Universal Preschool Education* (Cambridge University Press, 2006) and *The Tragedy of Child Care in America* (Yale University Press, in press). In this interview with *Educational Leadership,* Dr. Zigler expresses his views on Head Start, universal preschool, and child care

Your career has reflected a concern for the welfare, of young children, especially poor children. What inspired you to become an advocate for children?

You know, everybody's life is influenced by their own experiences. I'm the son of immigrants, growing up in deep poverty during the Great Depression. When I was a little boy, I never thought I'd wind up a Sterling Professor at Yale. So I have a built-in empathy for poor children, as well as a deep belief, based on my own life, that just because you're poor that doesn't mean you're inadequate. We all know how devastating poverty is, but if we help children, they can overcome poverty and move upward and onward.

I am basically an academic, not an advocate for children. I have done hundreds of studies on children. When I was being socialized as a scholar, I learned the way this game was played: You formulated the query; you developed hypotheses from it; you tested those hypotheses in rigorous studies; then you reported your findings in good journals, and about 300 of your colleagues read your report. If you did enough of this and were successful at it, you were promoted and given tenure. And that was your life.

I rebelled against this at a fairly early age. I thought, our subjects in all these studies are children. They are our partners in this learning enterprise, and we have a special responsibility to use this knowledge—not to fill up journals, but to make the lives of these children better. And that's what I have done with my life.

What did you and the others who designed Head Start in 1965 envision as its purpose?

Frankly, I wish we had been clearer. One of the great problems Head Start has had over the years is ambiguity concerning its goals. Clearly, nobody on the committee thought that by working with 4-year-olds we were going to end poverty in America. The goal was simply to help kids avoid poverty later in their own lives by making them more ready for school, but we didn't state that in our planning document. It wasn't until 1998 that Congress officially said that Head Start's goal was school readiness.

In the meantime, there was a kind of vacuum. And because school performance is heavily correlated with IQ, people decided that the goal was to increase children's IQs. That misconception was very harmful for Head Start, and we're still seeing it today. Politicians are trying to turn Head Start into a literacy-skills program focused on cognitive development. But cognitive development is just one part of human development.

There's been a debate going on for 50 years between the cognitive child approach and the whole child approach. In the former, the emphasis is on literacy, numeracy, getting back to the basics. We saw it when they sent up *Sputnik.* Hyman Rickover (U.S. Navy nuclear engineer) was saying, "Sure the Russians beat us—they're studying to be engineers, and our kids are finger painting."

The opposing view, which the Head Start planners held, is that you have to take a whole child approach. The brain is an integrated instrument. To most people, the brain means intelligence. But the brain mediates emotional and social development. Emotions and cognition are constantly interwoven in the lives of children. That's why the planning committee was determined that our program would be a whole child program.

There were two great achievements in the design of Head Start. First, the program emphasized social and emotional development. It emphasized health, comprehensive services, and social services to families. Our second victory was to introduce parent participation. Probably the most important single determinant of a child's growth is the behavior of the parents. Lots of research demonstrates that the more involved parents are in the education of their children, the better the children's education and performance. This is true of middle-class children, poor children—every child. Head Start pioneered this approach in a two-generation program with a great deal of parent involvement.

What can we say for sure, on the basis of the research, about the effects of Head Start?

It depends on what you want to read. Some people look at the evidence—for example, Doug Besharov at the American Enterprise Institute—and tend to be negative about the value of Head Start. These people, though, are a minority. The positive evidence is overwhelming.

The National Impact Study—a huge, rigorous, random-assignment experiment—is the best single study that we have, although it's only in its first year. I was one of its planners, and I worked with this administration to monitor it. The Bush administration and Besharov and a few others have pointed out how small the effects are. On the other hand, the Society for Research and Child Development has interpreted its findings as very healthy and positive.

But I don't look just at the National Impact Study. Deborah Phillips and Jens Ludwig at Washington University have written what I consider to be the best analysis to date; they conclude that Head Start is worth every dollar we've been spending on it. Other studies, like the Head Start Family and Child Experiences Survey, show that when Head Start kids get to kindergarten, they experience a boost, and they continue their learning through kindergarten.

You know, you look at a little 3- or 4-year-old child, be they black, brown, or white—they're all lovely. The last thing you think about is delinquency and criminality. But here's one of the most surprising findings about early intervention programs: The children who were in high-quality programs are less likely to become delinquent and criminal later on. When we began Head Start, we had no way to predict that. That is a huge savings for society.

If anything, the evaluations to date have underestimated the benefits of Head Start. One thing that's always bothered me—and it's true to this day—is that the evaluations don't look at effects on children's health. When I was running Head Start, we found that 34 percent of children were showing up in need of some kind of medical services. Many of these children hadn't been to a physician for the two years before Head Start entry. Many had never seen a dentist. I feel we've had a huge impact. Does anyone really believe that the health of a child is not important in determining his or her performance in school and later in life? Of course it is. If you just inoculate children, you're going to get a huge savings. If simple measures of health were included in these evaluations, Head Start would look a lot better.

The other big weakness in Head Start evaluations is that we never mention die siblings. Victoria Seitz and others have collected considerable evidence that shows that if you can get that mother involved and make her a better socializer and teacher to her own children, that benefit will accrue to the younger children. I'm still waiting for somebody to look at the siblings of Head Start children. I'm sure we'd find what studies of other programs have found—that it's helpful to siblings, too.

You support the idea of providing universal preschool, as opposed to just making targeted programs available to more disadvantaged kids. Why?

I sure do, loud and clear. This surprises some people because of my association with Head Start and my own poverty background. Why not worry about our most needy kids? I have an ongoing debate with economists James Heckman and Arthur Rolnick. They're pushing hard for directing preschool efforts to

---

Sources Mentioned in This Interview

Administration for Children and Families, U.S. Department of Health and Human Services. (2007), *Head Start family and child experiences survey (FACES), 1997–2010.* Washington, DC: Author, Available: www.acf.hhs.gov/programs/opre/hs/faces/index.html

Administration for Children and Families, U.S. Department of Health and Human Services. (2007). *Head Start impact study and follow-up, 2000–2009.* Washington, DC: Author. Available: www.acf.hhs.gov/programs/opre/hs/impact _study/index. html

Besharov, D. (2005). *Head Start's broken promise.* Washington, DC: American Enterprise Institute. Available: www.childcareresearch.org/location/ccrca7533

Mahoney, J. L, Lord, H., & Carryl, E. (2005). An ecological analysis of after-school program participation and the development of academic performance and motivational attributes for disadvantaged children. *Child Development, 76*(4), 811–825.

Merrow, J. (2002, September 25). The "failure" of Head Start. *Education Week.* Available: www.pbs.org/merrow/news/edweek.html

National Summit on America's Children. (2007 May), http://speaker.gov/issues?id=0032

Phillips, D. A., & Ludwig, J. (2007). *The benefits and costs of Head Start* (NBER Working Paper). Cambridge, MA: National Bureau of Economic Research.

Seitz, V., & Apfel, N. H. (1994). Parent-focused intervention: Diffusion effects on siblings. *Child Development, 65*(2), 677–683.

Society for Research in Child Development. (2007). *Placing the first-year findings of the National Head Start Impact Study in context.* Washington, DC: Author. Available: www.srcd.org/documents/policy/Impactstudy.pdf

poor children alone. But my experience in Head Start tells me that approach is wrong.

Now, I always take my direction from research, and research does show that you'll get bigger benefits for poor children from preschool than you will for middle-class children. If you're interested in more bang for your buck, you're going to get a bigger payoff by putting resources into preschool for poor children.

Why then, am I such a tough proponent of universal preschool? One reason is that in a targeted program, you're never going to get funding to serve all the children who need it.

John Merrow, a champion of preschool education, wrote a paper that startled me. He asserted that Head Start was a failure. But when I read this piece, I realized he was right. He said Head Start has been alive for 42 years and is only serving roughly 50 percent of eligible children. By definition, we have failed.

We know this program is good for poor kids. The evidence indicates that it works. Why aren't we funding it? Because poor people don't give money to congressional campaigns. They're not the voices that we listen to closely. We listen to powerful, rich people.

There's nothing wrong with a state starting a preschool program by serving poor children, like Connecticut is doing right now. Oklahoma and Georgia, two of the states that adopted universal preschool education early on, both started with poor children. But they learned the same lesson: If you want to get the state legislature to maintain and continue funding the program, the program has to have a constituency. Over time, you need to expand it to include all children. The only way you are going to have a preschool program that's safe from budget cuts and that gets funded for all the poor is by giving it to everybody.

And you'll be helping middle-class children—not as much as the poor children, but all children will benefit. The gap between middle-class children and rich children in school performance is just about the same as the gap between poor kids and middle-class kids. Our middle-class kids could do a lot better. Research shows that a good preschool program benefits them as well.

There is one final reason why I champion the universal approach. I'm not sure that it's moral to segregate children along socioeconomic lines, I'm not sure it meets John Dewey's notion of educating children to live in a democracy. If you put kids from all social classes together, they get the benefits of learning about one another. And research now indicates that poor children's education accomplishments are greater when they are in classes with middle-class children than when they are in classes only with other poor children.

What lessons have we learned about the best age to provide support for preschool children?

One lesson is to start earlier. It troubles me that most of the states are starting preschool at age 4. Most middle-class families send their children to preschool at age 3. That's when a child is ready for a preschool experience. It's particularly important for poor children. We have evidence from the National Institute of Early Education Research demonstrating that two years of intervention give you more benefits than one year. So we want a program for 3- and 4-year-olds.

But we have to reach down even earlier, as we did with Early Head Start. We've known for a long time the importance of the foundation years. Conception, not birth, is when development starts. The Early Head Start findings demonstrated that when mothers are pregnant, they're extremely interested in information and instruction.

After laying that foundation, we also need to have a good, solid, high-quality preschool program for 3s and 4s. And when they get to school at age 5, don't quit. You have to have a program that goes up through the 3rd grade. That's a turning point in children's lives and their school performance. If children are behind then, their chances of ever catching up are next to nil.

That's why I've been arguing for a conception-through-age-8 program. For years we've kept looking for some critical period of development, thinking if we could just get in there with a great program, we could fix everything. We've been ridiculous about it. Human development is a long and continuous process—stage built on top of stage. And at each stage, kids need different environmental nutrients.

Is it practical for public schools to provide the kind of continuous support you're talking about?

People say, "Oh, sure, some college professor's sitting there in his Ivy League sanctuary—he can spin pipe dreams for us all." Well, I'm a pragmatist. Everything I recommend is now being done in 1,400 schools across the United States that participate in the School of the 21st Century initiative.[1] Those schools provide early education, health services, parent support. And they meet what is probably the greatest need of U.S. parents—child care.

Does anyone really believe that the health of a child is not important in determining his or her performance in school and later in life?

Why should public schools get involved in child care?

The United States has no system of child care like other industrialized countries have. We have a hodgepodge of for-profits, not-for-profits, family day care, kith-and-kin care. The average quality of care in this country is somewhere between poor and mediocre, and a certain percentage is downright awful.

This nonsystem is compromising children's school readiness. A child's experiences before age 3 are among the most important factors in healthy development. Thirty-five percent of U.S. children show up at school unable to learn optimally. For poor kids, that's probably close to 50, 60 percent.

It's a tragedy because we're hurting our own children, who don't deserve this. And it's a shame because we came so close to developing a system of child care in the United States. Back in 1971, when I was head of the Office of Child Development, we wrote a bill that provided federal funding and set standards that every child care setting would have to meet to get funding. We were very far along. The bill passed both houses of Congress. But it was vetoed by President Nixon.

Just think where we would be today if we had put that system in place back in 1971. We would have had a system just like Denmark and Sweden have.

Great demographic changes have affected children's growth and development since World War II. One change is the number of women working outside the home. And the second is the number of children being raised by single-parent families. Society has got to build into its infrastructure the supports for the new kind of family that we now have in the United States. We're the only great industrialized country that has paid so little attention to this need. The same demographics exist in other countries. They decided to do something about it, and we decided not to.

And the child care crisis doesn't end with young children. Children need child care until they're 12, 13, 14. That's one promising area where we have made progress—school-age child care. Congress has provided funding for after-school care through the 21st Century Community Learning Center program, although our cunrrent president tried to cut it by 40 percent. I worked very hard in his hearings, and we held that off.

That program covers school-age child care for poor families, but we need it for all families. We know what high-quality after-school care is. It isn't two or three more hours of schooling. That's the mistake many schools make—they're determined to get those literacy scores up. But interestingly, recent research by Joe Mahoney has demonstrated that kids in programs that have a recreational, fun orientation, enriching the life of the child, show more academic progress than kids in after-school programs with a hard-nosed, academic approach—which this administration champions.

There are good times, and there are bad times. But you have to stay in the game.

What accomplishments so far have you been the most proud of? What would you like to be remembered for?

I think my greatest contribution is the work that I've done with my own students. I helped create a new field called child development and social policy, which combines our knowledge base with social action on behalf of children and families.

One of my students is the dean of the School of Education at Stanford. Another is the dean of the School of Education at Harvard. And I can give you 50 others who are national and international authorities. So they will change the world. I gave it my best shot. I've worked very hard in Washington and in state capitals to achieve some of these things, and I've failed more than I've succeeded. But I can go to my reward knowing that my students are making it all happen—200 to 250 absolutely top-notch people I've mentored are out there changing the world.

What current trends give you the greatest concern about the future of children? What trends give you the most hope?

The greatest enemy of children today is poverty. We're not doing enough. Our infant mortality rate has gone up for the first time in 40 years. And many of the younger people working in our field are now depressed because we've had a terrible time the last few years as far as progress for kids.

But there's always hope. They just held a wonderful children's summit on Capitol Hill. Many members of Congress came, and a lot of solutions were offered—ways federal policy could reflect scientific findings about child development. We know how to do it.

I tell my students, whatever your favorite cause, if you do not intend to pursue that effort for 25 years, do yourself a favor—don't start. You have to be prepared to hang in there for the long run. We couldn't get a reauthorization of Head Start through the last two Congresses, and Head Start suffered as a result. But we're finally getting one in this Congress.

I'm not partisan—I'm not talking Democrats or Republicans. We didn't do all that badly in the Nixon administration, except for the day-care bill. I have worked in some capacity for every administration since Lyndon Johnson. I'll work with anybody who would like to improve the lives of children.

Here's the strategy that I have used. It's taken me decades to learn it, and it has worked: In the good years, work very hard to win everything that's possibly winnable. In the bad years, work just as hard to keep your losses to a minimum. There are good times, and there are bad times. But you have to stay in the game.

Note

1. The School of the 21st Century initiative was launched in 1988 and is sponsored by the Edward Zigler Center in Child Development and Social Policy at Yale University. For more information, see www.yale.edu/21C/index2.html.

EDWARD ZIGLER is Director Emeritus of the Edward Zigler Center in Child Development and Social Policy and Sterling Professor of Psychology Emeritus at Yale University; edward_zigler@yale.edu. **DEBORAH PERKINS-GOUGH** is Senior Editor, Educational Leadership; dperkins@ascd.org.

From *Educational Leadership*, October 2007. Copyright © 2007 by ASCD. Reprinted by permission. The Association for Supervision and Curriculum Development is a worldwide community of educators advocating sound policies and sharing best practices to achieve the success of each learner. To learn more, visit ASCD at www.ascd.org

Including Children with Disabilities in Early Childhood Education Programs

Individualizing Developmentally Appropriate Practices

JOHN FILLER AND YAOYING XU

Early childhood educators are facing the challenge of creating quality educational programs for young children from an increasingly diverse mix of racial and cultural backgrounds. Programs that, in the past, have largely ignored the diversity of their participants must now re-examine approaches that emphasize the universality of linear lists of developmental milestones; they must pursue practices that reflect a pluralistic approach to both content and methods of instruction. Too many educators assume that children reach developmental milestones at similar points, leading to rather simplistic attempts to justify singular content and approach. Yet a multicultural, multiethnic, and multi-ability student population demands a unique and nontraditional approach, characterized by individualization and sensitivity to unique expressions of group identity.

The realities of diversity do not mitigate the fact that all children do seem to exhibit a finite set of accomplishments (milestones) that build, one upon the other, and proceed in an age-related fashion. We recognize the relevance of a developmental approach that is based upon the work of such theorists as Rousseau, Locke, Pestalozzi, Froebel, Piaget, and Vygotsky, exemplified by Itard's techniques, the Montessori approach, and the Head Start movement in the 1960s, as well as numerous other, more recent, examples of successful early childhood education programs. However, some children acquire skills at an earlier age than their age-mates, while others acquire those same skills much later than their peers or not at all. For example, not all children begin walking up stairs by placing both feet on each step before they move to the next step. Some alternate, placing only one foot on each step—a skill that Brigance (2004) claims one should expect to see exhibited 6 to 12 months after the two-feet per step approach. Some children seem to skip steps in a developmental sequence while others do not. Such variations are viewed as part of the "normal" range of individual differences, defined as falling less than one to two standard deviations above or below the theoretical mean for a given developmental area (such as cognitive, gross and fine motor, or social or language skills). Most of our attempts to adapt curriculum and strategies to diversity have been based upon either sociocultural

differences or ability differences that fall within the range of what might be termed "normal variation."

The realities of a multicultural, multi-ethnic, and multi-ability student population demand a unique and nontraditional approach, characterized by individualization and sensitivity to unique expressions of group identity.

Individually and Developmentally Appropriate Practices

Developmentally appropriate practice (DAP) is considered the foundation of early childhood education and serves as a guideline for curriculum development. The National Association of Education for Young Children (NAEYC) defined DAP in three dimensions (Bredekamp & Copple, 1997, p. 9):

- What is known about child development and learning—knowledge of age-related human characteristics that permits general predictions within an age range about what activities, materials, interactions, or experiences will be safe, healthy, interesting, achievable, and also challenging to children
- What is known about the strength, interests, and needs of each individual child in the group to be able to adapt for and be responsive to inevitable individual variations
- Knowledge of the social and cultural contexts in which children live to ensure that learning experiences are meaningful, relevant, and respectful for the participating children and their families.

On the one hand, this NAEYC statement views children as members of an overall group who follow similar predictable developmental patterns. Yet it also emphasizes the importance of valuing young children as individuals, with different personalities or temperaments and learning styles. Furthermore, children are considered part of a cultural group, members of the community in which children and their families live and by which they are influenced in every aspect of living. Additionally, the NAEYC statement encourages early childhood professionals to move from "either-or thinking" to "both-and thinking" (Gonzalez-Mena, 2000). As is often the case, what is developmentally appropriate is not always individually or culturally appropriate. Instead of having to make a falsely dichotomous choice, educators often need to combine all dimensions and know the child as a whole person with individual needs and cultural differences.

The nature of DAP encourages the placement of children, with and without disabilities, in the same setting. In fact, most professional organizations support the concept of inclusive programs for all children, regardless of the nature or severity of the disability. For example, the Division for Early Childhood of the Council for Exceptional Children issued its "Position Statement on Inclusion," which was endorsed that same year by NAEYC: "DEC supports and advocates that young children and their families have full and successful access to health, social, educational, and other support services that promote full participation in family and community life" (Sandall, McLean, & Smith, 2000, p. 150). The statement also proposed that young children participating in group settings (such as preschool, play groups, child care, or kindergarten) be guided by developmentally and individually appropriate curriculum. The Association for Childhood Education International published a brochure that discusses the benefits of inclusion for the children with disabilities, the children without disabilities, and the parents, school, and community (Kostell, 1997). The Association for Persons With Severe Handicaps (TASH) endorses the inclusion of children with severe disabilities in regular education settings and argues that inclusion implies more than just physical presence; it includes access to the curriculum that is taught in the regular education classroom (TASH, 2000).

Clearly, leading professional organizations endorse the concept of inclusive programming for children with disabilities; there also exists a strong legal basis for inclusion. The assumption of the universal relevance of the general education curriculum is readily apparent in the 2004 re-authorization of the Individuals With Disabilities Education Act (P.L. 108-446). This law requires that we reference the content of our curriculum for students with disabilities to that of their typically developing peers. For example, each student's individualized educational program (IEP), a written document that describes the needs of the child, must contain a statement of the child's present levels of educational performance, including how the child's disability affects his or her involvement and participation in appropriate activities. Furthermore, the IEP must include a statement of *measurable annual goals*, related to "meeting the child's needs that result from the child's disability to enable the child to be involved in and progress in the general curriculum" (Sec. 614; 20 USC 1414), and there must be a justification for non-participation in the regular class. Part C of P.L. 108-446 requires that

children from birth to 3 years of age receive early intervention services in environments that are *natural*, or normal for children the same age who have no disabilities (IDEA Rules and Regulations, 1998). This stipulation extends the requirements of the Americans With Disabilities Act (Public Law 101-336) by requiring each state to not only ensure reasonable access by infants with disabilities to child care/educare programs, but also deliver early intervention services in such settings.

Planning for Inclusion: Adapting Developmentally Appropriate Practices

While examples of curricula for young children can be found that do provide substantive suggestions for adapting to meet the needs of children with sensory, cognitive, motor, emotional, and/or learning disabilities (e.g., Bricker & Waddell, 2002a, 2002b; Hauser-Cram, Bronson, & Upshur, 1993), most do little by way of providing meaningful, practical suggestions to the early childhood teacher. This means that the task of planning to include these children will fall upon the shoulders of those whose formal training and experience may not have prepared them for such diversity (Gelfer, Filler, & Perkins, 1999; Heller, 1992). To be successful at what can, at first, appear to be a very daunting task, teachers will have to plan for modifications in both content and strategy. Numerous authors have recognized the importance of instructional flexibility and the need for an approach that includes the individual modifications that are often necessary in order to meet the needs of diverse groups of learners (Allen & Cowdery, 2004; Friend & Bursuck, 2002; Giangreco, Broer, & Edelman, 2002; Pretti-Frontczak & Bricker, 2004). Inclusion is not accomplished by simply placing a child with disabilities in a setting with his typically developing peers. It is realized only when we have succeeded in designing a set of activities that ensure the full participation of all children, including the child with disabilities. Participation and not mere geographical proximity is the necessary pre-condition for *achievement*, and so meaningful participation requires systematic planning.

Table 1 contains a description of the steps involved in planning for the inclusion of a child with disabilities in a typical early childhood program. The planning process begins with the selection of a team of knowledgeable individuals who will be responsible for developing the plan. Team planning is essential, because the success of efforts to include students with disabilities, especially those with severe disabilities, is not the sole responsibility of any single individual. This planning team should include the parents and/or any other family members who share in daily caregiving activities; the general education early childhood teacher and the early interventionist or early childhood special education teacher; and the program administrator and any related service personnel, such as speech or occupational therapists who may provide services to the child and family.

The second step in the planning process is to construct a simple schedule of the daily activities for the setting in which the target child with disabilities will be included from start to finish. When listing the activities, it is important to note the average length of time devoted to each activity and to include all activities in which the child will likely be included throughout the week, since activities may vary from day to day.

Step 3 involves a careful specification of the instructional goals for the target child, which are taken directly from the IEP or the Individualized Family Service Plan (IFSP). Since these documents contain goals and/or objectives that may cover six months to a year, only those that are currently being addressed are listed. Here, it is important to indicate the family's priorities for instruction. The family and the educators may feel differently about the relative importance of goals and objectives. For example, the family may not believe that the child learning a particular social behavior is as important as the child acquiring gross motor skills, while the teacher might think that more emphasis should be placed upon sharing and cooperative play than upon learning to throw and run. Such differences present opportunities to jointly discuss how both priorities can be addressed simultaneously in one or more activities. An important additional consideration is whether or not the child has a behavior support plan, the presence of which indicates the need to carefully and systematically pay attention to a recurring, potentially serious, form of inappropriate behavior.

Step 4 is, perhaps, the most important aspect of the planning process; it is the determination of exactly how many opportunities exist in the typical schedule to address the individual needs of the child with a disability and what program supports are needed to make an opportunity a successful reality. Each skill targeted in the IEP/IFSP must be referenced to the activities of the typical early childhood program. The team must ask (and answer) the question, "Does this activity provide an opportunity to address any of the skills in the IEP or IFSP?" and "If so, which ones?" In answering the questions, it becomes important to examine what the focus of the activity is for typically developing children. If it seems reasonable to the team that the activity may provide a context in which the needs of the child with disabilities can be addressed, *without completely altering the meaningfulness of the activity for typically developing children,* then the team can examine what adaptations may be needed. The effort to ensure that activities provide opportunities to address the needs of all children is central to what has been termed *activity-based instruction* (Pretti-Frontczak & Bricker, 2004).

As indicated in Table 1, adaptations may consist of two types. One involves individualizing the content of the activity by changing its focus or fundamental purpose for the target child. A modified content, or even a different content entirely, may be taught to the child with disabilities while the other children receive content appropriate for their needs. A second kind of adaptation involves changing the physical layout, modifying materials for the child, or even changing the way that staff conduct the activity. For example, while children with sensory disabilities, like blindness or low vision, may still function at age level and require no modification of content, they will require large print or Braille reading material. A child with cerebral palsy and an associated motor disability may require special equipment, such as a cut-out table and chairs with supports, wedges to facilitate upper body movement while in a prone play position, or a prone board to provide support in an upright

position (Campbell, 2006). In some situations, it may even be necessary to add staff during the activity to ensure adequate instructional support without sacrificing instructional time for the other children. This might be the case with a child who presents a significant challenging behavior that requires an involved support plan, the focus of which is to teach a positive incompatible replacement behavior (see Figure 2).

Step 5 involves determining what related services are required and how often and how long each related service session should be. Children with significant disabilities often require such services as occupational therapy and speech therapy, and may need to receive one-on-one instruction from an early childhood special educator. While the preference is to provide these services in the natural setting of the early childhood classroom, it may be necessary to remove the child to a different setting for the service. If that is the case, then the team must decide what classroom activity (or activities) is (are) least important and thus could be missed by the child. This is usually accomplished by viewing each activity in terms of the opportunities it provides for addressing skills from the IEP or IFSP, and then selecting times for the child to leave the classroom when activities are occurring that provide the fewest number of individually relevant instructional opportunities. Sometimes, however, the schedule of those professionals who are delivering the service may need to be taken into account when making the choice.

The final step, Step 6, is also an extremely important aspect of team planning. Parents and other family members have their own perspective on what, among all of the skills that may be included in the IEP or IFSP, is most important. It is critical that staff respect those priorities by making sure that, first, they are aware of parental priorities and, second, adequate opportunities exist to address high-priority skills during daily program activities. In addition, families may have concerns regarding skills or behaviors that are best addressed outside of the formal confines of the program setting. It is extremely important that the skills learned at the center also are taught and practiced in natural settings—those settings in which the skill or behavior is most likely to be demanded or exhibited. Natural settings are the environments where children with disabilities would participate or function if they did not have a disability. These environments may include the child's home, the neighborhood playground, community activity or child care centers, restaurants, Head Start programs, or other settings designed for children without disabilities (Cook, Klein, Tessier, & Daley, 2004). While it is unlikely that program staff will be able to provide continuous, direct instructional support at home or in the community, it still would be possible to make visits and provide occasional community-based instruction. Making suggestions to the family as to how to generalize procedures employed at the center is another important aspect of the child's program. These procedures need to be planned for as carefully as you would the daily activities.

The Activity Matrix

A good way to summarize and represent the results of this six-step planning process is to construct what has been referred to as an "Activity Matrix" (Fox & Williams, 1991). Figures 1 and 2

Table 1 Steps in Planning for Inclusion

STEP ONE: Form the inclusion planning team.	1.1 Invite the target child's parents and/or other significant caregivers to participate in planning for inclusion.
	1.2 Invite the EC program administrator to participate, along with the general early childhood education (EC) teacher and the special education (ECSE) teacher or early interventionist (EI).
	1.3 Determine if there are others who should be invited to participate on the planning team (e.g., speech or occupational or physical therapists who may be delivering related services).
STEP TWO: List each daily activity of the typical EC program	2.1 One member of the team (typically, the EC teacher) lists each activity from arrival to departure.
	2.2 If the daily activities vary from day to day, then care must be taken to include all activities.
	2.3 Note the typical length of time devoted to each daily activity.
STEP THREE: Determine the areas of instructional emphasis for the target child.	3.1 From the child's IEP or IFSP, list each current instructional target (these may be taken directly from the IEP objectives or child outcome statements that have not yet been met).
	3.2 Determine which of these objectives is a priority for the family.
	3.3 Note whether the child exhibits any particular behavior problems for which a support plan may have been developed.
	3.4 Inquire as to whether the family has any additional instructional concerns that may not have been noted in the IEP or IFSP. List these as well.
STEP FOUR: Determine what opportunities to address the needs of the target child may be provided by the daily EC program activities.	4.1 The team determines which of the activities in the typical program setting provide a reasonable opportunity to address the instructional needs of the target child.
	4.2 The team discusses and determines if an adaptation is required to address the instructional target.
	4.3 If an adaptation to the activity, as it is typically conducted, is needed to make a determination as to the nature of the adaptation; modification of content (changes in focus, rules, and/or materials); and/or modification in the way the activity is conducted (changes in physical setting, materials, and/or staffing).
STEP FIVE: Determine what modifications are necessary to meet the target child's possible need for related services.	5.1 From the IEP or IFSP, note the target child's need for a related service, the weekly schedule for each service, and the beginning date and length of time for each service visit.
	5.2 Discuss and determine whether the service can reasonably be delivered in the typical program setting by modifying an activity.
	5.3 If the service cannot reasonably be delivered in the natural setting of the classroom, then determine which activities the child will miss in order to receive the service in a different room or program setting.
STEP SIX: Determine what needs the family may see for addressing skills/ behavior at home or in the community.	6.1 Note any concerns of the family that are more appropriately addressed at home or in the community.
	6.2 Indicate which skills from the IEP/IFSP also can be addressed in these "other," more natural environments.

contain an example format for an activity matrix. Figure 1 is an Activity Matrix for Chu Chu, a Chinese American boy with moderate mental retardation. Figure 2 was developed for Nikki, an African American girl with autism spectrum disorder and moderate cognitive delay. Each of the daily activities of the typical early childhood program is written in one of the columns to the right of the box labeled "Activities" across the top of the form (planning Step 2). Directly below is a space for the "Length of Time," where the duration, in minutes, of each activity is entered. Since some children, particularly those with disabilities, may need to be involved in an alternative activity (e.g., speech therapy), space is provided to list those activities that could be substituted at an appropriate time for one of the regularly scheduled activities (planning Step 5). We have found it helpful to number each of these alternative activities directly above the activity

name and then refer to the activity by that number. Writing the number above one of the scheduled activities indicates that the alternative activity will occur instead of the scheduled activity. Down the left side of the matrix, room is provided for the individual instructional goals or objectives from the child's IEP or IFS (planning Step 3).

As suggested in Table 1, Step 4, the process continues by reading the first objective for the child and then looking at the first activity (arrival). You then ask yourself, "Does 'arrival' present an opportunity to address this objective?" Let's say, for the purpose of discussion, that the first objective for Chu Chu is from the "social skills/self-help" domain and it is "Chu Chu will greet his friends." Does "arrival" (i.e., coming into the room, hanging up his coat, putting his backpack away, and going to the table) present any opportunities for Chu Chu to

Child: __Chu Chu__ Age: __4.2 years__ Setting: __Rainbows__ Date: _____

Alternative Activities Listed by Number	1		2															Special Activities 1 2							Home/ Family
TYPICAL DAILY ACTIVITIES	Arrival	Free Choice Time	Outdoor Play	Large Group Time	Learning Centers	Closing Group Time	Outdoor Play	Departure										Speech Therapy	Special Ed. Resource (1:1)						Eats at Restaurant
Length of Time for Activity	15 mins	30 mins	30 mins	15 mins	30 mins	15 mins	30 mins	15 mins										30 mins	30 mins						
Adaptation: Modified Content	X		X				X																		
Adaptation: Modified arrangement / staffing	X		X				X	X																	

TARGET CHILD SKILL AREAS FROM CURRENT IEP or IFSP (√ indicates skill is a family priority)

Social Skill: Greets friends	√		√	√			√																		√
Language: Expressive vocab.	X	X	X	X	X	X	X	X	X																X
Self Help: Washes hands					X																				X
Fine Motor: Pincer grasp	X	X	X	X	X	X	X	X	X																X
Gross Motor: Kicks ball			X				X																		
Self Help: Signals need for BR	√	√	√	√	√	√	√	√	√																√
BEHAVIOR SUPPORT PLAN?																									

Figure 1 Early Childhood Activity Matrix

Child: __Nikki__ Age: __3.5 years__ Setting: __Ladybugs__ Date: _____

Alternative Activities Listed by Number	1		2															Special Activities 1 2							Home/ Family
TYPICAL DAILY ACTIVITIES	Arrival	Opening Group	Outdoor Play	Snack	Learning Centers	Closing Group Time	Outdoor Play	Departure										Speech Therapy	Special Ed. Resource (1:1)						Quietly occupies self during church service
Length of Time for Activity	15 mins	30 mins	30 mins	30 mins	30 mins	15 mins	30 mins	15 mins										30 mins	30 mins						
Adaptation: Modified Content	X		X				X																		
Adaptation: Modified arrangement / staffing		X	X	X	X		X	X																	X

TARGET CHILD SKILL AREAS FROM CURRENT IEP or IFSP (√ indicates skill is a family priority)

Social Skill: Plays and/or works cooperatively			√	√	√		√																		√
Language: Expressive vocab.	X	X	X	X	X	X	X	X	X																X
Language: Receptive vocab.					X																				X
Fine Motor: Pincer grasp	X	X	X	X	X	X	X	X	X																X
Self Help: Uses utensils				X																					
Self Help: Signals need for BR	X	X	X	X	X	X	X	X	X																√
BEHAVIOR SUPPORT PLAN?	yes	yes	yes	yes	yes	yes	yes	yes																	yes

Figure 2 Early Childhood Activity Matrix

acknowledge the presence of the other children by saying "hello"? Of course, that is a natural sub-activity involved in "arrival," so an "X" is placed in the box out from it and under "arrival" to indicate that a naturally occurring opportunity exists to practice the skills involved in "greeting friends" during this activity. What of the next activity? Does free choice time provide an opportunity to work on "greeting friends"? Probably not, so leave that box blank and look across the page, still on the row for the first objective, to the next activity, which is "outdoor play." Does it present any natural opportunities to practice greeting friends? Do the same thing for the next objective, and the next, until you have examined each activity in terms of its potential for each of Chu Chu's current IEP objectives. Those with high potential will have more Xs in the boxes under them; those with less potential will have fewer Xs. Skills that are of high priority to parents are indicated by a √ instead of an X. The last row in the matrix is left blank so that additions can be made if, upon reflection, the team feels a certain skill or behavior not included in the IEP or IFSP would benefit from focused attention.

It is important to remember that while an activity presents an opportunity to address the needs of a student with disabilities, it does not necessarily require *adaptations*. As indicated in Table 1, Step 4.3, an *adaptation* refers to the need to either change the content or substantive purpose of an activity, or change the way in which the activity is conducted by changing the setting arrangements, staffing patterns and responsibilities, or materials. Again, to use Chu Chu as the example, we have suggested in Figure 1 that arrival provides an opportunity to address his need to learn to greet his friends, a social skill goal taken from his IEP. Since this is not typically a skill that is the focus of instruction during arrival time, an adaptation of the first type (change in focus or content) is indicated by placement of an "X" to indicate Adaptation: Modified content/focus. But in order to accomplish this goal, the teacher will have to change how she behaves during the arrival of all of her students by focusing her attention specifically upon Chu Chu, prompting him to say "hello" and acknowledge others' greetings. Since this focused structure is not a typical part of the teacher's behavior during arrival, it would constitute an *adaptation* of the second type (Adaptation: Modified arrangement/staffing) and may require additional staff to help out with the other children while the teacher concentrates her attention on Chu Chu. Or, perhaps a "special friend" can be designated to help.

As is evident from Figure 1, arrival also provides an opportunity to address three other goals from Chu Chu's IEP: expressive vocabulary, pincer grasp, and signaling to use the bathroom should he need to do so. Because teaching these skills is not a part of the arrival activity for the other children, it needs further adaptation. Later, while outside, Chu Chu can practice greeting friends and using his expressive language and fine motor pincer grasp, but the signs indicating the need for an adaptation suggest that Chu Chu's caregivers will need to more carefully structure his activities so that he has sufficient opportunities to practice these skills each time he goes outside.

As required by his IEP, Chu Chu also will receive two types of related services, outside of the classroom (planning Step 5). Looking at Figure 1, it is evident that his team believed that the best time for him to miss a class activity to receive these services was during free choice time and part of the time devoted to learning centers. Additionally, Chu Chu's Activity Matrix indicates two family priority skills (planning Step 3.2): the social skill of greeting friends and the self-help skill of signaling his need to use the bathroom. The family also had indicated that they very much want Chu Chu to exhibit age-appropriate skills at restaurants, since they enjoy eating out as a family (planning Step 6). Staff plan to help identify non-obtrusive strategies that the family may use to reinforce Chu Chu's use of appropriate

social and communication skills in this community environment. Those that involve signaling his need to use the bathroom are of particular concern.

Figure 2 is similar to Figure 1. Activities of the early childhood (EC) program are listed in which Nikki, a 3-year-old with autism and moderate cognitive delay, is included. Skills that are the focus of instruction are taken directly from her IEP and are recorded down the left side of the matrix; an "X" is entered for each activity for each skill that may be addressed during that activity, and the need for adaptations is noted where necessary. As is the case with Chu Chu, Nikki's family's priorities are included. Attending church services is one of their top priorities. Therefore, their desire to have Nikki develop non-disruptive ways of occupying herself during the main service (so that they can all sit together as a family) is recorded in the matrix.

One major difference between Chu Chu's matrix and Nikki's is the indicated need for a behavior support plan for Nikki. She will often scream and hit when blocked from engaging in a behavior or if she is otherwise frustrated in an attempt to gain attention or access to a desired object. The support plan is the primary responsibility of those who are also responsible for the IEP, typically the ECSE teacher, behavior specialists with the public school district, and the family. However, since it will have to be implemented throughout the day in the regular early childhood setting, as well as in the community, it becomes essential that the EC program staff are involved in a determination of the adaptations that may be necessary to ensure success in the inclusive setting. Children with severe behavior problems often provide the greatest challenge to successful inclusion. We have found, however, that careful team planning with an eye toward modifications and supports, along with a willingness to try alternatives, will greatly reduce potential disruptions and go a long way toward creating an atmosphere of acceptance.

Conclusion

Developmentally appropriate practices in early childhood education programs must be implemented with a clear understanding of and appreciation for the extremes of individual variation that are likely to be encountered. Cultural, ethnic, and racial diversities are important and valued characteristics of the population of young children currently served by early childhood education programs. We now recognize the importance of curricula that celebrate different values and associated expressions of those values in both the content and strategy of instruction. As Noonan and McCormick (1993) noted, it is important to reference the early childhood curriculum to the child's social environment. However, recent social and legal imperatives have given additional meaning to "diversity." Children with a range of disabilities, including those with severe cognitive, motor, emotional, and behavioral disabilities, are a valuable aspect of the differences that we celebrate in our early childhood education programs. Their presence should cause us to pause and take a closer look at what we believe about how all children grow and learn and how we teach them.

If children are to benefit from the participation that inclusion brings, then educators, administrators, related service professionals, and parents must be ever-mindful that participation and achievement require that we emphasize the uniqueness of each child.

References

Allen, K. E., & Cowdery, G. E. (2004). *The exceptional child: Inclusion in early childhood education.* (5th ed.). Albany, NY: Thomson/Delmar Publishers.

Association for Persons with Severe Handicaps, The. (2000). *TASH Resolution on Quality Inclusive Education.* Baltimore: Author.

Bredekamp, S., & Copple, C. (Eds.). (1997). *Developmentally appropriate practice in early childhood programs* (Rev. ed.). Washington DC: National Association for the Education of Young Children.

Bricker, D., & Waddell, M. (2002a). *Assessment, evaluation and programming system (2nd ed.): Curriculum for birth to three years: Volume 3.* Baltimore: Paul H. Brookes.

Bricker, D., & Waddell, M. (2002b). *Assessment, evaluation and programming system (2nd ed.): Curriculum for three to six years: Volume 4.* Baltimore: Paul H. Brookes.

Brigance, A.H. (2004). *Brigance Diagnostic Inventory of Early Development* (2nd ed.). North Billerica, MA: Curriculum Associates.

Campbell, P. H. (2006). Addressing motor disabilities. In M. E. Snell & F. Brown (Eds.), *Instruction of students with severe disabilities* (6th ed., pp. 291–327). Upper Saddle River, NJ: Merrill.

Cook, R. E, Klein, M. D, Tessier, A., & Daley, S. (2004). *Adapting early childhood curricula for children in inclusive settings* (6th ed.). Upper Saddle River, NJ: Pearson Prentice Hall.

Fox, T. J., & Williams, W. (1991). *Implementing best practices for all students in their local school.* Burlington, VT: Center for Developmental Disabilities, The University of Vermont.

Friend, M., & Bursuck, W. D. (2002). *Including students with special needs: A practical guide for classroom teachers* (3rd ed.). Boston: Allyn and Bacon.

Gelfer, J., Filler, J., & Perkins, P. (1999). The development of a bachelor's degree in early childhood education: Preparation for teaching inclusive education. *Early Child Development and Care, 154,* 41–48.

Giangreco, M. F., Broer, S. M., & Edelman, W. (2002). "That was then, this is now!" Paraprofessional support for students with disabilities in general education classrooms. *Exceptionality, 10*(1), 47–64.

Gonzalez-Mena, J. (2000). *Foundations: Early childhood education in a diverse society.* Mountain View, CA: Mayfield.

Hauser-Cram, P., Bronson, M. B., & Upshur, C. C. (1993). The effects of the classroom environment on the social and mastery behavior of preschool children with disabilities. *Early Childhood Research Quarterly, 8,* 479–497.

Heller, H.W. (1992). A rationale for departmentalization of special education. In W. Stainback & S. Stainback (Eds.), *Controversial issues confronting special education* (pp. 271–281). Needham Heights, MA: Allyn and Bacon.

Individuals with Disabilities Education Act (IDEA), §303.18 of Rules and Regulations (1998).

Individuals with Disabilities Education Improvement Act, 20 U.S.C. 1414, §614 (2004).

Kostell, P. H. (1997). *Inclusion.* (ACEI Speaks brochure.) Olney, MD: Association for Childhood Education International.

Noonan, M. J., & McCormick, L. (1993). *Early intervention in natural environments: Methods and procedures.* Belmont, CA: Brookes/Cole Publishing.

Pretti-Frontczak, K., & Bricker, D. (2004). *An activity-based approach to early intervention* (3rd ed.). Baltimore: Paul H. Brookes.

Sandall, S., McLean, M. E., & Smith, B.J. (2000). *DEC recommended practices in early intervention/early childhood special education.* Longmont, CO: Sopris West.

JOHN FILLER is Professor, Department of Education, University of Nevada, Las Vegas. **YAOYING XU** is Assistant Professor, Department of Special Education and Disability Policy, Virginia Commonwealth University, Richmond.

From *Childhood Education,* Winter 2006/2007. Copyright © 2007 by the Association for Childhood Education International. Reprinted by permission of John Filler and Yaoying Xu and the Association for Childhood Education International, 17904 Georgia Avenue, Suite 215, Olney, MD 20832.

Creative Play

Building Connections With Children Who Are Learning English

How can teachers support young children, all of whom are English language learners? Play is a wonderful way to help all children gain the confidence and skills they need to succeed in school and life!

SARA J. BURTON AND LINDA CAROL EDWARDS

Six-year-old Ana Belen speaks Spanish. She is in the block center with an English-speaking friend named Malik. Ana Belen tries to get Malik's attention because she needs more blocks to complete her building. She calls out to Malik in Spanish, gesturing with her hands and asking for the block she needs. She looks at him with a confused look when he does not respond to her request. Ana Belen then walks around the block center and points toward the blocks for which she was asking. She then says, to Malik, "Tarugo" (block).

Malik complains to their teacher that he cannot understand Ana Belen and cannot play with her. When the teacher approaches, she explains to Malik, "Ana Belen is asking you to get her the square block—tarugo. Look, she is making a block shape with her hands, too!"

Immediately Malik understands how Ana Belen is communicating. His confused expression changes to a smile. Ana Belen smiles too, as Malik hands her a block. Both children understand that they can communicate, verbally and nonverbally. The teacher observes as the two children continue to play together.

Learning English: Opportunities for Everyone

English language learners (ELL) are learning to listen, speak, read, and write (Silvaggio, 2005). When speakers of other languages begin to acquire English, like all children, they develop at different rates. Teachers may encounter situations such as these with English language learners who already speak Spanish:

- Some children experience a silent period of 6 or more months.
- Other children practice learning by mixing or combining the two languages or use a form of "Spanglish."
- Some children may have the skills (appropriate accent, vocabulary, and vernacular) but they are not truly proficient.
- Other children quickly acquire English-language proficiency (National Association for the Education of Young Children, 1995).

Language acquisition is a very complex developmental process and it may take some students "a minimum of 12 years" to master a new language (Collier, 1989). Even when children seem to express themselves correctly, they may not have mastered the true complexity of the language.

Educators realize that children who are English language learners come to early childhood programs and schools with their own knowledge of the language used in their homes (NAEYC, 1995). Teachers of young children are encouraged to view the inclusion of children who are learning English as an enrichment opportunity for everyone: children who are learning English as a second language, the English-speaking students, and even themselves. Wise teachers embrace classroom diversity and create an atmosphere where all children can thrive and progress.

This article primarily considers children who come from homes where Spanish is spoken, but the premises and suggestions hold true for any of the "nearly 3 million ESL students" in the nation's schools (Shore, 2001). What better way to involve and encourage all children to learn than through play?

What Are the Benefits of Play for English Language Learners?

Play is the primary vehicle through which children learn about themselves and others and about the world in which they live and interact. Through play, children actively explore their world, build new skills, and use their imaginations. Best of all they do it for the simple *joy* of doing it.

Educators are well aware of the lasting benefits of play, but the idea of "playing with language, oral and especially written language, during dramatic play is not nearly as common as it ideally should be" (Korat, Bahar, & Snapir, 2002, p. 393).

Play is extremely beneficial in overcoming communication challenges between English speakers and speakers of other languages (Little, 2004–2005; Reeves, 2004–2005; Oliver & Klugman, 2002). For children who are learning English, self-directed play establishes an informal, non-threatening atmosphere that is one of the most valuable ways of learning.

When children are engaged in the process of play, they usually care very little about an end product. They are free to figure out what they want to do and when they want to do it. They engage in spontaneous activity. In other words, children are in control. Play is a hands-on activity in which children choose their own learning adventures. They learn while doing something they have decided to do. What are children learning through play?

- Children increase the size of their vocabularies and their ability to comprehend language.
- They develop skills in cooperation by sharing and taking turns.
- Play helps children to develop empathy and strengthens their ability to express emotions (Oliver & Klugman, 2002).
- Play enables children to develop patience and tolerance (Dorrell, 2000).
- During play, children feel comfortable enough to take risks. As they gain self-reliance and feel successful (Edwards, 2002) they begin to function more independently and eventually take more risks outside of the play environment.

Play is essential for the sound development of all children, but it is especially important in the growth and development of children who speak English as a second language. How did Ana Belen and Malik benefit from playing? They interacted in the block section, primarily with nonverbal communication, and both learned a new vocabulary word. After resolving their initial lack of knowledge about the Spanish and English words for *block,* they played together in such a way that both students felt comfortable.

Children who are learning a language benefit from play in several ways (Silver, 1999). Play helps establish bonds of friendship among children who do not communicate well in English (p. 67). During play, children who are learning English may exhibit independence and self-assurance that is not otherwise evident.

For example, Silver noted that children who were learning English tended to engage in solitary play when painting or doing cut-and-paste activities. As they got used to the routine, they became involved in play with rules and games. One child was very shy and used mostly telegraphic speech. After engaging in play, he gradually built up his confidence to volunteer to go first when playing a game. Silver concluded that only during periods of play was this child on "equal footing with the others in the class" (1999, p. 67).

Telegraphic speech: Use of only the words necessary to communicate. For example, "I want to be picked up," might be verbalized as "pick up."

How Can Teachers Support English Language Learners?

Teachers have a critical role in organizing their classrooms, structuring activities, and planning the use of materials in order to maximize all children's participation in play. Early childhood educators can celebrate children's strengths and allow them many ways to express their own interests and talents.

Many children born in the United States speak English at school, but speak their native language elsewhere. Speaking Spanish at home and among friends is one way that families cherish their ties to their home country. Silvaggio (2005) notes that children need adult help to negotiate this new world. It is not an easy task for teachers, who often lack resources to work with English language learners. As Shore (2001) explains, there are simple and practical ways that educators can help ESL children succeed. These are a few possibilities.

Assess needs. Find out where students' skill levels are, not only in English but in other areas of development as well. Families' perspectives, previous child care providers' insights, and regular observations are essential resources for understanding children.

Empathize. Imagine how overwhelming it is to walk into a classroom where you only understand part of what you hear. The first author of this article remembers studying in Spain during her college years and being truly scared during the first few months there. Even though she had studied the language for a number of years, she felt helpless, insecure, and disconnected. How much more difficult it must be for a young child!

Foster a sense of belonging. Make sure all children feel welcomed by being patient. Use body language and pictures to communicate while learning welcoming words in their languages. Take care to pronounce children's names correctly. Be aware of children's needs for personal space and privacy, too.

Assign buddies. All children yearn to feel important and included. English-speaking children can be terrific resources to those who speak other language by making sure they can find the way around school, count money at lunchtime, understand directions, and more.

Keep track of language progress. Maintain a portfolio of each child. Save photographs, recordings, artwork, and writing samples. Review records with the child (and family) to see progress over time. This is an important way to acknowledge children's strengths and accomplishments.

Encourage family involvement. Encourage parents of children who are learning English to feel like they are a part of the community and classroom. If needed, arrange for an interpreter at meetings and conferences. Learn more about each family's culture so that interactions with each other are always respectful. Study the language and learn important words and phrases.

Learn key words. Make sure all staff and children quickly learn basic vocabulary words in both languages, such as restroom, clock, teacher, and bus. Picture cards and labels with words are an excellent tool to use with children who are beginning to learn about written language.

Foster an appreciation of cultural diversity. Diverse cultures are an asset for any classroom. Respect each culture's customs, make and taste a variety of foods, learn vocabulary words, create maps, talk with family members, and encourage all children to share their traditions.

Ask and observe to find out how children prefer to be encouraged and supported to succeed—these strategies vary by culture and custom. "Children with high motivation, self-confidence, and low levels of anxiety are more successful second language learners" (Szecsi & Giambo (2004/2005, p. 104)).

Find out how children prefer to be encouraged.

In an ideal environment, children play independently, at their own pace, in their own unique way, and have the necessary materials to facilitate their play. "We need to play in English, not just speak English at school," said one student (Reeves, 2004/2005). Learning centers provide unique opportunities for all children to participate in free play, and this puts children who are learning English on "a level playing field" with their peers (Silver, 1999).

Dramatic Play Enhances Language Development

A dramatic play center is especially useful for children who are English language learners. Pretend play enables them to communicate in an informal setting and gather information that will be helpful to them, even beyond the classroom.

For example, during pretend play, children explore activities and relationships important to them in the real world. They typically investigate the role of family members, community helpers, and health care professionals (Texas Workforce Commission, 2002). Children bring their own knowledge into their play as they cooperate with one another.

In the dramatic play center, children build language and literacy skills. English language learners soon begin to communicate in effective and appropriate ways with both children and adults. They have many opportunities to "practice their language skills with peers" (deAtiles & Allexsaht-Snider, 2002) in a "language-rich environment" (Szecsi & Giambo, 2004/2005).

A language-rich environment is essential in any early childhood classroom. Include props such as telephone books, magazines, and restaurant menus for dramatic play. By labeling items, teachers expose all children to print in both languages. This enables children who are learning English to encounter reading and speaking while they play and gives them a "multisensory approach" (Gasparro & Falletta, 1994) to language acquisition.

For example, Luis Jose and Sophie are pretending to go to the subway station. The props are labeled with text and pictures of a train, ticket, money, a caution sign in both languages, so each child knows each object in his or her language. Even though they speak different languages, they are able to recreate what happens at the subway station.

Unscripted role play is a valuable way for children to interact informally and gain the confidence they need to speak aloud. Similarly, playing restaurant is efficient and helpful for children as they read menus, practice ordering, interact with a waiter, and use table manners. For children, it seems less important that they can engage in English or Spanish conversations. What does appear to matter to them is that they can interact and understand each other.

Teachers can choose relevant, diverse themes for dramatic play and provide props for each theme. Stock the area with tickets, pretend money, many types of groceries, tools, and toy animals. By using mostly familiar items, children find creative ways to play. Playing with real-life materials helps children feel more comfortable.

Teachers can also create a Reader's Theater. Children perform dramatic representations of a story read to them in class or by a friend (Szecsi & Giambo, 2004/2005). The list in the box contains a sample of books that may be helpful in working with Spanish speakers. These books can be integrated into many themes. Some books are also available in English so that children can "read" together.

Teachers who want children to feel at ease in the classroom must "reach past psychological and cultural barriers that lead students to prefer the safety of silence to the danger of speaking" (Reeves, 2004/2005). When children feel comfortable and relaxed, they will speak up and show what they have learned. "Drama places learners in situations that seem real," (Gasparro & Falletta, 1994) so when students use the goal language (English) for a specific purpose, the language is more easily internalized and remembered.

How Families Help Children Adjust to a New Language and Culture

- Read aloud in both languages to your children. Many reading skills transfer between languages.
- Get involved in community activities with your children. Go on local history tours, visit nature centers, and attend library story times. Link up with groups with similar interests, such as recreation departments, faith communities, and heritage festivals.
- Play board games. This will enrich skills such as counting, using money, and learning new words.
- Watch a few English-language children's educational television programs together such as *Reading Rainbow* or *Zoom!* The language is easy to understand and the characters are real. Talk about children's ideas afterwards, too.
- Become active in sports. Choose sports suitable for children's ages. These welcoming social interactions enable children to learn new expressions and casual rules of the language. Families are likely to gain new friendships. (adapted from Giambo & Szecsi, 2005)

Through a variety of play experiences, children who are learning English become more prepared to engage in everyday interactions with English speakers. They eventually gain the confidence to participate in the community.

What Role Do Families Play?

Parents and extended family members play a large role in helping children learn a new language and successfully adapt to the culture in which they live. Many families who speak another language and value their own culture face a difficult challenge when it comes to maintaining that culture and wanting their children to learn English as quickly as possible (Giambo & Szecsi, 2005).

Celebrate children's strengths.

Keeping children's fluency and literacy (if already acquired) in the native language while developing new language skills is a tremendous benefit because people "who are bilingual have an advantage in our increasingly global economy" (Giambo & Szecsi, 2005). Share these suggestions with families, who can help their children thrive in two cultures and languages.

Many school-related skills that parents teach their children in their native language transfer to their new language and class-room. Translators and resources in other languages are increasingly available in many communities. Families and teachers are urged to work together to facilitate each child's growth in language and in life.

Outlook for the Future

"Young children are just beginning to learn about the world, and because they are still amateurs, they make mistakes, they get confused, and they do not always get things just right. They need a positive reaction from the adults around them, and they need to be recognized for their own individual value" (Edwards, 2005, p. 2).

This challenge is true for teachers and their interactions with all children, including those who are learning another language. Young children construct knowledge by building on familiar experiences. Educators provide young children with an extensive array of meaningful experiences.

When children learn new vocabulary words and practice pronunciation and language conventions, they are gaining skills for life. Taking the time to help children learn English as well as key words in other languages enables them to succeed in their learning environment. They will gain the confidence and abilities to succeed in the diverse culture in which they live.

Hispanics are the largest minority population in the United States, with 39.9 million people as of July 2003 (U.S. Census Bureau, 2005). Hispanic youth also have a high dropout rate: "Nearly one in three students fails to graduate from high school" (Clearinghouse on Urban Education, 2000). Solutions are urgently needed to help children who speak Spanish become fluent in the language and gain skills they need to become productive, healthy adults.

Young children construct knowledge by building on familiar experiences.

Almost every teacher works with one or more English language learners every year. The education challenge is to make every situation a truly beneficial "teachable moment." Partnerships with children (and their families) will benefit children's language and literacy skills and build the confidence they need to succeed. After all, "People who can communicate in at least two languages are a great asset to the communities in which they live and work" (Cutshall, 2004/2005, p. 23).

Summary

As leaders and mentors, teachers can best help culturally and linguistically diverse children and families by respecting the importance of each child's home language and culture. Educators who embrace, respect, and preserve the many ethnic and linguistic backgrounds of students will enable them to increasingly contribute to this diverse culture.

Put These Ideas Into Practice!

Creative Play: Building Connections with Children Who Are Learning English

Sara J. Burton and Linda Carol Edwards

What Children Learn Through Play

- Children's vocabularies increase.
- Sharing and taking turns improves cooperation.
- Children develop empathy and express emotions.
- They develop patience and tolerance.
- Children gain self-reliance and feel successful.
- They become more independent.

Ways Teachers Support English Language Learners

- Find out their skill levels in all areas. Ask parents and previous child care providers to share their insights.
- Imagine what it is like to be in a group where you only understand part of what you hear.
- Be patient.
- Make sure children and families feel welcome. Learn a few words of their languages.
- Ask classmates to help each other during classroom routines.
- Regularly observe children and record progress. Keep a portfolio of photos, recordings, art, and (for older children) writing samples.
- Help families feel part of the community and classroom.
- Appreciate diversity.

Enrichment Experiences for Young Children

Focus on the dramatic play area. Add familiar props such as clothing, flowers, restaurant menus, pretend money, foods and tools, toy animals, magazines, and real-life materials. Label items in both languages for older preschoolers and primary children. Encourage informal, language-rich play.

Create a Reader's Theater. Offer age-appropriate and culturally relevant books, puppets, and dress-up clothing. Encourage role play of the stories in both English and children's own languages.

Offer everyday opportunities to use English. Pair an English language learner with an English-speaking student. Ask older English-speakers to read to younger ELL students. Encourage ELL students to read to younger peers.

Enrich learning opportunities. Ask older ELL students to interview a teacher, another student, or a member of the community. Students create their own interview questions, take photos, record the answers, and share the experience with classmates.

Suggestions to Share with Children's Families

- Read aloud in both languages to your children.
- Get involved in community activities with your children. Go on local history tours, visit nature centers, and attend library story times.
- Play board games. This will enrich skills such as counting, using money, and learning new words.
- Watch a few English-language children's educational television programs together. Talk about children's ideas afterwards.
- Become active in sports. Choose sports suitable for children's ages.

Adult Learning Experiences that Build on These Ideas

- Start learning children's languages. Perhaps a child's family member would like to tutor YOU.
- Get to know children's cultures. Shop in ethnic stores their families frequent. Attend community events. Read about diverse families to gain a better understanding of their strengths and challenges.
- Engage staff in a cultural immersion experience. Find a meeting moderator who speaks the chosen language, such as Spanish. Show a clip from a Spanish-language film. Each teacher receives a handout, in Spanish, about the film. After viewing the film, small groups discuss feelings, thoughts, reactions, and realizations as a result of this cultural experience.
- Ask an ELL parent to attend a staff meeting, with a translator, to talk about issues within the school and broader community.
- Identify translators who can attend parent meetings, translate written materials, and otherwise facilitate communication with families.

Note: *Dimensions of Early Childhood* readers are encouraged to copy this material for early childhood students as well as teachers of young children as a professional development tool.

References

Clearinghouse on Urban Education. (2000). *School practices to promote the achievement of Hispanic students.* ERIC Digest Number 153.

Collier, V.P. (1989). How long? A synthesis of research on academic achievement in a second language. *TESOL Quarterly, 23*(3), 509–531.

Cutshall, S. (2004/2005). Why we need "The Year of Languages." *Educational Leadership, 62*(4), 20–23.

deAtiles, J.R., & Allexsaht-Snider, M. (2002). *Effective approaches to teaching young Mexican immigrant children.* ERIC Digest Number 20021201.

Dorrell, A. (2000, March/April). All they do is play? Play in preschool. Early *Childhood News,* pp. 18–22.

Edwards, L.C. (2002). *The creative arts: A process approach for children and teachers* (3rd Ed.). Columbus, OH: Merrill/Prentice-Hall.

Gasparro, M., & Falletta, B. (1994). *Creating drama with poetry: Teaching English as a second language through dramatization and improvisation.* ERIC Digest Number 19940401.

Giambo, D., & Szecsi, T. (2005, Spring). Parents can guide children through the world of two languages. *Childhood Education, 81*(3), 164–165.

Korat, O., Bahar, E., & Snapir, M. (2002). Sociodramatic play as an opportunity for literacy development: The teacher's role. *Reading Teacher, 56*(4), 386–394.

Little, C. (2004/2005). A journey toward belonging. *Educational Leadership, 62*(4), 82–83.

Oliver, S.J., & Klugman, E. (2002). Playing the day away. *Child Care Information Exchange,* 66–70.

National Association for the Education of Young Children. (1995). Position Statement. *Responding to linguistic and cultural diversity: Recommendations for effective early childhood education.* Retrieved February 22, 2005, from www.naeyc.org/about/positions/PSDIV98.asp.

Reeves, D.B. (2004/2005). "If I said something wrong, I was afraid." *Educational Leadership, 62*(4), 72–74.

Shore, K. (2001). Success for ESL students. *Instructor, 110*(6), 30–33.

Silvaggio, A.M. ESL demand challenge schools. Retrieved January 11, 2005, from greenvilleonline.com/news/2005/01/11/2005011156589.htm

Silver, A. (1999). Play: A fundamental equalizer for ESL children. *TESL Canada Journal, 16*(2), 62–69.

Szecsi, T., & Giambo, D. (2004/2005, Winter). ESOL in every minute of the school day. *Childhood Education, 81*(2), 104–106.

Texas Workforce Commission. (2002, Spring). Learning centers: Why and how. *Texas Childcare,* 30–42.

U.S. Census Bureau. *Hispanic Heritage Month 2004.* Retrieved January 24, 2005, from census.gov/Press-Release/www/releases/archives/facts_for_features_special_edition.

SARA J. BURTON, BA, MAT, is a third grade teacher at Goodwin Elementary School in North Charleston, South Carolina. She holds a B.A. degree in Spanish from Wofford College and has traveled extensively to Spanish-speaking countries around the world. She earned her M.A.T. degree from the College of Charleston in Charleston, South Carolina. **LINDA CAROL EDWARDS,** EdD, is Professor, Department of Elementary and Early Childhood Education, College of Charleston, Charleston, South Carolina. Before she began teaching at the college level, she taught kindergarten in the North Carolina public schools. Edwards is the author of two books on early childhood education.

From *Dimensions of Early Childhood*, Spring/Summer 2006. Copyright © 2006 by Southern Early Childhood Association (SECA). Reprinted by permission.

Helping Young Hispanic Learners

**They bring many assets to the education process.
So why aren't they succeeding in U.S. schools?**

EUGENE E. GARCÍA AND BRYANT JENSEN

Although we may label various racial and ethnic groups "at risk" in terms of education outcomes, many are less at risk in certain areas than the majority population. Empirical studies have shown, for example, that compared with children from U.S.-born families, children from poor immigrant families have lower infant mortality rates, suffer from fewer physical and mental health problems, and are less likely to engage in such risky behaviors as substance abuse, early sexual intercourse, and delinquent or violent activity (Shields & Behrman, 2004).

These strengths, however, are not always sufficient to keep children on pathways to education success. Bearing in mind that child development is an amalgamation of individual, family, school, and community factors, research suggests a number of actions that education policymakers and practitioners can take to improve the early education trajectories of Hispanics, the largest and youngest ethnic group in the United States.

A Heterogeneous Group

In 2005, one in five children 8 years old or younger in the United States was Hispanic (Hernandez, 2006). Moreover, Hispanic children make up approximately 80 percent of the U.S. English language learner population (Capps et al., 2005). Born inside and outside the United States, children of Hispanic (or Latino) heritage come from diverse social, cultural, and linguistic backgrounds. Recent growth in the young Hispanic population in the United States has been driven primarily by immigration from Latin America (Ramirez & de la Cruz, 2003).

A majority of young Hispanic children are of Mexican origin (65 percent), but substantial proportions have origins in Puerto Rico (9 percent), Central America (7 percent), South America (6 percent), Cuba (2 percent), and the Dominican Republic (3 percent) (Hernandez, 2006). Two of three young children of Mexican and Cuban origins live in families that immigrated to the United States, as do 9 in 10 children with origins in the Dominican Republic and in Central or South America.

It is important to note that the vast majority of young Hispanic children in the United States are U.S.-born citizens.

Eighty-five percent of children with at least one South American–born parent, 88 percent of those with a Mexican-born parent, and approximately 92 percent of those with a parent born in the Dominican Republic or Central America were born in the United States and therefore are U.S. citizens (Capps, Fix, Ost, Reardon-Anderson, & Passel, 2004; Hernandez, 2006).

Their Strengths

Hispanic children and families demonstrate a number of positive attributes. In an analysis of census data, Hernandez (2006) found that 77 percent of young Hispanic children (from birth to age 8) lived with two parents in 2000. The proportion ranges from 81 to 86 percent for young children in immigrant families from Mexico, Central and South America, and Cuba. However, after the first generation, the proportion of children living with two parents decreases in families from those regions, and from the Dominican Republic and Puerto Rico as well.

Young Hispanic children typically live in families with a strong work ethic and desire to succeed. Ninety-three percent of these children have fathers who worked during the year previous to the 2000 U.S. Census. Moreover, Hispanic children are approximately three times more likely than other groups to have additional working adults living in the home (Hernandez, 2006).

In 2005, one in five children 8 years old or younger in the United States was Hispanic.

Despite low socioeconomic circumstances, Hispanic families demonstrate several positive physical health outcomes. Studies have consistently found that Hispanics have lower infant mortality rates, better birth outcomes, healthier diets, and lower rates of obesity than do whites (Escarce, Morales, & Rumbaut, 2006). These rates vary by group, however: Hispanics of Puerto Rican descent tend to have poorer health status than Hispanics of Mexican or Central American origin.

Although parents of young Hispanics, on average, do not have high levels of formal education, they express interest in enrolling their children in early education programs. A survey by the Tomás Rivera Policy Institute found that more than 90 percent of Hispanic parents believe that it is "very important" or "somewhat important" for children to attend preschool (Perez & Zarate, 2006). Hispanic parents also have high education aspirations for their children (Nuñez, Cuccaro-Alamin, & Carroll, 1998). Most significant, they are willing to work hard within and outside of education environments to advance their learning opportunities (García, 2005).

Many young Hispanic children are also poised to become fully bilingual in Spanish and English. Given the social, cognitive, and economic benefits of bilingualism, schools would be wise to provide Hispanic children with opportunities to maintain and develop their dual-language proficiency.

Their Challenges

Currently, Hispanics lag behind their white and Asian American peers at all proficiency levels of reading and mathematics throughout their K–12 schooling (Braswell, Daane, & Grigg, 2003; National Center for Education Statistics [NCES], 2003). Some differences in achievement among racial/ethnic groups result from socioeconomic factors. For example, on average, Hispanics have a lower socioeconomic status than whites and Asian Americans do. However, using data from the Early Childhood Longitudinal Study, Kindergarten Cohort (NCES, 2001), Reardon and Galindo (2006) found that Hispanic children scored lower in mathematics and reading than did their white peers in all five socioeconomic quintiles. In a separate analysis, Reardon (2003) noted that these achievement differences from kindergarten through 1st grade were attributable to factors both in and out of school. In other words, practices in the home and school greatly influence racial/ethnic and socioeconomic achievement gaps in early education (García, Jensen, & Cuéllar, 2006).

The home language environment plays a considerable role in school achievement. Using data from a national sample of children born between December 2001 and January 2002, López, Barrueco, and Miles (2006) described the home language environments of Hispanic infants. The largest group (34 percent) lived in homes in which Spanish was the primary language, with some English spoken. Twenty-two percent lived in a home in which English was the primary language, with some Spanish spoken. Twenty-one percent lived in English-only homes and 19 percent in Spanish-only homes. Consequently, approximately three of four Hispanic infants heard Spanish spoken in the home, and 53 percent of infants lived in a home in which Spanish was the primary or sole language spoken.

Reardon and Galindo (2006) found that reading and mathematics achievement patterns from kindergarten through 3rd grade varied by home language environments. Hispanic children living in homes in which Spanish was primarily spoken lagged further behind white children than did Hispanics who lived in homes in which English was primarily spoken. The academic risk for children from non-English-speaking homes has been documented as early as the preschool years (NCES, 1995).

However, not all young Hispanic English language learners are equally at risk for academic failure and reading difficulties. In their analyses of group differences in mathematics and reading outcomes from kindergarten through 3rd grade, Reardon and Galindo (2006) found that Hispanic children of Mexican, Central American, and Puerto Rican descent scored lower than those of South American and Cuban descent. Also, first- and second-generation children from Mexican backgrounds scored lower than children from the third or later generations. Because achievement differences between whites and Hispanics were found at all socioeconomic levels, early academic risk appears to result from a combination of factors that include family poverty, low parental education, limited-English-proficient parents, and single status of the mother (NCES, 1995).

Making a Difference

Academic achievement gaps for Hispanics—especially for those who enter school not speaking English—exist at the beginning of kindergarten, solidify in grades 3–8, and result in significantly lower rates of high school completion and college attendance. Reform initiatives have not produced the necessary robust changes in academic performance because they often ignore "what counts" for the academic success of young Hispanic students. Programs and curriculums often do not take into consideration the fact that the children speak a language other than English; that they need to acquire high levels of academic vocabulary, discourse, and inquiry in English to succeed in content areas; and that their own cultural and linguistic contexts are crucial ingredients in developing understanding of academic concepts.

With these considerations in mind, we offer several recommendations to improve education opportunities for young Hispanics in the United States. These recommendations highlight a double need: for policy and practice in early education to directly address language and for curriculum and instruction to reflect relevant culture and traditions.

Rich Language Environments

PreK–3 education environments of young Hispanic children should be rich in language. We define richness as a function of *frequency* and *quality*. In terms of frequency, research on cognitive development, language, and early experiences shows that the number of conversational exchanges between adults and young children is strongly associated with school readiness and academic success in formal schooling (Risley & Hart, 2006). Teachers, aides, and other school personnel should engage young Hispanic students in casual talk as much as possible and, where feasible, encourage parents to do the same.

In terms of quality, young Hispanics should hear English and Spanish spoken in the classroom and have many opportunities to express themselves in both languages, allowing for linguistic exploration. Meta-analyses and best-evidence syntheses suggest that bilingual or English-plus approaches to curriculum and instruction are preferable to English-only or English immersion programs (Rolstad, Mahoney, & Glass, 2005; Slavin & Cheung, 2005). For young children managing more than one language, academic skills are much more likely to develop and transfer between languages when environments provide access to knowledge through both languages in culturally relevant ways. Environments that do not provide this access can stifle cognitive development.

PreK-3 education environments of young Hispanic children should be rich in language.

Rich language environments that integrate Spanish and English also facilitate important parent-school associations. Spanish-speaking parents are more likely to involve themselves in schools and classrooms in which Spanish is regularly spoken.

Dual-Language Programs

Young Hispanic children should have access to high-quality dual-language programs (that is, two-way immersion), which teach English and Spanish language skills through content. Integrating native English and Spanish speakers in the same classroom fosters ethnic and linguistic equity among students. Dual-language programs also promote Hispanic students' literacy development in English without compromising their Spanish skills (August, Calderón, Carlo, & Nuttall, 2006). Moreover, research shows that when young Spanish-speaking Hispanics and their native English-speaking peers are enrolled in dual-language programs, the academic achievement levels of both groups are equivalent to, or in many cases superior to, outcomes of students in mainstream classrooms (August, Calderón, & Carlo, 2002).

Researchers at the Center for Applied Linguistics (2005) have provided a set of principles to help school personnel establish and maintain high-quality dual-language programs. Programs should

- Implement a curriculum that promotes and maintains the development of bilingual, biliterate, and multicultural competencies for all students.
- Use student-centered instructional strategies derived from research-based principles of dual-language education.
- Recruit and retain high-quality, dual-language staff.
- Have knowledgeable leadership that promotes equity among groups and supports the goals of additive bilingualism, biliteracy, and cross-cultural competence.
- Create positive, ongoing relations with students' families and the community.

Universal Prekindergarten

Hispanic children ages 3 and 4 should have access to free, state-funded preschool. Evidence suggests that high-quality prekindergarten programs improve school readiness for young Hispanic children and decrease achievement differences among racial/ethnic groups at kindergarten entry. These programs should have bilingual and culturally competent staff to effectively engage students and develop sustainable relationships with family members.

Spanish-speaking parents are more likely to involve themselves in schools and classrooms in which Spanish is regularly spoken.

Moreover, states would be wise to adopt prekindergarten curriculums in both Spanish and English. States and local communities should work together to offer high-quality education experiences with a variety of schedule options. In states where state-funded prekindergarten is not available to all children, policymakers and program administrators should expand definitions of eligibility to include children with limited English proficiency This intermediate step would increase Hispanic enrollments and serve more at-risk children until the state attains the broader goal of universal access.

High-Quality Teachers

Providing rich language environments and high-quality, dual-language programs in preK–3 requires high-quality, effective teachers. Teachers should be proficient in both English and Spanish and be knowledgeable about the cultural and linguistic circumstances of Hispanic families, particularly the academic strengths and needs of their children. Indeed, research shows that when teachers use Spanish in the classroom, it heightens the transfer of academic skills between languages and increases early achievement outcomes for young bilingual and emergent bilingual students (August et al., 2006). The most successful teachers are fluent in both languages; understand learning patterns associated with second-language acquisition; have mastered appropriate instructional strategies (such as cooperative learning, sheltered instruction, differentiated instruction, and strategic teaching); and have strong organizational and communication skills. These skills enable teachers to interact with Hispanic parents, encouraging them to engage in literacy activities with their children at home. Teachers with these skills can more easily learn important details about the linguistic backgrounds of their students and develop creative and accurate assessments of their students' linguistic ability and development.

When staff bilingualism is not feasible, schools should provide a language specialist. Language specialists serve as consultants and aids to teachers in the classroom to support Hispanic English language learners. They are proficient in Spanish and English and have extensive training in second-language acquisition and in multilingual and multicultural education. Having a language specialist in the classroom will help monolingual teachers make essential links with Spanish-speaking parents.

Vaughn, Linan-Thompson, Pollard-Durodola, Mathes, and Hagan (2006) offer several research-based principles to guide reading instruction for Hispanic English language learners. These include

- Designing effective reading programs based on commonalities between reading instruction in English and Spanish.
- Recognizing that English literacy will require more explicit instruction in both phonics and word reading.

- Making connections between students' knowledge in Spanish and its application to English.
- Offering as many opportunities as possible for students to use oral language (in Spanish or English) to address higher-order questions.
- Capitalizing on all opportunities to teach and engage students in building vocabulary and concept knowledge.
- Organizing effective use of peer and cooperative group work to enhance learning.

High-quality prekindergarten programs improve school readiness children.

A Call to Action

As U.S. educators welcome students to their classrooms, they frequently see a picture that differs from the school-day images of their own childhoods. Yet Hispanic children bring a set of welcome assets to the education process. It's high time we capitalize on these assets to improve the education outcomes of Hispanic students. By doing so, we will enhance not only the global competitiveness of the United States, but also the nation's social and economic well-being.

References

August, D., Calderón, M., & Carlo, M. (2002). *Transfer of skills from Spanish to English: A study of young learners.* Washington, DC: Center for Applied Linguistics.

August, D., Calderón, M., Carlo, M., & Nuttall, M. (2006). Developing literacy in English-language learners: An examination of the impact of English-only versus bilingual instruction. In P. D. McCardle & E. Hoff, *Childhood bilingualism: Research on infancy through school age* (pp. 91–106). Cleveland, UK: Multilingual Matters.

Braswell, J., Daane, M., & Grigg, W. (2003). *The nation's report card: Mathematics highlights 2003* (NCES 2004451). Washington, DC: U.S. Department of Education.

Capps, R., Fix, M., Murray, J., Ost, J., Passel, J., & Herwantoro-Hernandez, S. (2005). *The new demography of America's schools: Immigration and the No Child Left Behind Act.* Washington, DC: Urban Institute.

Capps, R., Fix, M., Ost, J., Reardon-Anderson, J., & Passel, J. (2004). *The health and well-being of young children of immigrants.* Washington, DC: Urban Institute.

Center for Applied Linguistics. (2005, March). *Guiding principles for dual language education.* Washington, DC: Author.

Escarce, J., Morales, L., & Rumbaut, R. (2006). The health status and health behaviors of Hispanics. In M. Tienda & F. Mitchell (Eds.), *Multiple origins, common destinies: Hispanics and the American future* (pp. 362–409). Washington, DC: National Research Council.

García, E. E. (2005). *Teaching and learning in two languages: Bilingualism and schooling in the United States.* New York: Teachers College Press.

García, E. E., Jensen, B. T., & Cuéllar, D. (2006). Early academic achievement of Hispanics in the United States: Implications for teacher preparation. *The New Educator, 2,* 123–147.

Hernandez, D. (2006). *Young Hispanic children in the U.S.: A demographic portrait based on Census 2000.* A report to the National Task Force on Early Childhood Education for Hispanics. New York: Foundation for Child Development.

López, M., Barrueco, S., &. Miles, J. (2006). *Latino infants and families: A national perspective of protective and risk factors for development.* A report to the National Task Force on Early Childhood Education for Hispanics.

National Center for Education Statistics. (1995). *Approaching kindergarten: A look at preschoolers in the United States.* Washington, DC: U.S. Department of Education.

National Center for Education Statistics (2001). *User's manual for the ECLS-K base year public-use data files and electronic codebook.* Washington, DC: U.S. Department of Education.

National Center for Education Statistics. (2003). *Status and trends in the education of Hispanics* (NCES 2003-007). Washington, DC: U.S. Department of Education.

Nuñez, A., Cuccaro-Alamin, S., & Carroll, C. D. (1998). *First-generation students: Undergraduates whose parents never enrolled in postsecondary education.* Washington, DC: U.S. Department of Education.

Perez, P., & Zarate, M. E. (2006). *Latino public opinion survey of pre-kindergarten programs: Knowledge, preferences, and public support.* Los Angeles: Tomás Rivera Policy Institute.

Ramirez, R. R., & de la Cruz, P. G. (2003, June). *The Hispanic population in the United States: March 2002.* Washington, DC: U.S. Census Bureau.

Reardon, S. (2003). *Sources of educational inequality: The growth of racial/ethnic and socioeconomic test score gaps in kindergarten and first grade.* University Park: Population Research Institute, Pennsylvania State University.

Reardon, S., & Galindo, C. (2006, April). *K–3 academic achievement patterns and trajectories of Hispanics and other racial/ethnic groups.* Paper presented at the annual meeting of the American Educational Research Association, San Francisco.

Risley, T. R., & Hart, B. (2006). Promoting early language development. In N. F. Watt et al. (Eds.), *The crisis in youth mental health* (Vol. 4, pp. 83–89). Westport, CT: Praeger.

Rolstad, K., Mahoney, K., & Glass, G. V. (2005). The big picture: A meta-analysis of program effectiveness research on English language learners. *Educational Policy, 19*(4), 572–594.

Shields, M., & Behrman, R. (2004). Children of immigrant families: Analysis and recommendations. *The Future of Children, 14*(2), 4-15.

Slavin, R. E., & Cheung, A. (2005). A synthesis of research on language of reading instruction for English language learners. *Review of Education Research, 75*(2), 247–284.

Vaughn, S., Linan-Thompson, S., Pollard-Durodola, S., Mathes, P., & Hagan, E. C. (2006). Effective interventions for English language learners (Spanish-English) at risk for difficulties. In D. K. Dickinson & S. B. Neuman, *Handbook of early literacy research* (Vol. 2, pp. 185–197). New York: Guilford Press.

EUGENE E. GARCÍA (eugene.garcia@asu.edu) is Vice President for Education Partnerships and **BRYANT JENSEN** (bryant.jensen@asu.edu) is a doctoral candidate in educational psychology at Arizona State University, Tempe, Arizona.

From *Educational Leadership,* March 2007. Copyright © 2007 by ASCD. Reprinted by permission. The Association for Supervision and Curriculum Development is a worldwide community of educators advocating sound policies and sharing best practices to achieve the success of each learner. To learn more, visit ASCD at www.ascd.org

UNIT 4

Supporting Young Children's Development

Unit Selections

Key Points to Consider

- How does a strong background in child development assist teachers when working with infants and toddlers?

- Why has childhood obesity become such an epidemic in our country today?

- What is it important for teachers to be knowledgeable about research related to the profession?

- Have you thought about the way children develop handedness? What can teachers do to support development in that area?

Student Web Site

www.mhcls.com/online

Internet References

Further information regarding these Web sites may be found in this book's preface or online.

Action for Healthy Kids
www.actionforhealthykids.org
American Academy of Pediatrics
www.aap.org

It has been a little over ten years since the first major research on early brain development began to emerge. Since that time hundreds of articles on the importance of early brain stimulation have been written. Some have prompted the development of programs such as Baby Einstein and a whole series of commercial materials. Others reinforce what parents for centuries have known; young children need a variety of active learning experiences to stimulate their minds and bodies. Pat Wingert and Martha Brant provide an up-to-date look at early brain development in their article "Reading Your Baby's Mind".

Care for our youngest citizens, infants and toddlers, requires caregivers to bring a special set of characteristics to the setting. Veteran infant/toddler researcher Alice Sterling Honig shares guidelines on interpreting the messages infants and toddlers are sending in, "Teaching to Temperaments". Continuing with the theme of the importance of teachers carefully observing children to determine their preferences, strengths, and needs is the article, "Which Hand?". Parents and teachers worry about handedness of children and are confused about the best ways to help children feel confident with hand use that feels most comfortable to them. For every successful left handed major league baseball pitcher with a multi-million dollar contract there are thousands of left handed children struggling to learn in a right handed world. About ten to twelve percent of the population is left handed. Strategies for helping all children strengthen motor skills that support learning are included.

The word "research" causes most early childhood educators to turn away and avoid further discussion. Responses such as, "I just want to teach young children and I'm not interested in research" are common from college and university students as well as some beginning teachers. However, when one understands research, a whole new world surrounding the importance of best practices comes to light. "Research 101: Tools for Reading and Interpreting Early Childhood Research" provides the reader with a quick and easy review of the importance of understanding how research is conducted, presented, and how to interpret the findings. All teachers of young children should make decisions based on research findings and evidence based practice. Don't shy away from research but instead embrace how understanding research can validate practices in place in your classroom as well as educate others on best practices.

Issues related to the health of young children continued to emerge this year. Childhood obesity is noticeable every time one enters a fast food restaurant and hears a child order a meal by its number on the menu because they are so familiar with

Laurence Mouton/Photoalto/PictureQuest

the selection at that particular restaurant. It is also evident on a playground where children just sit on the sideline not wanting to participate with their peers due to body image. In "What Can We Do to Prevent Childhood Obesity?," Julie Lumeng provides many suggestions for educators to follow that will help children develop appropriate eating habits and an active lifestyle. Parents and educators must work together to promote healthy living. Teachers should also participate in healthy living activities. Only then will our society begin to realize that a lifestyle that includes good nutrition and exercise is one of the best ways to lead a long and healthy life.

The title of this unit once again must be stressed: Supporting Young Children's Development. Teachers who see their job of working with young children as finding the approach that best supports each child's individual development will be most successful. We are not to change children to meet some idealistic model, but become an investigator whose job it is to ferret out the individual strengths and learning styles of each child in our care. Enjoy each day and the many different experiences awaiting you when you work with young children and their families.

Reading Your Baby's Mind

New research on infants finally begins to answer the question: what's going on in there?

PAT WINGERT AND MARTHA BRANT

Little Victoria Bateman is blond and blue-eyed and as cute a baby as there ever was. At 6 months, she is also trusting and unsuspecting, which is a good thing, because otherwise she'd never go along with what's about to happen. It's a blistering June afternoon in Lubbock, Texas, and inside the Human Sciences lab at Texas Tech University, Victoria's mother is settling her daughter into a high chair, where she is the latest subject in an ongoing experiment aimed at understanding the way babies think. Sybil Hart, an associate professor of human development and leader of the study, trains video cameras on mother and daughter. Everything is set. Hart hands Cheryl Bateman a children's book, "Elmo Pops In," and instructs her to engross herself in its pages. "Just have a conversation with me about the book," Hart tells her. "The most important thing is, do not look at [Victoria.]" As the two women chat, Victoria looks around the room, impassive and a little bored.

After a few minutes, Hart leaves the room and returns cradling a lifelike baby doll. Dramatically, Hart places it in Cheryl Bateman's arms, and tells her to cuddle the doll while continuing to ignore Victoria. "That's OK, little baby," Bateman coos, hugging and rocking the doll. Victoria is not bored anymore. At first, she cracks her best smile, showcasing a lone stubby tooth. When that doesn't work, she begins kicking. But her mom pays her no mind. That's when Victoria loses it. Soon she's beet red and crying so hard it looks like she might spit up. Hart rushes in. "OK, we're done," she says, and takes back the doll. Cheryl Bateman goes to comfort her daughter. "I've never seen her react like that to anything," she says. Over the last 10 months, Hart has repeated the scenario hundreds of times. It's the same in nearly every case: tiny babies, overwhelmed with jealousy. Even Hart was stunned to find that infants could experience an emotion, which, until recently, was thought to be way beyond their grasp.

And that's just for starters. The helpless, seemingly clueless infant staring up at you from his crib, limbs flailing, drool oozing, has a lot more going on inside his head than you ever imagined. A wealth of new research is leading pediatricians and child psychologists to rethink their long-held beliefs about the emotional and intellectual abilities of even very young babies.

In 1890, psychologist William James famously described an infant's view of the world as "one great blooming, buzzing confusion." It was a notion that held for nearly a century: infants were simple-minded creatures who merely mimicked those around them and grasped only the most basic emotions—happy, sad, angry. Science is now giving us a much different picture of what goes on inside their hearts and heads. Long before they form their first words or attempt the feat of sitting up, they are already mastering complex emotions—jealousy, empathy, frustration—that were once thought to be learned much later in toddlerhood.

They are also far more sophisticated intellectually than we once believed. Babies as young as 4 months have advanced powers of deduction and an ability to decipher intricate patterns. They have a strikingly nuanced visual palette, which enables them to notice small differences, especially in faces, that adults and older children lose the ability to see. Until a baby is 3 months old, he can recognize a scrambled photograph of his mother just as quickly as a photo in which everything is in the right place. And big brothers and sisters beware: your sib has a long memory—and she can hold a grudge.

Babies yet to utter an intelligent syllable are now known to feel a range of complex emotions like envy and empathy.

The new research is sure to enthrall new parents—See, Junior *is* a genius!—but it's more than just an academic exercise. Armed with the new information, pediatricians are starting to change the way they evaluate their youngest patients. In addition to tracking physical development, they are now focusing much more deeply on emotional advancement. The research shows how powerful emotional well-being is to a child's future health. A baby who fails to meet certain key "emotional milestones" may have trouble learning to speak, read and, later, do well in school. By reading emotional responses, doctors have begun to discover ways to tell if a baby as young as 3 months is showing early signs of possible psychological disorders, including depression, anxiety, learning disabilities and perhaps autism. "Instead of just asking if they're crawling or sitting, we're asking more questions about how they share their world with their caregivers," says Dr. Chet Johnson, chairman of the American Academy of Pediatrics' early-childhood committee. "Do they point to things? When they see a new person, how do they react? How children do on social and emotional and language skills are better predictors of success in adulthood than motor skills are." The goal: in the not-too-distant future, researchers hope doctors will routinely identify at-risk kids years earlier than they do now—giving parents crucial extra time to turn things around.

One of the earliest emotions that even tiny babies display is, admirably enough, empathy. In fact, concern for others may be hard-wired into babies' brains. Plop a newborn down next to another crying infant, and chances are, both babies will soon be wailing away. "People have always known that babies cry when they hear other babies cry," says Martin Hoffman, a psychology professor at New York University who did the first studies on infant empathy in the 1970s. "The question was, why are they crying?" Does it mean that the baby is truly concerned for his fellow human, or just annoyed by the racket? A recent study conducted in Italy, which built on Hoffman's own work, has largely settled the question. Researchers played for infants tapes of other babies crying. As predicted, that was enough to start the tears flowing. But when researchers played babies recordings of their own cries, they rarely began crying themselves. The verdict: "There is some rudimentary empathy in place, right from birth," Hoffman says. The intensity of the emotion tends to fade over time. Babies older than 6 months no longer cry but grimace at the discomfort of others. By 13 to 15 months, babies tend to take matters into their own hands. They'll try to comfort a crying playmate. "What I find most charming is when, even if the two mothers are present, they'll bring their own mother over to help," Hoffman says.

Part of that empathy may come from another early-baby skill that's now better understood, the ability to discern emotions from the facial expressions of the people around them. "Most textbooks still say that babies younger than 6 months don't recognize emotions," says Diane Montague, assistant professor of psychology at LaSalle University in Philadelphia. To put that belief to the test, Montague came up with a twist on every infant's favorite game, peekaboo, and recruited dozens of 4-month-olds to play along. She began by peeking around a cloth with a big smile on her face. Predictably, the babies were delighted, and stared at her intently—the time-tested way to tell if a baby is interested. On the fourth peek, though, Montague emerged with a sad look on her face. This time, the response was much different. "They not only looked away," she says, but wouldn't look back even when she began smiling again. Refusing to make eye contact is a classic baby sign of distress. An angry face got their attention once again, but their faces showed no pleasure. "They seemed primed to be alert, even vigilant," Montague says. "I realize that's speculative in regard to infants … I think it shows that babies younger than 6 months find meaning in expressions."

This might be a good place to pause for a word about the challenges and perils of baby research. Since the subjects can't speak for themselves, figuring out what's going on inside their heads is often a matter of reading their faces and body language. If this seems speculative, it's not. Over decades of trial and error, researchers have fine-tuned their observation skills and zeroed in on numerous consistent baby responses to various stimuli: how long they stare at an object, what they reach out for and what makes them recoil in fear or disgust can often tell experienced researchers everything they need to know. More recently, scientists have added EEGs and laser eye tracking, which allow more precise readings. Coming soon: advanced MRI scans that will allow a deeper view inside the brain.

When infants near their first birthdays, they become increasingly sophisticated social learners. They begin to infer what others are thinking by following the gaze of those around them. "By understanding others' gaze, babies come to understand others' minds," says Andrew Meltzoff, a professor of psychology at the University of Washington who has studied the "gaze following" of thousands of babies. "You can tell a lot about people, what they're interested in and what they intend to do next, by watching their eyes. It appears that even babies know that … This is how they learn to become expert members of our culture."

Meltzoff and colleague Rechele Brooks have found that this skill first appears at 10 to 11 months, and is not only an important marker of a baby's emotional and social growth, but can predict later language development. In their study, babies who weren't proficient at gaze-following by their first birthday had much less advanced-language skills at 2. Meltzoff says this helps explain why language occurs more slowly in blind children, as well as children of depressed mothers, who tend not to interact as much with their babies.

In fact, at just a few months, infants begin to develop superpowers when it comes to observation. Infants can easily tell the difference between human faces. But at the University of Minnesota, neuroscientist Charles Nelson (now of Harvard) wanted to test how discerning infants really are. He showed a group of 6-month-old babies a photo of a chimpanzee, and gave them time to stare at it until they lost interest. They were then shown another chimp. The babies perked up and stared at the new photo. The infants easily recognized each chimp as an individual—they were fascinated by each new face. Now unless you spend a good chunk of your day hanging around the local zoo, chances are you couldn't tell the difference between a roomful of chimps at a glance. As it turned out, neither could babies just a few months older. By 9 months, those kids had lost the ability to tell chimps apart; but at the same time, they had increased their powers of observation when it came to human faces.

Nelson has now taken his experiment a step further, to see how early babies can detect subtle differences in facial expressions, a key building block of social development. He designed a new study that is attempting to get deep inside babies' heads by measuring brain-wave activity. Nelson sent out letters to the parents of nearly every newborn in the area, inviting them to participate. Earlier this summer it was Dagny Winberg's turn. The 7-month-old was all smiles as her mother, Armaiti, carried her into the lab, where she was fitted with a snug cap wired with 64 sponge sensors. Nelson's assistant, grad student Meg Moulson, began flashing photographs on a screen of a woman. In each photo, the woman had a slightly different expression—many different shades of happiness and fear. Dagny was given time to look at each photo until she became bored and looked away. The whole time, a computer was closely tracking her brain activity, measuring her mind's minutest responses to the different photos. Eventually, after she'd run through 60 photos, Dagny had had enough of the game and began whimpering and fidgeting. That ended the session. The point of the experiment is to see if baby brain scans look like those of adults. "We want to see if babies categorize emotions in the ways that adults do," Moulson says. "An adult can see a slight smile and categorize it as happy. We want to know if babies can do the same." They don't have the answer yet, but Nelson believes that infants who display early signs of emotional disorders, such as autism, may be helped if they can develop these critical powers of observation and emotional engagement.

Halfway across the country, researchers are working to dispel another baby cliché: out of sight, out of mind. It was long believed that babies under 9 months didn't grasp the idea of "object permanence"—the ability to know, for instance, that when Mom leaves the room, she isn't gone forever. New research by psychologist Su-hua Wang at the University of California, Santa Cruz, is showing that babies understand the concept as early as 10 weeks. Working with 2- and 3-month-olds, she performs a little puppet show. Each baby sees a duck on a stage. Wang covers the duck, moves it across the stage and lifts the cover. Sometimes the duck is there. Other times, the duck disappears beneath a trapdoor. When they see the duck has gone missing, the babies stare intently at the empty stage, searching for it. "At 2½ months," she says, "they already have the idea that the object continues to exist."

A strong, well-developed ability to connect with the world—and with parents in particular—is especially important when babies begin making their first efforts at learning to speak. Baby talk is much more than mimickry. Michael Goldstein, a psychologist at Cornell University, gathered two groups of 8-month-olds and decked them out in overalls rigged up with wireless microphones and transmitters. One group of mothers was told to react immediately when their babies cooed or babbled, giving them big smiles and loving pats. The other group of parents was also told to smile at their kids, but randomly, unconnected to the babies' sounds. It came as no surprise that the babies who received immediate feedback babbled more and advanced quicker than those who didn't. But what interested Goldstein was the way in which the parents, without realizing it, raised the "babble bar" with their kids. "The kinds of simple sounds that get parents' attention at 4 months don't get the same reaction at 8 months," he says. "That motivates babies to experiment with different sound combinations until they find new ones that get noticed."

A decade ago Patricia Kuhl, a professor of speech and hearing at the University of Washington and a leading authority on early language, proved that tiny babies have a unique ability to learn a foreign language. As a result of her well-publicized findings, parents ran out to buy foreign-language tapes, hoping their little Einsteins would pick up Russian or French before they left their cribs. It didn't work, and Kuhl's new research shows why. Kuhl put American 9-month-olds in a room with Mandarin-speaking adults, who showed them toys while talking to them. After 12 sessions, the babies had learned to detect subtle Mandarin phonetic sounds that couldn't be heard by a separate group of babies who were exposed only to English. Kuhl then repeated the experiment, but this time played the identical Mandarin lessons to babies on video- and audiotape. That group of babies failed to learn any Mandarin. Kuhl says that without the emotional connection, the babies considered the tape recording just another background noise, like a vacuum cleaner. "We were genuinely surprised by the outcome," she says. "We all assumed that when infants stare at a television, and look engaged, that they are learning from it." Kuhl says there's plenty of work to be done to explain why that isn't true. "But at first blush one thinks that people—at least babies—need people to learn."

So there you have it. That kid over there with one sock missing and smashed peas all over his face is actually a formidable presence, in possession of keen powers of observation, acute emotional sensitivity and an impressive arsenal of deductive powers. "For the last 15 years, we've been focused on babies' abilities—what they know and when they knew it," says the University of Washington's Meltzoff. "But now we want to know what all this predicts about later development. What does all this mean for the child?"

Some of these questions are now finding answers. Take shyness, for instance. It's long been known that 15 to 20 percent of children are shy and anxious by nature. But doctors didn't know why some seemed simply to grow out of it, while for others it became a debilitating condition. Recent studies conducted by Nathan Fox of the University of Maryland show that shyness is initially driven by biology. He proved it by wiring dozens of 9-month-olds to EEG machines and conducting a simple experiment. When greeted by a stranger, "behaviorally inhibited" infants tensed up, and showed more activity in the parts of the brain associated with anxiety and fear. Babies with outgoing personalities reached out to the stranger. Their EEG scans showed heightened activity in the parts of the brain that govern positive emotions like pleasure.

Just because your baby is more perceptive than you thought doesn't mean she'll be damaged if she cries for a minute.

But Fox, who has followed some of these children for 15 years, says that parenting style has a big impact on which kind of adult a child will turn out to be. Children of overprotective parents, or those whose parents didn't encourage them to overcome shyness and childhood anxiety, often remain shy and anxious as adults. But kids born to confident and sensitive parents who gently help them to take emotional risks and coax them out of their shells can often overcome early awkwardness. That's an important finding, since behaviorally inhibited kids are also at higher risk for other problems.

Stanley Greenspan, clinical professor of psychiatry and pediatrics at George Washington University Medical School, is one of the leaders in developing diagnostic tools to help doctors identify babies who may be at risk for language and learning problems, autism and a whole range of other problems. He recently completed a checklist of social and emotional "milestones" that babies should reach by specific ages. "I'd like to see doctors screen babies for these milestones and tell parents exactly what to do if their babies are not mastering them. One of our biggest problems now is that parents may sense intuitively that something is not right," but by the time they are able to get their child evaluated, "that family has missed a critical time to, maybe, get that baby back on track."

So what should parents do with all this new information? First thing: relax. Just because your baby is more perceptive than you might have thought doesn't mean she's going to be damaged for life if she cries in her crib for a minute while you answer the phone. Or that he'll wind up quitting school and stealing cars if he witnesses an occasional argument between his parents. Children crave—and thrive on—interaction, one-on-one time and lots of eye contact. That doesn't mean filling the baby's room with "educational" toys and posters. A child's social, emotional and academic life begins with the earliest conversations between parent and child: the first time the baby locks eyes with you; the quiet smile you give your infant and the smile she gives you back. Your child is speaking to you all the time. It's just a matter of knowing how to listen.

With **T. Trent Gegax, Margaret Nelson, Karen Breslau, Nadine Joseph and Ben Whitford**

From *Newsweek*, August 15, 2005. Copyright © 2005 by Newsweek. Reprinted by permission via PARS International. www.newsweek.com

Teaching to Temperaments

Tuning into babies' individual temperaments paves the way for smooth and successful school days.

Alice Sterling Honig

Every baby expresses personality traits we call *temperament*. How a child responds emotionally to objects, events, and people is a reflection of his individual temperament. Researchers Thomas, Chess, and Birch described nine different temperament categories. These include:

- Activity level
- Mood
- Threshold for distress
- Rhythmicity
- Intensity of response
- Approach-Withdrawal
- Distractibility
- Adaptability
- Persistence

To determine a child's temperament, make the following observations:

1. **Notice the activity level.** Some babies are placid or inactive. Other babies thrash about a lot and, as toddlers, are always on the move. At this stage, they must be watched carefully.

2. **Observe the mood.** Some babies are very smiley and cheerful. Although securely attached emotionally to their teachers, others have a low key mood and look more solemn or unhappy.

3. **Figure out a child's threshold for distress.** Some babies are very sensitive. They become upset very easily when stressed. Other babies can more comfortably wait when they need a feeding or some attention.

4. **Consider the rhythmicity of children.** Some babies get hungry or sleepy on a fairly regular and predictable basis. Other babies sleep at varying times, urinate or have bowel movements at unpredictable times, and get hungry at different times. They are hard to put on a "schedule."

5. **Notice the intensity of response in each baby.** When a baby's threshold for distress has been reached, some babies act restless. Others act cranky or fret just a little. Still others cry with terrific intensity or howl with despair when they are stressed. They shriek with delight and respond with high energy when reacting to happy or challenging situations.

6. **See how they approach new situations.** Some infants are very cautious. They are wary and fearful of new teachers, being placed in a different crib, or being taken to visit a new setting. Other infants approach new persons, new activities, or new play possibilities with zest and enjoyment.

7. **Notice how easily they are distracted.** Some children can concentrate on a toy regardless of surrounding bustle or noise in a room. Others are easily distracted.

8. **Notice the adaptability of each child.** Some children react to strange or difficult situations with distress, but recover fairly rapidly. Others adjust to new situations with difficulty or after a very long period.

9. **Finally, observe each child's attention span.** Some children have a long attention span. They continue with an activity for a fairly long time. Others flit from one activity to another.

These temperament traits cluster into several groups: easy; cautious/fearful; feisty/irritable/difficult; or a mixture of the nine traits. Tailor your approach to each child's cluster of temperament traits. As you tune into temperament, you are likely to become more successful in helping all children adjust to situations and persons in ways that promote their social ease and competence.

From *Scholastic Early Childhood Today*, November/December 2003. Copyright © 2003 by Scholastic Inc. Reprinted by permission.

Which Hand?

Brains, Fine Motor Skills, and Holding a Pencil

- Right hand, left hand, or ambidextrous?
- What is handedness?
- How does handedness happen?
- Do left-handed people think any differently than right-handed ones?
- When should children begin to show a hand preference?
- How does handedness affect how we use tools—spoons, toothbrushes, and pencils?

At birth, parents and physicians make a quick check: 10 fingers, 10 toes—a symmetrical body. Both sides are the same. As babies grow, we expect reflexes, muscles, and movements to be fairly balanced on the two sides.

But it's not uncommon for infants to hold one hand more fisted than the other, to wave one arm more vigorously, or to turn the head to one side more often. Still, we can't say that a baby has a preference for the left or the right.

Though not an exact science, handedness can often be predicted by these early infantile movements. Why?

Handedness: Does It Start with the Brain?

Theorists speculate that handedness has to do with brain specialization. Different brain functions take place in different parts of the brain.

During prenatal development, while the brain and spinal cord are forming, nerves cross from one hemisphere or side of the brain, across the midline of the body, and connect to muscles on the opposite side of the body. The right hemisphere of the brain controls the muscles on the left side of the body, and the left hemisphere controls the right.

For right-handed people, the left side of the brain has a better developed nerve network that supports motor development and skills. For left-handed people, the opposite is true.

How We Develop Fine Motor Skills

Motor skills involve the movement of muscles throughout the body. Gross motor skills involve larger movements—swimming, walking, and dancing, for example. Fine motor skills describe the smaller actions of the hands, wrists, fingers, feet, toes, lips, and tongue. Fine and gross motor skills develop in tandem. Many activities depend on their coordination.

Infants. Newborns have little control over their hands. Typically the fist is closed. Hand movement results from reflex and not deliberate control. For example, if you place a rattle in an infant's hand, the infant may grasp it momentarily and then drop it as hand muscles relax. The infant has no awareness of the object or its absence. Typically, babies swipe at objects when they are 1 month old and discover and play with their hands at 2 months.

Between 2 and 4 months, babies begin to coordinate their eye and hand muscles. Babies see an object and try to grasp it—often unsuccessfully.

By 5 months, most infants can grasp an object within reach—without looking at their hands. This important milestone in fine motor development allows more prolonged but clumsy grasps. Eager to discover and learn, infants not only grasp objects but also taste them. Hand-to-mouth exploration is a standard and expected developmental leap.

By 9 months, most babies begin to show a preference for reaching with their right hand—even if the toy is placed on their left side. They will, however, continue to use the non-preferred hand much of the time.

By the end of the first year, babies will usually be able to grasp an object with the entire hand, swipe surfaces, and poke at an object with one finger. Significantly, the pincer grip—the ability to hold an object between the thumb and index finger—typically appears at about 12 months. The pincer grasp gives infants the ability to manipulate and grasp an object and to deliberately drop it. At 12 months, babies can usually hold an object in each hand, drop an object into a bucket, and perform stacking and nesting tasks.

Toddlers. Toddlers continue to strengthen hand and finger muscles. They develop the ability to use their fingers independently—twisting, pulling, poking, pushing—and with greater control. They are typically able to turn the page in a board book. They are also able to hold a fat crayon in a palmer grasp (all fingers wrapped around the crayon).

By 15 months, most toddlers can eat independently, first with fingers and then with a spoon. Toddlers can reach for objects smoothly and with minimal effort. They can hold two objects in one hand, fit objects together (puzzles and snap toys, for example), and stack a few blocks into a tower.

By 30 months, most toddlers can draw using a finger grasp (holding a crayon with four fingers pushing in opposition to the thumb). They can pour liquids from one container to another, take off socks and shoes independently, and turn the faucet on and off when hand washing.

It's during this period that children start to display a preference for one side—that is, they use the preferred side more consistently than the non-preferred. This is clear not only when they grasp objects with the hand, hold a spoon, and turn pages in a book but also when they kick a ball, roll play clay into a snake, and push a wheel toy along a path.

Preschoolers. The preschool child's central nervous system is still developing and maturing, a process that enables the brain to send complex messages to the fingers.

By age 3 or 4, most children are able to complete complex fine motor tasks. These include drawing deliberate shapes, stringing beads, cutting with scissors, spreading paint and paste with the index finger, dressing and undressing dolls, opening and placing a clothespin to hang artwork, and folding paper in halves and quarters. Each of these tasks reinforces a child's hand preference.

As these preferences become evident, you can accommodate them to maximize a child's hand strength. For example, for a child who shows a left hand preference, you can provide left-handed scissors.

Because preschoolers are still developing small muscle strength and hand-eye coordination, it is inappropriate to expect handwriting skills. Children this age are generally not ready for precise handwriting instruction.

Instead, introduce writing activities slowly and gently, recognizing that each child will have a different skill set and a unique developmental level. For example, a 4-year-old who does not show a hand preference is likely to have less overall muscle control and coordination.

Some tools for writing are easier to use than others. Some teachers like to start with markers because they require little pressure and minimal muscle strength. Other teachers start with crayons because they require more focus and muscle strength. Make sure you provide many tool choices and encourage children to use the tools to draw and paint before you expect them to write.

As children indicate their interest in writing letters and words—and you have observed and documented readiness—make writing tools available for exploration. Generally, markers and felt-tipped pens are easiest for inexperienced fingers to control.

School age. By the age of 5, children will show better fine motor development and consistent hand preference for most tasks. Children can typically draw a complete human figure; cut out shapes with scissors; trace forms; manipulate buttons, zippers, and snaps; and copy letters. Some can play piano; build models; knit, crochet, and sew; use a computer keyboard and mouse; and help with basic household chores like sweeping, dusting, and washing dishes.

School-age children (as well as adolescents and adults) experiment with using the non-preferred side. And researchers hold that such experimentation can be useful in maintaining brain function and dexterity.

How Do We Develop Handedness?

From the developmental review, it's clear that handedness is not just about hands. Consider:

- Which foot do you kick with?
- Which eye do you use to peer through a magnifying glass?
- Which hand do you use to unscrew a jar, hold your toothbrush, or sign your name?

Many people are consistent—all left-sided functions or all right-sided. Some have a combination of left and right dominance, sometimes determined by the task. For example, a right-handed knitter may be able to make stitches more quickly using the left hand. Sometimes handedness is determined by efficiency. For example, a person may complete a jigsaw puzzle or cut flowers with the preferred hand because it's less frustrating.

Consider these historical facts and current investigations.

- The percentage of left-hand dominant people has remained consistent (10 to 12 percent) in the population for generations.
- In colonial America, left-handed people were considered witches and were executed. More recently, well-meaning teachers used harsh methods—slapping wrists or tying the left hand behind the child's back—to "cure" left-handedness.
- Some research suggests that left-handed children are more likely to be creative, with high verbal and math ability. Other research finds no difference between left- and right-handed children.
- Children with autism and other developmental disabilities, as shown by some research, have a higher percentage of left-handedness than the general population.
- Dorothy Bishop (1990) concluded there is no consistent link between IQ and handedness.
- Can openers, spiral notebooks, telephone keypads, and automobile consoles are built for the convenience of right-handed users.
- Left-handed people are more likely to have a left-handed relative, but researchers have not identified a left-handed gene.
- Most researchers believe that handedness preference is on a scale. Few people are strictly right- or left-handed. Most link a hand to a specific task: throw a ball with the left hand but stir a pot with the right, for example.
- Truly ambidextrous people—those indifferent to hand preference—are rare.
- In India and Indonesia, eating with the left hand is considered impolite.
- When necessary, such as after injury to the dominant hand or under cultural pressure, humans can learn to use the non-preferred hand.

About 1 person in 10 is left-hand dominant—a challenge in a right-hand dominant classroom and world. Some neurologists seek to explain the causes of handedness (likely a combination of genetics and environmental factors). Others explore whether left-handed people think differently. And teachers and parents strive to make left-handed children comfortable and successful in a right-handed world.

Hand to the Task

When children are ready to write, make sure tools and materials support the intense effort. Handwriting is more than forming symbols on a page. Writing effectively—and efficiently—includes the selection of writing tools, gripping the tool, positioning the tool on paper, and having fine muscle strength, coordination, and control in the hand doing the writing.

Use these tips for helping all children—left- and right-handed—develop fine motor control and fluid writing skills.

- Observe children's pencil grips. The pencil should be loosely held with the fingers above the shaved tip—about an inch up from the point—in a tripod grip. The index finger is on top of the pencil, the thumb and middle finger holding two sides. There should be equal pressure between the thumb, the side of the middle finger, and the tip of the index finger. The ring and pinky fingers are relaxed and in line with the middle finger. See diagram at right.

  Watch for excessive pressure on the index finger and all fingers pulled into a fist with knuckles flexed. When a child holds a pencil too tightly, fatigue and frustration will interfere with writing efficiency.
- Observe children's posture and body mechanics. When a child holds a pencil, the eraser end should point to the shoulder. The wrist should rest on the table surface. The arm from thumb to elbow should be in a straight line—the hand doesn't hook back toward the body.

  Position paper so that the sheet is angled—the right corner higher for right-handed writers, and the left corner higher for left-handed writers. The non-dominant hand should hold the paper in place.
- Provide child-sized chairs and writing table. Make sure the chair's height enables the child's feet to rest comfortably on the floor with hips and knees at a 90-degree angle. The table should be just above elbow height and support the arms without tensing and lifting or shrugging the shoulders.
- Help left-handed children discover that the best place at a table is not next to a right-handed friend. Bumping elbows while writing—or eating soup—is messy and frustrating.
- Help children relax. When a child has clenched teeth and a tense neck and makes deep indentations on paper from pressing too hard, it's wise to end the writing session and encourage general relaxation. Check the position of the pencil and the wrist.
- Schedule whole-body writing time with non-traditional materials. Invite children to write letters in the air with their hands or feet. Offer finger paint, shaving cream, and sand trays for finger writing. Invite children to write with water on the sidewalk or a brick wall.
- Explore print with tactile tools like Wikki-stix® and clay. Fill zipper-top bags with hair gel and invite children to form letters and shapes with one finger.
- Provide colored markers—felt-tipped and of varying thicknesses. Often children refine their grip—and relax muscles—when they are absorbed in color on unlined paper.

1-middle finger
2-thumb
3-index finger

- Offer a variety of writing implements—pencils, fat pencils, colored pencils, and markers—that have a triangular and not round shape.
- Explore pencil grips. Mechanical pencils and gel pens often have built-in grips. Encourage children with awkward to tight pencil grips to use them.
- Provide stencils, alphabet charts, and tracing grids for fun writing practice. Crossword puzzles give children practice in precise letter spacing.

Activities for Left and Right

Eric Chudler, University of Washington, has a Web site called "Neuroscience for Kids." It includes games, quizzes, and links to brain development and function. The following activities are adapted from his work.

Each activity offers school-agers opportunities for charting and graphing, surveying, and evaluating evidence. Have plenty of chart paper and markers on hand. Encourage children to make notes of their observations. If your classroom has Internet access, children can upload their data and exploration results.

Left Hand or Right Hand?

Rather than ask children which hand they use, set up observation experiments that rely on more than self-reporting. Prepare observation charts with three columns: Left Hand, Right Hand, Either Hand. Have observers chart peers in tasks such as using a fork, painting at an easel, turning a door knob, and throwing a ball.

Left Foot or Right Foot?

Set up the same observation system as in the previous activity. Have observers chart their peers in tasks such as kicking a ball, walking up stairs (Which foot steps first?), time spent balanced on each foot, and stepping on a picture of a cockroach.

Left Eye or Right Eye?

Check for eyedness. Chart these tasks: looking through a paper tube, looking through a magnifying glass, and winking (Which eye winks more easily?).

You can chart eye dominance too. Cut a coin-sized hole in a sheet of construction paper. Ask the subject to hold the paper and look through the hole at a distant object using both eyes. Ask the subject to bring the paper closer and closer to the face while still looking at the object. As the paper comes close to the face, only one eye will be looking through the hole. Which one?

Left Ear or Right Ear?

Chart which ear is preferred in different tests. Which ear does the subject cup to help make a whisper louder? Which ear does the subject hold against a small box when trying to determine what's inside? Which ear does the subject hold against a door to hear what's going on outside?

References

Chudler, Eric. *Neuroscience for Kids.* http://faculty.washington. edu/chudler/experi.html.

Encyclopedia of Children's Health. 2006. "Fine motor skills." www. answers.com/topic/fine-motor-skills.

Liddle, Tara Losquadro and Laura Yorke. 2003. *Why Motor Skills Matter: Improving Your Child's Physical Development to Enhance Learning and Self-Esteem.* New York: McGraw-Hill.

LiveScience. 2006. "What Makes a Lefty? Myths and Mysteries Persist." www.livescience.com/humanbiology/060321_left_hand.html.

Needlman, Robert. 2001. "What is 'Handedness'?" www.drspock. com/article/0,1510,5812,00.html.

Smith, Jodene Lynn. 2003. *Activities for Fine Motor Skills Development.* Westminster, Calif.: Teacher Created Materials.

From *Texas Child Care,* Spring 2007. Copyright © 2007 by Texas Workforce Commission. Reprinted by permission.

Research 101: Tools for Reading and Interpreting Early Childhood Research

Angela C. Baum and Paula McMurray-Schwarz

Studies suggest that the quality of a child care setting can have important implications for children's development (Howes, Phillips, & Whitebook, 1992).

Research demonstrates an important link between parent involvement and young children's literacy development (Fitton & Gredler, 1996).

Findings suggest that opportunities for recess can have a positive impact on children's cognitive performance and adjustment to school (Pellegini & Bohn, 2005).

Research findings, such as those in the above examples, provide us with important information. As teachers, we frequently hear or read such statements and consider them as we make daily decisions about what is best for the young children with whom we work. To those without specialized training in research methodology, however, the task of reading and interpreting original research can be intimidating and confusing. The language is sometimes difficult to understand and the format may seem incomprehensible. The purpose of this article is to help make the research reading experience more manageable. This editorial breaks the typical research manuscript down into several parts and offers a brief description of the purpose of each, as well as some tips for developing more clear interpretations and understandings.

Why Is Reading Research Important?

Research Guides Our Decision-Making

Every day, teachers of young children are faced with the task of making many decisions. These decisions range in complexity; deciding what to serve for snack may be relatively easy, but deciding how best to support a child who is struggling to develop positive relationships with her peers poses more of a challenge, one that requires careful thought and reflection. Research can be a valuable resource as we strive to provide high quality care and education for young children and their families. Consider the following example. Mr. Frank, who has taught third grade for five years, has a clearly defined guidance plan for his classroom. As a consequence for off-task behavior, he requires that children make up the wasted time during their scheduled recess period. This seems to be working well. The children love recess and will try to avoid losing even a few minutes of their favorite part of the day. Recently, however, Mr. Frank read a research article describing the positive impact that experiences during recess can have on the development of children's social skills. The article described recess as a time where children learn to negotiate, take turns, and consider another's perspective (Jarrett, 2002). After some consideration, Mr. Frank has decided to re-evaluate his recess policy. He has decided to find another method of discouraging off-task behavior; one that will not deprive children of important opportunities for social interaction. Mr. Frank found that research findings influenced his philosophy about guidance and decided to alter his practices to reflect his newfound understanding. As illustrated by this example, reading and reflecting on research can help teachers ensure that their decisions surrounding their work in the classroom reflect current knowledge and understandings regarding best practice.

Research Strengthens Our Work as Advocates

Knowledge of current research is also important as we become advocates for young children by communicating with families, community members, and policymakers. In order to be effective in advocating for best practice in our schools and programs, we must be well informed and provide evidence in support of our opinions. As stated by Crosser (2005), "There must be a body of knowledge supported in research that indicates what is best practice. Decisions in classrooms and board rooms need to be based on that body of knowledge rather than on simple opinion, gut feelings, and common sense" (p. 4). In my work with preservice teachers, I often share the following example to illustrate this point. Many of us have heard comments such as, "I wish my major was Early Childhood Education. All you do is play all day." It's true . . . we do play . . . a lot. But effective educators know that play is an important part of developmentally appropriate experiences for young children (Bredekamp & Copple, 1997).

Many research studies suggest that children learn most effectively through play-oriented activities (Edwards, 2002). While we, as early childhood educators, do not need to be convinced of the importance of play, we may be required to convince others. This requires us to explain *why* play is best practice. Beyond simply being fun, how does it benefit young children? Many studies have been conducted that help us answer this question and we should take advantage of this information. In a climate of increased accountability, it becomes an important responsibility to communicate these findings and their applicability as we strive to be effective advocates for young children (Crosser, 2005).

Research Enhances Our Professional Development and Growth

Research also can play an important role in our professional development and growth as early childhood educators. Katz (1995) states that after beginning teachers have become skilled at basic survival in the classroom, it is not uncommon for them to seek ways to expand their knowledge and develop a renewed sense of enthusiasm for their work with young children. Often they may become interested in participating in professional development activities, such as professional reading, to explore new ideas, strategies, and philosophies. As high-quality teachers of young children, we have committed to a life-long learning process. Reading educational research challenges us to avoid complacency as we strive to continually improve the quality of early experiences for young children.

The Research Article
Introductory Information

While the first thing you probably notice about a research article is its title, you should also take a moment to consider who wrote the article, as well as who published the piece. While this may seem fairly straightforward, it can offer some important information. For example, when noting the author and publisher information, it is useful to look at whether or not they may be associated with any particular interest group. It makes sense to use this information as a way to identify any possible source of bias in the research study. For example, Crosser (2005) suggests that an organization may not necessarily be likely to publish findings that are contrary to their mission or that government agencies may be more likely to report findings that reflect their political priorities or policies. While affiliation with a particular interest group does not automatically discredit or reduce the validity of the study, it is important information to consider as you make decisions about the applicability of the findings.

Abstract

An abstract provides a short (usually 100–150 words) overview of the purpose of the study. Often the abstract also contains information regarding the methods used to conduct the research, as well as some of the main findings of the project. The abstract provides a manageable way to decide if you are interested in reading the article in its entirety. Ask yourself . . . does this article provide the information that I am searching for in relation to my practice or interests? If so, you should move forward and read the article in its entirety. An important point to keep in mind is that reading the abstract should never substitute for reading the complete article. You should not rely on information in the abstract as the final word on the topic. It is important to read the full article in an effort to obtain a clear picture of what the author is trying to communicate and for you to make personal judgments about the importance or quality of the research findings. In essence, an abstract is an important tool that can save you the frustration of investing precious time in reading a full article, only to find that it doesn't really provide the information you were seeking.

Literature Review and Purpose

Most research articles begin by explaining the rationale for the author's chosen topic of study. This typically involves describing what is currently known about the topic of interest, sometimes including a brief overview of other studies that have been conducted in the area. This is done to provide a framework for the current study; a reason that the topic needs to be explored. In other words, the author explains what is already known about the topic as a foundation for the next logical step of exploration. Usually, this "next step" is the purpose of the current article. It is common for this section to include (often toward the end) the research questions that the author is attempting to answer in his or her research. Upon the completion of this section, you should be able to answer the following questions: What is the researcher trying to accomplish? What is currently known about this topic? Why is this topic important to explore?

Methods and Procedures

Once the research questions are established, the researcher must decide *how* to proceed in answering those questions. It is important that these methods are clearly explained, allowing the reader to make decisions regarding the quality and applicability of the researcher's findings. Do you believe that the researcher used the best possible methods to gather the data? Do the findings of the study seem to be applicable to your situation? Consider the following scenario. Mrs. Telmer teaches second grade in an urban school district. The children in her class come from diverse backgrounds and all of their families' incomes fall below the poverty level. Mrs. Telmer has recently become interested in exploring some new strategies to help the children in her class improve their reading skills. During her research, she comes across an article describing the implementation of an innovative strategy to teach reading to young children. Upon reading the abstract, Mrs. Telmer discovers that the authors found many benefits when implementing this new strategy, including improved scores on reading tests and an increase in children's interest surrounding reading activities. While Mrs. Telmer believes that this sounds promising as an option for the children in her class, she decides to read the full article to learn more. She makes an interesting discovery. When reading about the methods used to gather data, Mrs. Telmer found that the authors conducted their study in a suburban area primarily inhabited by Caucasian families with middle to upper income levels. After some thought, Mrs. Telmer begins to wonder if the children in her class would experience the same benefits. Their daily lives are so different from the lives of the children in the study! Would this strategy work for her children, too? While she understands that this difference doesn't necessarily mean that the study isn't worthwhile, she decides that she must do some further research before implementing this new strategy in her classroom.

Analyses and Results

After the researcher collects data, he or she must decide what the data mean. As a reader of research, this may be the place in the article where you are tempted to give up. There are endless ways to analyze data, many of them involving complicated statistical methods and analysis techniques. Entire classes are devoted to these strategies and it is beyond the scope of this article to delve into the "nitty-gritty" of statistical analysis. The goal here is to encourage you to forge on even if this information seems incomprehensible. You may ask, however, "How can I develop confidence in the researcher's findings if I don't understand the processes used to analyze the data? This is a valid question and may inspire you to pursue some additional training in the understanding of statistics. Statistics courses are not for you? This does not mean that you can't read research articles and benefit from them.

There are other ways to evaluate the quality of data analysis. One way is to examine the medium in which the article is published. Often there are measures in place to ensure that the study is statistically sound before it is published. For example, articles appearing in refereed journals are not published until they have been reviewed by a panel of experts and an editor. If there are questions related to the appropriateness of analysis techniques, it is likely that the issue will be addressed before it is even in print. This is not a failure proof method, of course, but it should instill confidence in the reader that the article has most likely been reviewed by someone who has expertise in the area.

Discussion, Interpretation, and Implications

Once you have successfully waded through to this point, you will likely find this to be the most useful section of the research manuscript. In this portion of the article, the researcher examines his or her analysis and offers interpretations and explanations as to what the results might mean. This section often includes advice or suggestions, based on the findings, that are useful for the reader when incorporating the research into his or her work with young children. This section also allows the researcher to discuss variables that may have influenced the results and offer explanations for why the findings are significant. Additionally, this section may include suggestions for others wishing to continue this line of research in the future. After completing this section, you will have an idea of what the researcher believes is the important information to take away from the article.

After reflecting on the author's perspective, the final and most important question to ask yourself is "What does this mean to me and how does it impact my work with young children"? High quality research is useful. It should allow us to become better educators and improve experiences for young children. It should encourage us to think about current issues in the field and ways that we can apply this knowledge in our work with children and their families.

Summary and Conclusion

As early childhood educators, it is our professional responsibility to be aware of current advances in the field. An important piece of this involves reading, evaluating, and implementing educational research. This process may seem overwhelming at times, but remains a crucial aspect of our work with young children. This article provides information that can serve as a first step to becoming actively involved in the process of utilizing research as a means of strengthening classroom practice. When coupled with other available resources such as reviews and handbooks of research, reading research allows us to better align our practice with the field's most current knowledge and understandings of best practice. In closing, the following list provides a summary of questions to ask while reading research and can serve as a tool to guide your thinking as you explore ways to enhance your teaching by developing a foundation of research.

Introductory Information

- Are the authors or the publishers associated with any special interest groups?

Abstract

- What information is provided in the abstract?
- Do you want to take the time to learn more about this study?

Literature Review and Purpose

- What is currently known about this topic?
- What is the purpose of the study?
- What are the research questions?

Methods and Procedures

- Who are the participants in the study? What are their characteristics?
- How did the research(s) collect data?

Analyses and Results

- How did the researcher(s) analyze the data?
- What are the results of the research study?

Discussion, Interpretations, and Implications

- How did the researcher interpret the results?

Finally, and most importantly, ask yourself . . .

- What does this mean to me and how does it impact my work with young children?

References

Bredekamp, S., & Copple, C. (1997). *Developmentally appropriate practice in early childhood programs*. Washington, DC.: NAEYC.

Crosser, S. (2005). *What do we know about early childhood education? Research based practice*. New York: Thomson Delmar Learning.

Edwards, L. C. (2002). *The creative arts: A process approach for teachers and children*. Upper Saddle River, NJ: Merrill Prentice Hall.

Fitton, L., & Gredler, G. (1996). Parent involvement in reading remediation with young children. *Psychology in the Schools, 33(4)*, 325–332.

Jarrett, O. S. (2002). Recess in elementary school: What does the research say? ERIC Digest number (ERIC Document Reproduction Service No. ED466331).

Howes, C., Phillips, D. A., & Whitebook, M. (1992). Thresholds of quality: Implications for the social development of children in center-based child care. *Child Development, 63*, 449–460.

Katz, L. G. (1995). *The developmental stages of teachers. Talks with teachers of young children.* Norwood, NJ: Ablex.

Pellegrini, A. D., & Bohn, C. M. (2005). The role of recess in children's cognitive performance and school adjustment. *Educational Researcher, 34,* 13–19.

Angela C. Baum: Instruction and Teacher Education, University of South Carolina, 820 Main Street, 107 Wardlaw, Columbia, SC 29208, USA and Correspondence should be directed to Angela C. Baum. Instruction and Teacher Education, University of South Carolina, 820 Main Street, 107 Wardlaw, Columbia, SC 29208, USA. emails: bauma@gwm.sc.edu; mcmurray@ohio.edu; and **Paula McMurray-Schwarz:** Health and Human Services, Ohio University–Eastern, 4525 National Road, 341 Shannon Hall, St. Clairsville, OH 43950, USA.

From *Early Childhood Education Journal*, June 2007, pp. 367–370. Copyright © 2007 by Springer Science and Business Media. Reprinted by permission via Copyright Clearance Center/Rightslink.

What Can We Do to Prevent Childhood Obesity?

Julie Lumeng

Center for Human Growth and Development, University of Michigan

Childhood obesity is a real and pressing public health problem in the United States. Moreover, the obesity epidemic is accelerating—even among babies and toddlers. Contrary to popular opinion, all the information available to date indicates that a child less than 3 years old who is overweight is no more likely to be overweight as a young adult than is a toddler who is not overweight. However, the same research indicates that an overweight 3-year-old child is nearly 8 times as likely to become an overweight young adult as is a typically developing 3-year-old (Whitaker, Wright, Pepe, Seidel, & Dietz, 1997). In other words, by the time a child is 3, she may be on the path to obesity in adulthood. If we assume that the weight status of a 3-year-old has taken some time to develop, we must conclude that factors predisposing children to overweight begin operating in children in the first 3 years of life.

What factors in the experience of infants and toddlers seem likely to account for childhood overweight? What evidence do we have to suggest that these factors do, in fact, influence obesity risk? If research findings are scarce (or shaky), what advice about preventing obesity can practitioners offer to parents and caregivers of babies and toddlers? What can we do at a public health and policy level to change our obesigenic (obesity producing) environment? This article is an effort to answer these questions as fully as reliable research findings will allow. We will also define some terms that are used in medical discussions about childhood obesity; attempt to dispel some common misunderstandings about the causes of childhood obesity; and suggest some promising approaches for practice, research, and policy.

Definitions and Data

What is obesity in early childhood? *Obesity* is a term for excessive body fat. We measure body fat in anyone older than 24 months by calculating body mass index (BMI; weight in kilograms divided by the square of height in meters). Clinicians can plot a child's BMI on gender-specific charts pro-

vided by the National Center for Health Statistics (NCHS) of the Centers for Disease Control (CDC) (http://www.cdc.gov/growthcharts/). There are no BMI-for-age references or consistent definitions for overweight for children younger than 2 years. However, nutrition programs such as the Special Supplemental Nutrition Program for Women, Infants and Children have used weight-for-length recommendations to determine overweight and thus program eligibility. Consequently, overweight in this age group is defined as at or above the 95th percentile of weight for length (Ogden, Flegal, Carroll, & Johnson, 2002). Thus, for the remainder of this discussion, we will use the term "overweight" to describe children aged 2 years to 18 years whose BMI falls at the 95th percentile or above.

> **An overweight 3-year-old child is nearly 8 times as likely to become an overweight young adult as is a typically developing 3-year-old.**

Why does BMI mean something different for adults than for children? Adults have stopped growing. Because an adult's height remains the same, one can look at the weight and height of an adult and calculate BMI in a straightforward fashion. But think about children. Who appears to be naturally "chubbier"—a healthy 3-year-old or a 5-year-old? The 3-year-old—because she is still losing her "baby fat." *All* children are naturally at their "skinniest" when they are between 4 and 6 years old. Then their BMI slowly increases. Compare a 10-year-old girl about to enter puberty to a 5-year old girl. The 10 year-old's BMI is higher, but that is as it should be, given her stage of development. In other words, different degrees of "adiposity" (fatness) are normal at different ages during childhood. Babies *should* be "fat"—but fat within the normal range on the NCHS weight-for-length

At a Glance

- Rates of childhood obesity are increasing.
- Children less than 3 years old who are overweight are no more likely to be overweight in adulthood than are children who are not overweight, but 3-year-olds who are overweight are likely to be overweight in adulthood.
- Children learn many of their food preferences from their peers and from advertisements—not from their parents.
- Researchers have studied many possible factors in childhood obesity, such as genetics; the family's access to supermarkets and fresh, healthy foods; parents' attempts to limit when a child eats; and parents' attempts to make children eat more vegetables.

charts. The 3-year-olds who are in the top 5% of the weight-for-length bell curve are much more likely to continue to be overweight into adulthood. And adults who are at the top end of the BMI bell curve are at increased risk for serious health problems.

Terminology aside, more of America's children are becoming overweight, and today's overweight children tend to be heavier than overweight children were in past years. These data are concerning for a number of reasons. First of all, the obesity epidemic is accelerating—even among our youngest children. For example, between 1976 and 2000, the prevalence of overweight in 6- to 23-month-old children increased from 7% to nearly 12%. Most of this increase occurred from 1990 to 2000. Among 2- to 5-year-old children, the prevalence of overweight more than doubled (from 5% to more than 10%), again with most of the increase between 1990 and 2000 (Ogden et al., 2002).

Even among very young children, we are seeing significant—and growing—racial disparities in the prevalence of overweight. The greatest increases in the prevalence of overweight between 1971 and 1994 occurred in children of black and Hispanic race/ethnicity (Ogden et al., 1997). Racial disparities with respect to overweight appear to grow and interact with socioeconomic status as children grow older. For example, in 1986, the prevalence of overweight among 12-year-old upper-income White girls and low-income African American and Hispanic boys of the same age was nearly identical—6.5%. By 1998, the prevalence of overweight in upper-income White girls was essentially unchanged at 8.7%, but had more than quadrupled among low-income African American and Hispanic boys, at 27.4% (Strauss & Pollack, 2001). Unfortunately, we do not yet understand the causes underlying these alarming racial and socioeconomic disparities in the prevalence of overweight among children.

Chubby Babies, Fat Adults?

As noted above, all of the information available to date indicates that a child who is overweight at less than 3 years of age is no more likely to be overweight as a young adult than is a child who is not overweight. However, a child who is overweight at 3 years or older is nearly 8 times as likely to be overweight as a young adult than is a 3-year-old who is not overweight (Whitaker et al., 1997). Why and how is overweight in early childhood tied to adult obesity? Not surprisingly, current hypotheses focus on genes and the environment.

Genetic factors that predispose to obesity in a family may already be expressing themselves in early childhood. Genetic factors related to obesity may include: metabolism rates, behavioral predispositions to food preferences, eating behavior, and patterns of physical activity. Even among children younger than 3 years, a child with one parent who is obese is 3 times as likely to become an obese adult as is a child with two parents of normal weight. A child with two obese parents is more than 13 times as likely to become an obese adult as is a child with parents of normal weight (Whitaker et al., 1997). This phenomenon undoubtedly reflects a complex interplay of biology and behavior. In other words, as we have come to recognize that with respect to most aspects of child development, the old dichotomy of nature versus nurture represents an oversimplification of a complex issue.

We do know that the dramatic increase in the prevalence of overweight in the general population and among children since 1990 absolutely cannot be accounted for by genetic shifts in the population. Genetic changes simply do not occur this quickly. It *is* possible, however, that genetic predispositions toward certain behaviors (e.g., preferences for sweet or high-fat foods) vary within the population. When the environment changes, these genetic predispositions may be more apt to express themselves than formerly; the result is overweight or obesity. The overarching message? Our genes have not changed recently; our environment has. What does this conclusion tell us about the strong transmission of overweight risk from parent to child?

Parents' modeling of behavior and their shaping of a child's relationship to food have been areas of active research in child development for quite some time. Accounts in the lay press do not hesitate to hold parents responsible for childhood overweight. For example, recent articles in national newspapers have been headlined, "Overweight kids? You might deserve a big slice of the blame" (Lee, 2004), or "If parents can't say no, then their children won't learn to either" (Hart, 2003). Blaming parents for a problem that is growing more quickly—and at epidemic proportions—in disadvantaged minority populations than in the population as a whole immediately raises concerns about the validity of this conceptualization of the problem. If parents are generally and primarily to blame for the increased prevalence of child overweight since 1990, one or both of the following statements would have to be true: (a) Parenting practices as a whole have shifted dramatically in the last 15 years, and (b) low-income parents (especially mothers) have a reasonable chance of overcoming the influence of both food advertising that is targeted at their children and the economic conditions in which they live.

Who Influences Children's Eating Behavior?

If poor parenting is to blame for the growing prevalence of childhood obesity, then something must have changed since 1990 in the ways in which parents teach their children about food, set limits around food, and promote healthy eating habits. This assertion is difficult to support, for a variety of reasons. For example, if parents have a powerful influence over children's eating behavior and development of food preferences, then family members' food preferences should be very much alike. In fact, very little correlation exists between parent and child food preferences (even when the children have grown to be adults; Rozin, 1991). Parents are not very effective at transmitting preferences for foods to their children (a finding that will not surprise any parent or caregiver who has struggled to encourage a child to sample a new food!).

Today's overweight children tend to be heavier than overweight children were in past years.

Although parents have limited control over what children are willing to eat while sitting at the dinner table parents *do* control what food is in the cupboards. Given that obesity is more common in low-income minority populations, perhaps efforts should focus on encouraging low-income mothers with young children to stock the house with a range of healthy food options for their children. Unfortunately, this recommendation is problematic from a public health perspective. Consider, for example, the research finding that families who live closer to supermarkets are more likely to consume a healthier diet than are families who live further away, presumably because those living closer have readier access to a range of fresh and healthy foods (Morland, Wing, & Roux, 2002). However, the number of supermarkets per capita is nearly 6 times greater in White neighborhoods than it is in neighborhoods of primarily minority race/ethnicity (Morland, Wing, Roux, & Poole, 2002). The reasons for these stark disparities are undoubtedly complex, and not fully understood. These differences, however, would potentially be amenable to public policy intervention.

Where *do* children learn their food preferences? The bulk of the evidence suggests that even children as young as 2 years learn food preferences from their peer group. In one study, researchers in a preschool setting seated children who didn't like broccoli next to children who did. The broccoli eaters ate their green vegetable in full view of their broccoli-averse classmates. Over time, the children who hadn't liked broccoli began to eat it (Birch, 1980). In a more recent experiment, teachers in a preschool setting and peer models were put head-to-head to determine who was more likely to influence a child's food preferences. The children were significantly more powerful influences than the adults were (Hendy & Raudenbush, 2000).

Evolutionary biology suggests two principal reasons why peers may be more powerful than adults in shaping children's food preferences:

- *Young children's reluctance to sample new foods is biologically wired.* Reluctance to try new foods begins to emerge at around age 2 years and lessens as children approach school age. The unfamiliar foods that children are most reluctant to try are vegetables (Cooke, Wardle, & Gibson, 2003). That children become reluctant to sample new foods just as they are becoming mobile, independent explorers seems to be more than mere coincidence. It would be to the human species' survival advantage for its young to be reluctant to eat unfamiliar plant life (e.g., vegetables): Plants can be poisonous. Instead of tasting any new item that they encounter, human children (in fact, nearly all mammals) determine what to eat by observing others around them.
- *Modeling eating behavior after peers may provide young children with some survival advantage.* A biological perspective suggests that the nutritional needs of the young human are more similar to those of other young humans than to those of full-grown adults. For example, because children's bodies are smaller than those of adults and to some extent less able to protect against infection, foods that adults can eat or drink safely in reasonable quantities could prove toxic to a young child (e.g., sushi, steak tartar, unpasteurized apple cider, and alcohol).

In brief, if nature had tried to equip children's brains with a preset system for recognizing which foods are safe to eat, a system that led children to imitate the behavior of the organisms most like themselves (i.e., other children), would clearly be the best design. This appears to be, indeed, the food-selection system that children use.

Unfortunately, advertisers seem to have recognized the power of peers to influence children's food preferences long before the rest of us. Anyone who has ever watched television recognizes that to sell food to children, advertisers use other children (e.g., "Mikey") or characters designed to appeal to and resonate with children. No cereal or candy company would ever attempt to sell a product to a child with a commercial featuring a firm (yet kind and gentle) adult model eating the product while enthusiastically explaining to the child how "yummy" it is. Paradoxically, this is exactly the method by which parents try to get children to eat healthy foods. Perhaps reframing our efforts at changing childhood eating behavior is in order. Food advertisements on television are powerful. Children's consumption of specific foods correlates with their having viewed advertisements for these foods. Obese children are more likely than are children of normal weight to recognize food advertisements on television (Halford, Gillespie, Brown, Pontin, & Dovey, 2004). Even children as young as 2 years are more likely to select a food that they recently saw advertised in a 30-second commercial embedded in a cartoon than are children who have watched the cartoon without the commercial (Borzekowski & Robinson, 2001). Unless the government can be convinced to provide sufficient funding to advertise vegetables, whole grains, and milk on television with the same vigor and enormous advertising budget of the junk-food industry, hawking healthy food to children through television may be an unreachable goal. However, children who attend preschool and child care are exposed to peers in eating situations every day. These interactions may be prime opportunities for promoting the transmission of healthy food preferences between and among children.

What Is the Right Way to Parent to Prevent Obesity?

Parents do exert some control over how their children learn to prefer healthy foods and regulate food intake. Therefore, professionals who work with the parents of young children should base their recommendations about nutrition and feeding on solid scientific evidence. Unfortunately, although professionals frequently give families advice on these topics, we have little data to back up our suggestions.

Although parents have limited control over what children are willing to eat . . . parents do control what food is in the cupboards.

For example, early childhood professionals and clinicians generally believe that young infants should be fed "on demand." (Whether or not parents actually accept and implement this advice is an unanswered question.) But although feeding an infant on demand may certainly promote a sense of security and help the infant to calm and self-regulate, we have no evidence to suggest that feeding a baby on demand has anything to do with her eventual ability to regulate appetite. Interestingly, at some point in the early childhood years, however, general professional opinion and advice seem to shift from feeding "on demand" to feeding at scheduled snack and mealtimes. We encourage parents to have a child wait until dinner for food, even if he or she is clearly hungry. The theory is that the child will then "have a good appetite" and will "eat a good dinner." On the other hand, some professionals advise parents to allow young children to "graze"

on healthy foods all day long. They counsel parents to allow their child to eat a snack when they ask for one, with the thought that the child is learning to respond to his hunger cues accurately. Feeding children when they say that they are hungry, these professionals and parents believe, will teach children that "we eat when we are hungry," not that "we eat because it is dinnertime."

Evidence to support either method of regulating food intake is scanty. Some data suggest that restricting children's access to palatable foods makes children like and want these foods even more over time (Birch, Zimmerman, & Hind, 1980) and promotes overeating when the restricted foods are actually available (Fisher & Birch, 1999). The more that mothers control how much, what, and when children eat at age 5 years (regardless of the child's weight status at that age), the more likely the child is to eat without being hungry (i.e., to be insensitive to hunger cues and therefore apt to overeat) by age 9 years (Birch, Fisher, & Davison, 2003). These data suggest that parents who set strict limits on their young children's eating may actually promote obesity. This information might, therefore, prompt professionals to instruct mothers *not* to restrict the amount, timing, or content of children's meals. However, such advice runs directly counter to how much of the general public views the cause of today's childhood obesity epidemic—lax, inconsistent parenting with little limit-setting.

Similar confusion exists concerning strategies to get children to eat more vegetables. Simply encouraging parents to put vegetables on the dinner table each evening does not result in children's becoming more familiar with a food and therefore more likely to eat it. Children must actually taste a vegetable repeatedly before they begin to like it (Birch, McPhee, Shoba, Pirok, & Steinberg, 1987). If simply prompting a child to "take one bite" could make a typical child easily and pleasantly take a bite of a disliked vegetable, parenting (and obesity prevention) would certainly be a much simpler endeavor than it is. Unfortunately, as we have seen, children have an inherent reluctance to sample new vegetables, and parental modeling, as described above, has limited power to overcome this reluctance. If these methods fail, parents often then resort to rewarding the child for trying one bite of the vegetable. Most commonly, parents will tell a child that she may not leave the table, or may not have dessert, or may not have any more servings of a preferred food until the target vegetable is sampled. Unfortunately, it seems that these methods of reward actually result in a decreased preference for the target vegetable over time—certainly not the desired outcome (Birch, Marlin, & Rotter, 1984).

Synthesis of the Research to Date

Do we have evidence that any feeding practices in the first few years of life influence obesity risk? It is relatively well-accepted among researchers that breast-feeding reduces the risk of obesity (Hediger, Overpeck, Kuczmarski, & Ruan, 2001), although questions remain concerning whether this correlation is simply due to the presence of confounders, such as the general health consciousness of mothers who breast-feed (Parsons, Power, & Manor, 2003). If one accepts that a relationship exists between breast-feeding and lowered risk of obesity, one should note that breast-feeding in infancy has not been found to be associated with protection against overweight among children of preschool age in all populations. Among low-income children, for example, the relationship between breast-feeding and protection against overweight is present only in white children—not in black or Hispanic children (Grummer-Strawn & Mei, 2004). The reason for this discrepancy remains unclear. Researchers are also debating whether or not the timing of a baby's introduction to solid foods is associated with an increased risk of child overweight. Most recent research seems to indicate that introduction of solid foods before 4–6 months does not seem to be associated with infant weight status, at least at 12 months of age. We have no data about timing of solid food introduction and weight status at age 3 years or later. The use of food as a reward (for example, to avert a tantrum) has been associated with children's increased preference for the food that has been used as a reward (Birch et al., 1980). However, the children of mothers who report that they use food as a reward do not seem, as a group, to be particularly obese (Baughcum et al., 2001).

Because of the high prevalence of obesity among children living in poverty, several researchers have studied the feeding practices of low-income mothers of young children. However, efforts to relate children's weight status at 11 to 24 months of age to self-reported maternal feeding practices in low-income populations have not uncovered any clear associations. Baughcum and her colleagues (2001) found that low-income mothers of children who were overweight did not report being more concerned about their infant's hunger, being less aware of their infant's hunger and satiety cues, feeding their infant more on a schedule, being more likely to use food to calm their infant, or having less social interaction during feeding than did low-income mothers of children of normal weight. However, low-income obese mothers in this study were more likely to be concerned about their baby's being underweight than other mothers. Given their concern, obese mothers may have been more apt to overfeed their babies, and thereby place them at greater risk for overweight. Regardless of the weight status of child or mother, low-income mothers are more likely to be concerned about their child's hunger than are higher-income mothers (Baughcum et al., 2001). Low-income mothers said that they found it difficult to withhold food from a child who said he or she was hungry, even if the child had just finished a meal.

Results from the same authors for children 23 to 60 months of age provide equally confusing information for the practitioner who wants to provide straightforward advice to a family. The researchers found that obese mothers and low-income mothers were more likely to engage in what professionals consider age-inappropriate feeding practices

than were non-obese or upper-income mothers (Baughcum et al., 2001). For example, low-income toddlers and preschoolers were more likely than upper-income young children to eat in front of the TV or walking around the living room rather than having a meal at a table with a place setting. Lower-income mothers said that they had less difficulty feeding their children than did higher-income mothers, but low-income mothers reported a tendency to push their children to eat more. However, none of these frowned-upon feeding practices were associated with increased risk of overweight at age 5 years.

Some data suggest that restricting children's access to palatable foods makes children like and want these foods even more over time.

In summary, we find no evidence from mothers' reports that overweight children experience a different feeding style from their mothers than do non-overweight children. Although lower-income mothers do feed their young children differently than do upper-income mothers, we have no evidence that these different feeding practices are actually related to an increased risk of child overweight. In other words, the fact that a low-income mother chooses to have unstructured mealtimes, encourages her child to eat more, allows her child to have a bottle during the day, or will feed the child herself if the child does not want to eat, may reflect sociocultural differences between lower-income and upper-income parents in their beliefs about feeding practices. Professionals have no basis on which to make a value judgment about these practices as they pertain to child overweight outcomes.

What *Should* Professionals Recommend to Parents?

We have reviewed the research on young children's eating behavior and parental feeding practices (with a particular focus on low-income minority children) and their relationship to childhood overweight. We have found an absence of robust research to guide us in advising parents about how to prevent childhood overweight. What advice *should* professionals give to parents of young children about feeding practices? Research suggests four guidelines for practice:

1. *Acknowledge the limits of parental influence in the face of an obesigenic environment.*

Especially when working with disadvantaged parents, acknowledge that although parents influence their children's eating and will do the best job they can to prevent obesity in their child, individual parents are constantly battling a myriad of societal and biological influences on their child's eating behavior.

2. *Empower parents to advocate for systemic change.*

Parents are in a prime position to advocate for change in their children's child-care and preschool settings with regard to the foods served and the mealtime atmosphere. Parents are also important voices in advocating for more and safer playgrounds in their neighborhoods so that children can get exercise outdoors.

3. *Refrain from urging parents to change their feeding practices when we have little scientific evidence to suggest that these are actually "wrong."*

Although allowing a child to walk around all day with a bottle of juice is certainly problematic from an oral health perspective, professionals tend to frown on other feeding practices without compelling evidence that these practices increase children's risk of poor health outcomes. For example, telling a mother to have structured mealtimes rather than allowing her young child to "graze" has little basis in science, and may only serve to alienate a mother from the health care provider. She is likely to be feeding her child as her mother fed her, and as her cultural and socioeconomic peers feed their children.

4. *Advocate, advocate, advocate.*

Although working with individual families to reduce their child's risk for overweight is important, advocating for change on a public health and policy level is critical. Providing low-income families in both urban and rural areas with ready access to fresh and palatable fruits and vegetables would be an important change for the better. Increasing the availability of healthy, tasty, and inexpensive fast food could also make a big difference in children's health. Although an upper-income working family can find palatable (albeit expensive) rather healthy take-out food in some communities, cost and availability preclude this option for most low-income families. Yet few low-income mothers have the time or energy after a long day at work to take public transportation (which doesn't exist in many communities) with several children in tow to buy fresh food at a supermarket (which may not exist in the vicinity of many low-income families' homes), and then cook while the children vie for her attention. Because many low-income families do not feel safe allowing their children to play outside in their home neighborhoods, it is important to ensure that, along with healthy meals and snacks, children get adequate opportunity for physical activity in child-care, preschool, school, and after-school programs. Of course our long-term goal should be safe child- and family-friendly communities with ample sources of affordable, healthy food to purchase and accessible resources for information and physical exercise (including community gardening).

In Conclusion

The early childhood professional can play a critical role in stemming the tide of childhood overweight. However, this role may not play out in the home of the individual family as much as it may in the Early Head Start or Head Start classroom or the community meeting hall. Preventing childhood overweight will, as the saying goes, take a village.

References

Baughcum, A., Powers, S., Johnson, S., Chamberlin, L., Deeks, C., Jain, A., et al. (2001). Maternal feeding practices and beliefs and their relationships to overweight in early childhood. *Journal of Developmental & Behavioral Pediatrics, 22*(6), 391–408.

Birch, L. (1980). Effects of peer models' food choices and eating behaviors on preschoolers' food preferences. *Child Development, 51,* 489–496.

Birch, L., Fisher, J., & Davison, K. (2003). Learning to overeat: Maternal use of restrictive feeding practices promotes girls' eating in the absence of hunger. *American Journal of Clinical Nutrition, 78*(2), 215–220.

Birch, L., Marlin, D., & Rotter, J. (1984). Eating as the "means" activity in a contingency: Effects on young children's food preference. *Child Development, 55,* 432–439.

Birch, L., McPhee, L., Shoba, B., Pirok, E., & Steinberg, L. (1987). What kind of exposure reduces children's food neophobia? *Appetite, 3,* 353–360.

Birch, L., Zimmerman, S., & Hind, H. (1980). The influence of social affective context on the formation of children's food preferences. *Child Development, 51*(3), 856–861.

Borzekowski, D., & Robinson, T. (2001). The 30-second effect: An experiment revealing the impact of television commercials on food preferences of preschoolers. *Journal of the American Dietetic Association, 101*(1), 42–46.

Cooke, L., Wardle, J., & Gibson, E. (2003). Relationship between parental report of food neophobia and everyday food consumption in 2–6-year-old children. *Appetite, 41*(2), 205–206.

Fisher, J., & Birch, L. (1999). Restricting access to palatable foods affects children's behavioral response, food selection, and intake. *American Journal of Clinical Nutrition, 69,* 1264–1272.

Grummer-Strawn, L., & Mei, Z. (2004). Does breastfeeding protect against pediatric overweight? Analysis of longitudinal data from the Centers for Disease Control and Prevention Nutrition Surveillance System. *Pediatrics, 113*(2), e81–e86.

Halford, J., Gillespie, J., Brown, V., Pontin, E., & Dovey, T. (2004). Effect of television advertisements for foods on consumption in children. *Appetite, 42*(2), 221–225.

Hart, B. (2003, November 16). If parents can't say no, then their children won't learn to either. *Chicago Sun-Times,* p. 36.

Hediger, M., Overpeck, M., Kuczmarski, R., & Ruan, W. (2001). Association between infant breastfeeding and overweight in young children. *Journal of the American Medical Association, 285,* 2453–2460.

Hendy, H., & Raudenbush, B. (2000). Effectiveness of teacher modeling to encourage food acceptance in preschool children. *Appetite, 34,* 61–76.

Lee, E. (2004, May 30). Overweight kids? You might deserve a big slice of the blame. *Atlanta Journal-Constitution,* p. 1A.

Morland, K., Wing, S., & Roux, A. D. (2002). The contextual effect of the local food environment on residents' diets: The atherosclerosis risk in communities study. *American Journal of Public Health, 92*(11), 1761–1768.

Morland, K., Wing, S., Roux, A. D., & Poole, C. (2002). Neighborhood characteristics associated with the location of food stores and food service places. *American Journal of Preventive Medicine, 22,* 23–29.

Ogden, C., Flegal, K., Carroll, M., & Johnson, C. (2002). Prevalence and trends in overweight among US children and adolescents, 1999–2000. *Journal of the American Medical Association, 288,* 1728–1732.

Ogden, C., Troiano, R., Briefel, R., Kuczmarski, R., Flegal, K., & Johnson, C. (1997). Prevalence of overweight among preschool children in the United States, 1971 through 1994. *Pediatrics, 99*(4), e1.

Parsons, T., Power, C., & Manor, O. (2003). Infant feeding and obesity through the life-course. *Archives of Disease in Childhood, 88*(9), 793–794.

Rozin, P. (1991). Family resemblance in food and other domains: The family paradox and the role of parental congruence. *Appetite, 16,* 93–102.

Strauss, R., & Pollack, H. (2001). Epidemic increase in childhood overweight. *Journal of the American Medical Association, 286*(22), 2845–2848.

Whitaker, R., Wright, J., Pepe, M., Seidel, K., & Dietz, W. (1997). Predicting obesity in young adulthood from childhood and parental obesity. *New England Journal of Medicine, 337,* 869–873.

From *Zero to Three,* January 2005, pp. 13–19. Copyright © 2005 by National Center for Infants, Toddlers and Families. Reprinted by permission.

UNIT 5

Educational Practices

Unit Selections

Key Points to Consider

- What is causing the pressure to push the curriculum down from the primary grades into preschool? How can teachers of young children resist that pressure?

- What caused the large increase in scripted curriculum programs on the market?

- Make a brief listing of the components of developmentally appropriate practice that you believe are vital.

- How can teachers and parents assist young children as they move from preschool to kindergarten?

- What are some of the best design features of a preschool classroom where you have worked or observed?

- Why are transition grades not the best way to educate children?

- Why is the ability to make choices a crucial skill to learn in the early years?

- Describe some of the important reasons for and against homework.

Student Web Site

www.mhcls.com/online

Internet References

Further information regarding these Web sites may be found in this book's preface or online.

Association for Childhood Education International (ACEI)
http://www.acei.org/
Early Childhood Education Online
http://www.umaine.edu/eceol/
Reggio Emilia
http://www.ericdigests.org/2001-3/reggio.htm

I am struck with the increasing push to have young children do things at an earlier and earlier age as the life expectancy keeps increasing. Children born today have an excellent chance of living into their 90s and beyond. There is no great need to rush and acquire skills that can easily be learned when the child is a little older at the expense of valuable lifelong lessons that are best learned when children are young. How to get along with others, make choices, negotiate, develop a sense of compassion and communicating needs are all skills that require introduction and practice during the preschool years. "Back to Basics" by Jill Englebright Fox focuses on the importance of developmentally appropriate play experiences for young children not the basics many think would be core academic skills. The basics to which Fox refers are a solid foundation in understanding how things work, many opportunities to explore and manipulate materials, and opportunities for creative expression. How this can all be accomplished in the new world of standards is the balancing act under which many teachers now operate.

The passage of No Child Left Behind legislation has many implications for early childhood care and educational practices. As academic assessment and accountability measures are implemented, many publishers have rushed to develop scripted curriculum for teachers to use. Most of these programs are centered on teaching reading. In "Scripted Curriculum" Anita Ede examines the politics behind the development of scripted curriculum and both positive and negative research findings. The reader might want to read article 19 "Research 101: Tools for Reading and Interpreting Early Childhood Research" prior to reading this article.

We now know teaching IS rocket science and does require committed individuals who are well prepared to deal with a variety of development levels and needs as appropriate learning experiences are planned for all children. Good teaching does make a difference and children deserve no less than adults who truly are passionate about being with young children on a daily basis. Teaching cannot be viewed as a great profession for someone who wants their summers off. Teachers well prepared to provide exemplary learning experiences for their children can make a real difference in the lives of their students.

Both Francis Wardle in "*Rethinking* Early Childhood Practices" and Vera Estok in "One District's Study on the Propriety of Transition-Grade Classrooms" ask us to give careful consideration to a variety of common practices in programs for young children. Teachers often put great thought and time into preparing lesson plans, but give little attention to developing the daily schedule, grouping children, or recommending children for a transitional grade. Teachers must make research based decisions. Any teacher who carefully studied the research would not support transitional grades. We must take our cues from those in the medical community, read, and follow the research.

Lars Niki

The word "transition" is used a different way in the next article. In "Successful Transition to Kindergarten" the author provides ways teachers and parents can help young children make the major transition to kindergarten. For some children, kindergarten is their first experience with formal schooling. For many others it means a different school, classroom, and teacher than they had during their preschool years. With this new experience come many different expectations. When I sent my two sons off to college I thought about the many ways their universities prepared them, and their parents, for this major transition. First year orientation, welcome week, and parents' weekend were all carefully planned to assist the new students with adjusting to college. We do little to help five year olds also making a major transition in their life. It is time preschool teachers, kindergarten teachers, and families collaborate to ensure a smooth progression to the next learning experience.

In "Making the Case for Play Policy" the author addresses the need to protect children's right to play as an avenue of cognitive, emotional, and academic growth. The reader should also recognize that to be beneficial to growth and development, play needs to be channeled and supported. Teachers are encouraged to provide appropriate props and materials to foster the type of play that extends learning.

The last article in this unit, "The Case For and Against Homework," deals with this most misunderstood topic. Once again understanding and applying the research is the theme of this article. Teachers who are familiar with the many issues surrounding homework will be best able to structure the experience to meet the needs of children and the changing demands of families and teachers. Homework should not be an all-or-nothing experience and can be designed to be effective. Homework today is not what you may remember as homework of your youth. Be open to learning about the importance of enriching experiences outside of class and how they can assist children.

Back to Basics

Play in Early Childhood

Jill Englebright Fox, PhD

Kyle plays with blocks and builds a castle. Tony and Victoria play fire station and pretend to be firefighters. Kenzo and Carl play catch with a ball. Children playact with playmates in the playhouse. Playgroups on the playground choose players to play ball. As an early childhood professional, you probably use the word "play" a hundred times per day.

Research indicates that children learn best in an environment which allows them to explore, discover, and play. Play is an important part of a developmentally appropriate child care program. It is also closely tied to the development of cognitive, socio-emotional, and physical behaviors. But what exactly does it mean to play and why is play so important for young children?

What Is Play?

Although it is simple to compile a list of play activities, it is much more difficult to define play. Scales, et al., (1991) called play "that absorbing activity in which healthy young children participate with enthusiasm and abandon" (p. 15). Csikszentmihalyi (1981) described play as "a subset of life . . . an arrangement in which one can practice behavior without dreading its consequences" (p. 14). Garvey (1977) gave a useful description of play for teachers when she defined play as an activity which is: 1) positively valued by the player; 2) self-motivated; 3) freely chosen; 4) engaging; and 5) which "has certain systematic relations to what is not play" (p. 5). These characteristics are important for teachers to remember because imposing adult values, requirements, or motivations on children's activities may change the very nature of play.

According to *Webster's Desk Dictionary of the English Language,* the word play has 34 different meanings. In terms of young children and play, the following definitions from Webster's are useful:

- light, brisk, or changing movement (e.g., to pretend you're a butterfly)
- to act or imitate the part of a person or character (e.g., to play house)
- to employ a piece of equipment (e.g., to play blocks)
- exercise for amusement or recreation (e.g., to play tag)
- fun or jest, as opposed to seriousness (e.g., to play peek-a-boo or sing a silly song)
- the action of a game (e.g., to play duck-duck-goose)

Why Is Play Important?

According to Fromberg and Gullo (1992), play enhances language development, social competence, creativity, imagination, and thinking skills. Frost (1992) concurred, stating that "play is the chief vehicle for the development of imagination and intelligence, language, social skills, and perceptual-motor abilities in infants and young children" (p. 48).

Garvey (1977) states that play is most common during childhood when children's knowledge of self, comprehension of verbal and non-verbal communication, and understanding of the physical and social worlds are expanding dramatically.

Fromberg (1990) claims that play is the "ultimate integrator of human experience" (p. 223). This means that when children play, they draw upon their past experiences—things they have done, seen others do, read about, or seen on television—and they use these experiences to build games, play scenarios, and engage in activities.

Children use fine and gross motor skills in their play. They react to each other socially. They think about what they are doing or going to do. They use language to talk to each other or to themselves and they very often respond emotionally to the play activity. The integration of these different types of behaviors is key to the cognitive development of young children. According to Rogers and Sawyer (1988), "until at least the age of nine, children's cognitive structures function best in this unified mode" (p. 58). Because children's play draws upon all of these behaviors, it is a very effective vehicle for learning.

Play and Cognitive Development

The relationship between play and cognitive development is described differently in the two theories of cognitive development which dominate early childhood education—Piaget's and Vygotsky's.

Piaget (1962) defined play as assimilation, or the child's efforts to make environmental stimuli match his or her own concepts. Piagetian theory holds that play, in and of itself, does not necessarily result in the formation of new cognitive structures. Piaget claimed that play was just for pleasure, and while it allowed children to practice things they had previously learned, it did not necessarily result in the learning of new things. In other words, play reflects what the child has already learned but does not necessarily teach the child anything new. In this view, play is seen as a "process reflective of emerging symbolic development, but contributing little to it" (Johnsen & Christie, 1986, p. 51).

In contrast, Vygotskian theory states that play actually facilitates cognitive development. Children not only practice what they already know, they also learn new things. In discussing Vygotsky's theory, Vandenberg (1986) remarks that "play not so much reflects thought (as Piaget suggests) as it creates thought" (p. 21).

Observations of children at play yield examples to support both Piagetian and Vygotskian theories of play. A child who puts on a raincoat and a firefighter's hat and rushes to rescue his teddy bear from the pretend flames in his playhouse is practicing what he has previously learned about firefighters. This supports Piaget's theory. On the other hand, a child in the block center who announces to his teacher, "Look! When I put these two square blocks together, I get a rectangle!" has constructed new knowledge through her play. This supports Vygotsky's theory.

Whether children are practicing what they have learned in other settings or are constructing new knowledge, it is clear that play has a valuable role in the early childhood classroom.

Play—Indoors and Out

Early childhood teachers have long recognized the value of play in programs for young children. Unfortunately, teachers often fail to take advantage of the opportunities play provides for observing children's development and learning. Through such observations teachers can learn about children's social interactions, cognitive and language abilities, motor skills, and emotional development.

Frost (1992) recommends that observing children at play be a daily responsibility for early childhood professionals. Regular observations provide teachers with assessment information for identifying children with special needs, planning future play experiences, evaluating play materials, determining areas of strength and weakness for individual children, planning curriculum for individual children, reporting to parents, and checking on a child's on-going progress. The increased use of authentic assessment strategies is making observations of children's play more commonplace in early childhood classrooms.

Hymes (1981) recommends that children have two classrooms—one indoors and one outdoors. The outdoor play environment should be used as an extension of the indoor classroom. It should be a learning environment as carefully planned as the indoor activity centers and should encourage motor and social skills as well as help children refine existing cognitive structures and construct new ones. Used in this way, the outdoor play environment provides a basis for observational assessment in all areas of development.

Fox (1993) researched the practicality of observing young children's cognitive development during outdoor play. Her observations of four- and five-year-old children during outdoor play found examples of addition and subtraction, shape identification, patterning, one-to-one correspondence, number sense, sequencing of events, use of ordinal numbers, knowledge of prepositions, and identification of final and initial consonants. Fox's outdoor observations also found multiple examples of problem-solving, creative thinking, social competence, language use, and gross and fine motor skills. Although outdoor observations do not replace classroom assessment, they can provide valuable information for teachers of young children. As Fox stated, "These observations can be performed unobtrusively, without intruding upon the children's activities and without placing children in a stressful testing situation" (p. 131).

Parten's Five Types of Play

Play for young children assumes many different forms. Mildred Parten (1932) was one of the early researchers studying children at play. She focused on the social interactions between children during play activities. Parten's categories of play are not hierarchical. Depending on the circumstances, children may engage in any of the different types of play. Parten does note, however, that in her research with two- to five-year-olds, "participation in the most social types of groups occurs most frequently among the older children" (p. 259).

Extra playtime allows children to become involved in more complex and productive play activities

- **Onlooker behavior**—Playing passively by watching or conversing with other children engaged in play activities.
- **Solitary independent**—Playing by oneself.
- **Parallel**—Playing, even in the middle of a group, while remaining engrossed in one's own activity. Children playing parallel to each other sometimes use each other's toys, but always maintain their independence.
- **Associative**—When children share materials and talk to each other, but do not coordinate play objectives or interests.
- **Cooperative**—When children organize themselves into roles with specific goals in mind (e.g., to assign the roles of doctor, nurse, and patient and play hospital).

How Much Should Children Play?

Indoors and outdoors, children need large blocks of time for play. According to Christie and Wardle (1992), short play periods may require children to abandon their group dramatizations or constructive play just when they begin to get involved. When this happens a number of times, children may give up on more sophisticated forms of play and settle for less advanced forms that can be completed in short periods of time. Shorter play periods reduce both the amount and the maturity of children's play, and many important benefits of play, such as persistence, negotiation, problem solving, planning, and cooperation are lost. Large blocks of time (30 to 60 minutes, or longer) should be scheduled for indoor and outdoor play periods. Christie and Wardle remind teachers that extra playtime does not result in children becoming bored. Instead, it prompts children to become involved in more complex, more productive play activities.

The Teacher's Role

The early childhood teacher is the facilitator of play in the classroom. The teacher facilitates play by providing appropriate indoor and outdoor play environments. Safety is, of course, the primary concern. Age and developmental levels must be carefully considered in the design and selection of materials. Guidelines for selecting safe and appropriate equipment for outdoor play environments are available through the U.S. Consumer Product Safety Commission's Handbook for Public Playground Safety and the Playground Safety Manual by Jambor and Palmer (1991). Similar guidelines are also available for indoor settings (Torelli & Durrett, 1996; Caples, 1996; Ard & Pitts, 1990). Once appropriate environments and materials are in place, regular safety checks and maintenance are needed to ensure that the equipment is sound and safe for continued play.

Teachers also facilitate play by working with children to develop rules for safe indoor and outdoor play. Discussion about the appropriate use of materials, the safe number of participants on each piece of equipment, taking turns, sharing, and cleaning up provides the children with information to begin their play activities. These discussions need to be ongoing because some children may need frequent reminders about rules and because new situations may arise (e.g., new equipment).

By providing play materials related to thematic instruction, early childhood teachers can establish links between the children's indoor and outdoor play and their program's curriculum. Thematic props for dramatic play can be placed in the dramatic play center or stored in prop boxes and taken outside to extend the dramatic play to a new setting. An art center in the outdoor play environment may encourage children to explore the possibilities of using leaves, twigs, pebbles, and sand in their three-dimensional art productions. Painting easels and water tables may also be moved outside periodically for children's use during outdoor play periods. Finally, a collection of books stored in a wagon to be taken outside during play time may offer some children a needed alternative to more active play.

As facilitators of children's play, teachers should closely observe children during play periods not only for assessment purposes, as stated earlier, but also to facilitate appropriate social interactions and motor behaviors. It is important that children be the decision-makers during play, choosing what and where to play, choosing roles for each player, and choosing how play will proceed. Occasionally, however, some children will need adult assistance in joining a play group, modifying behavior, or negotiating a disagreement. Careful observation will help the teacher to decide when to offer assistance and what form that assistance should take.

Conclusion

Although play is a difficult concept to define, it is very easy to recognize. Children actively involved in play may be engaged in a variety of activities, independently, with a partner, or in a group. Because play is closely tied to the cognitive, socio-emotional, and motor development of young children, it is an important part of developmentally appropriate early childhood programs.

JILL ENGLEBRIGHT FOX, PHD, is an assistant professor of early childhood education at Virginia Commonwealth University. She taught kindergarten and first grade in the Texas public schools for eight years, and is currently an active member of the International Play Association-USA. Her research interests focus on play and aesthetic development in young children, and professional development schools.

From *Earlychildhood NEWS*, March/April 2006, pp. 12–15. Copyright © 2006 by Excelligence Learning Corporation. Reprinted by permission.

Scripted Curriculum

Is It a Prescription for Success?

Anita Ede

Imagine walking down the halls of your school and hearing the same sentences read, the same questions asked, and the same teacher comments coming from each classroom. "Impossible," you say to yourself. "This could not possibly be happening." But it is. This scenario is becoming more and more commonplace throughout schools in the United States as scripted curriculum materials are implemented more widely. In 2001, one in every eight schools in California used Open Court, a scripted reading program (Posnick-Goodwin, 2002). Nationwide, 1,551 elementary schools in 48 states use Success for All, another scripted reading program (Dudley-Marling & Murphy, 2001). Scripted curriculum materials are instructional materials that have been commercially prepared and require the teacher to read from a script while delivering the lesson (Moustafa & Land, 2002). Scripted materials reflect a focus on explicit, direct, systematic skills instruction and are touted as a method to boost sagging standardized test scores and narrow the achievement gap between children growing up in poverty and those who are more affluent (Coles, 2002).

Politics and the Scripted Curriculum

The goal of the education system in the United States has long been to provide an effective public education for all children in order that they may realize their full potential. Precisely how this is to be achieved, however, is the subject of a great deal of debate.

In April 1999, the National Reading Panel (NRP), based on its review of 100,000 studies of how children learn to read, provided a guide for scientifically based reading instruction (cited in Coles, 2002). Those numbers are a little misleading, however. The NRP began by looking at 100,000 studies on reading that had been conducted since 1966. It then established criteria that limited the studies to those relating to instructional material that the panel decided, ahead of time, represented key areas of good reading instruction. The field was further narrowed to studies that had been conducted "scientifically"; that is, using only quantitative data. When all was said and done,

the 100,000 studies had been pruned to 52 studies of phonemic awareness, 38 studies of phonics, 14 studies of reading fluency, and 203 studies related to comprehension instruction (Coles, 2002). After examination of the aforementioned 307 studies, the NRP concluded that the most effective course of reading instruction included explicit and systematic instruction in phonemic awareness and phonics (Metcalf, 2002)—that is, the scripted curriculum.

> **It is important for teachers to understand the politics of the scripted curriculum, as well as who profits, its basic structure, current research as to its effectiveness, and concerns about its effect on students as well as teachers.**

One week after becoming president, George W. Bush sent Congress an education reform bill that referred to the NRP's research findings; he promised to eliminate reading inequalities and ensure that all children would read at grade level by the time they reached the 3rd grade. This would be achieved through the use of scientifically based reading instruction. These education reforms became law when the No Child Left Behind Act (NCLB) was passed in 2002.

The Reading First initiative, the portion of NCLB that applies to reading instruction, provides funding to schools on the condition that they adopt "scientifically based" reading programs. The "scientifically based" (quantitative) research by the NRP that resulted in the funding for "scientifically based" reading programs by Reading First is the basis for the scripted reading curriculum. Programs qualifying as scientifically based are those that incorporate explicit and systematic instruction in phonemic awareness, phonics, fluency, vocabulary, and comprehension. Two such highly scripted and very profitable curriculum programs are Open Court and Success for All (SFA).

Profits and the Scripted Curriculum

The Reading First initiative provides an enormous amount of taxpayer dollars to states in the form of grants. States then dispense the money to individual school districts in the form of subgrants. For example, Oklahoma received a multi-year Reading First grant in 2003 that provided $12.5 million to schools implementing scientifically based reading programs (The National Right to Read Foundation, 2003) in its first year. Over the next six years, Oklahoma will receive a total of $82 million to further implement these programs. Taking into account that 49 other states will also receive federal funds to implement scientifically based reading programs, it stands to reason that the companies publishing these programs will make a resounding profit. In the third quarter of 2003, SRA/McGraw-Hill, which publishes Open Court, one of the most frequently used scripted reading programs, posted an increased net income of $14.1 million (5.1 percent) over the same period in the previous year (McGraw-Hill Newswire, 2003). Success for All (SFA), another highly scripted reading curriculum, published by a nonprofit foundation, has flourished into a $45 million-a-year business (Mathews, 2000).

Scripted curriculum materials are a costly solution for school districts that are having difficulty raising their students' academic achievement.

Socioeconomics and the Scripted Curriculum

Students in high poverty areas have a much higher likelihood of being taught in schools using a scripted curriculum than those living in more affluent school districts. Schools in which more than 50 percent of all students are on free or reduced-price lunches qualify for Title I funds from the federal government. Currently, Title I regulations specify that "all participating schools must use program funds to implement a comprehensive school reform program that employs proven methods and strategies based on scientifically based research" (Comprehensive School Reform Program, n.d., p. 2). In essence, these regulations prescribe the use of scripted curriculum materials because these are the only ones that qualify as being scientifically based. Schools that do not receive Title I funds (i.e., those located, in general, in more affluent areas) are free to spend their district's funds on the curriculum of their choice.

The Scripted Curriculum

As noted, two of the most widely used scripted reading curriculum programs are Open Court and Success for All. Both deliver explicit, systematic instruction by way of a script the teacher is required to follow in the areas of phonemic awareness, phonics, fluency, vocabulary, and comprehension. Open Court and SFA share certain characteristics. Both publishers advocate grouping students by reading level during the reading portion of the

lesson. Both programs are available in English as well as Spanish and are available for a wide range of age and grade levels. Open Court is available for students ranging from Pre-K to 6th grade and SFA is available for students ranging from Pre-K to 8th grade.

Depending on the teacher's familiarity with either the Open Court or SFA material and the students' abilities, up to three hours of class time every day may be needed to cover the lesson script, thus leading to a significant narrowing of the curriculum. In a survey conducted in the fall of 2003 by the Council for Basic Education, principals reported that their schools currently spent 37 percent less time teaching civics and 35 percent less time teaching geography than they had previously (Perkins-Cough, 2004). Other principals surveyed for this study reported that their schools spent 29 percent less time teaching languages and 36 percent less time teaching the arts than they had in the past (Perkins-Cough, 2004). Given that many schools have already curtailed children's exposure to geography, civics, languages, and art, one must question if these subjects would be completely eliminated following the implementation of a scripted curriculum.

The diverse ethnic and cultural makeup of today's classrooms makes it unlikely that one single curriculum will meet the needs and interests of all students.

Reading Achievement and the Scripted Curriculum
Positive Research Findings

One study in an urban Title I school (no geographic information was given) compared the word recognition, reading comprehension, vocabulary growth, and spelling achievement of three groups of 1st- and 2nd-grade students. They were taught using one of three methods: Open Court, the district's standard curriculum, and less direct instruction embedded in a connected text (Foorman, Fletcher, Francis, Schatschneider, & Mehta, 1998). The latter approach emphasized the teacher-as-facilitator, children's active construction of meaning using learning centers, and portfolio assessment. Achievement test scores at the end of the year indicated that the children who had used Open Court approached the national average in their decoding skills (43rd percentile) and passage comprehension (45th percentile). The group using the district's standard curriculum scored in the 27th percentile for decoding skills and the 33rd percentile for passage comprehension. The group using less direct instruction embedded in the text scored in the 29th percentile for word decoding and the 35th percentile for passage comprehension. Spelling skills were not significantly different for any of the groups.

On first impression, it appears that the performance of students taught using Open Court clearly exceeded that of students taught using different methods. However, even though the

285 students in this study were randomly grouped by age, gender, and ethnicity, no mention is made of the students' ability levels prior to their assignment to a group. Without knowing the ability levels of the participants and ensuring that they were evenly distributed among all three groups, it would be difficult to attribute performance increases to a particular instructional method.

In a study conducted in Memphis, Tennessee, students from eight SFA schools were matched with students in statistically similar non-SFA schools. After two years of SFA instruction, the students in the SFA schools performed significantly better than their comparison groups on measurements of reading, language, science, and social studies (Slavin & Madden, 2001). In Baltimore, where SFA actually began, a longitudinal study conducted from 1987–93 comparing Comprehensive Test of Basic Skills (CTBS) scores of students in the five original SFA schools to students in five control schools indicated that SFA students' scores exceeded those of students in the control group at each grade level (Slavin & Madden, 2001).

It must be noted that subsequent researchers disagreed with these findings. Pogrow (2002) notes that only students who had been in the same school for five years were included in this study and that almost no special education students were included. In other words, the group of students that reflected the greatest gain from SFA was not representative of the population as a whole. He further notes that when the same data were reevaluated, this time including all students who were assessed, students' reading levels ranked, on average, three years below grade level by the time they got to 6th grade. SFA has since been dropped by the Baltimore city school district.

Negative Research Findings

A study of 2nd- through 5th-grade students in California comparing the Stanford Achievement Test, Ninth Edition (SAT 9) scores of children in urban schools using Open Court to students in comparable schools using non-scripted materials found no evidence that Open Court fosters higher reading achievement (Moustafa & Land, 2002). In an all-grade comparison study of SAT 9 scores, 28 percent of the students in non-scripted programs were in the bottom quartile, compared to 57 percent of the students using Open Court. The researchers found that 72 percent of the students from non-scripted programs scored above the bottom quartile, compared to only 43 percent of the students taught using Open Court.

A study comparing the standardized test scores of Title I elementary school students using SFA to the scores of students in comparable Title I schools using a different reading program found that, over a three-year period, students in non-SFA schools experienced an average gain of 17 percent in the reading proficiency section, compared to an average gain of 8.5 percent in the reading proficiency of students in schools using the SFA reading curriculum (Greenlee & Bruner, 2001).

English Language Learners

Both Open Court and SRA offer program adaptations in Spanish that may be used in Spanish-only, Spanish-English, and English-only classrooms. Literature compiled by Open Court states that the English scores of 2nd-grade students rose in all but four of Sacramento's 60 elementary schools in 1998 (Open Court, 2002). Slavin and Madden (2001), the founders of SFA, cite studies in California and Arizona in which English language learners using SFA scored higher on English reading measures than did comparable students who were using a different curriculum. In contrast, a three-year study of Miami-Dade County schools in Florida found that English language learners who attended SFA schools actually made smaller gains in English language proficiency than did comparable students at schools not using SFA (Pogrow, 2002).

Concerns

As scripted curriculum materials become more and more commonplace, certain concerns must be addressed. The diverse ethnic and cultural makeup of today's classrooms makes it unlikely that one single curriculum will meet the needs and interests of all students. Curriculum must be flexible so that teachers are able to construct lessons that will be of high interest to their unique group of students, and actively engage them in creating knowledge. Reading aloud scripted lessons that have been created for a generic group is unlikely to accomplish this goal.

Another concern is whether scripted curriculum challenges gifted learners as well as supports those who are struggling. A typical classroom consists of students with a wide spectrum of learning strengths and needs. Classroom teachers are in the best position to identify individual strengths and needs and adjust a curriculum to address them. Again, reading aloud scripted lessons that have been created for a generic group is unlikely to accomplish this goal.

What about the long-term success of students who are read aloud scripted lessons? If the focus of curriculum is on test-driven instruction and rote memorization, will critical-thinking skills and comprehension be overlooked? Students learn when curriculum is relevant to their lives, when it is of personal interest to them, and when they are actively engaged in the pursuit of knowledge.

What about time? If it takes between two to three hours to deliver a script, will science, social studies, art, music, and physical education be eliminated? All of these subject areas contribute to children's overall learning, and their elimination would result in a watered-down educational experience.

What about the teacher? Will teachers be willing to spend their days reading from a script, rather than planning and facilitating lessons that further their students' construction of knowledge? Perhaps teachers with the most experience and education would transfer to school districts that do not use a scripted curriculum, leaving the least experienced teachers to read the script to students with the greatest needs.

These concerns must be addressed in order to determine whether or not the use of a scripted curriculum is truly a prescription for success or a one-size-fits-all approach that does not reflect sound pedagogical practice.

References

Coles, G. (2002). Learning to read scientifically. *Rethinking Schools Online.* Retrieved February 2, 2005, from www. rethinkingschools.org/special_reports/bushplan/Read154.shtml

Comprehensive School Reform Program. (n.d.) Guide to U.S. Department of Education Programs. Retrieved April 3, 2005, http://wdcrobcolp01.ed.gov/CFAPPS/GTEP_PUBLIC/index

Dudley-Marling, C., & Murphy, S. (2001). Changing the way we think about language arts. *Language Arts, 78*(6), 574–578.

Foorman, B. R., Fletcher, J. M., Francis, D. J., Schatschneider, C., & Mehta, P. (1998). The role of instruction in learning to read: Preventing reading failure in at-risk children. *Journal of Educational Psychology, 90*(1), 37–55.

Greenlee, B. J. & Bruner, D. Y. (2001). Effects of Success for All reading programs on reading achievement in Title I schools. *Education, 122*(1), 177–188.

Mathews, J. (2000, January). Prepackaged school reform. *The School Administrator.* Retrieved April 2, 2005, from www.aasa.org/publications/sa/2000_/mathews.htm

McGraw-Hill Companies. (2003, October). *Investors: News releases.* Retrieved April 2, 2005, from http://investor.mcgraw-hill.com

Metcalf, R. (2002, January). Reading between the lines. *The Nation.* Retrieved April 2, 2005, from www.thenation.com/docprint. mhtml?i=20020128&s=metcalf

Moustafa, M., & Land, R. E. (2002). The reading achievement of economically disadvantaged children in urban schools using Open Court vs. comparably disadvantaged children using non-scripted reading programs. 2002 Yearbook of the *Urban Learning, Teaching, and Research Special Interest Group of the American Educational Research Association,* 44–53.

National Right to Read Foundation, The. (2003, February). Paige announces $12.5 million Reading First grant for Oklahoma children. Retrieved February 6, 2005, from www.nrrf.org/pr_OK-RF_2-6-03.htm

Open Court. (2002). *Programs & Practices.* Retrieved on April 3, 2005, from www.sra4kids.com

Perkins-Gough, D. (2004). The eroding curriculum. *Educational Leadership, 62*(1), 84–85.

Pogrow, S. (2002, February). Success for All is a failure. *Phi Delta Kappan, 83*(6), 463–468.

Posnick-Goodwin, (2002). Scripted learning: A slap in the face? *California Educator, 6*(7), 6–16.

Slavin, R. E., & Madden, N. (2001). Research on achievement outcomes of Success for All. *Phi Delta Kappan, 82*(1), 38–66.

ANITA EDE is a doctoral student, College of Education, Oklahoma State University, Stillwater.

From *Childhood Education,* Fall 2006. Copyright © 2006 by the Association for Childhood Education International. Reprinted by permission of Anita Ede and the Association for Childhood Education International, 17904 Georgia Avenue, Suite 215, Olney, MD 20832.

Rethinking Early Childhood Practices

Francis Wardle, PhD

All professions have a canon of beliefs and practices. Some of these come from research and best practices; many simply develop and are passed on without critical examination. The early childhood field is no exception. Not only should any "self-renewing" profession continually re-examine itself on a regular basis, but, in this period of postmodern thought, we have the opportunity to carefully evaluate many beliefs that our profession accepts as the truth.

Critical theory is one way to examine our common beliefs and practices. Critical theory is, "an umbrella term for a range of perspectives . . . (that) all assume knowledge is socially constructed . . . From a critical theory perceptive, therefore, no universal truths or set of laws or principals can be applied to everyone." (Ryan & Glieshaber, 2004, p. 45) However, this article does not suggest we simply deconstruct our profession from one specific point of view for several reasons. First, a critical theory critique presupposes our current early childhood practices come from some kind of logic and order—one of power and oppression. Secondly, the power orientation creates straw arguments: in early childhood education an attack on developmentally appropriate practice (DAP) (Hatch, Bowman, Jortlan, Morgan, Hart, Soto, Lubeck & Hyson, 2002; Lubeck, 1998.). As you will see in this article, many early childhood practices should be more DAP, not less (particularly because, in spite of the view of many critics, most of our early childhood programs are not DAP) (Dunn & Kontos, 1997). Finally, when I teach my qualitative methods graduate classes I strongly advise students against threats to theoretical validity—the temptation to force or morph all data into an existing and popular theoretical orientation (Burke, 1997). It's not hard to make 'the data fit'.

The question, of course, is where have our practices come from? Critical theorists say from research on white, middle class students, and from dead white men (Ryan & Grieshaber, 2004). I believe they have largely developed as a downward extension of school practices (Wardle, 2003). It seems to me, historically, that our approach to everything regarding young children—building design, playgrounds, health/safety, bus safety, scheduling, curriculum, etc., can be characterized as a reaction against the traditional home, farm and village upbringing, and a belief that school is better and early school is even better (Johnson, Christie & Wardle, 2005).

Same-Age Grouping

Part of the history of U.S. public schools is the one-room schoolhouse, which was characterized by vertical grouping of children, with older children assisting younger ones as they themselves learned about service and caring for others. But in 1843 Horace Mann returned from visiting the Prussian military, and decided the regimented, same-age grouping would be an improvement (Wiles & Bondi, 1998).

While same-age grouping has dominated K–12 schools, it is slowly becoming the norm in most early childhood programs. Many Head Start programs, for example, have children grouped by "older 4s" and "younger 4s". The pedagogical rationale for this approach is to target curricula content and instruction to specific age groups. However, the arguments against same-age grouping of children in early childhood programs are overwhelming:

The tremendous diversity within age groups, due to gender; race/ethnicity social-economic status, experience, and exceptionality (special needs and gifted) make curriculum targeting well neigh impossible.

The reduced size of most US families (Berger, 2005) requires that children have multiage experiences in their early childhood programs.

Vygotsky argues learning takes place when an 'expert' assists the learner to learn within his zone of proximal development; and the best expert is often a child who is slightly more advanced than the learner (Berk & Winsler, 1995).

Piaget argues that one of the best ways for a child to learn is when a child is 'forced' to expand his existing schemas to match overwhelming evidence from the environment. One of the best ways to expose a child to this evidence is by interacting with a child who is one level higher than the learner (Brainerd, 1978).

It would seem that, along with language, race/ethnicity and income, age differences are forms of diversity we should expose our children to.

Character education curricula in early childhood programs stress a sense of caring and responsibility (Wardle, 2004). One of the best ways to develop these values is to have children practice helping, caring for, and protecting younger, more vulnerable children. The result may be fewer issues with bullying and harassment in the later school years.

The Importance of a Daily Schedule

A regular, daily schedule teaches children a needed sense of security, especially children from low-income and minority homes. Almost all early childhood textbooks and research articulate this belief. For example, "Daily routines form the framework for a young child's day; some children depend on them for a sense of security. . . . But no matter what type of schedule the early childhood program follows, there are certain routines that should occur daily" (Gonzalez-Mena, 2001, p. 262). And, according to Gordon & Browne, (2004), "Children are more secure in a place that has a consistent schedule; they can begin to anticipate the regularity of what comes next and count on it" (p. 367) "Routines are the framework of programs for young children. A routine is a constant; each day certain events are repeated, providing continuity and a sense of order. Routines are reassuring to children, and they take pride in mastering them" (Gordon & Browne, 2004, p. 366).

The argument for this canon goes something like this: "Children need regular routines to enable them to develop a sense of security in a predictable environment". And, of course, the more "unstructured" their home life, the more they need structure and routine in a program. Argument against this fixation on routine include:

Research has shown time and again that the most important form of security for young children is a consistent, warm, responsive, long-term relationship with a caregiver (Bowlby, 1969; Honig, 2002; Lally, 1998). Yet there is an embarrassing dearth of suggestions in the literature about ways to achieve this important relationship, which requires providing caregivers with adequate salaries, benefits, and working conditions. Is our fixation on schedules and routines due to the inability to provide consistent and long-term care with one provider?

Children have no sense of time as adults' know it. Certainly the sequence of activities provides important mental scripts that children use in cognitive and language development (Berger, 2005). Many argue that one reason for schedules is to teach children about time, and the behaviors needed to function in an adult world fixated on schedules. Members of one of my early childhood classes argued vehemently that children who don't follow a strict timetable would not be able to function effectively in the adult world. After I pointed out that each of them were late for class, they dropped the argument!

Children from less structured, more chaotic environments desperately need time to fully complete important projects they are personally and socially invested in, without being interrupted by a more powerful adult. Research suggests that children who lack a sense of control over their learning eventually reduce commitment to on-task behavior (Johnson, Christie & Wardle, 2005). Thus it would seem to me that all children, but particularly children from unstructured environments, need programs that encourage them to pursue projects and interactions until they decide they are finished.

The new brain research has reinforced the need for stimulation, change, challenge, involvement, and meaningful learning (Shore, 1997), which is often much easier to achieve with a less

structured schedule, and more difficult to achieve with more structure. Structure begets bored children, frustrated teachers, and stressful transitions.

Learning is continuous. Young children learn in continuous ways, relating new learning to past experiences and accomplishments. Children learn best when a project, idea, or activity veers off into new and different directions, "emerging" into new and exciting learning (Dewey, 1938).

The American workplace is less and less structured by traditional routines, and more often organized by projects, flextime, team activities, and self-directed problem solving. Early childhood programs need to develop workers who can structure their own time, and who do not feel confused when work demands require varied and flexible schedules.

Meals Must be Provided at Regular Intervals

One of the areas where early childhood programs insist on a schedule is eating. While this is often dictated by the reality of the kitchen schedule, catering service, and use of the cafeteria, we also seem to deeply believe that children should be fed "on schedule". However, it is fairly well established that infants should be fed, "on demand".

Most of us will stop off at a store to pick up a snack when we get hungry, and go to the refrigerator when we cannot last till the next full meal. Why not allow children to do the same? Does our meal schedule—and the accompanying need for children to clean off their plate before they get desert—contribute to our child obesity problem? After all, if a child thinks they won't get food until a specific time (or maybe, if they won't get it till very late at home), they might "stuff themselves" so they won't get hungry. Providing healthy snacks in a refrigerator in the classroom for children to eat when they are hungry might be a good idea.

Sleep-Time Should be Scheduled

The biggest struggle my wife and I had with our children's child care was naptime. We insisted our children not have a nap because when they did they would not get tired until 11 at night. At the opposite end of the spectrum, some teachers complain that parents keep their children up so late that they fall asleep before naptime. Maybe early childhood programs should provide a quiet area away from the noise and activity of the classroom, where children can lie down when they get tired.

A Curriculum Is at the Center of All Good Educational Programs

According to Diane Trister Dodge and Toni Bickart (2003), "Curriculum and assessment drive our work with young children every day. If we do them well we achieve positive outcomes for children. Good input means good output" (p. 28). The No Child Left Behind Act and the Head Start outcomes have refueled this belief in the veracity of a curriculum. A curriculum is, "a plan for learning" (Wiles & Bondi, 1998), and most are driven by specific outcomes—those that some expert has decided are needed to reach the next rung on the educational ladder (usually developmentally inappropriate kindergarten entry-level skills). Several questions, however, must be asked:

Does, in fact, input result in output? Is the educational model so simple, mechanical, linear, and businesslike? Doesn't this kind of model deny any sense of inner direction, child-center learning, and spirituality and soul? (Steiner, 1926).

Does following the prescribed rungs of the ladder develop the kind of people we want? There are many examples of famous people who did not follow these rungs: Einstein, Erikson, Bill Gates, home-schooled students, and the very successful graduates of the free schools in the 1960s and 1970s. A mother told me a story of her daughter who dropped out of high school. When she finally decided to go to college she negotiated with the college to take the first two semesters on a trial basis—without ever getting a high school diploma or GED. Not only did she pass with flying colors, she is now a pediatrician!

Who develops the plan, and how do they know what is best for our children? John Dewey (1938) talked a lot about basing curricula of children's own experiences, interests, and aspirations.

Why do we not trust children and teachers to collaborate with parents to develop their own curriculae? This reliance on a curriculum is a strong indictment against the professionalism of teachers; it's also obviously a deep belief that children will not learn what is needed without a curriculum-by-numbers approach.

What happens if the plan is wrong? More specifically, what happens if the plan misses important outcomes, such as teaching a second language beginning in preschool, focusing extensively on the epidemic of childhood obesity, spending more time and energy on emotional, and social development and conflict resolution, and integrating effective diversity education? Are we developing a bunch of fat, asocial citizens who cannot relate to others, who are intolerant of differences, and who cannot compete in the global marketplace because they only speak English, but who can read, write, and work on a computer at home?

Minority Students Are Unsuccessful Due to a Eurocentric Approach to Education

Multiculturalists insist that the failure of minority children in our educational programs is because these programs are Eurocentric—developed to work only for the white children. Early childhood multiculturalists have fully embraced this cannon (Ramsey, 1998; York, 2003). Clearly, there is a tragic achievement gap between white and Asian students on the one hand, and Native American, Black and Hispanic students on the other hand. But is this gap due solely to an Eurocentric approach?

Asian children as a group, who are clearly a minority, not only do as well as white children, but in some cases do better (Thernstrom & Thernstrom, 2003).

Picture young Mayan children in their ragged clothes and bare feet writing on small slate tablets with stubs of chalk in a 'school'—a four-post structure with a laminar (corrugated iron) roof. These little children learned their lesson enthusiastically. The fact the building was primitive and lacked resources, the instructor white, and the material Eurocentric, did not bother them. They were motivated to learn because their parents were learning with them, and because they were starved for basic literacy instruction.

We must admit that, while we have children in this country from a variety of cultural backgrounds, all of them are American—especially African American, Native American, and Hispanic families that have been here for generations. As such, these children and their families generally subscribe to the American values of competition, individualism, legal justice, materialism, gender differences, the value of education, and religious freedom.

The fact a disproportionate number of minorities are placed in special education is, I believe, more of a function of the U.S. deficit approach to disabilities (IDEA), than a Eurocentric idea. After all, far fewer students in Europe are diagnosed with special needs than the U.S., and more boys, including white boys (the ultimate symbol of white privilege) are in special education (Berger, 2005).

The strongest statistical correlation with school success is income (Hout, 2002). The problem is that minority families are statistically more represented in the low-income category. Schools in low-income areas tend to have fewer resources, less experienced teachers, and more discipline problems (Hout, 2002)

School success is largely dependent on family support of education. I have proposed what I call a three-legged-stool model of school success: home, school and community. Each leg must provide the optimal stimulation, support, structure and expectations needed. The seat connects all 3 legs together, in a unified manner, much like Bronfenbrenner's mesosystem (1979). Without the seat the stool falls; without open, supportive two-way communication between home, school and community, the minority child will not succeed.

Is a Eurocentric approach really bad for our minority children? Many claim that because DAP is Eurocentric it is detrimental to minority children (Lubeck, 1998; Ramsey 1998; York, 2003). But a DAP approach calls for adjusting the curriculum to meet individual needs, working closely with families and the community, responding to "the whole child", and considering cultural and linguistic diversity (Bredekamp & Copple, 1997). How is this bad? As our population becomes more and more diverse we need a more DAP approach, and a less standards-based approach (Wardle & Cruz-Janzen, 2004).

Further, our very approach to special needs, linguistic diversity, and the right of each individual child to succeed in our schools is based on this country's Eurocentric belief in individual rights, educational opportunity, and legal justice. The academic divide is a tragedy in a society that depends heavily on its schools to provide equal opportunity. We must solve this dilemma. To do so, we must challenge our orthodoxies about the causes of the problem.

The Calendar Activity

In 1996 I was asked by Partners of the Americas to build a play ground for a low income crèche in Brazil (Wardle, 1999). While I was checking out the site I toured the dingy classrooms. There were no books, building blocks, or paints. There was no house-keeping area or place for the children to nap, and the kitchen was very poorly equipped. But they did have a calendar proudly affixed to the wall (with names and numbers in Portuguese, of course). Recently in a graduate psychology class I discussed with my students that, according to Piaget, preoperational children cannot possibly do the calendar activity in a meaningful way (Wardle, 2001). Then a kindergarten teacher asked me the obvious question: why do we teach this activity? And it seems like we teach it all over the world!

I have already discussed that children's ideas of time are based on activity—what we do—not the passage of time. Further, in today's world it's extremely easy to know the date by checking a watch, computer or newspaper. Important concepts of such as past, present and future, sequence, repetition, can all be taught in much more effective ways.

Universal ECE Standards Will Improve the Image of Our Profession

Clearly our profession is not well regarded by much of the public: Many see us as "just babysitters"; the teaching profession still perpetuates the notion that school starts at kindergarten. I recently met a Head Start education manager who believes the new outcomes are very positive, "because now we are not just babysitters". And many colleges prefer to graduate teachers with an elementary education degree with a few ECE classes tacked on, rather than a full ECE degree (Silva & Johnson, 1999). Others deeply believe if it's something that any parent can do, then it can't be that difficult.

When the public's view of the counseling profession plummeted after the 'free love' approach of many therapists during the sixties, counseling organizations quickly established professional codes of ethics and developed training standards for their field. The early childhood profession is doing the same thing, creating codes of ethics (NAEYC, 1989, 1992, 1998), codifying a ladder of professional development, and professing the value of standards. Head Start now requires college degrees for teachers; the No Child Left Behind act requires degrees for public school paraprofessionals.

But this will not increase the status of the early childhood profession. First, professionals must be paid like professionals and get the kind of benefits professionals deserve. In France ECE teachers are paid the same as regular teachers, have the same professional requirements, are paid the same benefits, and have the same number of paid in-service and further education classes each year (and, of course, paid substitutes) (Hurless, 2004). Secondly, in my mind one of the things that perpetuate the public's low view of our profession is a total lack of ethical behavior. And I'm not talking about teachers. From my personal experience in Head Start, corporate child care, and early child-

hood leadership groups, I have come to realize that members at the top of our profession do not follow the ethical standards that we ask of our teachers.

And, as we are discovering with K-12 standards, the negatives of standards for the early childhood field far outweighs any positives. These include:

Children who cannot achieve the standards are viewed as failures or placed in special education.

All the schools resources—space, energy, professional support, money—are focused 100 percent toward the standards. Everything else is secondary: special education, emotional/mental health, school climate, diversity, anti-obesity efforts, working with parents, etc.

The standards are not DAP. A central component of DAP is individual differences (Bredekamp & Copple, 1997). Declaring that every child should be reading at a third grade level denies this individual difference.

The entire concept of standard implies lack of a standard. While we are trying to change the stigma of children with special needs, we are creating a stigma that children who cannot meet a standard are somewhat abnormal. In some states, for example, special education students are still required to take each of the standardized tests.

There are many instances where important learning activities are being withheld from children because they have performed poorly on a standardized test. This includes withholding recess, physical education, computers, and extra classes such as music and art. These activities are the very thing these children desperately need; yet they are being withheld to improve their scores in literacy, math, and science.

Since we teach to the standards and their tests, an area that is not tested is simply unimportant. Thus art, music, dance, social development, emotional development, character education, conflict resolution, and physical education are shortchanged.

Conclusion

All professions develop a canon of beliefs and practices that are passed from generation to generation. Unfortunately, if these canons are not carefully examined, we can end up perpetuating harmful practices in the name of professional behavior. This article highlighted areas important for careful examination, and most importantly areas where a change of approach might be beneficial to the children in early childhood programs.

References

Berger, K. (2005). *The developing person. Through the lifespan.* (6th ed.). New York, NY: Worth Publisher.

Berk, L.E. & Winsler, A. (1995). *Scaffolding children's learning: Vygotsky and early childhood education.* Washington, DC: NAEYC.

Bowlby, J. (1969). Attachment. *Vol.1 of attachment and loss.* New York: Basic Books.

Brainerd, C.J. (1978). *Piaget's theory of Intelligence.* Englewood Cliffs, NJ: Prentice-Hall.

Bredekamp, S., & Copple, C. (1997). *Developmentally appropriate practice* (rev. ed.). Washington, DC: NAEYC.

Bronfenbrenner, U. (1979). *The ecology of human development.* Cambridge, MA: Harvard University Press.

Burke, J. R. (1997). Examining the validity structure of qualitative research. *Education,* 118 (2), 282–293.

Dodge, D.T., & Bickart, T. (2003). Curriculum, assessment, and outcomes. Putting them all in perceptive. *Children and Families,* XVII (1), 28–31.

Dewey, J. (1938). *Education and experience.* New York, NY: McMillan.

Dunn, L., & Kontos, S. (1997). Research in review: What we have learned about developmentally appropriate practice. *Young Children,* 52(4), 4–13

Gonzalez-Mena, J. (2001). Foundations. *Early Childhood education in a diverse society.* (2nd ed.) Mountain View, CA: Mayfield.

Gordon, A.M. & Browne, K.W (2004). *Foundations in early childhood education.* (6th ed.) Clifton Park, NJ: Delmar Learning.

Hatch, A. Bowman, B., Jor'dna, J., Morgan, Hart, C., Soto, J, Lubeck, S., and Hyson, M. (2002). Developmentally appropriate practice: Continuing the dialogue. *Contemporary Issues in Early Childhood,* 3, 439–57.

Honig, A.S. (2002). The power of positive attachment. *Scholastics Early Childhood Today.* (April), 32–34.

Hout, M. (2002). Test scores, education, and poverty. In J.M. Fish (Ed.) *Race and Intelligence: Separating Science from Myth* (329–354). Mahwah, NJ: Lawrence Erlbaum Associates.

Hurless, B.R. (Sept, 2004). Early childhood education in France. A personal perspective. *Beyond the Journal: Young Children on the Web.* Retrieved, Oct, 2004.

Johnson, J., Christie, J., & Wardle, F. (2005). *Play, development, and early education.* Boston, MA: Allyn and Bacon.

Lally, J.R. (1998). Brain research, infant learning and child care curriculum. *Child Care Information Exchange* (May/June), 46–48.

Lubeck, S. (1998). Is developmentally appropriate practice for everyone? *Childhood Education,* 74 (5) 283–92.

National Association for the Education of Young Children (1989, 1992, 1998). *Code of ethical conduct and statement of commitment: Guidelines for responsible behavior in early childhood education.* (Rev. ed.). Brochure. Washington, DC: Author.

Ramsey, PG. (1998). *Teaching and learning in a diverse world: Multicultural education for young children.* (2nd ed). New York, NY: Teachers College Press.

Ryan, S., & Grieshaber, S. (2004). It's more than child development: Critical theories, research, and teaching young children. *Young Children,* 59 (6), 44–52.

Shore, R. (1997). *Rethinking the brain. New insights into early development.* New York, NY: Families and Work institute.

Silva, D.Y., & Johnson, J.E. (1999). Principals' preference for the N-3 certificate. *Pennsylvania Educational Leadership,* 18 (2), 71–81.

Steiner, R. (1926). *The essentials of education.* London: Anthroposophical Publishing Co.

Thernstrom, A., & Thernstrom, S. (2003). *No excuses: Closing the racial gap in learning.* New York, NY: Simon and Schuster.

Wardle, F. (1999). The story of a playground. *Child Care Information Exchange,* 128 (July/Aug), 28–30.

Wardle, F. (2001). Developmentally appropriate math: How children learn. *Children and Families. XVII* (2), 14–15.

Wardle, F. (2003). Introduction to early childhood education: A multidimensional approach to child-centered care and learning. Boston, MA: Allyn and Bacon.

Wardle, F. (2004). Character education: Seeing a bigger picture. *Child Care Information Exchange.* 160 (Nov/Dec.) 41–43.

Wardle, F., & Cruz-Janzen, M. I. (2004), *Meeting the needs of multiethnic and multiracial children in schools.* Boston, MA: Allyn and Bacon.

Wiles, J. & Bondi, J. (1998). *Curriculum development: A guide to practice* (5th ed.) Upper Saddle River, NJ: Merrill.

York, S. (2003). *Roots and Wings: Affirming culture in early childhood programs* (Rev. ed). St. Paul, MN: Redleaf Press.

FRANCIS WARDLE, PHD, teaches for the University of Phoenix (Colorado) and is the executive director for the Center for the Study of Biracial Children. He has just published the book with Marta Cruz Jansen, *Meeting the Needs of Multiethnic and Multiracial Children,* available from Allyn & Bacon, www.ablongman.com.

From *Earlychildhood NEWS,* January/February 2005. Copyright © 2005 by Excelligence Learning Corporation. Reprinted by permission.

One District's Study on the Propriety of Transition-Grade Classrooms

Vera Estok

The end of the school year brought the usual cheers from the children, a flurry of exchanging phone numbers, and promises to keep in touch. As a pre-first teacher, I too cheered, traded phone numbers, and promised to keep in touch with my colleagues.

> **Our task . . . was to review the district's pre-first classrooms, in which kindergartners considered developmentally unprepared for first grade attend an extra-year transitional program.**

During the previous six months, my fellow teachers and I had become close partners in reviewing our program's approach to individualized education and the use of sound early childhood practice. We had served on a committee formed by Springfield (Ohio) Local Schools to align our district philosophy with developmentally appropriate practice to meet the individual needs of young children. Our task—now completed—was to review the district's pre-first classrooms, in which kindergartners considered developmentally unprepared for first grade attend an extra-year transitional program.

We began our six-month journey by comparing our practices with those advocated by NAEYC (Bredekamp 1987; Bredekamp & Copple 1997). Many questions arose. Committee members wanted to know what had prompted the district's adoption of pre-first 23 years earlier. They were also interested in what research shows about the academic achievement and self-esteem of children placed in pre-first classrooms. We wondered where professional organizations stand on pre-first programs. Finally, all of us wanted to examine existing alternatives, those that would best align our early childhood classes with current best practices. This article outlines the process followed by our district's teachers and administrators to improve our early childhood program.

History of Pre-first Programs

Pre-first classrooms were first introduced in the United States in the 1940s as reading readiness programs for children who lacked necessary skills for formal reading instruction (Harris 1970). Each pre-first classroom had a low teacher-child ratio, a flexible curriculum, and an interactive environment with learning centers (Horm-Wingerd, Carella, & Warford 1993; Patton & Wortham 1993). In the late 1970s, with pressure mounting for more academic emphasis in kindergarten and first grade and reliance on standardized testing for promotion and placement, interest in pre-first programs was renewed. In response to this emphasis on academics, Springfield Local Schools added a pre-first classroom. The implementation of the new class was featured in *Changing to a Developmentally Appropriate Curriculum—Successfully* (Uphoff 1989).

Today, some school districts still initiate pre-first classes as intervention programs for children who, regardless of chronological age, are considered "unready" or "immature" for placement in a regular first grade. Generally, the purpose of an additional year of instruction is to allow children to mature and develop those skills necessary for success in a regular first grade curriculum (Smith & Shepard 1987). An assumption of pre-first grade placement is that participating children will experience academic success and demonstrate higher levels of achievement than would have been possible if they had gone straight to first grade. Some studies (for example, Bohl 1984) support transitional programs based on a maturational theoretical perspective by considering them a "gift of time."

What the Research Shows

The committee weighed the research information carefully. We realized that transitional placement—a decision that requires an additional year of school life—should not be taken lightly. We turned our attention toward finding research that would support pre-first's success at promoting children's higher academic achievement and greater self-esteem.

Views on Grade Retention

"When individual children do not make expected learning progress, neither grade retention nor social promotion are used; instead, initiatives such as more focused time, individualized instruction, tutoring, or other individual strategies are used to accelerate children's learning."

—*NAEYC*

"Delaying children's entry into school and/or segregating them into extra-year classes actually labels children as failures at the outset of their school experience. These practices are simply subtle forms of retention. Not only is there a preponderance of evidence that there is no academic benefit from retention in its many forms, but there also appear to be threats to the social-emotional development of the child subjected to such practices."

—*NAECS/SDE*

"Students recommended for retention but advanced to the next level end up doing as well as or better academically than non-promoted peers. Children who have been retained demonstrate more social regression, display more behavior problems, suffer stress in connection with being retained, and more frequently leave high school without graduating."

—*NAECS/SDE*

Sources: From NAEYC position statement on developmentally appropriate practice, online pp. 16–17: www.naeyc.org/about/positions/pdf/PSDAP98.PDF and NAECS/SDE position statement on kindergarten entry and placement, online pp. 4 and 10: www.naeyc.org/about/positions/pdf/Psunacc.pdf

Our investigation found the use of transition programs questionable (Shepard & Smith 1989). Gredler (1984) suggests it is counterproductive to wait for children to mature.

Academic Achievement

Three studies offer an extended and in-depth analysis of academic achievement of children in transitional programs. Shepard and Smith (1989); Mantzicopoulos and Morrison (1991); and Ferguson, Jimerson, and Dalton (2001) used recognized testing and screening measures and a host of variables to compare children in transitional classes with peers who had been promoted to first grade. The carefully designed studies show little or no improvement in achievement between children who attended extra-year programs and their peers who moved into first grade. Moreover, when placement in a transitional program did improve/increase academic achievement, the benefits prove to be short-lived. In all three studies the differences between test scores of children in transitional classes and comparison groups diminished and were nonexistent by the end of fourth grade.

Self-esteem

While objective measures of the cognitive functioning of children are highly developed, measuring social and emotional functioning is less exact, lacking comparable reliability and validity. Still, Sandoval and Fitzgerald (1985) and Rihl (1988) document a negative or insignificant difference in the self-concept and emotional development of children assigned to extra-year classrooms.

When placement in a transitional program did improve/increase academic achievement, the benefits were found to be short-lived.

Examination of the research was beginning to sway the committee toward an alternative to the pre-first program that would solidify our early childhood program, but what would that be? We concluded that professional organizations might offer some guidance.

What Professional Organizations Recommend

In 1987, following the release of its position statement on developmentally appropriate practice, NAEYC noted that tracking young children into ability groups is developmentally *inappropriate* practice (Bredekamp 1987). David Elkind, NAEYC past president, calls transitional classes simply "another programmatic strategy for dealing with the mismatch between children and first grade curriculum" (1987, 175). More recently, NAEYC has recommended, "Children who fall behind [should] receive individualized support, such as tutoring, personal instruction, focused time on areas of difficulty, and other strategies to accelerate learning progress" (Bredekamp & Copple 1997, 176).

Now that we knew what was needed to enhance our program, implementing a full-day kindergarten program was the next step.

The National Association of Early Childhood Specialists in State Departments of Education (NAECS/SDE) also finds transitional classes unacceptable. The NAECS/SDE states in a position paper that "all children should be welcomed into regular heterogeneous classroom settings and not be segregated into transitional programs following kindergarten" (1987, 10). In a newer, revised position statement, NAECS/SDE points out, "Reducing class size, making the curriculum less abstract and therefore more related to children's conceptual development, insisting that only the most appropriately trained, competent, child-oriented teachers are placed in kindergarten programs, and assuring every child access to a high-quality prekindergarten program are among better means to achieving the educational goal of success for all students" (2000, 14).

Our committee turned to our own state board of education for more guidance. Following a longitudinal study, the Ohio Department of Education concluded that kindergarten and first grade classrooms need developmentally appropriate programs to address children's diverse needs (Ohio Department of Education 1992). The study offers three ways to accomplish this task: (1) implement a preschool program in public schools, (2) establish Chapter 1 reading services, and (3) expand alternate-day and half-time kindergartens to full-day programs. Of the three suggestions, extension to a full-day kindergarten program is reported to reduce grade retention rates and produce the fewest remedial placements. This was the new direction we had been seeking.

We encourage any district that still has a pre-first in its early childhood program to analyze the appropriateness of such classes and find better ways to educate young children.

Implementing Our Plan

Now that we knew what was needed to enhance our program, implementing a full-day kindergarten program was the next step. As is almost always the case, financing proved to be the most difficult part of the project. Knowing what the addition of full-day kindergarten could mean in the growth of our district, our administrative staff pulled together. They tightened the budget by eliminating the pre-first program and asked the high school and middle school to make as many cuts as they could. State funds already allocated to our district were redirected toward funding the project.

At the final school board meeting of the school year, board members were so impressed with our commitment and dedication to the project that they gave unanimous approval for full-day kindergarten. It would be implemented the next school year.

Will the addition of a full-day kindergarten experience provide added support to the children in our school system? Our committee did its homework well, and we are confident that we are following guidelines to ensure that every child has a successful school experience. We encourage any district that still has a pre-first in its early childhood program to analyze the appropriateness of such classes and find better ways to educate young children.

I am no longer a pre-first teacher but a kindergarten teacher eagerly waiting to join in as children cheer for the new school year.

References

Bohl, N. 1984. A gift of time: The transition year. *Early Years* (January): 14.

Bredekamp, S., ed. 1987. *Developmentally appropriate practice in early childhood programs serving children from birth through age 8.* Exp. ed. Washington, DC: NAEYC.

Bredekamp, S., & C. Copple, eds. 1997. *Developmentally appropriate practice in early childhood programs.* Rev. ed. Washington, DC: NAEYC.

Elkind, D. 1987. *Miseducation: Pre-schoolers at risk.* New York: Knopf.

Ferguson, P., S. Jimerson, & M. Dalton. 2001. Sorting out successful failures: Exploratory analyses of factors associated with academic and behavioral outcomes of retained students. *Psychology in the Schools 38* (4): 327–41.

Gredler, G.R. 1984. Transition classes: A viable alternative for the at-risk child? *Psychology in the Schools* 21: 463–70.

Harris, A.J. 1970. *How to increase reading ability.* 5th ed. New York: David McKay.

Horm-Wingerd, D., P. Carella, & S. Warford. 1993. Teacher's perceptions of the effectiveness of transition classes. *Early Education and Development* 4 (2): 130–38.

Mantzicopoulos, D., & P. Morrison. 1991. Transitional first grade referrals. *Journal of Educational Psychology* 90 (1): 122–33.

NAECS/SDE (National Association of Early Childhood Specialists in State Departments of Education). 1987. Unacceptable trends in kindergarten entry and placement. Position statement. ERIC ED 297 856.

NAECS/SDE. 2000. Still unacceptable trends in kindergarten entry and placement. Position statement. Online: www.naeyc. org/about/positions/pdf/Psunacc.pdf and http://naecs.crc.uiuc. edu/position/trends2000.html

Ohio Department of Education, Division of Early Childhood Education. 1992. *Effects of pre-school attendance and kindergarten schedule: Kindergarten through grade 4. A longitudinal study.* 1992. ERIC ED 400 038.

Patton, M., & S. Wortham. 1993. Transition classes, a growing concern. *Journal of Research in Childhood Education* 8 (1): 32–40.

Rihl, J. 1988. *Pre-first: A year to grow. A follow-up study.* ERIC ED 302 332.

Sandoval, J., & P. Fitzgerald. 1985. A high school follow-up of children who were nonpromoted or attended a junior first grade. *Psychology in the Schools* 22: 164–70.

Shepard, L.A., & M.L. Smith. 1989. Effects of kindergarten retention at the end of the first grade. *Psychology in the Schools* 16 (5): 346–57.

Smith, M.L., & L.A. Shepard. 1987. What doesn't work: Explaining policies of retention in the early grades. *Phi Delta Kappan* 69: 129–34.

Uphoff, J. 1989. *Changing to a developmentally appropriate curriculum—successfully.* Rosemont, NJ: Programs for Education.

VERA ESTOK, ME, is a full-day kindergarten teacher with Springfield Local Schools in Holland, Ohio. Vera taught pre-first classes for six years and has four years of experience in a variety of kindergarten classrooms.

From *Young Children*, March 2005, pp. 1–8. Copyright © 2005 by National Association for the Education of Young Children. Reprinted by permission.

Successful Transition to Kindergarten

The Role of Teachers and Parents

PAM DEYELL-GINGOLD

While new kindergartners are worrying about whether or not anyone will be their friend and if they'll be able to find the bathroom, their preschool teachers are wondering if they've succeeded at preparing their small students for this big transition. In recent years the role of kindergarten has changed from an extension of preschool to a much more academic environment because of new standards in the public schools that "push back" academic skills to earlier grades.

How can we ensure that our students make a smooth transition? Are our students mature enough? What can we do to make them "more" ready? This article will explore the skills that constitute kindergarten "readiness," how preschool teachers can collaborate with parents and kindergarten teachers to make the process more rewarding for all, and activities to help prepare children for what will be expected of them in kindergarten.

The Transition Process

Children go through many transitions throughout their lives, but one of the most important transitions is the one from a preschool program to kindergarten. "During this period behavior is shaped and attitudes are formed that will influence children throughout their education" (PTA and Head Start, 1999). Children's transitions are most strongly influenced by their home environment, the preschool program they attend, and the continuity between preschool and kindergarten (Riedinger, 1997).

In 1995, Head Start and the Parent Teacher Association (PTA) began a plan to create a partnership between the two organizations in order to create effective transition practices and to promote continuity in parent and family involvement in the schools. Three pilot programs were studied to determine "best practice" in kindergarten transition, and to foster the continued strong involvement of families in their children's education. They worked with elementary schools to create parent-friendly environments and to develop strategies that lessen the barriers to involvement (Head Start & PTA, 1999). Even Start, a federal program for low-income families implemented to improve educational opportunities for children and adults, also helps parents to work with the school system to help their children

succeed. Their research found that parents felt that the way in which Even Start focuses on the family strengths rather than weaknesses and allows the families to identify their own needs, empowered them more than anything else to help them to support their children in school (Riedinger, 1997).

Kindergarten Readiness

A 1998 study by the National Center for Early Development & Learning of nearly 3,600 kindergarten teachers nationwide indicated that 48 percent of children have moderate to serious problems transitioning to kindergarten. Teachers are most often concerned about children's skills in following directions, academics, and working independently. There seems to be a discrepancy between the expectations of teachers and the actual skills of kindergarten children. Therefore, a need for kindergarten teachers to collaborate with both parents and preschool teachers exists (Pianta & Cox, 1998). School readiness is more than a matter of academics, though. As reported in a National Education Goals Panel in 1998; "The prevailing view today, however, is that readiness reflects a range of dimensions, such as a child's health and physical development, social and emotional development, approaches to learning, language and communication skills, and cognitive and general knowledge" (California Department of Education, 2000).

Historically, kindergarten was a "children's garden": a place to interact for the first time with a group of agemates, and to learn basic skills through play. Today, because of increasing numbers of working mothers, single-parent families, and strict welfare regulations, many children begin having group experiences in a child care program or family child care home at a much earlier age. Together with the concern that America's children are not getting adequate education to compete in a global market, our schools began to make the transition from the children's garden to "curriculum escalation" (Shepard & Smith, 1988) and "academic trickle-down" (Cunningham, 1988). While the trend towards focusing on academic skills continues at a fast pace, early childhood professionals argue for a more integrated curriculum that addresses the developmental needs of each child.

Social Adjustment

Although academics may be becoming increasingly more important, research shows that social skills are what most affect school adjustment (Ladd & Price, 1987; Ladd, 1990). Preschool teachers should not feel pressured into teaching academics beyond what is developmentally "best practice" (Bredekamp & Copple, 1997) but should continue to focus on social and emotional development. Children who have been rejected by their peers in kindergarten tend to have poor school performance, more absences, and negative attitudes towards school that last throughout their school years. "Three particular social skills that are known to influence children's peer acceptance: play behavior, ability to enter play groups, and communication skills" (Maxwell & Eller, 1994).

Play Behavior and Communication Skills

Specific behaviors that cause rejection by fellow students include things like rough play, arguing, upsetting things in class, trying to get their own way, and not sharing. Children who exhibit these behaviors also tend to be less independent and less cooperative than their peers. Most children prefer playing with others who are polite, caring, and attentive. Preschool teachers and parents need to teach young children social skills, especially how to enter social groups. For example, children who say, "Looks like that's a fun game, can I play?" are more likely to be accepted than those who shove others aside and whine, "I want a turn!"

Another important social skill is the ability to participate in complicated fantasy games and take part in making up and extending the story. Children who lack sufficient experience playing with agemates may feel frustrated at not being able to keep up with the capabilities of their classmates. "A generous amount of guided social experience with peers prior to kindergarten helps children do well in this new world" (Maxwell & Eller, 1994). Some children need assistance to learn how to play make-believe. A teacher can help model this by giving verbal cues like, "You be the mommy, and I'll be your little girl. Can I help you make dinner, Mommy?" Some children need reminders to keep them focused on their roles. Others may need help to read the emotions on people's faces. "Look at Nick's face. He is sad because you pulled the hat away from him." Because young children do not have a large enough vocabulary to express themselves, teachers can help them find words to express their feelings such as, "You're feeling frustrated. Let's go find a puzzle with fewer pieces."

Communication skills, such as being able to take part in a conversation, listen to others, and negotiate are also important. For example, children who speak directly to peers, are attentive to others in the group, and respond to the initiations of others tend to be liked by the other children. Disliked children are more likely to make irrelevant comments, reject the initiations of other children without reasons or explanations, and often make comments without directing them to anyone (Maxwell & Eller, 1994). Part of a teacher's task is to quietly remind children to look at the person they're talking to, and listen to what another child is saying.

Immaturity and Redshirting

A common practice when dealing with children who are not socially mature is to keep them out of school for a year, in the hope that "readiness will emerge." In academic circles this is referred to as "redshirting," a term borrowed from college athletics. However, "Research shows that redshirts are not gaining an academic advantage, and the extra year does not solve the social development problems that caused initial concern" (Graue, 1994). Parents who are told that their children need to stay home for a year should ask for the reasons.

"Developmentally appropriate practice is less common in kindergarten, and primary teachers face many constraints and pressures that teachers of younger children are not yet experiencing in the same intensity [although preschool appears to be next in line for "pushdown" curriculum]." (Jones, Evans, & Rencken, 2001). "If we think inclusively we have to problem-solve in ways to accommodate the incredible diversity presented by the characteristics of kindergartners. . . . Redshirting and retention are outmoded tools that should be replaced by more appropriate practices. One step in the right direction is collaboration between preschool and elementary school educators" (Graue, 1994). A second step is to have parents understand what experiences can help their child have a successful transition.

Learning About Classroom Styles

In collaborating with kindergarten teachers, preschool teachers and parents need to visit the school and pay close attention to details that may affect their students in kindergarten. "When teachers and parents agree on a philosophy of education, children usually adjust more easily" (Maxwell & Eller, 1994). Children feel more secure in their new environment if they feel that their parents support the teacher and the school.

The first step may be either a meeting with the kindergarten teacher or a class field trip to the elementary school. "Observe kindergarten classrooms to identify teaching styles, classroom management techniques, and routines. Also try to identify skills that are needed to be successful in participating in the kindergarten classroom" (Karr-Jelinek, 1994).

In her research, Karr-Jelinek used a checklist of what parents (and teachers) should look for in a kindergarten classroom, to see if their children—both normally developing and with special needs—are ready for the classroom they visit (Karr-Jelinek, 1994):

- How many steps are given at a time in directions?
- What types of words are children expected to understand?
- How does each individual child compare to the other children?
- How long are children expected to sit still in a group?
- How often do children speak out of turn or move around when they should be sitting?
- How much independence is expected?
- What type of work is being done? (small groups, seatwork, etc.)
- Where might my special needs students need extra help?
- What kind of special information can I pass along to the teacher about each child?

Although expectations vary by teacher and school district, by the time children reach kindergarten they should be able to listen to a story in a group, follow two or three oral directions, take turns and share, follow rules, respect the property of others, and work within time and space constraints. They need to learn the difference between work and play, knowing when and where each is appropriate. "Most five-year-olds can express themselves fluently with a variety of words and can understand an even larger variety of words used in conversations and stories" (Nurss, 1987).

Many kindergartens make use of learning centers, small group instruction, and whole group language activities. However, others use "structured, whole group paper-and-pencil activities oriented to academic subjects, such as reading and mathematics. The curriculum in these kindergartens often constitutes a downward extension of the primary grade curriculum and may call for the use of workbooks, which are part of a primary level textbook series. Many early childhood professionals have spoken out on the inappropriateness of such a curriculum" (Nurss, 1987).

Preparing Parents for the Transition

High-quality preschool programs encourage parent involvement in the home and in the classroom. Volunteering to read during story time, to share cultural traditions, or to be a lunch guest are all ways for parents to feel that they are a part of their child's school life. According to the National PTA, parent and family involvement increases student achievement and success. If preschool teachers can make parents feel welcome helping in the classroom, they will be more likely to remain involved in their child's future education.

Many parents worry about their children entering elementary school because of their own negative school experiences. They may feel intimidated by teachers and uncomfortable showing up at school events—even for orientation and enrolling their children in school (Reidinger, 1997). Parents' expectations of how well children will do in school influence children's performance. It appears that parents who expect success may provide more support, encouragement and praise, which may give their children more self-esteem and confidence. The most important thing is that children who believe in their own abilities have been found to be more successful in school (Dweck, 1991).

To assist parents, preschool teachers can arrange visits to the school and take parents along on the kindergarten field trip. They can ask for children to be paired with a kindergarten "buddy" who can take them around, while parents meet with the teacher or go to the office to register their child. A study done by Rathbun and Hauskin (2001) showed that the more low-income students that were enrolled in a school, the less parental involvement there was. Involving low-income families in the schools may help to break the cycle of poverty of future generations.

One way to really help the family with transition is to empower the parents to act as advocates for their children. Par-

Kindergarten Readiness Is . . .

A Child Who Listens
To directions without interrupting
To stories and poems for five or ten minutes without restlessness

A Child Who Hears
Words that rhyme
Words that begin with the same sound or different sounds

A Child Who Sees
Likenesses and differences in pictures and designs
Letters and words that match

A Child Who Understands
The relationship inherent in such words as up and down, top and bottom, little and big
The classifications of words that represent people, places and things

A Child Who Speaks and Can
Stay on the topic in class discussions
Retell a story or poem in correct sequence
Tell a story or relate an experience of her own

A Child Who Thinks and Can
Give the main idea of a story
Give unique ideas and important details
Give reasons for his opinions

A Child Who Adjusts
To changes in routine and to new situations without becoming fearful
To opposition or defeat without crying or sulking
To necessity of asking for help when needed

A Child Who Plays
Cooperatively with other children
And shares, takes turns and assumes his share of group responsibility
And can run, jump, skip, and bounce a ball with comparative dexterity

A Child Who Works
Without being easily distracted
And follows directions
And completes each task
And takes pride in her work

*Adapted from Howlett, M.P. (1970, February 18). Teacher's edition: *My Weekly Reader Surprise*, Vol. 12, Issue 20.

ent meetings and newsletters can help parents learn how to work with school staff, learn about volunteer opportunities at school, as well as how to prepare their child at home for kindergarten. They may need some advice on how to help their children and themselves cope with anxieties related to transitions from preschool to kindergarten.

Preparing Children for Transition

In the last few weeks of summer, children start getting excited about going to kindergarten, and are apprehensive at the same time. It is important for parents to treat the child's entrance into kindergarten as a normal occurrence and not build up the event in children's minds. An important way to provide continuity for the child is to find preschool classmates or other children who will be in their kindergarten class. According to research, children who have a familiar peer in a new group setting have fewer problems adjusting to new environments (Howes, 1988).

Transition Activities for Parents and Children

The more you discuss this transition in a matter-of-fact way, the more comfortable children will become. Encourage parents to prepare their child for kindergarten with the following:

- Visit the school so the children can meet the kindergarten teacher and see what kindergarten is really like. Try to arrange for them to see more than one type of classroom activity, such as seatwork time and free choice time.
- Show them where the bathroom and cubbies are located.
- Find out what lunchtime will be like. If the children are going to be getting a school lunch, they may have to learn how to open new kinds of containers.
- Read books about kindergarten.
- Answer children's questions in a straight forward way about what they will do in kindergarten. Tell them they will listen to stories, do counting activities, have group time, and play outside.
- Explore how long the kindergarten day is and what the daily routine will be like. They will want to know what will be the same as preschool and what will be different.
- If the children are going to a school that presents more diversity than they are familiar with, talk honestly with them about racial and ethnic differences and disabilities.
- If children are going to be taking the schoolbus for the first time, you will need to discuss schoolbus safety rules.
- Reassure children that they will be picked up from school every day just as they are in preschool.
- Check to make sure your pre-kindergarten children are capable of basic kindergarten "readiness" skills. (See sidebar.)

Conclusion

The transition from preschool to kindergarten can be a stressful time for both children and parents. However, if preschool teachers can facilitate collaboration between parents and kindergarten and familiarize children with the workings of kindergarten, it will be a smoother process. Parents need to try to find a developmentally appropriate class for their child by observing different classrooms and talking to teachers about educational philosophies. Preschool teachers, with their knowledge of different learning styles and the temperaments of their students, can help everyone with this important transition.

References

Bredekamp, S. & Copple, C. (1997). *Developmentally appropriate practice for early childhood programs*. Revised edition. Washington, DC: NAEYC.

California Dept of Ed., (2000). *Prekindergarten learning and development guidelines*. Sacramento, CA.

Cunningham, A. 1988. Eeny, meeny, miny, moe: Testing policy and practice in early childhood. Berkeley, CA: National Commission on Testing and Public Policy In Graue, E (2001, May) What's going on in the children's garden today? *Young Children*.

Dweck, C.S. (1991). Self-theories and goals: their role in motivation, personality and development. In *Nebraska symposia on motivation*, Vol. 36, ed. by R. Dienstbier, 199–235, Lincoln: University of Nebraska Press. [In Maxwell, Eller, 1994]

Graue, E. (2001, May) What's going on in the children's garden today? *Young Children*, pp. 67–73.

Howes, C. (1988). Peer interaction of young children. Monographs of the Society for Research in Child Development 53 (2. Serial No. 217). In Maxwell, K. and Eller, C. (1994, September) Children's Transition to Kindergarten, *Young Children*.

Howlett, M.P. (1970, February 18). Teacher's edition: *My Weekly Reader Surprise*, Vol. 12, Issue 20.

Jones, E., Evans, K., & Rencken, K. (2001) *The Lively Kindergarten*, NAEYC publications.

Karr-Jelinek, C. (1994). *Transition to kindergarten: Parents and teachers working together*. Educational Resources Information Center.

Ladd, G.W., 1990. Having friends, keeping friends, making friends and being liked by peers in the classroom: Predictors of children's early school adjustment? *Child Development* (61) 1081–100.

Ladd, G.W., & J.M. Price. 1987. Predicting children's social and school adjustment following the transition from preschool to kindergarten. *Child Development*, (58) 1168–89.

Maxwell, K. & Eller, S. (1994, September). Children's transition to kindergarten. *Young Children*, pp. 56–63.

National PTA & National Head Start Association. (1999). *Continuity for success: Transition planning guide*. National PTA, Chicago, IL. National Head Start Association, Alexandria, VA.

Nurss, J. 1987, *Readiness for Kindergarten*, ERIC Clearinghouse on Elementary and Early Childhood Education, Urbana, IL; BBB16656.

Pianta, R. & Cox, M. (1998). Kindergarten Transitions. Teachers 48% of Children Have Transition Problems. *NCEDL Spotlights Series*, No. 1, National Center for Early Development & Learning: Chapel Hill, NC.

Rathbun, A. & Hauskin, E. (2001). How are transition-to-kindergarten activities associated with parent involvement during kindergarten? Paper presented at the Annual meeting of the American Educational Research Foundation: Seattle, WA.

Riedinger, S. (1997), *Even Start: Facilitating transitions to kindergarten*. Dept. of Education: Washington, DC: Planning and Evaluation Service.

Shepard, I.A. & M.I. Smith. (1988) Escalating academic demand in kindergarten: counterproductive policies. *The Elementary School Journal*, (89) 135–45. In Maxwell, K. and Eller, C. (1994, September) Children's Transition to Kindergarten, *Young Children*.

PAM DEYELL-GINGOLD is a graduate student in Human Development at Pacific Oaks College. She works as master teacher at Head Start, teaches child development classes for Merced Community College, and is a freelance writer and anti-bias curriculum enthusiast. Her home is in the Sierra foothills near Yosemite National Park, California.

From *Earlychildhood NEWS*, May/June 2006, pp. 14–19. Copyright © 2006 by Excelligence Learning Corporation. Reprinted by permission.

Making the Case for Play Policy

Research-Based Reasons to Support Play-Based Environments

DOLORES A. STEGELIN

Play is a child's life and the means by which he comes to understand the world he lives in.

—Susan Isaacs,
Social Development in Young Children

Contemporary early childhood classrooms are complex places where the opportunities for play are few. The need for effective play policy has never been greater. We early childhood professionals know that physically and mentally engaging, play-based activity is essential for overall healthy child development. But these days we often find ourselves defending play-based curriculum and instructional approaches to families, administrators, even colleagues.

This article can help teachers and directors become eloquent and effective advocates of play-based early learning environments. It defines play and play policy and discusses distinct research areas that support play policy and practice for physical, cognitive, social, and emotional development within diverse early childhood settings. Also presented are three anecdotal examples of current challenges to play-based curriculum. I hope the information serves as a useful tool for developing strategies for organizing a play policy effort.

Defining Play and Play Policy

Play research has many important dimensions, and play policy is an untapped and fertile area for research (Stegelin 2002b). An appropriate definition of play is necessary for effective play policy development and implementation. Definitions of play emerge from three perspectives: (1) the exploratory and open-ended nature of play; (2) the intrinsic, evolutionary, and synergistic nature of play; and (3) the developmental aspects of play (Anderson 1998).

The *exploratory nature* of play has been studied extensively (Pellegrini & Perlmutter 1989; O'Neill-Wagner, Bolig, & Price 1994; Bolig et al. 1998) and is captured in this definition:

"Play is an essential part of every child's life and vital to his/her development. It is the way children *explore* the world around them and develop practice skills. It is essential for physical, emotional, and spiritual growth; for intellectual and educational development; and for acquiring social and behavioral skills" (Hampshire Play Policy Forum 2002, 1). Play and exploration behaviors are characteristic behaviors of both young humans and primates and are observable in a variety of contexts that include specific conditions, such as availability of toys and objects for manipulation and freedom from excessive anxiety. Play behaviors are often preceded by exploration, so it is important that the environment encourages exploration.

The *evolutionary and intrinsic* nature of play is reflected in the creative aspect of play that is open-ended, unpredictable, unique, and "comedic" or imbued with "surprise" (Salthe 1991). From the child's perspective, the opportunity to play is an invitation that turns into a "self-fueled, synergistic, inherently rewarding, but not necessarily rewarded process called play" (Anderson 1998, 103). The resulting patterns of play activity lead to a summative experience known as "fun" (Anderson 1998). Thus, a definition of play should include the *intrinsic, evolutionary, synergistic,* and *motivating* aspects of play.

Play behaviors are often preceded by exploration, so it is important that the environment encourages exploration.

The *developmental* aspects of play include the more predictable structures of play associated with children's social, cognitive, language, physical, and creative development from infancy through the primary years. At every stage of development, play activity takes on some degree of predictability but still allows for spontaneous, fluid, repetitive, and turn-taking behaviors. The responsibility of the early childhood professional and the policy advocate is to provide appropriate contexts in which these predictable and developmental behaviors can occur, as delineated in the Hampshire play policy statement (2002) above.

Explaining a Literacy Approach to a Family

Ms. Ruhnquist is a veteran child care director of a large for-profit preschool center that provides comprehensive services for more than 100 children. Ms. Ruhnquist has a master's degree in educational administration and a bachelor's in child development. Well-organized and attentive to detail, she is respected for her understanding of early childhood development, her engaging style of family and staff interactions, and her business skills.

Today, as she enrolls four-year-old Mariah, the parents ask her about the center's approach to "teaching reading." Somewhat surprised, she listens attentively and then asks what their main concern is.

"Well, we want Mariah to know the alphabet and be able to read when she starts kindergarten. We want her to be ahead of the others and ready for higher academic work. Do you use a recognized reading curriculum?"

Ms. Ruhnquist explains that the center uses a nationally recognized early childhood curriculum that focuses on all aspects of a child's development, including language development.

"We use a play-based, child-directed approach that focuses on developing autonomy and self-reliance," she says. "In terms of language development, we have a literacy center, lots of books, and we encourage the exploration of reading and writing in six different learning centers. We focus on storytelling, exploration of different kinds of books and literature, and on phonemic awareness. But we do not teach reading per se. We believe that helping Mariah learn to love books and gain confidence in her own abilities will help her be ready for the early reading experiences in kindergarten. If you'd like to observe the classroom and talk to Mariah's teacher, you're welcome to do so before finalizing her enrollment."

The parents observe the classroom and complete Mariah's enrollment but make it clear they will be watching her progress in prereading skills.

In summary, play policy advocates can use the following essential features to define play:

- Play requires specific *conditions of safety and psychological security* that are essential for the child to engage in relaxed, open-ended, and exploratory behaviors.
- Play includes *exploratory behaviors* that involve manipulation of objects, toys, and other materials, and this exploratory nature of play often precedes actual focused play behavior.
- Play is an important *evolutionary behavior* that is essential for healthy development to occur across all areas: social, cognitive, language, physical, and creative.
- Play is behavior that *sustains the healthy development of the individual* and the larger sociocultural fabric of society and reflects the contexts in which the child lives (home, community, and the larger society).

Defending Learning Centers to the Assistant Principal

Mr. Hemminger, a first-year kindergarten teacher, graduated top of his class with a bachelor's degree in early childhood education. He impresses everyone with his enthusiasm, eagerness to learn about new teaching approaches, and obvious delight in working with five-year-olds.

Mr. Hemminger advocates and models a highly interactive, hands-on approach to learning, and his classroom is known for creative expression, high levels of family involvement, and a learning environment that invites everyone to come in, observe, and participate. The classroom includes five learning centers, small-group cooperative-learning opportunities, and a high level of child-initiated planning and assessment of learning experiences.

Mr. Hemminger is guided by state and local school curriculum guidelines, content expectations, and assessment procedures. He uses many different assessment strategies, including observation, work sampling, portfolios, and periodic testing.

During Mr. Hemminger's first evaluation, the assistant principal asks about his use of center-based learning. "Isn't that for preschool children? There have been some complaints by other teachers about the noise level in this classroom. Is there some way you can tone it down a bit? Shouldn't the children be doing more seat work, silent reading, and worksheets? After all, they'll soon be taking a standardized test."

Mr. Hemminger explains that he has specific learning objectives and outcomes in mind for all daily activities. He points out that research supports active, exploratory learning at the kindergarten level. He is so confident in his center-based approach to teaching that he says he is not concerned about testing outcomes in the spring. "The children are learning *and* they are having fun. I believe that if they are involved in the planning of the day's activities, have a chance to create hypotheses and then explore them, and have daily interactions with their peers, they will learn much more than they would in isolation or in completing seat work."

"Well, we'll see how it goes this year," says the assistant principal. "I'll be noting the noise level and the way your children perform in April."

Linking Play to Play Policy

Many contemporary play policy initiatives have originated in the United Kingdom, while systematic play research has been done in the United States and other parts of the world. Effective play policy is founded on clear articulation of what is meant by play and a commitment to respond to children's needs and wishes (PLAYLINK 2001). But what is a play policy? According to Play Wales (2002), a play policy is a statement of both an organization's current play provision and its aspirations for change and development. Play policy usually includes the following important criteria (PLAYLINK 2001; Play Wales 2002):

- the objectives of play and play-related services and activities;
- the connection between acceptable levels of risk and healthy play;
- an assumption of inclusive play settings for all children (ethnic and developmental diversity);
- the criteria for evaluating a quality play environment;
- the essential and inherent aspect of play as part of a child's cultural life; and
- the need to create and integrate play opportunities in the general environment.

Effective play policy is founded on clear articulation of what is meant by play and a commitment to respond to children's needs and wishes.

Developing and implementing effective play policy takes time, commitment, and perseverance. Effective play policy at the local, state, national, and international levels evolves over time and is the result of many attempts. The primary aim of play policy is to

- articulate and promote the importance of play for all children,
- recognize that all children have the right to play, as stated in the 1989 United Nations Convention on the Rights of the Child, and
- enable all children to have equal access to good quality play environments in their local communities. (Hampshire Play Policy Forum 2002)

Early childhood professionals involved in play policy development can use the above definitions of play and play policy to bolster their play policy rationales and to strengthen their role as advocates. Essential to policy development is the use of research-based information for integrating systematic play into child care, Head Start, preschool, and K–3 settings. Three critical research areas support the rationale for play-based environments.

Research Focus 1: Active Play and Health-related Indicators

The first area of research that addresses the critical need for play-based learning environments—especially physically active and vigorous play—is health related. The rapidly increasing rates of childhood obesity and weight-related health problems are exacerbated by physical inactivity and sedentary routines. Experts point to the prevalence of junk food marketed to children, too much television and other sedentary entertainment,

Using Manipulatives and Other Play-Based Approaches in First Grade

Mrs. Alvarez is an experienced primary teacher in a large public school system. She has twice been named Teacher of the Year at the elementary school and is now working toward a master's degree in elementary education.

Today, during unit meetings, three other first grade teachers want to know why Mrs. Alvarez does not use the rigorous math and science curriculum recommended by the school district. The new curriculum is heavily teacher-directed, uses daily worksheets and drills, and requires standardized testing every nine weeks.

Mrs. Alvarez says, "You know, I really thought about making a change this year. The new textbooks are attractive, and in some ways the curriculum seems easier in terms of planning and teaching. But then I thought about how much my students really look forward to math and science and how well they have done the past several years on the school district's end-of-the-year tests. I decided that even though it takes more time and resources, I really believe in a hands-on approach to learning.

"Besides," she adds, "six-year-olds need time and space to explore, suggest activities, make up their own hypotheses, and feel their ideas really do count. My math and science activities require the children to think, work together, and record their own answers. I like the opportunities for creative thinking, for students to think for themselves and to move around and take charge of their time. For now, I'm going to keep using manipulatives.

"And yes," she says, "I know my classroom is louder and messier than most of yours, but so far the parents agree with my approach. I'm convinced that six-year-olds learn best with interactive, cooperative learning experiences."

and fewer families sitting down together to eat (American Heart Association 2005).

In addition, mental health research points out the link between physical exercise and the reduced incidence of anxiety, depression, and behavioral problems in young children (U.S. Department of Health and Human Services 1996). Physical activity through play alleviates stress and helps children learn to manage feelings and gain a sense of self-control (Aronson 2002; Sanders 2002). Therefore, integrated and physically demanding play requires the use of both mind and body (Larkin 2002).

Physical activity through play alleviates stress and helps children learn to manage feelings and gain a sense of self-control.

The Link between Physical Inactivity and Health Problems

Rates of childhood obesity in the United States and England have doubled since 1970 (Edmunds, Waters, & Elliott 2001; Elliott 2002). Even some infants and toddlers are being diagnosed as obese by their second or third birthdays. According to the American Heart Association (2005) the U.S. obesity epidemic is now affecting the youngest children, with more than 10 percent of two- to five-year-olds overweight—up from 7 percent in 1994. Childhood obesity is related to five critical health and psychosocial problems: (1) high blood pressure, (2) Type 2 diabetes, (3) coronary heart disease, (4) social rejection, and (5) school failure and dropout (Freedman et al. 2001).

Early childhood professionals and play advocates can bolster the case for physically active and play-based environments by citing current information from national and international entities. For example, in the United States the Centers for Disease Control and Prevention (CDC) assumes a preventive health stance, advocating for greater physical activity, balanced nutrition, and much more active life-styles. Because 25 percent of American children are obese and 61 percent of adults are overweight (Guo et al. 2002), it is difficult to overstate the dimensions of the problem. The CDC uses the Body Mass Index (BMI) with children as a predictor of adult obesity (Guo et al. 2002). Advocates for physically active play environments can use these facts to emphasize the seriousness of health issues for children in sedentary care and learning environments and stress the need for all types of play, both indoor and outdoor.

The Health Benefits of Physically Active Play

Daily schedules, play objects, and adult-child interactions can be contrasted in high- and low-quality early childhood settings to make advocacy points. For example, high-quality early childhood classrooms incorporate (1) daily schedules that routinely include active indoor and rough-and-tumble outdoor play (Rivkin 2000); (2) kinesthetic movement as part of concept learning; (3) integration of music, movement, and creative expression; and (4) adult-child interactions that model moderate to high levels of physical activity. In contrast, low-quality settings (1) do not have predictable schedules for indoor and outdoor play; (2) employ more passive and sedentary learning strategies such as television viewing or adult-directed teaching; (3) minimize opportunities for kinesthetic movement and learning; and (4) do not encourage creative expression through physical exercise, dance, and movement.

At the elementary school level, organized sports and physical education also provide play opportunities. Supporters of sports as a form of play suggest that sports contain many of the elements used to describe play (Frost, Wortham, & Reifel 2001). The policy issue of regular and scheduled outdoor recess in public schools is being studied, but research indicates that children need recess for a variety of reasons, including socialization opportunities, respite from attention to classroom tasks, a break that allows them to give maximum attention to their work once again, and the obvious benefits of physical activity

to counter sedentary lifestyles and patterns of obesity (Pelligrini & Bjorklund 1996; Jarrett 2002).

In summary, play advocates can state the following health benefits of active play to bolster their play advocacy efforts:

- large muscle development through reaching, grasping, crawling, running, climbing, skipping, and balancing;
- fine motor skill development and eye-hand coordination as the child handles objects in play;
- increased metabolism and energy consumption through routine physical activity;
- decreased weight and heart-related problems;
- reduced levels of chronic stress; and
- increased feelings of success, self-control, and social competence. (Piaget 1962; Piaget & Inhelder 1969)

This research area may represent the most urgent rationale for physically active and rigorous play for all children. Teachers, parents, and administrators should place health concerns high on their priority list when developing play policy. What can be more important than the overall health of young children?

Research Focus 2: Brain Research—The Critical Link between Play and Optimal Cognitive and Physical Development

Brain research now documents observable differences in the quantity and quality of brain cell development between young children with stimulating and nonstimulating early learning experiences during the first 36 months of life. Children's play behaviors become more complex and abstract as they progress through childhood (Piaget 1962; Johnson, Christie, & Yawkey 1987). In very concrete terms, the recent flurry of research related to brain growth and development clearly supports and under-girds the necessity of active, physical, and cognitively stimulating play for *all* young children (Zwillich 2001).

Children's play behaviors become more complex and abstract as they progress through childhood.

Information gathered through new brain-imaging techniques is already playing a major role in how public policy decisions are made. Cognitive skills advance during problem solving with play materials, ideas, events, and people. This begins in infancy—for example, when a baby makes the startling discovery that shaking a rattle causes a sound reaction. Stimulating play environments facilitate progress to higher levels of thought throughout childhood. Functional magnetic resonance imaging (fMRI), positron emission tomography (PET), and other brain-scanning tools are for the first time providing meaningful insights into the way human brains change and develop during the early years of life (Zwillich 2001).

Neuroscientists point out that the connections between brain cells that underlie new learning become hard-wired if they are used repeatedly but can be diminished if they are not (Morrison 2004). However, caution is warranted here: we should not interpret brain research findings to label or place limits on children whose brains do not appear to be "normal" at very young ages. What is clear among the varied brain research findings is that younger children need (1) physical activity, (2) hands-on activities that develop large and fine motor skills, (3) opportunities for eye-hand coordination activities, (4) auditory and visually stimulating environments, and (5) consistent daily routines that actively engage the child both in the home and preschool environments.

Stimulating play environments facilitate progress to higher levels of thought throughout childhood.

Research Focus 3: The Link between Play, Early Literacy, and Social Competence

Research on play and its relationship to social and language development has been conducted for many years (for example, Parten 1932). Current research on early literacy outcomes shows a relationship between active, socially engaging play and early language and literacy development (Neuman & Roskos 1993; Owocki 1999; Morrow 2001). Social skills also grow through play experiences as the child moves from enjoying simple contact with another person to learning to cooperate, take turns, and play by the rules. Social skills, oral language development, and dramatic play go hand in hand. Children who are provided play opportunities in same-age and multi-age settings broaden their own understandings of the social world and of language diversity (Roskos et al. 1995).

Relationships between Social Play, Language, and Early Literacy Development

The growing emphasis on the teaching of early literacy skills in child care, Head Start, and other early learning settings stems from this important research linkage (Neuman & Roskos 1993). Play policy advocates can find much support in the research literature for social play as a significant contributor to early language development and later literacy indicators (Strickland & Strickland 1997; Christie 1998; Owocki 1999; Morrow 2001; International Reading Association 2002). A noted group of early literacy specialists (Neuman & Roskos 1993; Goldhaber et al. 1996; Morrow 1997; Strickland & Strickland 1997; Christie 1998; Morrow 2001) are documenting the significant effect of hands-on, socially engaging early

literacy experiences on the literacy readiness and prereading skills of young children in preschool and kindergarten settings. Although not always regarded as "reading" in a formal sense, acquisition of these print-meaning associations is viewed as an important precursor to more skilled reading (Mason 1980; Goodman 1986).

Literacy props, especially developmentally appropriate books and writing tools, placed in learning centers *beyond* the traditional reading and meeting areas increase both the quality and quantity of early literacy play-based experiences.

Play advocates can argue for a "materials intervention" strategy that involves making play areas resemble the literacy environments that children encounter at home and in their communities (Christie 1998). Since not all families offer equal opportunities for young children to engage in rich literacy events, it is especially important that child care and other early learning settings provide these play-based experiences for equal access to literacy building skills. And children are more likely to engage in play-related reading and writing activities if available materials invite these types of activities (Morrow & Rand 1991; Vukelich 1991; Christie & Enz 1992).

Research shows that the following play-based activities in the early childhood setting promote social awareness and early literacy development:

- *Use of literacy props*—puppets, stuffed animals, dramatic-play items, books, markers, signs, paper of many types—along with adult modeling and encouragement, fosters greater print awareness, verbal expression, and social interactions (Christie & Enz 1992; Neuman & Roskos 1992; Goldhaber et al. 1996). Literacy props, especially developmentally appropriate books and writing tools, placed in learning centers *beyond* the traditional reading and meeting areas (such as block, puzzle and manipulative, dramatic play, and natural science) increase both the quality and quantity of early literacy play-based experiences (Goldhaber et al. 1996; Neuman & Roskos 1993). One study (Neuman & Roskos 1993) found a significant increase in book handling, reading, and writing choices by children (98% African-American and 2% Hispanic) after Head Start teachers set up and participated in a play "office" setting.
- *Integration of art activities* (such as painting, finger painting, and drawing) in the curriculum promotes writing and print awareness (Morrow 2001). Play in the visual arts is immediate and responsive rather than planned out and goal-directed (Johnson 1998); children learn to "invent" their own words, represent letters of the alphabet, and otherwise re-create their imaginary world through forms of printing and drawing.

- *Emphasis on environmental print* (such as labeling of blocks, learning centers, and materials within centers), along with print-rich learning environments (which include maps, newspapers, magazines, many types of books, and posters) encourages alphabet awareness, understanding that print has meaning, and the assimilation of new words in children's vocabularies (Morrow 2001).
- *Incorporation of poetry, songs, chants, storytelling, and sharing of big books* on a daily basis encourages children to verbalize their feelings, learn letter sounds (phonemic awareness) and words, and begin to understand written language through repetition with adults and peers. This is especially important for preschoolers who may have limited exposure to oral language, rituals, and storytelling at home (Morrow 2001; Stegelin 2002a).
- *Teachers should provide adequate time for children to play* and should be sensitive to matching authentic play-based literacy materials to the cultural and developmental characteristics of the children (Neuman & Roskos 1991; Christie & Wardle 1992).

In short, play policy advocates can find an abundance of current research on the positive effects of play-based early literacy experiences that increase the likelihood of positive outcomes in language and literacy development.

Research Linking Play to Social Competence

Much research-based evidence supports the common-sense notion that play with others is necessary for the development of social competence, and that it in turn has a direct relationship to success in school. In fact, a convincing body of evidence has accumulated to indicate that unless children achieve minimal social competence by about age six, they have a higher probability of being at risk in adolescent and adult development (McClellan & Katz 2001). Other studies (Hartup & Moore 1990; Ladd & Profilet 1996) suggest that a child's long-term social and emotional adaptation, academic and cognitive development, and citizenship are enhanced by frequent childhood opportunities to strengthen social competence.

Early childhood educators and play advocates alike should be able to articulate this critical relationship. In addition, we can cite specific studies that document important social outcomes. For example, in the area of pretend play, research (Piaget 1962; Fein 1981; Smilansky 1990; Nourot 1998) reveals that pretend and dramatic play strengthens the child's understanding of the real world and provides opportunities for imagination to develop. Sociodramatic play provides the matrix for understanding and representing the perspectives of others and for opportunities to compromise and to stand firm in one's beliefs and intentions (Nourot 1998).

Pretend and dramatic play strengthens the child's understanding of the real world and provides opportunities for imagination to develop.

Fabes and colleagues (2003) studied the role that young children's same-sex peer interactions play in influencing early school competence. In observing 98 young children (median age of 54.77 months), they found that patterns differed for boys and girls related to school outcomes and specific play interactions. This study invites follow-up research to determine more specific gender-related differences in play. Further, these studies show that informal interactions with peers in play situations foster the social competence behaviors necessary for learning and development.

Summary

All of us can become play advocates who influence play policy in varied settings such as child care, Head Start, and public school kindergarten and primary classrooms. Early childhood professionals wanting to become more active in play policy development can point to research-based evidence that active play leads to optimal outcomes for young children. There are clear positive outcomes in the following areas:

1. *Physical and mental health indicators* reflect a direct correlation between rigorous, physically active play and reduced levels of obesity, heart-related problems, and chronic stress.
2. *Cognitive development* is optimized through active, exploratory play, as evidenced through brain scans and research that document that active, stimulating play on a regular basis promotes optimal brain development in young children.
3. *Language and early literacy development* is enhanced through print-rich learning environments that engage children in active, reciprocal, and systematic interaction with their peers and supportive adults through books, writing experiences, manipulatives, and story-sharing routines.
4. *Social competence*, largely developed by age six, is best nurtured in young children through sociodramatic and pretend play with peers, social interactions in small group settings, and assimilation of routines and reciprocal engagement with peers and caring adults.

We make a strong case for the importance of play in early childhood education when we are able to cite research that strongly supports play and play-based environments. Play-based instructional strategies and environments are a widely discussed topic in the field these days. Many forces counter the play movement, promoting accelerated academic requirements at earlier ages, standardized testing, and accountability mandates, while also citing scheduling issues in elementary schools and safety factors. We early childhood professionals must be prepared to assume an advocacy role in the area of play policy. Parents, teachers, and administrators must be willing to speak up and speak out on behalf of the play needs of our children.

References

American Heart Association. 2005. *Heart disease and stroke statistics—2005 update*. Dallas, TX: Author. Online: www.americanheart.org/downloadable/heart/1103829139928HDSStats2005Update.pdf

Anderson, M. 1998. The meaning of play as a human experience. In *Play from birth to twelve and beyond*, eds. D. Fromberg & D. Bergen, 103–08. New York: Garland.

Aronson, S.S., ed., comp. with P. Spahr. 2002. *Healthy young children: A manual for programs*. 4th ed. Washington, DC: NAEYC.

Bolig, R., C.S. Price, P.L. O'Neill-Wagner, & S.J. Suomi. 1998. Reactivity and play and exploration behaviors of young Rhesus monkeys. In *Play and culture studies*, Vol. 1, ed. S. Reifel, 165–77. Greenwich, CT: Ablex.

Christie, J., & F. Wardle. 1992. How much time is needed for play? *Young Children* 47 (3): 28–32.

Christie, J.F. 1998. Play as a medium for literacy development. In *Play from birth to twelve and beyond*, eds. D. Fromberg & D. Bergen, 50–55. New York: Garland.

Christie, J.F., & B. Enz. 1992. The effects of literacy play interventions on preschoolers' play patterns and literacy development. *Early Education and Development* 3: 205–20.

Edmunds, L., E. Waters, & E. Elliott. 2001. Evidence-based management of childhood obesity: Evidence-based pediatrics. *British Medical Journal* 323 (7318): 916–9.

Elliott, V. 2002. Adult options for childhood obesity? Doctors say the high number of extremely overweight young people is serious enough to consider radical interventions. *American Medical News* 45 (20): 27.

Fabes, R.A., C.L. Martin, L.D. Hanish, M.C. Anders, & D.A. Madden-Derdich. 2003. Early school competence: The roles of sex-segregated play and effortful control. *Developmental Psychology* 39 (5): 848–59.

Fein, G.G. 1981. Pretend play in childhood: An integrative review. *Child Development* 52: 1095–1118.

Freedman, D., L. Khan, W. Dietz, S. Srivinasian, & G.S. Berenson. 2001. Relationship of childhood obesity to coronary heart disease risk factors in adulthood. *Pediatric* 108 (3): 712.

Frost, J.L., S.C. Wortham, & S. Reifel. 2001. *Play and child development*. Columbus, OH: Merrill/Prentice-Hall.

Goldhaber, J., M. Lipson, S. Sortino, & P. Daniels. 1996. Books in the sand box? Markers in the blocks? Expanding the child's world of literacy. *Childhood Education* 73 (2): 88–92.

Goodman, Y. 1986. Children coming to know literacy. In *Emergent literacy*, eds. W. Teale & E. Sulzby, 1–14. Norwood, NJ: Ablex.

Guo, S.S., W. Wu, W.C. Chulea, & A.F. Roche. 2002. Predicting overweight and obesity in adulthood from body mass index volume in childhood and adolescence. *Journal of Clinical Nutrition* 76 (3): 653–56.

Hampshire Play Policy Forum. 2002. *Hampshire play policy position statement*. Online: www.hants.gov.uk/childcare/playpolicy.html

Hartup, W.W., & S.G. Moore. 1990. Early peer relations: Developmental significance and prognostic implications. *Early Childhood Research Quarterly* 5 (1): 1–18.

International Reading Association. 2002. *What is evidence-based reading instruction?* Reading standards statement. Online: www.reading.org/advocacy/standards

Jarrett, O.S. 2002. Recess in elementary school: What does the research say? *ERIC Digest* EDO-PS-02-5.

Johnson, H.A. 1998. Play in the visual arts: One photographer's way-of-working. In *Play from birth to twelve and beyond*, eds. D. Fromberg & D. Bergen, 435–41. New York: Garland.

Johnson, J., J. Christie, & T. Yawkey. 1987. *Play and early childhood development*. Glenview, IL: Scott, Foresman.

Ladd, G.W., & S.M. Profilet. 1996. The Child Behavior Scale: A teacher-report measure of young children's aggressive, withdrawn, and prosocial behaviors. *Developmental Psychology* 32 (6): 1008–24.

Larkin, M. 2002. Defusing the "time bomb" of childhood obesity. *The Lancet* 359: (9310): 987.

Mason, J. 1980. When do children begin to read?: An exploration of four-year-old children's word reading competencies. *Reading Research Quarterly* 15: 203–27.

McClellan, D.E., & L.G. Katz. 2001. Assessing young children's social competence. *ERIC Digest* EDO-PS-01-2.

Morrison, G.M. 2004. *Early childhood education today*. 9th ed. Columbus, OH: Merrill/Prentice-Hall.

Morrow, L.M. 1997. *The literacy center*. York, ME: Stenhouse.

Morrow, L.M. 2001. *Literacy development in the early years*. 4th ed. Boston: Allyn & Bacon.

Morrow, L.M., & M.K. Rand. 1991. Preparing the classroom environment to promote literacy during play. In *Play and early literacy development*, ed. J.F. Christie, 141–65. Albany: State University of New York.

Neuman, S.B., & K. Roskos. 1991. Peers as literacy informants: A description of young children's literacy conversations in play. *Early Childhood Research Quarterly* 6: 233–48.

Neuman, S.B., & K. Roskos. 1992. Literacy objects as cultural tools: Effects on children's literacy behaviors in play. *Reading Research Quarterly* 27: 202–25.

Neuman, S., & K. Roskos. 1993. Access to print for children of poverty: Differential effects of adult mediation and literacy-enriched play settings on environmental and functional print tasks. *American Educational Research Journal* 30 (1): 95–122.

Nourot, P.M. 1998. Sociodramatic play—Pretending together. In *Play from birth to twelve and beyond*, eds. D. Fromberg & D. Bergen, 378–91. New York: Garland.

O'Neill-Wagner, P.L., R. Bolig, & C.S. Price. 1994. Do play activity levels tell us something of psychosocial welfare in captive monkey groups? *Communication and Cognition* 27: 261–72.

Owocki, G. 1999. *Literacy through play*. Portsmouth, NH: Heinemann.

Parten, M. 1932. Social participation among preschool children. *Journal of Abnormal and Social Psychology* 27: 243–69.

Pelligrini, A.D., & D.F. Bjorklund. 1996. The place of recess in school: Issues in the role of recess in children's education and development. *Journal of Research in Childhood Education* 11: 5–13.

Pelligrini, A., & M. Perlmutter. 1989. Classroom contextual effects of children's play. *Child Development* 25: 289–96.

Piaget, J. 1962. *Play, dreams, and imitation in childhood*. New York: Norton.

Piaget, J., & B. Inhelder. 1969. *The psychology of the child*. New York: Basic.

PLAYLINK. 2001. *Articulating play policy*. London, UK: Author.

Play Wales. 2002. *Defining play policy*. Cardiff, UK: Author.

Rivkin, M.S. 2000. Outdoor experiences for young children. *ERIC Digest* EDO-RC-007.

Roskos, K., J. Vukelich, B. Christie, B. Enz, & S. Neuman. 1995. *Linking literacy and play*. Newark, DE: International Reading Association.

Salthe, S.N. 1991. *Development and evolution: Complexity and change in biological systems*. Cambridge, MA: MIT Press.

Sanders, S.W. 2002. *Active for life: Developmentally appropriate movement programs for young children*. Washington, DC: NAEYC.

Smilansky, S. 1990. Sociodramatic play: Its relevance to behavior and achievement in school. In *Children's play and learning: Perspectives and policy implications*, eds. E. Klugman & S. Smilansky, 18–42. New York: Teachers College Press.

Stegelin, D.A. 2002a. *Early literacy education: First steps toward dropout prevention*. Clemson, SC: National Dropout Prevention Center, Clemson University.

Stegelin, D.A. 2002b. Play policy: A survey of online and professional literature. Unpublished paper presented to the Play, Policy, and Practice Forum, NAEYC Annual Conference, Nov. 20–23, New York, New York.

Strickland, D., & M. Strickland. 1997. Language and literacy: The poetry connection. *Language Arts* 74 (3): 201–05.

U.S. Department of Health and Human Services. 1996. *Physical activity and health: A report of the Surgeon General*. Atlanta, GA: Author, Centers for Disease Control and Prevention.

Vukelich, C. 1991. Learning about the functions of writing: The effects of three play settings on children's interventions and development of knowledge about writing. Unpublished paper presented at the National Reading Conference, December, Palm Springs, California.

Zwillich, T. 2001. Brain scan technology poised to play policy. Online: www.loni.ucla.edu/thompson/MEDIA/RH/rh.html

DOLORES A. STEGELIN, PhD, is associate professor and program coordinator of early childhood education in the Eugene T. Moore School of Education at Clemson University in South Carolina. Active in policy research and professional activities for 20 years, Dee is the public policy chair for South Carolina AEYC and the author of two books and numerous articles.

From *Young Children*, March 2005. Copyright © 2005 by National Association for the Education of Young Children. Reprinted by permission.

The Looping Classroom

Benefits for Children, Families, and Teachers

MARY M. HITZ, MARY CATHERINE SOMERS, AND CHRISTEE L. JENLINK

The second week of school, the second-graders work intently in small groups or individually. They require little direct teacher instruction and clearly understand their responsibilities and the teacher's expectations. How did this independence develop so early? What did the teacher do?

Welcome to a looping classroom! "Looping—which is sometimes called multiyear teaching or multiyear placement—occurs when a teacher is promoted with her students to the next grade level and stays with the same group of children for two or three years" (Rasmussen 1998, 1). What results is a continuity of relationship with their teacher that enables children to flourish (Wynne & Walberg 1994).

American's one room schoolhouse was a looping classroom, with the teacher teaching the same children over a period of several years.

Looping Origins

The practice of looping is not a new concept in education. America's one room schoolhouse was a looping classroom, with the teacher teaching the same children over a period of several years. In Germany in 1919 Rudolf Steiner developed the Waldorf School model. Oppenheimer suggests that one unusual aspect of education in the Waldorf School "Is a system called looping, whereby a homeroom teacher stays with a class for more than a year . . . from first through eighth grade" (1999, 82). Also in the early 1900s, Italian pediatrician Maria Montessori introduced the Montessori Method, characterized by relationship development over several years on the part of the teacher, child, and parents (Seldin n.d).

The Multiage Classroom

Two or more grade levels are intentionally placed in a single classroom. Children are taught as a class and regrouped as necessary for different activities based on interests and/or abilities rather than on chronological age or grade level. At the end of each year, the older students move to a new class, and a group of younger students joins the class. In a multiage grouping, children can experience being both younger and older among the students in their class.

Generally, in modern Germany, student groups formed in first grade remain together over the next four years (Zahorik & Dichanz 1994). In China, grouping is by grade level, with a homeroom teacher who stays with students two to three years in elementary school and for three years in both junior and senior high schools. Many subject area teachers also choose to teach the same students for two to three years (Liu 1997).

In 1974 Deborah Meier founded the Central Park East Elementary School in New York City. Because she believed it takes time to build relationships, in this school the children and teachers stayed together for two years (Meier 1995).

In other instances, U.S. schools developed looping classrooms to solve scheduling problems or manage the significant population shifts in enrollment numbers per grade. This led to teachers being assigned to different or combined grades especially in small rural schools where school populations fluctuate each year. The multiage model is another popular form of looping (see "The Multiage Classroom").

Introducing Looping Today

It is not expensive or difficult to begin a school looping program. Two teachers volunteer for the assignment on any two contiguous grade levels. For example, teacher A teaches first grade and teacher B teaches second grade. The next year, teacher A moves with her class to teach second grade, and teacher B cycles back to begin with a group of new first-graders. Prior to looping, the two teachers and their administrator thoughtfully plan for this structural change (see "Starting a Looping Program").

Benefits of Looping for Children

In today's rapidly altering world, many children's lives are filled with change: of residence, in family structure, in economic status. Numerous children come from single parent homes or have two parents both working full-time away from home. Children can benefit from the looping classroom's stability and teacher continuity (Nichols & Nichols 2002).

Children in typical settings. Because children typically attend school six or more hours a day, five days a week, the teacher is a significant adult in their lives. Staying together two years or longer enhances the bonding and trust established between children and teacher (Grant, Johnson, & Richardson 1996). Pianta and LaParo, in discussing how to improve early school success, conclude that "relationships that children have with adults and other children in families, child care, and school programs provide the foundation for their success in school" (2003, 27). When children form secure relationships with teachers and other caregivers, both social and cognitive competence show improvement (Kontos & Wilcox-Herzog 1997; Gallagher & Mayer 2006).

In the looping classroom children build relationships over time with an adult confidant. Grant and Johnson suggest, "For a lot of children today, their teacher is often the most stable, predictable adult in their life" (1995, 34). Several examples of benefits follow from two coauthors' (Hitz and Somers) primary grades looping classrooms.

> Makayla, an eight-year-old, was one of four children, including a sister who was very bright and two brothers with cognitive disabilities. She brought a great deal of pent-up anger to school. During the first year in the looping class, her many angry outbursts involved lashing out at anyone nearby. By her second year in the looping class, she trusted us enough to tell us what was happening. When necessary, Makayla could choose to move to a more isolated area to work alone or, with teacher permission, could go to the office to talk with the assistant principal. Makayla's aggressive expressions lessened, and she gained a sense of control over her emotions.

With additional time together, teachers can become more familiar with each child's learning style, interests, strengths, and needs and respond with individualized learning experiences (Seldin n.d.). In a looping classroom children are not apprehensive about their second or next years; they already know their teacher and classmates (Lacina-Gifford 2001). The familiar environment also allows a shy child to blossom. For example,

> At the beginning of his first looping year, Eric cried when called upon during any kind of discussion. Later in the year he would raise his hand to volunteer, only to shrink inside himself at being recognized. Once in a while he worked with another child.

Starting a Looping Program

- Form a proposal study group
- Read about looping programs
- Enlist and build support form administrators and other teachers
- Involve parents in the planning
- Design the program to allow for change
- Provide time for staff development
- Visit other looping programs
- Invite teachers to volunteer for looping classrooms
- Work with administrators on the careful selection of the teachers for looping

> Knowing we would have Eric for two years, we did not feel the pressure to force participation in the first year. We offered support and encouragement when he attempted to participate but also allowed him needed time to mature.
>
> Although Eric struggled in reading all that first year, during the second year he volunteered more often and answered questions. Eric was on grade level at the end of the year. His mother was glad he was in a looping classroom. He was still quiet, but he knew he could do well in a new third grade classroom.

In a looping classroom, the teacher and the children experience a sense of community. The bonds between children grow strong; they share achievements and disappointments, resolve problems, and learn to trust each other. Teachers personalize their teaching and talk about their individual interests and their families.

One of the most positive elements of looping is that it allows a child to grow at his or her own pace, not at an arbitrary fixed-grade rate. John Goodlad reminds us that children "don't fit into a nice, neat age-grade package, either collectively or individually. Each individual child differs in regard to the various areas of accomplishment" (Stone 1999, 265). An example from our classroom follows:

> Austin, a young first-grader, worked hard in class and at home with his parents. By the end of the year, however, he was barely able to read at the preprimary level. His mother asked if we should retain Austin in first grade. We suggested waiting, since as a looping class we could monitor Austin's progress in the coming year.
>
> Austin bloomed that second year. Reading became his favorite activity, and by the end of the year he was reading above grade level. In third grade he moved into the gifted program. Had Austin been in a nonlooping classroom, he might have been retained.

English-language learners. The looping classroom supports children and their families for whom English is a second language. As English-language learners (ELLs) adjust to a new school and become comfortable with their teacher, they develop confidence in practicing their new language. Eventually they may help others who are new to the class or have little knowledge of U.S. culture. When children who are ELLs are members of a class, the other children can learn firsthand from a peer about another culture and country. The experience results in respect and understanding among all the students (Haslinger, Kelly, & O'Lare 1996).

Maritza uses both English and Spanish. One day, in her second year, she and three other Spanish-speaking friends chose a book to read to the class and designed follow-up activities. They read the story aloud—in Spanish. The other children gained an idea of what ELL students experience when learning a second language. Because Maritza and her friends felt safe and secure in their classroom, they could make this presentation to their peers.

Looping Pluses for Others

Looping provides time for teachers to get to know each child and family in a personal way, and it fosters stronger bonds between teachers and families.

Teachers. In nonlooping classrooms, each year teachers spend the first four to six weeks determining each child's skills, abilities, and interests. In contrast, in the second year of a looping classroom cycle, the teacher already knows the students and is able to immediately support their learning, thus making better use of instructional time (Little & Dacus 1999). Effective teaching and learning can begin on the first day of the second year after a brief review of rules and procedures (Burke 1996).

Many teachers provide summer learning packets to help children bridge from one year to the next. In looping classrooms the children are returning to the same classroom and teacher, and it is easy to design packets and follow up with them the second year. Children are excited to share journals kept over the summer, stories they wrote, or special books they read. The looping teacher can build on children's previous year's experiences and use the summer packets to lead into the second year's curriculum.

One of the most positive elements of looping is that it allows a child to grow at his or her own pace, not at an arbitrary fixed-grade rate.

Usually teachers choose to loop because they believe in developmentally appropriate practices, including the importance of encouraging emotional development (Dunn & Kontos 1997). Such teachers understand young children's need for stability and how the looping classroom addresses that need.

In looping classrooms, collaborating teachers learn new skills and curriculum (Albrecht et al. 2000) by sharing materials and ideas. They have a chance to know more about the children—where they live, who needs extra motivation, who works best

with whom (Burke 2000). Units of study can extend into the next year. Looping gives teachers an extra year to consider high-stakes decisions regarding retention or referral for testing for special services (Jacobson 1997; Liu 1997; Bracey 1999).

Families. Looping classrooms foster stronger bonds between families and teachers. "Because parents are the most significant people in a child's life, the relationship between the teacher and the parents is paramount" (Albrecht et al. 2000, 24). Parents tend to place more trust in a teacher the second year, with the development of a relaxed relationship conducive to a positive attitude toward the teacher (Nichols & Nichols 2002). Conversely, the teacher values input from the home, a direct result of the collaborative relationship that has been forged in this type of classroom setting.

Parents get to know the teacher's philosophy of education and how it relates to their child. Because a trusting relationship builds over the long span of a looping classroom, families may be more willing to accept a teacher's constructive suggestions (Chirichello & Chirichello 2001) and tend to be comfortable sharing the challenges they face with their child at home. Our looping classroom provides this example:

Zach had difficulty completing classroom assignments on time. At home, his family reported he was never ready on time and every morning was a fight to get dressed for school. Zach's mother called one morning to say he would be at school on time, but in his pajamas. We were proud of the other children for not making fun of Zach or teasing him. But ever after, Zach was always ready for school.

For the families of children who are English-language learners, the stability of having the same teacher for a span of two years helps them gain confidence in talking with the teacher about their children's progress. The teacher can also smooth this transition by having materials translated as frequently as possible into the family's home language and arranging for translators to attend conferences.

A looping classroom favors both the child and the teacher and adds stability to children's lives.

What Concerns Might Arise in Looping?

While the advantages of a looping classroom are many, some concerns do arise. One issue parents express is a fear of their child being locked in for two years with a possibly ineffective teacher. Other potential problems include a teacher-child personality conflict, a child who simply does not get along with the other children, or a parent who does not get along with the teacher. Although looping teachers report that these occurrences are rare; each school needs to have procedures for reviewing class placements. The school principal plays an important role in identifying teacher-child personality conflicts as well as ensuring that teachers have the skills and work ethic necessary to create a successful looping classroom.

In our looping classroom two sets of parents came to us with concerns about their children. In both instances the issues reflected differences about teaching philosophy. After discussions, with both sets of parents, we jointly decided to place each child in a traditional classroom. Involvement of the school principal is essential in such situations to ensure making the best decision for the child.

Another challenge involves a new child entering the program, especially in the second year when children are already familiar with each other and the classroom. The looping teacher must prepare and encourage the children to welcome and accept the new student and help the child become part of the community.

Conclusion

At the end of the school year, it is always difficult to say good-bye, but when a teacher and children have been together for two years, it is doubly difficult. The class is a learning community that has shared joys as well as the sadness of departure. Some teachers plan special events to highlight their two years together. The children outline their advice to the incoming group of younger students and write letters to their future teachers to introduce themselves. Receiving teachers visit the looping class to be introduced to their new students when possible.

Good-bye is a bittersweet time. Sometimes it's harder for parents. Not only do looping teachers have to reassure the children that they will succeed, but also they have to reassure the families.

The concept of a looping classroom is being revisited by many teachers today. It favors both the child and the teacher and adds stability to children's lives. It provides time—time for children to grow and develop at their own rates and time for teachers to get to know each child and family in a personal way.

Looping may not be a good fit for everyone nor solve all the problems in education. But teacher proponents express it this way: Looping provides the most rewarding opportunity for helping children succeed (Rasmussen 1998).

References

Albrecht, K., M. Banks, G. Calhoun, L. Dziadul, C. Gwinn, B. Harrington, B. Kerr, M. Mizukami, A. Morris, C. Peterson, & R.R. Summers. 2000. The good, the bad and the wonderful! Keeping children and teachers together. *Child Care Information Exchange* (136): 24–28.

Bracey, G.W. 1999. Going loopy for looping. *Phi Delta Kappan* 81 (2): 169–70.

Burke, D.L. 1996. Multi-year teacher/student relationships are a long-overdue arrangement. *Phi Delta Kappan* 77 (5): 360–61.

Burke, D.L. 2000. Learning to loop and loving it. *The School Administrator Web Edition.* Online: www.aasa.org. publications/content.cfm?ItemNumber=3831

Chirichello, M., & C. Chirichello. 2001. A standing ovation for looping: The critics respond. *Childhood Education* 78 (1): 2–10.

Dunn, L., & S. Kontos. 1997. What have we learned about developmentally appropriate practice? *Young Children* 52 (5): 4–13.

Gallagher, K.C., & K. Mayer. 2006. Teacher-child relationships at the forefront of effective practice. *Young Children* 61 (6): 44–49.

Grant, J., & B. Johnson. 1995. *A common sense guide to multiage practices, primary level.* Columbus, OH: Teachers' Publishing Group.

Grant, J., B. Johnson, & I. Richardson. 1996. *Our best advice: The multiage problem solving handbook.* Petersborough, NH: Crystal Springs Books.

Haslinger, J., P. Kelley, & L. O'Lare. 1996. Countering absenteeism, anonymity, and apathy. *Educational Leadership* 54 (1): 47–49.

Jacobson, L. 1997. 'Looping' catches on as way to build strong ties. *Education Week* 17 (7): 1–3.

Kontos, S., & A. Wilcox-Herzog. 1997. Teachers' interactions with children: Why are they so important? *Young Children* 52 (2): 4–12.

Lacina-Gifford, L.J. 2001. The squeaky wheel gets the oil, but what about the shy student? *Education* 122 (2): 320–21.

Little, T.S., & N.B. Dacus. 1999. Looping: Moving up with the class. *Educational Leadership* 57 (1): 42–45.

Liu, J. 1997. The emotional bond between teachers and students: Multi-year relationships. *Phi Delta Kappan* 78 (2): 156–57.

Meier, D. 1995. *The power of their ideas: Lessons for America from a small school in Harlem.* Boston, MA: Beacon.

Nichols, J.D., & G.W. Nichols. 2002. The impact of looping classroom environments on parental attitudes. *Preventing School Failure* 47 (1): 18–25.

Oppenheimer, T. 1999. Schooling the imagination. *The Atlantic Monthly* 284 (2): 71–83.

Pianta, R.C., & K. LaParo. 2003. Improving early school success. *Educational Leadership* 60 (7): 24–29.

Rasmussen, K. 1998. Looping: Discovering the benefits of multiyear teaching. *Education Update* 40 (2): 41–44.

Selden, T. N.d. Montessori 101: Some basic information that every Montessori parent should know. Online: www.montessori.org/ sitefiles/Montessori_101_nonprintable.pdf.

Stone, S.J. 1999. A conversation with John Goodlad. *Childhood Education* 75 (5): 264–68.

Wynne, E.A., & H.J. Walberg. 1994. Persisting groups: An overlooked force for learning. *Phi Delta Kappan* 75 (7): 527–30.

Zahorik, J.A., & H. Dichanz. 1994. Teaching for understanding in German schools. *Educational Leadership* 51 (5): 75–77.

From *Young Children*, March 2007, pp. 80–84. Copyright © 2007 by National Association for the Education of Young Children. Reprinted by permission.

The Case For and Against Homework

**Teachers should not abandon homework.
Instead, they should improve its instructional quality.**

ROBERT J. MARZANO AND DEBRA J. PICKERING

Homework has been a perennial topic of debate in education, and attitudes toward it have been cyclical (Gill & Schlossman, 2000). Throughout the first few decades of the 20th century, educators commonly believed that homework helped create disciplined minds. By 1940, growing concern that homework interfered with other home activities sparked a reaction against it. This trend was reversed in the late 1950s when the Soviets' launch of *Sputnik* led to concern that U.S. education lacked rigor; schools viewed more rigorous homework as a partial solution to the problem. By 1980, the trend had reversed again, with some learning theorists claiming that homework could be detrimental to students' mental health. Since then, impassioned arguments for and against homework have continued to proliferate.

We now stand at an interesting intersection in the evolution of the homework debate. Arguments against homework are becoming louder and more popular, as evidenced by several recent books as well as an editorial in *Time* magazine (Wallis, 2006) that presented these arguments as truth without much discussion of alternative perspectives. At the same time, a number of studies have provided growing evidence of the usefulness of homework when employed effectively.

The Case for Homework

Homework is typically defined as any tasks "assigned to students by school teachers that are meant to be carried out during nonschool hours" (Cooper, 1989a, p. 7). A number of synthesis studies have been conducted on homework, spanning a broad range of methodologies and levels of specificity (see fig. 1). Some are quite general and mix the results from experimental studies with correlational studies.

Arguments against homework are becoming louder and more popular.

Two meta-analyses by Cooper and colleagues (Cooper, 1989a; Cooper, Robinson, & Patall, 2006) are the most comprehensive and rigorous. The 1989 meta-analysis reviewed research dating as far back as the 1930s; the 2006 study reviewed research from 1987 to 2003. Commenting on studies that attempted to examine the causal relationship between homework and student achievement by comparing experimental (homework) and control (no homework) groups, Cooper, Robinson, and Patall (2006) noted,

> With only rare exceptions, the relationship between the amount of homework students do and their achievement outcomes was found to be positive and statistically significant. Therefore, we think it would not be imprudent, based on the evidence in hand, to conclude that doing homework causes improved academic achievement. (p. 48)

The Case Against Homework

Although the research support for homework is compelling, the case against homework is popular. *The End of Homework: How Homework Disrupts Families, Overburdens Children, and Limits Learning* by Kralovec and Buell (2000), considered by many to be the first high-profile attack on homework, asserted that homework contributes to a corporate-style, competitive U.S. culture that overvalues work to the detriment of personal and familial well-being The authors focused particularly on the harm to economically disadvantaged students, who are unintentionally penalized because their environments often make it almost impossible to complete assignments at home. The authors called for people to unite against homework and to lobby for an extended school day instead.

A similar call for action came from Bennett and Kalish (2006) in *The Case Against Homework: How Homework Is Hurting Our Children and What We Can Do About It*. These authors criticized both the quantity and quality of homework. They provided evidence that too much homework harms students' health and family time, and they asserted that teachers are not well trained in how to assign homework. The authors suggested that individuals and parent groups should insist that teachers reduce the amount of homework, design more valuable assignments, and avoid homework altogether over breaks and holidays.

FIGURE 1 Synthesis Studies on Homework

Synthesis Study	Focus	Number of Effect Sizes	Average	Percentile Gains
Graue, Weinstein, & Walberg, 1983[1]	General effects of homework	29	.49	19
Bloom, 1984	General effects of homework	—	.30	12
Paschal Weinstein, & Walberg, 1984[2]	Homework versus no homework	47	.28	11
Cooper, 1989a	Homework versus no homework	20	.21	8
Hattie, 1992; Fraser, Walberg, Welch, & Hattie, 1987	General effects of homework	110	.43	17
Walberg, 1999	With teacher comments	2	.88	31
	Graded	5	.78	28
Cooper, Robinson, & Patall, 2006	Homework versus no homework	6	.60	23

Note: This figure describes the eight major research syntheses on the effects of homework published from 1983 to 2006 that provide the basis for the analysis in this article. The "Number of Effect Sizes" column includes results from experimental/control group studies only.

1 Reported in Fraser, Walberg, Welch, & Hattie, 1987.
2 Reported in Kavale, 1988.

In a third book, *The Homework Myth: Why Our Kids Get Too Much of a Bad Thing* (2006a), Kohn took direct aim at the research on homework. In this book and in a recent article in *Phi Delta Kappan* (2006b), he became quite personal in his condemnation of researchers. For example, referring to Harris Cooper, the lead author of the two leading meta-analyses on homework, Kohn noted,

> A careful reading of Cooper's own studies . . . reveals further examples of his determination to massage the numbers until they yield something—anything—on which to construct a defense of homework for younger children. (2006a, p. 84)

He also attacked a section on homework in our book *Classroom Instruction that Works* (Marzano, Pickering, & Pollock, 2001).

Kohn concluded that research fails to demonstrate homework's effectiveness as an instructional tool and recommended changing the "default state" from an expectation that homework *will* be assigned to an expectation that homework *will not* be assigned. According to Kohn, teachers should only assign homework when they can justify that the assignments are "beneficial" (2006a, p. 166)—ideally involving students in activities appropriate for the home, such as performing an experiment in the kitchen, cooking, doing crossword puzzles with the family, watching good TV shows, or reading. Finally, Kohn urged teachers to involve students in deciding what homework, and how much, they should do.

Some of Kohn's recommendations have merit. For example, it makes good sense to only assign homework that is beneficial to student learning instead of assigning homework as a matter of policy. Many of those who conduct research on homework explicitly or implicitly recommend this practice. However, his

misunderstanding or misrepresentation of the research sends the inaccurate message that research does not support homework. As Figure 1 indicates, homework has decades of research supporting its effective use. Kohn's allegations that researchers are trying to mislead practitioners and the general public are unfounded and detract from a useful debate on effective practice.[1]

The Dangers of Ignoring the Research

Certainly, inappropriate homework may produce little or no benefit—it may even decrease student achievement. All three of the books criticizing homework provide compelling anecdotes to this effect. Schools should strengthen their policies to ensure that teachers use homework properly.

If a district or school discards homework altogether, however, it will be throwing away a powerful instructional tool. Cooper and colleagues' (2006) comparison of homework with no homework indicates that the average student in a class in which appropriate homework was assigned would score 23 percentile points higher on tests of the knowledge addressed in that class than the average student in a class in which homework was not assigned.

Perhaps the most important advantage of homework is that it can enhance achievement by extending learning beyond the school day. This characteristic is important because U.S. students spend much less time studying academic content than students in other countries do. A 1994 report examined the amount of time U.S. students spend studying core academic subjects compared with students in other countries that typically outperform the United States academically, such as Japan, Germany, and France. The study found that "students abroad are required to work on demanding subject matter at least twice as long" as are U.S. students (National Education Commission on Time and Learning, 1994, p. 25).

To drop the use of homework, then, a school or district would be obliged to identify a practice that produces a similar effect within the confines of the school day without taking away or diminishing the benefits of other academic activities--no easy accomplishment. A better approach is to ensure that teachers use homework effectively. To enact effective homework policies, however, schools and districts must address the following issues.

Grade Level

Although teachers across the K–12 spectrum commonly assign homework, research has produced no clear-cut consensus on the benefits of homework at the early elementary grade levels. In his early meta-analysis, Cooper (1989a) reported the following effect sizes (p. 71):

- Grades 4–6: ES = .15 (Percentile gain = 6)
- Grades 7–9: ES = .31 (Percentile gain = 12)
- Grades 10–12: ES = .64 (Percentile gain = 24)

The pattern clearly indicates that homework has smaller effects at lower grade levels. Even so, Cooper (1989b) still recommended homework for elementary students because

homework for young children should help them develop good study habits, foster positive attitudes toward school, and communicate to students the idea that learning takes work at home as well as at school. (p. 90)

The Cooper, Robinson, and Patall (2006) meta-analysis found the same pattern of stronger relationships at the secondary level but also identified a number of studies at grades 2, 3, and 4 demonstrating positive effects for homework. In *The Battle over Homework* (2007), Cooper noted that homework should have different purposes at different grade levels:

- For students in the *earliest grades,* it should foster positive attitudes, habits, and character traits; permit appropriate parent involvement; and reinforce learning of simple skills introduced in class.
- For students in *upper elementary grades*, it should play a more direct role in fostering improved school achievement.
- In *6th grade and beyond,* it should play an important role in improving standardized test scores and grades.

Time Spent on Homework

One of the more contentious issues in the homework debate is the amount of time students should spend on homework. The Cooper synthesis (1989a) reported that for junior high school students, the benefits increased as time increased, up to 1 to 2 hours of homework a night, and then decreased. The Cooper, Robinson, and Patall (2006) study reported similar findings: 7

to 12 hours of homework per week produced the largest effect size for 12th grade students. The researchers suggested that for 12th graders the optimum amount of homework might lie between 1.5 and 2.5 hours per night, but they cautioned that no hard-and-fast rules are warranted. Still, researchers have offered various recommendations. For example, Good and Brophy (2003) cautioned that teachers must take care not to assign too much homework. They suggested that

homework must be realistic in length and difficulty given the students' abilities to work independently Thus, 5 to 10 minutes per subject might be appropriate for 4th graders, whereas 30 to 60 minutes might be appropriate for college-bound high school students. (p. 394)

Cooper, Robinson, and Patall (2006) also issued a strong warning about too much homework:

Even for these oldest students, too much homework may diminish its effectiveness or even become counterproductive. (p 53)

Cooper (2007) suggested that research findings support the common "10-minute rule" (p. 92), which states that all daily homework assignments combined should take about as long to complete as 10 minutes multiplied by the student's grade level. He added that when required reading is included as a type of homework, the 10-minute rule might be increased to 15 minutes.

Focusing on the amount of time students spend on homework, however, may miss the point. A significant proportion of the research on homework indicates that the positive effects of homework relate to the amount of homework that the student completes rather than the amount of time spent on homework or the amount of homework actually assigned. Thus, simply assigning homework may not produce the desired effect—in fact, ill-structured homework might even have a negative effect on student achievement. Teachers must carefully plan and assign homework in a way that maximizes the potential for student success (see Research-Based Homework Guidelines).

Parent Involvement

Another question regarding homework is the extent to which schools should involve parents. Some studies have reported minimal positive effects or even negative effects for parental involvement. In addition, many parents report that they feel unprepared to help their children with homework and that their efforts to help frequently cause stress (see Balli, 1998; Corno, 1996; Hoover-Dempsey, Bassler, & Burow, 1995; Perkins & Milgram, 1996).

Epstein and colleagues conducted a series of studies to identify the conditions under which parental involvement enhances homework (Epstein, 2001; Epstein & Becker, 1982; Van Voorhis, 2003). They recommended *interactive* homework in which

- Parents receive clear guidelines spelling out their role.
- Teachers do not expect parents to act as experts regarding content or to attempt to teach the content.
- Parents ask questions that help students clarify and summarize what they have learned.

Good and Brophy (2003) provided the following recommendations regarding parent involvement:

> Especially useful for parent-child relations purposes are assignments calling for students to show or explain their written work or other products completed at school to their parents and get their reactions (Epstein, 2001; Epstein, Simon, & Salinas, 1997) or to interview their parents to develop information about parental experiences or opinions relating to topics studied in social studies (Alleman & Brophy, 1998). Such assignments cause students and their parents or other family members to become engaged in conversations that relate to the academic curriculum and thus extend the students' learning. Furthermore, because these are likely to be genuine conversations rather than more formally structured teaching/learning tasks, both parents and children are likely to experience them as enjoyable rather than threatening. (p. 395)

Going Beyond the Research

Although research has established the overall viability of homework as a tool to enhance student achievement, for the most part the research does not provide recommendations that are specific enough to help busy practitioners. This is the nature of research—it errs on the side of assuming that something does not work until substantial evidence establishes that it does. The research community takes a long time to formulate firm conclusions on the basis of research. Homework is a perfect example: Figure 1 includes synthesis studies that go back as far as 60 years, yet all that research translates to a handful of recommendations articulated at a very general level.

In addition, research in a specific area, such as homework, sometimes contradicts research in related areas. For example, Cooper (2007) recommended on the basis of 60-plus years of homework research that teachers should not comment on or grade every homework assignment. But practitioners might draw a different conclusion from the research on providing feedback to students, which has found that providing "feedback coupled with remediation" (Hattie, 1992) or feedback on "test-like events" in the form of explanations to students (Bangert-Drowns, Kulik, Kulik, & Morgan, 1991) positively affects achievement.

Riehl (2006) pointed out the similarity between education research and medical research. She commented,

> When reported in the popular media, medical research often appears as a blunt instrument, able to obliterate skeptics or opponents by the force of its evidence and arguments. . . . Yet repeated visits to the medical journals themselves can leave a much different impression. The serious medical journals convey the sense that medical research is an ongoing conversation and quest, punctuated occasionally by important findings that can and should alter practice, but more often characterized by continuing investigations. These investigations, taken cumulatively,

can inform the work of practitioners who are building their own local knowledge bases on medical care. (pp. 27–28)

If relying solely on research is problematic, what are busy practitioners to do? The answer is certainly not to wait until research "proves" that a practice is effective. Instead, educators should combine research-based generalizations, research from related areas, and their own professional judgment based on firsthand experience to develop specific practices and make adjustments as necessary. Like medical practitioners, education practitioners must develop their own "local knowledge base" on homework and all other aspects of teaching. Educators can develop the most effective practices by observing changes in the achievement of the students with whom they work every day.

Research-Based Homework Guidelines

Research provides strong evidence that, when used appropriately, homework benefits student achievement. To make sure that homework is appropriate, teachers should follow these guidelines:

- Assign purposeful homework. Legitimate purposes for homework include introducing new content, practicing a skill or process that students can do independently but not fluently, elaborating on information that has been addressed in class to deepen students' knowledge, and providing opportunities for students to explore topics of their own interest.
- Design homework to maximize the chances that students will complete it. For example, ensure that homework is at the appropriate level of difficulty. Students should be able to complete homework assignments independently with relatively high success rates, but they should still find the assignments challenging enough to be interesting.
- Involve parents in appropriate ways (for example, as a sounding board to help students summarize what they learned from the homework) without requiring parents to act as teachers or to police students' homework completion.
- Carefully monitor the amount of homework assigned so that it is appropriate to students' age levels and does not take too much time away from other home activities.

If a district or school discards homework altogether, it will be throwing away a powerful instructional tool.

Note

1. For a more detailed response to Kohn's views on homework, see Marzano & Pickering (2007) and Marzano & Pickering (in press).

References

Balli, S. J. (1998). When mom and dad help: Student reflections on parent involvement with homework. *Journal of Research and Development in Education, 31*(3), 142–148.

Bangert-Drowns, R. L., Kulik, C. C., Kulik, J. A., & Morgan, M. (1991). The instructional effects of feedback in test-like events. *Review of Educational Research, 61*(2), 213–238.

Bennett, S., & Kalish, N. (2006). *The case against homework: How homework is hurting our children and what we can do about it.* New York: Crown.

Bloom, B. S. (1984). The search for methods of group instruction as effective as one-to-one tutoring. *Educational Leadership, 41*(8), 4–18.

Cooper, H. (1989a). *Homework.* White Plains, NY: Longman.

Cooper, H. (1989b). Synthesis of research on homework. *Educational Leadership, 47*(3), 85–91.

Cooper, H. (2007). *The battle over homework* (3rd ed.). Thousand Oaks, CA: Corwin Press.

Cooper, H., Robinson, J. C., & Patall, E. A. (2006). Does homework improve academic achievement? A synthesis of research, 1987–2003. *Review of Educational Research, 76*(1), 1–62.

Corno, L. (1996). Homework is a complicated thing. *Educational Researcher, 25*(8), 27–30.

Epstein, J. (2001). *School, family, and community partnerships: Preparing educators and improving schools.* Boulder, CO: Westview.

Epstein, J. L., & Becker, H. J. (1982). Teachers' reported practices of parent involvement: Problems and possibilities. *Elementary School Journal, 83*, 103–113.

Fraser, B. J., Walberg, H. J., Welch, W. W., & Hattie, J. A. (1987). Synthesis of educational productivity research [Special issue]. *International Journal of Educational Research, 11*(2), 145–252.

Gill, B. P., & Schlossman, S. L. (2000). The lost cause of homework reform. *American Journal of Education, 109*, 27–62.

Good, T. L., & Brophy, J. E. (2003). *Looking in classrooms* (9th ed.). Boston: Allyn & Bacon.

Graue, M. E., Weinstein, T., & Walberg, H. J. (1983). School-based home instruction and learning: A quantitative synthesis. *Journal of Educational Research, 76*, 351–360.

Hattie, J. A. (1992). Measuring the effects of schooling. *Australian Journal of Education, 36*(1), 5–13.

Hoover-Dempsey, K. V., Bassler, O. C., & Burow, R. (1995). Parents' reported involvement in students' homework: Strategies and practices. *The Elementary School Journal, 95*(5), 435-450.

Kavale, K. A. (1988). Using meta-analyses to answer the question: What are the important influences on school learning? School *Psychology Review, 17*(4), 644–650.

Kohn, A. (2006a). *The homework myth: Why our kids get too much of a bad thing.* Cambridge, MA: Da Capo Press.

Kohn, A. (2006b). Abusing research: The study of homework and other examples. *Phi Delta Kappan. 88*(1), 9–22.

Kralovec, E., & Buell, J. (2000). *The end of homework: How homework disrupts families, overburdens children, and limits learning.* Boston: Beacon.

Marzano, R. J., & Pickering, D. J. (2007). Response to Kohn's allegations. Centennial, CO: Marzano & Associates. Available: http://marzanoandassociates.com/documents/KohnResponse.pdf

Marzano, R. J., & Pickering, D. J. (in press). Errors and allegations about research on homework. *Phi Delta Kappan.*

Marzano, R. J., Pickering, D. J., & Pollock, J. E. (2001). *Classroom instruction that works: Research-based strategies for increasing student achievement.* Alexandria, VA: ASCD.

National Education Commission on Time and Learning (1994). *Prisoners of time.* Washington, DC: U.S. Department of Education.

Paschal, R. A., Weinstein, T., & Walberg, H. J. (1984). The effects of homework on learning: A quantitative synthesis. *Journal of Educational Research, 78*, 97–104.

Perkins, P. G., & Milgram, R. B. (1996). Parental involvement in homework: A double-edge sword. *International Journal of Adolescence and Youth, 6*(3), 195–203.

Riehl, C. (2006). Feeling better: A comparison of medical research and education research. *Educational Researcher, 35*(5), 24–29.

Van Voorhis, F. (2003). Interactive homework in middle school: Effects on family involvement and science achievement. *Journal of Educational Research, 96*, 323–338.

Walberg, H. J. (1999). Productive teaching. In H. C. Waxman & H. J. Walberg (Eds.), *New directions for teaching practice research* (pp. 75–104). Berkeley, CA: McCutchen.

Wallis, C. (2006). Viewpoint: The myth about homework. *Time, 168*(10), 57.

ROBERT J. MARZANO is a Senior Scholar at Mid-Continent Research for Education and Learning in Aurora, Colorado; an Associate Professor at Cardinal Stritch University in Milwaukee, Wisconsin; and President of Marzano & Associates consulting firm in Centennial, Colorado; robertjmarzano@aol.com. **DEBRA J. PICKERING** is a private consultant and Director of Staff Development in Littleton Public Schools, Littleton, Colorado; djplearn@hotmail.com.

From *Educational Leadership*, March 2007, pp. 74-79. Copyright © 2007 by ASCD. Reprinted by permission. The Association for Supervision and Curriculum Development is a worldwide community of educators advocating sound policies and sharing best practices to achieve the success of each learner. To learn more, visit ASCD at www.ascd.org

UNIT 6

Helping Children to Thrive in School

Unit Selections

Key Points to Consider

- What does it mean to be a ready school?

- Why is emotional stability so important to develop during the preschool years?

- Is it possible to prevent disruptive behavior before it occurs?

- How can a teacher build positive relationships with children?

- What skills other than physical can children develop on the playground?

Student Web Site

www.mhcls.com/online

Internet References

Further information regarding these Web sites may be found in this book's preface or online.

Future of Children
http://www.futureofchildren.org
Busy Teacher's Cafe
http://www.busyteacherscafe.com
Tips for Teachers
http://www.counselorandteachertips.com
You Can Handle Them All
http://www.disciplinehelp.com

Early childhood teaching is all about being proactive and establishing policies that support young children's development and learning. Good teachers are problem solvers just as children work to solve problems. Every day, teachers make decisions about how to guide children socially and emotionally. In attempting to determine what could be causing a child's emotional distress, teachers must take into account a myriad of factors. They consider physical, social, environmental, and emotional factors, in addition to the surface behavior of a child. Whether it is an individual child's behavior or interpersonal relationships, the pressing problem involves complex issues that require careful reflection and analysis. Even the most mature teachers spend many hours thinking and talking about the best ways to guide and support young children's behavior: What should I do about the child who is out of bounds? What do I do to best prepare the learning environment to meet the needs of all children? How can I develop effective relationships with children and their families? These are some of the questions teachers ask as they interact with young children on a day to day basis.

When those outside of the education profession talk about getting children ready to learn many early childhood professionals instinctively say to themselves, "Children come to us already learning. Our job is to make our schools and classrooms ready to accept all children". That is the theme of "Ready or Not, Here We Come" by Dowker, Schweinhart and Daniel-Echols. It is our responsibility to accommodate the learning environment and provide the support for children and their families to successfully transition to the next phase in their learning.

Many of the articles in this unit start with teachers establishing positive relationships with children. "Teacher-Child Relationships at the Forefront of Effective Practice" and "'You Got It!" are just two chosen for this edition that support the need for positive relationships as the cornerstone for building rapport. The other theme that is woven throughout the articles in this unit is the importance of social and emotional development on all areas of development. Teachers who rush to teach academic skills at the expense of fostering the children's social and emotion development will find there are many unexpected hurdles to jump. Children who are not secure or confident in their surroundings or comfortable with the adults in their life will not be strong learners. "Fostering Positive Transitions for School Success" highlights the importance of social emotional development and sets a proactive tone by providing teachers with an overview of the importance of children feeling secure about themselves and their place in life. Children who believe they are accepted and respected in the classroom feel confident and are able to develop genuine relationships with their peers and teacher. Teachers who have a limited number of disruptive children in their class are those teachers who take precautionary steps to establish firm rules, establish a supportive environment and help children learn about consequences of their behavior.

Laurence Mouton/Photoalto/PictureQuest

Determining strategies of guidance and discipline is important work for an early childhood teacher. Because the teacher-child relationship is foundational for emotional well-being and social competence, guidance is more than applying a single set of guidance techniques. Instead of one solitary model of classroom discipline strictly enforced, a broad range of techniques is more appropriate. It is only through careful analysis and reflection that teachers can look at children individually, assessing not only the child but the impact of family cultures as well, and determine what is appropriate and effective guidance.

Children crave fair and consistent guidelines from caring adults in their world. They want to know the consequences of their behavior and how to meet the expectations of others. When the expectations are clear and the students see a direct relation between their behavior and the consequences they begin to develop the self control that will be so important as they move through life.

Ready or Not, Here We Come

What It Means to Be a Ready School

PAULA M. DOWKER, WITH LARRY SCHWEINHART AND MARIJATA DANIEL-ECHOLS

In the game hide-and-seek, one player counts to 10 while the others run and hide. Now, depending on how fast the one who is "it" counts, some players may find they are not ready and hiding when that person comes looking for them. The problem of not being ready could stem from many causes: perhaps the player did not have the proper shoes, which made running difficult; maybe the player did not understand the rules and was not sure what to do; or perhaps the player had never played the game before. We educators of young children, prekindergarten through grade 3, encounter many of the same readiness issues when it comes to the children in our classrooms, because each child enters school with a completely different set of experiences and abilities.

Planning effectively for children with diverse backgrounds, learning styles, and school-readiness levels can be daunting. To better understand and respond to such challenges, early elementary educators need to become familiar with what it means to be a ready school, so they can assess and implement strategies to ensure success for all students. Those of us working with young children who will soon be entering school need to provide quality early childhood education and care that extends beyond preschool settings. When children move from high-quality early childhood experiences into ready schools, they benefit from having a strong foundation and access to superior tools with which to continue building upon that foundation.

We all have a stake in seeing that our children's schools are ready schools. A ready school is a comprehensive vision of what a school can do to ensure that all children who enter its doors will fulfill their potential as learners:

> The idea of a ready school broadens the definition of school readiness. Instead of only focusing on whether or not children arrive at school ready to learn, a more inclusive definition of readiness also considers whether or not school policies and practices support a commitment to the success of every child. The concept of school readiness must align the best of early childhood practices and elementary education in ways that build upon the strengths of each and locus equally on child outcomes, adult behaviors, and institutional characteristics. It is expected that children should come to school ready to learn and schools should

open their doors able to serve all children. (High/Scope Educational Research Foundation 2006, 1)

Is your school, or the school that the young children you serve will attend, a ready school? Are its classrooms ready classrooms? Consider your answers to the following assessment, which will give you some idea of how to evaluate a school in terms of readiness:

- Does the principal communicate a clear vision for the school—a vision that is committed to the success of every child?
- Are parents of incoming children contacted about registration and school entry three or more months before school starts?
- Do kindergarten teachers communicate with preschool/child care staff about children and curriculum on an ongoing basis?
- Do classrooms have a variety of manipulative materials and supplies for art, building, and hands-on learning?
- Are procedures in place for monitoring the fidelity of implementation of all instructional materials/methods?
- Does the school promote community linkages by making and following up on appropriate referrals of children and families to social service and health agencies?
- Do classroom activities provide accurate, practical, and respectful information regarding peoples' cultural backgrounds and experiences?
- Does the school employ improvement strategies that are based on an assessment of the quality of the classroom as well as children's progress? (High/Scope Educational Research Foundation 2006)

Between 2003 and 2006 the High/Scope Educational Research Foundation, funded by a grant from the W.K. Kellogg Foundation, researched, designed, and developed the Ready School Assessment. The assessment focuses on eight key dimensions that teachers and schools should evaluate when asking, "Are we a ready school?" The work of the National Education Goals Panel (Shore 1998) was an important source in identifying these dimensions. The dimensions were developed after researchers conducted intensive research and reality testing with practitioners throughout the nation. Assessment using the dimensions, listed here, can assist educators in evaluating their individual school's state of readiness:

1. **Leaders and leadership.** The principal, with the assistance of the teachers, advocates for and leads the ready school. For example, the principal encourages teachers to take responsibility for and implement ready school strategies. The principal provides professional development and resources on these strategies.

2. **Transitions.** Teachers, staff, and parent groups work with families, children, and the preschool teachers and caregivers before kindergarten and with families and children during kindergarten to smooth the transition from home to school. For example, teachers and staff at feeder early childhood programs are informed about registration before school starts so they can pass on to families information about kindergarten roundup dates, orientation dates, and any other planned transition activities.

3. **Teacher supports.** Classrooms, schedules, teams, and activities are organized to maximize the support for all adults to work effectively with children during the school day. For example, teachers from feeder early childhood programs (including those not part of the school) are invited to participate in professional development programs along with K–3 staff. This allows *all* adults to work effectively with children in both teaching venues and it allows teachers to share curriculum goals and benchmarks with each other.

4. **Engaging environments.** The school's learning environments employ elements that make them warm and inviting and actively engage children in a variety of learning activities. For example, classrooms have a variety of manipulative materials and supplies for art, building, and hands-on learning.

5. **Effective curricula.** The teachers and school diligently employ educational materials and methods shown to be effective in helping children achieve objectives required for grade-level proficiency. For example, teachers and staff are well informed about and well trained in developmentally appropriate methods and strategies for early childhood learners.

6. **Family, school, and community partnerships.** The teachers and school take specific steps to enhance parents' capacities to foster their children's readiness and to support children's learning in and outside of school. For example, teachers use an open-door policy that allows for, welcomes, and involves families' participation in classroom activities at all times of the day.

7. **Respecting diversity.** The teachers and school help all children succeed by interacting with children and families in ways that are compatible with individual needs, family backgrounds, and life experiences. For example, classrooms include many materials that reflect a variety of cultural backgrounds and experiences. Teachers plan classroom activities that provide accurate, practical, and respectful information regarding peoples' cultural backgrounds, traditions, languages, and experiences.

8. **Assessing progress.** Teachers and staff engage in ongoing improvement based on information that rigorously and systematically assesses classroom experiences, school practices that influence them, and children's progress toward curricular goals. For example, teachers address clearly defined and clearly stated curricular goals for each group/subgroup of children. In addition, the quality of the classroom experiences is assessed using a standardized, systematic approach. This results in teachers taking a focused look at what they are doing and making changes to the classroom experience so all students can achieve success (High/Scope Educational Research Foundation 2006).

A ready school is many things. It is a place where instruction is gauged to meet the learning level of each student, where diversity is welcome, where teachers have the support they need to do their best work for every learner. In this place partnerships between school, families, and community reinforce the education process. Most important, a ready school is a place that builds on its strengths and addresses challenges through the process of focused, ongoing school improvement.

Is your school, or the school that the young children you serve will attend, a ready school? For more information about becoming a ready school or about the Ready School Assessment, please contact Paula Dowker (pdowker@highscope.org) at the High/Scope Educational Research Foundation.

References

High/Scope Educational Research Foundation. 2006. Ready School Assessment. Ypsilanti, MI: High/Scope Press. Online: www.readyschool assessment.org.

Shore R. 1998. *Ready Schools.* A report of the Goal 1 Ready Schools Resource Group. Washington, DC: National Education Goals Panel. Online:http://govinfo.library.unt.edu/negp/Reports/readysch.pdf.

PAULA DOWKER is education specialist at High/Scope Educational Research Foundation in Ypsilanti, Michigan. Paula has been involved in Michigan's public education system for 16 years. She has been a teacher, administrator, and curriculum director. Paula is responsible for the dissemination of information regarding the Ready School Assessment nationwide and also is the designer and facilitator of the Ready School Training modules. **LAWRENCE J. SCHWEINHART,** PhD, is president of High/Scope Educational Research Foundation. A former member of the NAEYC Governing Board, Larry served as chair of the NAEYC Program Panel on Quality, Compensation, and Affordability. **MARIJATA C. DANIEL-ECHOLS,** PhD, is chair of the research division at the High/Scope Educational Research Foundation. She has served as the project director for High/Scope's W.K. Kellogg Foundation-funded Ready School Assessment instrument development project.

From *Young Children,* March 2007, pp. 68–70. Copyright © 2007 by National Association for the Education of Young Children. Reprinted by permission.

Heading Off Disruptive Behavior

How early intervention can reduce defiant behavior— and win back teaching time

HILL M. WALKER, ELIZABETH RAMSEY, AND FRANK M. GRESHAM

More and more children from troubled, chaotic homes are bringing well-developed patterns of antisocial behavior to school. Especially as these students get older, they wreak havoc on schools. Their aggressive, disruptive, and defiant behavior wastes teaching time, disrupts the learning of all students, threatens safety, overwhelms teachers—and ruins their own chances for successful schooling and a successful life.

In a poll of AFT teachers, 17 percent said they lost four or more hours of teaching time per week thanks to disruptive student behavior; another 19 percent said they lost two or three hours. In urban areas, fully 21 percent said they lost four or more hours per week. And in urban secondary schools, the percentage is 24. It's hard to see how academic achievement can rise significantly in the face of so much lost teaching time, not to mention the anxiety that is produced by the constant disruption (and by the implied safety threat), which must also take a toll on learning.

But it need not be this way in the future. Most of the disruption is caused by no more than a few students per class[1]—students who are, clinically speaking, "antisocial." Provided intervention begins when these children are young, preferably before they reach age 8, the knowledge, tools, and programs exist that would enable schools to head off most of this bad behavior—or at least greatly reduce its frequency. Schools are not the source of children's behavior problems, and they can't completely solve them on their own. But the research is becoming clear: Schools can do a lot to minimize bad behavior—and in so doing, they help not only the antisocial children, they greatly advance their central goal of educating children.

In recent decades, antisocial behavior has been the subject of intense study by researchers in various disciplines including biology, sociology, social work, psychiatry, corrections, education, and psychology. Great progress has been made in understanding and developing solutions for defiant, disruptive, and aggressive behavior (see Burns, 2002). The field of psychology, in particular, with its increasingly robust theories of "social learning" and "cognition," has developed a powerful empirical literature that can assist school personnel in coping with, and ultimately preventing, a good deal of problematic behavior. Longitudinal and retrospective studies conducted in the United States, Australia, New Zealand, Canada, and various western European countries have yielded knowledge on the long-term outcomes of children who adopt antisocial behavior, especially those who arrive at school with it well developed (see Reid et al., 2002). Most importantly, a strong knowledge base has been assembled on interventions that can head off this behavior or prevent it from hardening (Loeber and Farrington, 2001).

To date, however, this invaluable knowledge base has been infused into educational practice in an extremely limited fashion. A major goal of this article (and of our much larger book) is to communicate and adapt this knowledge base for effective use by educators in coping with the rising tide of antisocial students populating today's schools. In our book, you'll find fuller explanations of the causes of antisocial behavior, of particular forms of antisocial behavior like bullying, and of effective—and ineffective—interventions for schools. And all of this draws on a combination of the latest research and the classic research studies that have stood the test of time.

In this article, we look first at the source of antisocial behavior itself and ask: Why is it so toxic when it arrives in school? Second, we look at the evidence suggesting that early intervention is rare in schools. Third, we look at a range of practices that research indicates should be incorporated into school and classroom practice. Fourth, in the accompanying sidebars we give examples of how these practices have been combined in different ways to create effective programs.

I. Where Does Antisocial Behavior Come from and What Does That Mean for Schools?

Much to the dismay of many classroom teachers who deal with antisocial students, behavior-management practices that work so well with typical students do not work in managing antisocial behavior. In fact, teachers find that their tried and true behavior-management practices often make the behavior of antisocial students much worse. As a general rule, educators do not have a thorough understanding of the origins and developmental course of such behavior and are not well trained to deal with moderate to severe levels of antisocial behavior. The older these students become and the further along the educational track they progress, the more serious their problems become and the more difficult they are to manage.

How can it be that behavior-management practices somehow work differently for students with antisocial behavior patterns? Why do they react differently? Do they learn differently? Do they require interventions based on a completely different set of learning principles? As we shall see, the principles by which they acquire and exercise their behavioral pattern are quite typical and predictable.

Frequent and excessive noncompliance in school (or home) is an important first indicator of future antisocial behavior.

One of the most powerful principles used to explain how behavior is learned is known as the Matching Law (Herrnstein, 1974). In his original formulation, Herrnstein (1961) stated that the rate of any given behavior matches the rate of reinforcement for that behavior. For example, if aggressive behavior is reinforced once every three times it occurs (e.g., by a parent giving in to a temper tantrum) and prosocial behavior is reinforced once every 15 times it occurs (e.g., by a parent praising a polite request), then the Matching Law would predict that, on average, aggressive behavior will be chosen five times more frequently than prosocial behavior. Research has consistently shown that behavior does, in fact, closely follow the Matching Law (Snyder, 2002). Therefore, how parents (and later, teachers) react to aggressive, defiant, and other bad behavior is extremely important. The Matching Law applies to all children; it indicates that antisocial behavior is learned—and, at least at a young enough age, can be unlearned. (As we will see in the section that reviews effective intervention techniques, many interventions—like maintaining at least a 4 to 1 ratio of praising versus reprimanding—have grown out of the Matching Law.)

First Comes the Family . . .

Antisocial behavior is widely believed to result from a mix of constitutional (i.e., genetic and neurobiological) and environmental (i.e., family and community) factors (Reid et al., 2002). In the vast majority of cases, the environmental factors are the primary causes—but in a small percentage of cases, there is an underlying, primarily constitutional, cause (for example, autism, a difficult temperament, attention deficit/hyperactivity disorder [ADHD], or a learning disorder). Not surprisingly, constitutional and environmental causes often overlap and even exacerbate each other, such as when parents are pushed to their limits by a child with a difficult temperament or when a child with ADHD lives in a chaotic environment.

Patterson and his colleagues (Patterson et al., 1992) have described in detail the main environmental causes of antisocial behavior. Their model starts by noting the social and personal factors that put great stress on family life (e.g., poverty, divorce, drug and alcohol problems, and physical abuse). These stressors disrupt normal parenting practices, making family life chaotic, unpredictable, and hostile. These disrupted parenting practices, in turn, lead family members to interact with each other in negative, aggressive ways and to attempt to control each others' behavior through coercive means such as excessive yelling, threats, intimidation, and physical force. In this environment, children learn that the way to get what they want is through what psychologists term "coercive" behavior: For parents, coercion means threatening, yelling, intimidating, and even hitting to force children to behave. (Patterson [1982] conducted a sequential analysis showing that parental use of such coercive strategies to suppress hostile and aggressive behavior actually increased the likelihood of such behavior in the future by 50 percent.)

For children, coercive tactics include disobeying, whining, yelling, throwing tantrums, threatening parents, and even hitting—all in order to avoid doing what the parents want. In homes where such coercive behavior is common, children become well-acquainted with how hostile behavior escalates—and with which of their behaviors ultimately secure adult surrender. This is the fertile ground in which antisocial behavior is bred. The negative effects tend to flow across generations much like inherited traits.[2]

By the time they are old enough for school, children who have developed an antisocial profile (due to either constitutional or environmental factors) have a limited repertoire of cooperative behavior skills, a predilection to use coercive tactics to control and manipulate others, and a well-developed capacity for emotional outbursts and confrontation.

. . . Then Comes School

For many young children, making the transition from home to school is fraught with difficulty. Upon school entry, children must learn to share, negotiate disagreements, deal with conflicts, and participate in competitive activities. And, they must do so in a manner that builds friendships with some peers and, at a minimum, social acceptance from others (Snyder, 2002). Children with antisocial behavior patterns have enormous difficulty accomplishing these social tasks. In fact, antisocial children are more than twice as likely as regular children to initiate unprovoked verbal or physical aggression toward peers, to reciprocate peer aggression toward them, and to continue aggressive behavior once it has been initiated (Snyder, 2002).[3]

From preschool to mid-elementary school, antisocial students' behavior changes in form and increases in intensity. During the preschool years, these children often display aversive behaviors such as frequent whining and noncompliance. Later, during the elementary school years, these behaviors take the form of less frequent but higher intensity acts such as hitting, fighting, bullying, and stealing. And during adolescence, bullying and hitting may escalate into robbery, assault, lying, stealing, fraud, and burglary (Snyder and Stoolmiller, 2002).

Although the specific form of the behavior changes (e.g., from noncompliance to bullying to assault), its function remains the same: Coercion remains at the heart of the antisocial behavior. As children grow older, they learn that the more noxious and painful they can make their behavior to others, the more likely they are to accomplish their goals—whether that goal is to avoid taking out the trash or escape a set of difficult mathematics problems. An important key to preventing this escalation (and therefore avoiding years of difficult behavior) is for adults to limit the use of coercive tactics with children—and for these adults to avoid surrendering in the face of coercive tactics used by the child. This has clear implications for school and teacher practices (and, of course, for parent training, which is not the subject of this article).

Frequent and excessive noncompliance in school (or home) is an important first indicator of future antisocial behavior. A young child's noncompliance is often a "gate key" behavior that triggers a vicious cycle involving parents, peers, and teachers. Further, it serves as a port of entry into much more serious forms of antisocial behavior. By treating noncompliance effectively at the early elementary age (or preferably even earlier), it is possible to prevent the development of more destructive behavior.

II. Early Intervention Is Rare

How many children are antisocial? How many are getting help early? To study the national incidence of antisocial behavior among children, researchers focus on two psychiatric diagnoses: oppositional defiant disorder and conduct disorder. Oppositional defiant disorder, the less serious of the two, consists of an ongoing pattern of uncooperative, angry behavior including things like deliberately trying to bother others and refusing to accept responsibility for mistakes. Conduct disorder is characterized by severe verbal and physical aggression, property destruction, and deceitful behavior that persist over time (usually one or more years). Formal surveys have generally indicated that between two and six percent of the general population of U.S. children and youth has some form of conduct disorder (Kazdin, 1993). Without someone intervening early to teach these children how to behave better, half of them will maintain the disorder into adulthood and the other half will suffer significant adjustment problems (e.g., disproportionate levels of marital discord and difficulty keeping a job) during their adult lives (Kazdin, 1993). (It is worth noting that on the way to these unpleasant outcomes, most will disrupt many classrooms and overwhelm many teachers.) When we add in oppositional defiant disorder (which often precedes and co-occurs with conduct disorder), estimates have been as high as 16 percent of the U.S. youth population (Eddy, Reid, and Curry, 2002).

In contrast, school systems typically identify (through the Individuals with Disabilities Education Act [IDEA]) slightly less than one percent of the public school population as having emotional and behavioral problems. Further, the great tendency

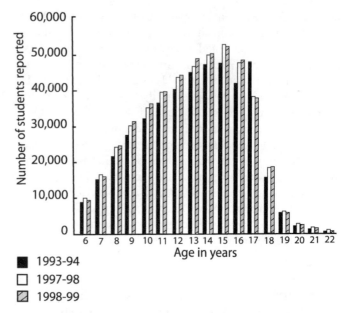

Figure 1 Students with emotional disturbance served by age, selected school years

of schools is to identify these behavioral problems quite late in a child's school career.

The figure above provides a stark example of this practice, which is more typical than not in today's public school systems. Walker, Nikiosha, Zeller, Severson, and Feil (2000) examined the number of K–12 students in the 1993–94, 1997–98, and 1998–99 school years who were certified as emotionally disturbed (the IDEA category that captures antisocial students). As the figure shows, the number of students certified as emotionally disturbed peaks around age 15 (approximately 50,000 cases) during the 1997–98 and 1998–99 school years. Similarly, the older data, from the 1993–94 school year, show the peak in referrals spread over the ages 14, 15, and 17. These results suggest that a large number of students, who were no doubt in need of supports and services for emotional disturbance in their elementary and middle school years, were not referred, evaluated, or served under special education.[4] Only in adolescence, when their behavior problems had become so intractable and difficult to accommodate, were many of these students finally identified and served. This practice of delayed referral is the polar opposite of what research clearly shows is necessary.

Our society's social, cultural, and economic problems are spilling over into our schools. They are greatly complicating schools' central task of educating students safely and effectively. But the research is clear and growing: Even though many children and youth come from and return to chaotic, coercive home environments on a daily basis, they can still acquire sufficient behavioral control to succeed in school—and to allow classmates to learn in an orderly environment.

We have substantial knowledge about how to divert at-risk children, youth, and families from destructive outcomes.[5] We believe the problem is not one of knowing what to do, but of convincing schools to effectively use research-based intervention programs over the long term.

The remainder of this article is devoted to providing educators with guidelines and programs for early intervention that greatly reduce antisocial behavior. There are no magic bullets in the material presented herein. Dealing with the antisocial student population is difficult, frustrating, and, because schools tend to intervene too late, often without identifiable rewards. However, of all those who suffer from conditions and disorders that impair school performance, these students are among those with the greatest capacity for change—particularly when they first start school.

III. What Can Schools Do?

Schools are not the source of children's antisocial behavior, and they cannot completely eliminate it. But schools do have substantial power to prevent it in some children and greatly reduce it in others.

First, and in some ways most importantly, schools can help by being academically effective. The fact is, academic achievement and good behavior reinforce each other: Experiencing some success academically is related to decreases in acting out; conversely, learning positive behaviors is related to doing better academically. Kellam and his colleagues (1994), for example, showed experimentally that gains in first-grade academic achievement, as measured by standardized achievement tests, resulted in substantially reduced levels of aggression, according to behavior ratings by their teachers. And, confirming what common sense tells us, Caprara, Barbaranelli, Pastorelli, Bandura, and Zimbardo (2000) found that positive behaviors (like cooperating, sharing, and consoling) among very young children contributed to their later academic achievement.

Second, schools can, to a large and surprising extent, affect the level of aggression in young boys just by the orderliness of their classrooms. An intriguing longitudinal study dramatically illustrates the role of this variable in the development or prevention of aggressive behavior from first grade to middle school (Kellam, Rebok, Ialongo, and Mayer, 1994). After randomly assigning students to first-grade classrooms, researchers found that nearly half of the classrooms were chaotic and the remainder were reasonably well-managed. Of the boys in the study who began schooling in the top quartile of aggressive behavior (as rated by their teachers), those assigned to orderly classrooms had odds of 3:1 in favor of being highly aggressive in middle school. However, those boys assigned to chaotic classrooms had odds of 59:1 for being highly aggressive in middle school. This seminal finding suggests that poor classroom management by teachers in grade one is a huge, but preventable, factor in the development of antisocial behavior—and, conversely, that effective classroom management can have an enormous long-term positive effect on behavior. Thus, working closely with first-grade teachers (and, presumably, other early-grade teachers) on their behavior management can yield substantial future benefits for students and their schools by offsetting destructive outcomes.

Aggressive first-grade boys assigned to orderly classrooms had odds of 3:1 in favor of being highly aggressive in middle school. Those assigned to chaotic classrooms had odds of 59:1 for being highly aggressive in middle school.

But to some extent, this just begs the larger question: How can schools and their teachers create and sustain orderly classrooms? We summarize here the key findings and conclusions from 40 years of research. First, we present a three-tiered intervention model that matches the extent of children's behavioral problems to the power (and, therefore, cost) of the programs implemented. Second, we offer tools that can accurately and effectively identify students as young as kindergarten (and, in daycare or preschool settings, even at-risk three-year-olds can be identified) who are likely to become school behavior problems (and, later in life, delinquents and even adult criminals). Third, we review five techniques that, in combination, are at the heart of preventing antisocial behavior. Fourth, we describe specific programs with substantial and growing records of effectiveness that successfully incorporate all of the above into entirely doable, economical, and feasible school interventions. These programs can be purchased by schools from a variety of for-profit publishers and non-profit child and family services organizations. Some are inexpensive; the more expensive interventions tend to be individualized to meet the needs of highly aggressive children. All of the programs described in this article can be funded with either IDEA resources or school improvement funds. Programs for antisocial children, such as those described here, can also be funded in partnership with mental health agencies and/or through grants available through the Safe and Drug Free Schools division of the U.S. Department of Education. (See box, Funding Early Interventions.)

A. Three Levels of Intervention

Research has shown that the best way to prevent antisocial behavior is actually to start with an inexpensive school-wide intervention and then add on more intensive interventions for the most troubled kids. Building on work done by the U.S. Public Health Service, Hill Walker and his colleagues developed a model with three progressively more intensive levels of intervention to address challenging behavior within schools (Walker, Horner, Sugai, Bullis, Sprague, Bricker, and Kaufman, 1996). This model has proved to be very popular among educational researchers and has been broadly adopted by practitioners as a way to select and coordinate interventions. It is sometimes referred to in educational forums as "the Oregon Model." However, this approach is clearly a matter of public domain and is not owned by anyone. The three levels of intervention are known as "universal," "selected," and "indicated." Each is briefly described below.

Funding Early Interventions

With the research reviewed here, building support for the idea of early interventions should not be difficult—but finding funds could be if you don't know where to look. One source is Title I. Schools in which at least 40 percent of the students are poor should look into using the schoolwide provision of Title I to fund universal interventions. Under Title I schoolwide, you can combine several federal, state, and local funding streams to support school improvement programs. Insofar as students are identified as emotionally disturbed, their interventions can be funded by IDEA. The federal government also provides funding to reduce behavior problems through the Safe and Drug Free Schools and Communities Act. In this case, state education agencies receive funds to make grants to local education agencies and governors receive funds to make complementary grants to community-based organizations. Schools can also partner with mental health agencies, enabling services to be covered by insurance such as Medicaid and the State Children's Health Insurance Program. Plus, most states have funding streams that could support the programs described in this article. (For more information on funding, see chapter two of *Safe, Supportive, and Successful Schools: Step by Step*, available from Sopris West for $49; order online at www.sopriswest.com/swstore /product.asp?sku=872)

"Universal" interventions are school or classroom practices that affect all students. Examples of universal interventions relevant to behavior are classwide social skills training and well-enforced school discipline codes. (Outside of education, the polio vaccination is an example of a "universal intervention.") It may seem odd to implement a program for all students when most teachers can easily identify children who have, or are developing, antisocial behavior. But schoolwide programs accomplish three things. First, they improve almost all students' behavior—and most students, even if they don't qualify as troublemakers, still need some practice being well-behaved. Second, universal interventions have their greatest impact among students who "are on the margins"—those students who are just beginning to be aggressive or defiant. Sometimes, systematic exposure to a universal intervention will be sufficient to tip them in the right direction. Third, the universal intervention offers a foundation that supports the antisocial students throughout the day by reinforcing what they are learning in their more intensive selected and indicated interventions; these latter interventions are more efficient and have a greater impact when they are applied in the context of a prior, well-implemented, universal intervention.

Approximately 80 to 90 percent of all students will respond successfully to a well-implemented universal intervention (Sugai et al., 2002). Once the school environment is orderly, the antisocial students pop up like corks in water. These students have "selected" themselves out as needing more powerful "selected" interventions that employ much more expensive and labor-intensive techniques. The goal with these students is to decrease the frequency of their problem behaviors, instill appropriate behaviors, and make the children more responsive to universal interventions (Sugai et al., 2002). While selected interventions typically are based in the school, to be their most effective they often require parental involvement. Nevertheless, even when parents refuse to participate, selected interventions still have positive effects and are well worth the effort.

The vast majority of antisocial students will start behaving better after being involved in universal and selected interventions, but schools can expect that a very small percentage of antisocial students (about one to five percent of the total youth population) will not. These are the most severe cases—the most troubled children from the most chaotic homes—and they require extremely intensive, individualized, and expensive interventions. These interventions, called "indicated," are typically family focused, with participation and support from mental health, juvenile justice, and social service agencies, as well as schools. Most non-specialized schools will find that running such an intervention is beyond their capacity. It's for such students that alternative education settings are necessary.

This three-tiered intervention model offers a structure that educators can use when they are reviewing and trying to coordinate programs. It ensures that all students' needs will be met efficiently—each child is exposed to the level of intervention that his behavior shows he needs. This is a very cost-effective model for schools because interventions become much more expensive as they become more specialized.

But it all begins with effective early screening.

B. Early Screening and Identification of Potentially Antisocial Students

Many fields have well-established practices to identify problems early and allow for more effective treatments. For instance, in medicine, routine screening procedures such as prostate-specific antigen (PSA) tests to detect prostate cancer, mammograms to detect breast cancer, and Papanicolaou (Pap) tests to detect the early states of cervical cancer have been routine for years. Unfortunately, similar proactive, early identification approaches are not commonly used to identify children with, or at risk of developing, antisocial behavior.

But research shows that early identification is absolutely critical: Children who have not learned appropriate, non-coercive ways to interact socially by around 8 years of age (the end of third grade) will likely continue displaying some degree of antisocial behavior throughout their lives (Loeber and Farrington, 1998). We also know that the longer such children go without access to effective and early intervention services (particularly after the age of 8), the more resistant to change their behavior problems will be (Gresham, 1991) and the more expensive it will be to induce the change.

Yet, as discussed previously, schools offer special education services to just one percent of students, though two to 16 percent manifest some form of antisocial behavior—and virtually no special education services are provided before students become adolescents. The technology (usually simple normed checklists and observation instruments, as described below) for identifying such children is gradually becoming more accurate for children at younger and younger ages (Severson and Walker, 2002).

A particularly valuable approach to screening is known as "multiple gating" (Loeber, Dishion, and Patterson, 1984). Multiple gating is a process in which a series of progressively more precise (and expensive) assessments or "gates" are used to identify children who need help with their behavior. One such screening procedure is the Systematic Screening for Behavior Disorders (SSBD) (Walker and Severson, 1990).

This screening procedure offers a cost-effective, mass screening of all students in grades one to six in regular education classrooms. The SSBD is made up of a combination of teacher nominations (Gate 1), teacher rating scales (Gate 2), and observations of classroom and playground problem behavior (Gate 3). It was nationally standardized on 4,500 students for the Gate 2 measures and approximately 1,300 students for the Gate 3 measures. It represents a significant advance in enabling the systematic and comprehensive screening of behavioral problems among general education students (Gresham, Lane, and Lambros, 2002). The major advantage of the SSBD is first, its ease of use, and second, its common set of standards for teachers to use in evaluating students' behavior; these standards remove most of the subjectivity that is endemic to the referral process commonly used in schools (Severson and Walker, 2002). If all schools employed universal screening (and backed it up with effective early interventions), an enormous amount of defiant and destructive behavior could be prevented—and innumerable teaching hours could be preserved.

Researchers have found that teachers do tend to praise their regular students for good behavior, but they tend not to seize opportunities to praise antisocial students when they are behaving well.

C. Key Features of Effective Interventions

When dealing with well-established antisocial behavior, a combination of the following techniques is usually required in order to successfully bring about behavior change: (1) a consistently enforced schoolwide behavior code, (2) social-skills training, (3) appropriately-delivered adult praise for positive behavior, (4) reinforcement contingencies and response costs, and (5) time-out (see Wolf, 1978). Each of these techniques is briefly explained below.

Over the past three decades, an extensive body of research has developed on the effectiveness of these techniques for preventing and remediating problem behavior within the context of schools. Studies of the use of these techniques show that

positive strategies (appropriate praise, social-skills training, providing free-time privileges or activities) are generally sufficient for developing and maintaining the appropriate behavior of most students. However, students with challenging behavior often also require sanctions of some type (e.g., time-out or loss of privileges) in order to successfully address their problems. Extensive research clearly shows that, to be most effective, intervention programs or regimens incorporating these techniques should be applied across multiple settings (classrooms, hallways, playgrounds, etc.), operate for a sufficient time period for them to work, and should involve teachers and parents in school-home partnerships whenever possible.

No single technique applied in isolation will have an enduring impact. Used together, however, they are effective—especially for antisocial students age 8 or younger. Assembling these techniques into feasible and effective daily routines can be done by individual teachers in well-run schools. But it is difficult, time-consuming, and fraught with trial and error. Among the fruits of the past several decades of research on this topic is a group of carefully developed and tested programs that integrate these techniques into entirely doable programs that don't overly distract teachers from their main job: teaching. Several are briefly described in this and the following section.

1. A Well-Enforced Schoolwide Behavior Code

A schoolwide behavior code creates a positive school climate by clearly communicating and enforcing a set of behavioral standards. The code should consist of 5 to 7 rules—and it's essential to carefully define and provide examples of each rule. Ideally, school administrators, teachers, related services staff, students, and parents should all be involved in the development of the code. But writing the code is just the first step. Too often, teachers and others complain, a behavior code is established—and left to wither. To be effective, students must be instructed in what it means, have opportunities to practice following the rules, have incentives for adhering to it (as described in the third and fourth techniques), and know that violating it brings consequences.

One excellent, inexpensive program for teaching the schoolwide behavior expectations reflected in a code is called Effective Behavior Support (EBS). The principal features of EBS are that all staff (administrative, classroom, lunchroom, playground, school bus, custodial, etc.) recognize and abide by the same set of behavioral expectations for all students. The behavior expectations are explicitly taught to students and they are taught in each relevant venue. In groups of 30 to 45, students are taken to various parts of the school (e.g., the bus loading zone, cafeteria, main hallway, gym, and classrooms) to discuss specific examples of behaviors that would, and would not, meet the behavior expectations. Once they have learned the expectations, they are motivated to meet them by earning rewards and praise for their good behavior.

2. Social Skills Training

As discussed earlier, many antisocial students enter school without adequate knowledge of—or experience with—appropriate social skills. These skills must be taught, practiced, and reinforced. This is the purpose of social skills training. Skills taught include empathy, anger management, and problem solving. They are taught using standard instructional techniques and practiced so that students not only learn new skills, but also begin using them throughout the school day and at home. While the training is vital for antisocial students, all students benefit from improving their social skills—especially students "on the margin" of antisocial behavior. Social skills curricula are typically taught in one or two periods a week over the course of several months and in multiple grades.

3. Adult Praise

Adult praise (from teachers, parents, or others) is a form of focused attention that communicates approval and positive regard. It is an abundantly available, natural resource that is greatly underutilized. Researchers have found that teachers do tend to praise their regular students for good behavior, but they tend not to seize opportunities to praise antisocial students when they are behaving well (Mayer & Sulzer-Azaroff, 2002). This is indeed unfortunate because praise that is behavior specific and delivered in a positive and genuine fashion is one of our most effective tools for motivating all students and teaching them important skills. Reavis et al. (1996) note that praise should be immediate, frequent, enthusiastic, descriptive, varied, and involve eye contact. We would also suggest that the ratio of praise to criticism and reprimands be at least 4:1—and higher if possible. Although antisocial students may not immediately respond to praise because of their long history of negative interactions with the adults in their lives, when paired with other incentives (such as the type of reward system described below), the positive impact of praise will eventually increase.

4. Reinforcement Contingencies and Response Costs

Rewards and penalties of different sorts are a common feature of many classroom management strategies. Research shows that there are specific "best" ways to arrange these reinforcements to effectively motivate students to behave appropriately. These strategies are called individual reinforcement contingencies, group reinforcement contingencies, and response costs. Individual contingencies are private, one-to-one arrangements between a teacher or parent and a student in which specified, positive consequences are made available dependent ("contingent") upon the student's performance. Earning a minute of free time for every 10 or 15 math problems correctly solved, or attempted, is an example of an individual contingency.

Group contingencies are arrangements in which an entire group of individuals (e.g., a class) is treated as a single unit and the group's performance, as a whole, is evaluated to determine whether a reward is earned, such as an extra five minutes of recess. (Note: A group can fail to earn a reward, such as an extra five minutes of recess, but should not be penalized, such as by losing five minutes of the normal recess.) This strategy gets peers involved in encouraging the antisocial student to behave better. For example, if the antisocial student disrupts the class, instead of laughing at his antics, other students will encourage him to quiet down so that they can all earn the reward. To make it easier to keep track of students'

behavior, reinforcement contingencies are often set up as point systems in which students must earn a certain number of points within a certain time period in order to earn a reward.

"Response costs" are a form of penalty that is added to the package of contingencies when working toward a reward is not quite enough to change students' behavior. Teachers can increase the effectiveness of contingencies by adding a response cost so that good behavior earns points and bad behavior subtracts points—making it much harder to earn a reward. (Response costs are the basis for late fees, traffic tickets, penalties in football, foul shots in basketball, and other sanctions in public life.)

5. Time-Out

Time-out is a technique of last resort in which students are removed for just five to 15 minutes from situations in which they have trouble controlling their behavior and/or their peers' attention is drawn to their inappropriate behavior. We recommend both in-classroom time-out for minor infractions and out-of-classroom time-out (the principal's office or a designated time-out room) for more serious infractions. Students should be given the option of volunteering for brief periods of time-out when they temporarily cannot control their own behavior, but teachers should *never* physically try to force students into time-out. Finally, *in-class* time-out should be used sparingly and should *not* be used with older students. Older students who need to be removed from a situation can be sent to the principal's office or another "cooldown" room instead of having an in-class time-out.

The research foundation for these techniques is quite strong and the empirical evidence of their effectiveness is both persuasive and growing. For the past 40 years, researchers in applied behavior analysis have worked closely with school staff and others in testing and demonstrating the effectiveness of these techniques within real world settings like classrooms and playgrounds. Literally hundreds of credible studies have documented the effectiveness of each of these techniques—as well as combinations of them—in remediating the problems that antisocial children and youth bring to schooling. The research has also surfaced guidelines for the effective application of the techniques in school contexts (Walker, 1995).

IV. Effective Programs for Preventing Antisocial Behavior

In spite of huge advances in our knowledge of how to prevent and treat antisocial behavior in the past decade, the Surgeon General's Report on Youth Violence indicates that less than 10 percent of services delivered in schools and communities targeting antisocial behavior patterns are evidence-based (see Satcher, 2001). As these children move through schools without effective intervention services and supports, their problems are likely to become more intractable and ever more resistant to change. This is simply not necessary. Effective, manageable programs exist.

Effective programs require an upfront investment of time and energy, but they more than "pay for themselves" in terms of teaching time won back.

We highlight three promising interventions—Second Step, First Step to Success, and Multisystemic Therapy—as examples of, respectively, universal, selected, and indicated interventions. The coordinated implementation of these or similar programs can make a remarkable difference in the orderliness of schools and classrooms and in the lives of antisocial youth (not to mention the victims of their aggression).

Second Step, a social skills training program for K-9 students, is described in detail. It was recently rated as the number one program for ensuring school safety by a blue ribbon panel of the U.S. Department of Education. Evaluations of Second Step have found results ranging from decreases in aggression and disruption among 109 preschool and kindergarten children from low-income, urban homes (McMahon, 2000) to less hostility and need for adult supervision among over 1,000 second- to fifth-grade students (Frey, Nolen, Van Schoiack-Edstrom, and Hirschstein, 2001).

First Step, is an intensive intervention for highly aggressive K-3 students. Experimental studies with kindergartners have found great improvments in their overall classroom behavior and academic engagement, and substantial reductions in their aggression during implementation and over many years following the end of intervention (see Walker, Kavanagh, Stiller, Golly, Severson, and Feil, 1998; Epstein and Walker, 2002). Similarly, studies involving two sets of identical twins enrolled in regular kindergarten programs found that exposure to the program produced powerful behavior changes upon introduction of the intervention that were maintained throughout the program's implementation (Golly, Sprague, Walker, Beard, and Gorham, 2000). These types of positive effects have also been replicated by other investigators. The First Step program has been included in six national reviews of effective early interventions for addressing oppositional and/or aggressive behavior in school.

Multisystemic Therapy (MST) is a family-focused intervention conducted by a trained therapist. It is aimed at the most severely at-risk youth, those who have been or are about to be incarcerated, often for violent offenses. Very often, the student has already been assigned to an alternative education setting. The therapist teaches parents the skills they need to assist their antisocial child to function more effectively across a range of social contexts. Daily contact between the student and therapist is common in the early stages of MST and reduces to several times per week as the intervention progresses. Therapists periodically talk to teachers to find out about the children's behavior, attendance, and work habits. Most importantly, teachers need to let therapists know when they perceive incremental improvements in the children's behavior—the therapists use this information to guide their work with the families. According to

the Blueprints for Violence Prevention Project, MST has been found to reduce long-term rates of being re-arrested by 25 to 70 percent, to greatly improve family functioning, and to lessen mental health problems (Blueprints, 2003). (To find out if MST is available in your area, visit www.mstservices.com).

As the research clearly shows, these three programs have the potential to prevent countless acts of aggression and positively influence both school and family functioning.

Disruptive student behavior will decrease and teaching time will increase, allowing all children to learn more. Office discipline referrals will decrease, freeing up school staff to address other school needs like supporting instruction. Effective programs do require an upfront investment of time and energy, but over the school year, and certainly over the school career, they more than "pay for themselves" in terms of teaching time won back.

An obvious subtext in the article has been that elementary schools—and especially K-3 teachers—must bear the burden of preventing antisocial behavior. This may come as a surprise since behavior problems seem so much more severe as children age. But if there's one uncontestable finding from the past 40 years of research on antisocial children, it's this: The longer students are allowed to be aggressive, defiant, and destructive, the more difficult it is to turn them around. While high schools can, and should, do what they can to help antisocial students control themselves, elementary schools can, and should, actually help antisocial children to become socially competent.

Notes

1. In the AFT's poll, of the 43 percent of teachers who said they had students in their classes with discipline problems, more than half said the problems were caused by one to three students. Poll conducted by Peter D. Hart Research Associates, October 1995.

2. It is important to note that the kind of coercive interaction described is very different from parents' need to establish authority in order to appropriately discipline their children. This is accomplished through the clear communication of behavioral expectations, setting limits, monitoring and supervising children's behavior carefully, and providing positive attention and rewards or privileges for conforming to those expectations. It also means using such strategies as ignoring, mildly reprimanding, redirecting, and/or removing privileges when they do not. These strategies allow parents to maintain authority without relying on the coercion described above and without becoming extremely hostile or giving in to children's attempts to use coercion.

3. This unfortunate behavior pattern soon leads to peer rejection (Reid, Patterson and Snyder, 2002). When behaviorally at-risk youth are rejected and forsaken by normal, well-behaved peers, they often begin to form friendships amongst themselves. If, over several years (and particularly in adolescence), these friendships solidify in such a way that these youth identify with and feel like members of a deviant peer group, they have a 70 percent chance of a felony arrest within two years (Patterson et al., 1992).

4. Kauffman (1999) suggests that the field of education actually "prevents prevention" of behavioral disorders through well-meaning efforts to "protect" difficult children from being labeled and stigmatized by the screening and identification process.

5. Successful model programs have been reviewed and described extensively by Catalano, Loeber, and McKinney (1999), by Loeber and Farrington (2001), and by Reid and his colleagues (2002).

References

Blueprints for Violence Prevention (2003). Multisystemic Therapy online at www.colorado.edu/cspv/blueprints/model/programs/MST.html

Burns, B. (2002). Reasons for hope for children and families: A perspective and overview. In B. Murns & K.K. Hoagwood (Eds.), *Community treatment for youth: Evidence-based interventions for severe emotional and behavioral disorders* (pp. 1–15). New York: Oxford University Press.

Caprara, G., Barbaranelli, C., Pastorelli, C., Brandura, A., & Zimbardo, P. (2000). Prosocial foundations of children's academic achievement. *Psychological Science, 11*(4), 302–306.

Catalano, R., Loeber, R., & McKinney, K. (1999). School and community interventions to prevent serious and violent offending. *Juvenile Justice Bulletin.* U.S. Department of Justice, Office of Juvenile Justice and Delinquency Prevention, Washington, D.C.

Eddy, J.M., Reid, J.B., & Curry, V. (2002). The etiology of youth antisocial behavior, delinquency and violence and a public health approach to prevention. In M.R. Shinn, H.M. Walker, & G. Stoner (Eds.), *Interventions for academic and behavior problems II: Preventive and remedial approaches,* (pp. 27–51). Bethesda, Md.: National Association for School Psychologists.

Epstein, M. & Walker, H. (2002). Special education: Best practices and First Step to Success. In B. Burns & K. Hoagwood (Eds.), *Community treatment for youth: Evidence-based intervention for severe emotional and behavioral disorders* (pp. 177–197). New York: Oxford University Press.

Frey, K.S., Nolan, S.B., Van Schoiack-Edstrom, L., and Hirschstein, M. (2001, June). "Second Step: Effects on Social Goals and Behavior." Paper presented at the annual meeting of the Society for Prevention Research, Washington, D.C.

Golly, A., Sprague, J., Walker, H.M., Beard, K., & Gorham, G. (2000). The First Step to Success program: An analysis of outcomes with identical twins across multiple baselines. *Behavioral Disorders, 25*(3), 170–182.

Gresham, F.M. (1991). Conceptualizing behavior disorders in terms of resistance to intervention. *School Psychology Review, 20,* 23–36.

Gresham, F.M., Lane, K., & Lambros, K. (2002). Children with conduct and hyperactivity attention problems: Identification, assessment and intervention. In K. Lane, F.M. Gresham, & T. O'Shaughnessy (Eds.), *Children with or at risk for emotional and behavioral disorders* (pp. 210–222). Boston: Allyn & Bacon.

Grossman, D., Neckerman, M., Koepsell, T., Ping-Yu Liu, Asher, K., Beland, K., Frey, K., & Rivara, F. (1997). Effectiveness of a violence prevention curriculum among children in elementary school: A randomized, control trial. *Journal of the American Medical Association, 277*(20), pp. 1605–1611.

Herrnstein, R. (1961). Relative and absolute strength of response as a function of frequency of reinforcement. *Journal of the Experimental Analysis of Behavior, 4,* 267–272.

Herrnstein, R. (1974). Formal properties of the matching law. *Journal of the Experimental Analysis of Behavior, 21,* 486–495.

Kauffman, J. (1999). How we prevent emotional and behavioral disorders. *Exceptional Children, 65,* 448–468.

Kazdin, A. (1993). Adolescent mental health: Prevention and treatment programs. *American Psychologist, 48,* 127–141.

Kellam, S., Rebok, G., Ialongo, N., & Mayer, L. (1994). The course and malleability of aggressive behavior from early first grade into middle school: Results of a developmental epidemiologically based prevention trial. *Journal of Child Psychology and Psychiatry, 35*(2), 259–281.

Loeber, D. & Farrington, D. (2001). *Child delinquents: Development, intervention and service needs.* Thousand Oaks, Calif.: Sage.

Loeber, R., Dishion, T., & Patterson, G. (1984). Multiple-gating: A multistage assessment procedure for identifying youths at risk for delinquency. *Journal of Research in Crime and Delinquency, 21,* 7–32.

Loeber, R. & Farrington, D. (Eds.). (1998). *Serious and violent juvenile offenders: Risk factors and successful interventions.* Thousand Oaks, Calif.: Sage.

Loeber, R. & Farrington, D.P. (2001) *Serious and violent juvenile offenders: Risk factors and successful interventions.* Thousand Oaks, Calif.: Sage.

Mayer, G.R. & Sulzer-Azanoff, B. (2002). Interventions for vandalism and aggression. In M. Shinn, H. Walker, & G. Stoner (Eds.), *Interventions for academic and behavior problems II: Preventive and remedial approaches* (pp. 853–884). Bethesda, Md.: National Association of School Psychologists.

McMahon, S.D., et al. (2000). "Violence Prevention: Program Effects on Urban Preschool and Kindergarten Children." *Applied and Preventive Psychology, 9,* 271–281.

Patterson, G. (1982). *A social learning approach, Volume 3: Coercive family process.* Eugene, Ore.: Castalia.

Patterson, G.R., Reid, J.B., & Dishion, T.J. (1992). *Antisocial boys.* Eugene, Ore.: Castalia.

Reavis, H.K., Taylor, M., Jenson, W., Morgan, D., Andrews, D., & Fisher, S. (1996). *Best practices: Behavioral and educational strategies for teachers.* Longmont, Colo.: Sopris West.

Reid, J.B., Patterson, G.R., & Snyder, J.J. (Eds.). (2002). *Antisocial behavior in children and adolescents: A developmental analysis and the Oregon Model for Intervention.* Washington, D.C.: American Psychological Association.

Satcher, D. (2001). *Youth violence: A report of the Surgeon General.* Washington, D.C.: U.S. Public Health Service, U.S. Department of Health and Human Services.

Severson, H. & Walker, H. (2002). Proactive approaches for identifying children at risk for sociobehavioral problems. In K. Lane, F.M. Gresham, & T. O'Shaughnessy (Eds.), *Interventions for children with or at-risk for emotional and behavioral disorders,* pp. 33–53. Boston: Allyn & Bacon.

Snyder, J. (2002). Reinforcement and coercion mechanisms in the development of antisocial behavior: Peer relationships. In J. Reid, G. Patterson, & L. Snyder (Eds.), *Antisocial behavior in children and adolescents: A developmental analysis and model for intervention,* pp. 101–122. Washington, D.C.: American Psychological Association.

Snyder, J. & Stoolmiller, M. (2002). Reinforcement and coercive mechanisms in the development of antisocial behavior. The family. In J. Reid, G. Patterson, & J. Snyder (Eds.), *Antisocial behavior in children and adolescents: A developmental analysis and model for intervention* (pp. 65–100). Washington, D.C.: American Psychological Association.

Sugai, G. & Horner, R., & Gresham, F. (2002) Behaviorally effective school environments. In M. Shinn, H. Walker, & G. Stoner (Eds.). *Interventions for academic and behavior problems II: Preventive and remedial approaches* (pp. 315–350). Bethesda, Md.: National Association of School Psychologists.

Walker, H.M. (1995). *The acting-out child: Coping with classroom disruption.* Langmont, Colo.: Sopris West.

Walker, H.M., Horner, R.H., Sugai, G., Bullis M., Spraque, J.R., Bricker, D. & Kaufman, M.J. (1996). Integrated approaches to preventing antisocial behavior patterns among school-age children and youth. *Journal of Emotional and Behavioral Disorders, 4,* 193–256.

Walker, H., Kavanagh, K., Stiller, B., Golly, A., Severson, H., & Feil, E. (1997). *First Step to Success: An early intervention program for antisocial kindergartners,* Longmont, Colo.: Sopris West.

Walker, H., Kavanagh, K., Stiller, B., Golly, A., Severson, H., & Feil, E. (1998). First Step: An early intervention approach for preventing school antisocial behavior. *Journal of Emotional and Behavioral Disorders, 6*(2), 66–80.

Walker, H. & Severson, H. (1990). *Systematic screening for behavioral disorders.* Longmont, Colo.: Sopris West.

Walker, H.M., Nishioka, V., Zeller, R., Severson, H., & Feil, E. (2000). Causal factors and potential solutions for the persistent under-identification of students having emotional or behavioral disorders in the context of schooling. *Assessment for Effective Intervention, 26*(1) 29–40.

Wolf, M.M. (1978). Social validity: The case for subjective measurement, or how applied behavior analysis is finding its heart. *Journal of Applied Behavior Analysis, 11,* 203–214.

HILL M. WALKER is founder and co-director of the Institute on Violence and Destructive Behavior at the University of Oregon, where he has been a professor since 1967. Walker has published hundreds of articles; in 1993 he received the Outstanding Research Award from the Council for Exceptional Children and in 2000 he became the only faculty member to receive the University of Oregon's Presidential Medal. **ELIZABETH RAMSEY** is a school counselor at Kopachuck Middle School in Gig Harbor, Wash., and a co-author of the Second Step program. **FRANK M. GRESHAM** is distinguished professor and director of the School Psychology Program at the University of California-Riverside. He is co-author of the Social Skills Rating System and co-principal investigator for Project REACH. The Division of School Psychology in the American Psychological Association selected him for the Senior Scientist Award. Together, Walker, Ramsey, and Gresham wrote Antisocial Behavior in School: Evidence-Based Practices, on which this article is based.

From *American Educator,* Winter 2003-2004 , pp. 6, 8–21, 46. Copyright © 2004 by Hill M. Walker, Elizabeth Ramsey and Frank M. Gresham. Reprinted with permission of the American Educator, the quarterly journal of the American Federation of Teachers, AFL-CIO, and reprinted with permission of the authors.

Teachers and Children

Relationships at the Forefront of Effective Practice

KATHLEEN CRANLEY GALLAGHER AND KELLEY MAYER

Azim's parents carry him into the Caterpillar Toddler room at 7:30 A.M., hurrying to get to work by 8:00 A.M. Two-year-old Azim is sleepy, and his eyes are red from crying. Azim does not like transitions, and his parents typically spend time reading and discussing the activities for the day before leaving Azim in the lap of his teacher, Rachelle. But today is different, his parents are in a hurry, and Azim is not happy. Rachelle greets his parents, and then Azim, saying "Busy mornings are hard". Rachelle reassures Azim's parents, and encourages them to say good-bye, hug Azim as usual, and take their leave. Rachelle takes a crying Azim to the window, where they blow kisses to Mom and Dad. Azim then buries his head into Rachelle's shoulder. Rachelle takes Azim to a chair, where she begins reading a book. She points to pictures, encouraging him to look, and asks wondering questions about what will happen next. By the story's midpoint, Azim is calm, and pointing to pictures himself. It is now 7:45 as Azim turns and smiles to Rachelle. As the story's ends, he climbs down from her lap and begins to examine a new bin of trucks.

This could have been a very difficult morning for all involved, but Azim's relationship with his teacher provided the support he needed during this morning transition. Rachelle's program provided the support she needed to spend 1:1 time with Azim and help him transition into play. These supports include low child: staff ratios, small group sizes, and places in the classroom that allow for quiet interaction. Additionally, Rachelle has learned the importance of these early transition times. Rachelle puts her relationships with children at the forefront of her morning activities; paperwork and planning will get done later. Research provides extensive evidence that teacher-child relationships are important for social-emotional and cognitive development, as well as later academic learning (Goosens & IJzendoorn, 1990; Howes, Galinsky, & Kontos, 1998). Developmentally appropriate practice (DAP) puts rela-

tionships on center stage, with the goal of "helping children and adults achieve their full potential in the context of relationships that are based on trust, respect, and positive regard" (Bredekamp & Copple, 1997).

The importance of teachers' relationships with young children has been addressed by numerous research studies (Gallagher, Mayer, Sylvester, Bundy, & Fedora, 2006; Hamre & Pianta, 2001, 2005; Pianta, Hamre, & Stuhlman, 2003; Rimm-Kaufman et al., 2002). Children who have warm, close, supportive relationships with their early childhood teacher, are more likely to have better relationships with other children, do well academically, and have fewer behavior problems in early childhood and elementary classrooms. Research on brain development and self-regulation (Gallagher, 2005; Schore, 2001; Shonkoff & Phillips, 2000; Shore, 1997) suggests that early relationships virtually train children's young minds about what to expect from relationships and how to interact with others. Additionally, high quality early relationships provide the secure base children need to explore and learn (Bowlby, 1988). While this knowledge has long been reflected in early childhood practice recommendations (Bredekamp & Copple, 1997), research continues to confirm its importance.

The purpose of this article is to reflect on what it means for teachers to put relationships with children as the priority in their practice. We will focus on four themes of relationships that we believe are at the heart of what it means to have a relationship: recognition, familiarity, respect, and commitment. We developed these themes in response to research on close relationships (Bowlby, 1988; Simpson & Tran, 2006; Thompson, 1999; Watson, 2003). Recognition refers to acknowledging another person's presence and preferences. Familiarity refers to deeper knowledge of a person's abilities, preferences, contexts, and history, including other important people in his/her life. Respect refers to treating the other person as a highly valued individual, consistent with how one wishes to be valued by others. Finally, commitment refers to demonstrating to an individual your intent to remain in a relationship with this person. These themes can apply to all relationships, but we don't always think about them applying to our relationships with children. Recognizing that behaviors that support relationships vary with children's developmental level (Bredekamp & Copple, 1997), we will outline practice ideas for teachers at each level of child development.

Infants

To build a high quality relationship with an infant requires attention and time, two things that are essential to quality care. Infants cycle through states of alertness, including sleep, drowsiness, hunger, and alertness. Infants should be greeted upon arrival, and again each time they enter an alert state. Teachers of infants need to carefully monitor and "catch" children's alert states, greeting them with a gentle smile and a few words, including the child's name. Upon awaking from his nap, Damian can be greeted with, "Hello, Damian, I see you are awake. I hope you had a good nap." Ideally, teachers will give such a greeting while 8–10 inches from the infant's face, and when the infant is looking. Infants typically respond to these greetings with a gaze and a smile. Becoming familiar with an infant includes understanding the child's typical sleep-wake cycle, and the child's preferences for transitioning among these cycles. For example, Azim may prefer to be held upon awakening, while Sara may prefer to remain in her crib for a few minutes. Developing a relationship with an infant means attending to (sometimes subtle) cues through which the baby expresses her preferences and needs, and responding to those cues appropriately and fairly quickly.

For infants, respect is also about attending and responding, and recognizing that each infant is a unique individual, with his or her own emerging personality and behavior style. Respecting infants' individual needs and preferences (often expressed through emphatic crying) is an important element of quality care. Children whose needs are addressed quickly and appropriately actually fuss less over time, and demonstrate fewer behavior problems later on (Sroufe, 2000). Finally, teachers of infants need to demonstrate their commitment to individual children. This isn't always easy, since "I'll be back tomorrow" is not easily understood by infants. One way teachers do this is by responding to infants' needs consistently and as quickly as possible. Practices that enhance infant-teacher relationships include: assigning each child to a primary teacher, developing a consistent, individualized diapering routine, and taking extra time to reconnect after an absence, such as illness, vacation or even a weekend.

Toddlers

Building relationships with toddlers can be a challenging and engaging adventure. Toddlers need to explore in safe environments and they need warm, responsive interactions with their teachers. Toddlers typically ask for independence while also seeking comfort, sometimes not stopping to give cues about exactly what they need at a given moment in time. Nonetheless, it is the teacher's job to ensure toddlers' health and safety while allowing them to explore the world and return to the arms of the teacher for reassurance. Again, it is essential to greet a toddler when he arrives in the program, and again after waking up from a nap. Greetings should include eye contact when possible, the child's name, and a question of interest. For example, upon Hannah's arrival at school her teacher might say, "Good morning, Hannah. I'm glad you're here. I see you came here with your dad today. Did you bring your big brother, Alex, to school, too?"

Toddlers' language skills are growing daily, and modeling the words used to convey good manners is valuable. Saying "please", "thank you" and "excuse me" when talking with toddlers, models practical language while showing respect for children. Toddlers assert their individual differences, but lacking the language skills needed to express themselves, they are not always effective in communicating their needs and wants. It is important to get to know individual interests and activity levels and respect each child's need for those activities, while also encouraging new ones. Toddlers may become intrigued with one kind of toy—perhaps cars—and may want only to do car activities. It makes sense for the teacher to both support that interest, and encourage a range of activities around cars. Teachers can build relationships with toddlers around their interests, bringing pictures, books, and other media to share, as well as focusing conversations around the toddlers' interests. Toddlers are very interested in their families and enjoy talking about them. It is important for teachers to get to know families and learn about their home routines. While toddlers can't always express themselves verbally, teachers can capitalize on toddlers' receptive language, asking questions and talking about the child's family in ways that help the child feel cared for and understood.

Finally, toddlers thrive on predictability and consistency. Teachers can convey a sense of commitment by acknowledging the importance of a toddler's routine. Teachers can make certain to notify and explain changes in routines to the child as they arise. For example, the teacher may say, "Eliza, today we won't be able to go outside and play today because the playground is too muddy." and following with, "What fun things might we do inside? Let's look at the toys in the big motor room. Most toddlers understand much more language than they are able to produce.

Preschoolers

Preschoolers are ready to be full and active partners in relationships. With lots of language, coordination, and a bit of self-regulation under their belts, preschoolers can initiate and participate in social relationships at a new level. Most preschoolers can make friends, and begin to be able to understand others' perspectives. This does not mean, however, that preschoolers don't need support and special relationships with their teachers. Teachers need to be ready for preschoolers' diverse, and sometimes passionate interests.

By around three years old, children "get" relationships, but their ideas about social interaction are often somewhat scripted: they have expectations about what to expect from adults, and what is expected from them, and they sometimes struggle with being flexible with their expectations. For example, preschoolers often apply social rules (such as sharing) to others, but not to themselves. Preschool teachers' efforts at modeling social respect are very important. Teachers can remind children of the rules, but at the same time invite children to see the perspective of another person, "Yes, Sonja, I see that you need help with your tower. I would like to help you, and I will as soon as I finish helping Miguel with his artwork. I want to help you with your very tall tower. Would you like to help Miguel and me, and then we will both help you?" When teachers scaffold children's perspective-taking, they are providing a strong foundation for children to build quality relationships. Despite their emerging peer relationships, preschoolers still need an individual relationship with a teacher. The same guidelines apply as for younger children. Preschoolers need more extensive greetings: teachers should use children's name, inquire as to their well-being, and ask about their previous evening or morning. They can ask about children's pets, hobbies, and family members, such as siblings, grandparents, aunts and uncles. Getting to know families well helps teachers connect children to various activities and classroom projects. For example, teachers may choose class or group activities that reflect children's experiences with their family. A kite activity could follow a child's experience with a kite festival over the weekend. A learning center based on travel, complete with suitcases and tickets, could precede a child's first trip on an airplane to visit a grandparent.

Preschool teachers should have deep familiarity with children's interests, and support those interests in the classroom. When preschoolers develop specific passions, such as interest in dinosaurs or space travel, teachers can respond by designing a variety of activities that address the child's interests while also providing experiences that build skills and knowledge.

School-Age Children

Children in the early elementary grades benefit greatly from a good relationship with their teacher (Hamre & Pianta, 2001, 2005). In *More Than Meets the Eye*, Donna Skolnick shares her experiences building relationships with young elementary school children by focusing on literacy. Before school begins, Skolnick sends a postcard to each child in the class, welcoming each child to her class. She also tries to meet each child before the school year starts, scheduling a home visit with the child's family, and inviting families to visit their classroom. Activities, such as open houses and home visits, help children negotiate the transition from preschool to kindergarten and from kindergarten to first grade by initiating a teacher-child relationship before the school year begins.

Once the school year begins, teachers can use group activities to recognize and greet children, connecting with each child for a moment before beginning a busy day. Center time provides opportunities for teachers to connect with children individually. When teachers are able to observe and interact with children individually and small groups in centers, they are able to learn more about each child and can more readily provide the emotional support necessary for early learning. Teachers may answer children's questions, provide feedback or assistance, and extend children's learning. For example, when a teacher observes Nadya struggling to build her name with magnet letters, her teacher may say, "Nadya, I see you are having trouble finding the letters in your name. May I help you?" At this point,

Ideas for Building Supportive Relationships with Children of All Ages

- **Get to know each child as an individual.** Make home visits to get to know the child's family and home life and use what you learn to build individual supportive relationships.
- **Choose books with individual children in mind.** Read books that address children's individual needs, interests, and emotions, while sharing some one-on-one time.
- **Take time to observe children's behavior and reflect** on the quality of your relationship with that child. Videotape interactions with different children at various times of the day and during a variety of activities, and use the video to become familiar with children's interests. Use this new knowledge to build your relationship with the child.
- **Review information on child development** on a regular basis. Understanding children's development is crucial for understanding children's needs. Development guides the choices we make in interacting and building relationships with children (Bredekamp & Copple, 1997). For example, knowing that toddlers' use of language is often limited, teachers may help a child develop "signals" for when extra attention is needed. This may mean sitting on a special chair or using a sign to communicate, "I need you to be with me now".
- **Learn about children's family relationships,** such as the history of their attachments with parents. Knowing if a child has had separations, or if a parent has experienced difficulty, can help teachers understand and adjust to a child's needs. For example, when a child experiences the birth of a sibling, many attachment emotions can be enacted. The experience of becoming a big brother or sister may mean the child needs extra care and connection. A child with a new sibling may require reassurance and extra attention in order to feel valued.
- **Ask families how children like to be comforted,** and use those strategies in the classroom. Having a special toy or song can help a child to feel safe and open to a new relationship more quickly.

Nadya's teacher may adjust the activity by reducing the number of letters from which Nadya is choosing. Or the teacher may give Nadya clues for finding the letters. Once Nadya has successfully located the letters, her teacher may provide specific, positive feedback, saying "You worked hard to find the letters in your name today. I am proud of you." When teachers provide specific, positive feedback on children's efforts, the quality of the child's relationship with the teacher and success in the classroom are enhanced.

Finally, it is important to always deliver individual guidance in private. No teacher would want to be corrected in the presence of peers. Nor do children. Respecting young children means delivering feedback in private, and assisting children in finding alternatives to problem behavior. Respecting school-age children requires that teachers remember that, despite their physical and verbal maturity, young elementary students are still learning what it means to participate in relationships. Young children will make mistakes in this regard. When a teacher takes time to build a quality relationship with an individual child, she is simultaneously teaching the child what it means to be a partner—a skill that will benefit a child for life.

Conclusion

As with infants, toddlers, and preschoolers, relationships with school-age children are developed one at a time, over time. Each relationship is precious. Teachers build relationships with children by recognizing, becoming familiar, respecting, and making a commitment to each child. Teachers may identify children that need more attention and time, as evidence suggests that the teacher-child relationship may be even more valuable for children with behavior and learning problems (Hamre & Pianta, 2005). Regardless of the age of the child one teaches, making a difference starts with making a relationship.

References

Bowlby, J. (1988). *A secure base*. Basic Books.

Bredekamp, S., & Copple, C. (Eds.). (1997). *Developmentally appropriate practice in early childhood programs* (Revised ed.). Washington, DC: National Association for the Education of Young Children (NAEYC).

Gallagher, K. C. (2005). Brain research and early childhood development: A primer for DAP. *Young Children, 60*(4), 12–20.

Gallagher, K. C., Mayer, K. L., Sylvester, P., Bundy, M. P., & Fedora, P. (2006). *Teacher-child relationships and developing literacy and social-emotional skills in pre-kindergarten*. Paper presented at the Annual Meeting of the American Educational Research Association, San Francisco, CA.

Goosens, F. A., & van IJzendoorn, M. H. (1990). Quality of infants' attachments to professional caregivers: Relation to infant-parent attachment and day-care characteristics. *Child Development, 61*, 832–837.

Hamre, B. K., & Pianta, R. C. (2001). Early teacher-child relationships and the trajectory of children's school outcomes through eighth grade. *Child Development, 72*(2), 625–638.

Hamre, B. K., & Pianta, R. C. (2005). Can instructional and emotional support in the first-grade classroom make a difference for children at risk for school failure? *Child Development, 76*(5), 949–967.

Howes, C., Galinsky, E., & Kontos, S. (1998). Child care caregiver sensitivity and attachment. *Social development, 7*(1), 25–36.

Pianta, R. C., Hamre, B., & Stuhlman, M. (2003). Relationships between teachers and children. In W. M. Reynolds & G. E. Miller (Eds.), *Comprehensive Handbook of Psychology* (Vol. 7, pp. 199–234). New York: Wiley.

Rimm-Kaufman, S. E., Early, D. M., Cox, M. J., Saluja, G., Pianta, R. C., & Payne, C. (2002). Early behavioral attributes and teachers' sensitivity as predictors of competent behavior in the kindergarten classroom. *Applied Developmental Psychology, 23*, 451–470.

Schore, A. N. (2001). Effects of a secure attachment relationship on right brain development, affect regulation, and infant mental health. *Infant Mental Health Journal, 22*(1–2), 7–66.

Shonkoff, J. P., & Phillips, D. A. (Eds.). (2000). *From neurons to neighborhoods: The science of early childhood development*. Washington D.C.: National Academy Press.

Shore, R. (1997). *Rethinking the Brain: New Insights into Early Development*. New York: Families and Work Institute.

Simpson, J. A., & Tran, S. (2006). The needs, benefits, and perils of close relationships. In P. Noller & J. A. Feeney (Eds.), *Close relationships: Functions, forms, processes*. New York: Psychology Press.

Sroufe, A. L. (2000). Early relationships and the development of children. *Infant Mental Health Journal, 21*(1–2), 67–74.

Thompson, R. A. (1999). Early attachment and later development. In J. Cassidy & P. R. Shaver (Eds.), *Handbook of Attachment: Theory, Research, and Clinical Applications* (pp. 265–286). New York: The Guilford Press.

Watson, M. (2003). Attachment theory and challenging behaviors: Reconstructing the nature of relationships. *Young Children, 58*(4), 12–20.

From *Young Children*, November 2006, pp. 44–49. Copyright © 2006 by National Association for the Education of Young Children. Reprinted by permission.

"You Got It!"

Teaching Social and Emotional Skills

LISE FOX AND ROCHELLE HARPER LENTINI

Early educators report that one of their biggest challenges is supporting young children who have problem behavior beyond what might be expected (Buscemi et al. 1995; Hemmeter, Corso, & Cheatham 2005). Some children engage in problem behavior that is typical of a particular stage of development as they build relationships with peers and adults and learn to navigate the classroom environment. For example, a toddler might grab a cracker from another child's plate because she is still learning to use words to ask for what she wants or needs. What troubles teachers is how to meet the needs of children who have persistent problem behavior that does not respond to positive guidance or prevention practices. The extent of this problem is highlighted by recent reports on the rates of expulsion of children from preschool programs (Gilliam 2005).

The Teaching Pyramid

The teaching pyramid model (Fox et al. 2003) describes a primary level of universal practices—classroom preventive practices that promote the social and emotional development of all children—built on a foundation of positive relationships; secondary interventions that address specific social and emotional learning needs of children at risk for challenging behavior; and development of individualized interventions (tertiary level) for children with persistent problem behavior (see the diagram "The Teaching Pyramid"). The model is explained more fully in "The Teaching Pyramid: A Model for Supporting Social Competence and Reinventing Challenging Behavior in Young Children," in the July 2003 issue of *Young Children*.

The foundation for universal practices begins with nurturing and responsive caregiving that supports children in developing a positive sense of self and in engaging in relationships with others. At this level, teachers focus on their relationships with children and families. Universal classroom practices include developmentally appropriate, child-centered classroom environments that promote children's developing independence, successful interactions, and engagement in learning. While universal practices may be enough to promote the development of social competence in the majority of children in the classroom, teachers may find that there are children whose lack of social and emotional skills or whose challenging behavior requires more focused attention.

In this article we look at the secondary level of the teaching pyramid, which emphasizes planned instruction on specific social and emotional skills for children at risk for developing more challenging behavior, such as severe aggression, property destruction, noncompliance, or withdrawal. Children who may be considered at risk for challenging behavior are persistently noncompliant, have difficulty regulating their emotions, do not easily form relationships with adults and other children, have difficulty engaging in learning activities, and are perceived by teachers as being likely to develop more intractable behavior problems.

> **Teachers may find that there are children whose lack of social and emotional skills or whose challenging behavior requires more focused attention.**

Research shows that when educators teach children the key skills they need to understand their emotions and the emotions of others, handle conflicts, problem solve, and develop relationships with peers, their problem behavior decreases and their social skills improve (Joseph & Strain 2003). Emphasis on teaching social skills is just one component of multiple strategies to support a child at risk for challenging behavior. Additional critical strategies include collaborating with the family; addressing the child's physical and mental health needs; and offering the support of specialists and other resources to address the child or family's individual needs.

Reframing Problem Behavior

The teaching pyramid model guides teachers to view a child's problem behavior as serving a purpose for that child. Some children may use problem behavior instead of socially

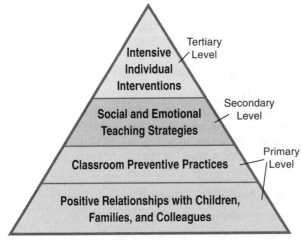

The Teaching Pyramid

Social and Emotional Skills to Teach

- Following rules, routines, and directions
- Identifying feelings in oneself and others
- Controlling anger and impulses
- Problem solving
- Suggesting play themes and activities to peers
- Sharing toys and other materials
- Taking turns
- Helping adults and peers
- Giving compliments
- Understanding how and when to apologize
- Expressing empathy with others' feelings
- Recognizing that anger can interfere with problem solving
- Learning how to recognize anger in oneself and others
- Learning how to calm down
- Understanding appropriate ways to express anger

conventional and appropriate behavior to avoid or join interactions and activities, obtain or avoid attention, and obtain objects. For example, a child who wants another child's toy may hit the other child instead of asking to have a turn with the toy. Other children may use problem behavior to express their disappointment or anger to the teacher, rather than asking for help or sharing their feelings with words. For example, a child may throw toys or destroy materials when frustrated rather than asking a teacher for help.

Reasons for Challenging Behavior

Children may use problem behavior to get their needs met for a variety of reasons. For example, a child may have language development problems, social-emotional delays, difficulties with peer interactions, or developmental disabilities; she may have experienced neglect or trauma; or she may simply have not had opportunities to learn appropriate social or communication skills before entering preschool.

When teachers view challenging behavior as actions children use to get their needs met, they can reframe problem behavior as a skill-learning or skill-fluency issue. *Skill fluency* refers to a child's ability to use a skill consistently and independently. Children with problem behavior may not have appropriate social or communication skills or may not use those skills well in a variety of situations. Reframing problem behavior as a skill-instruction issue opens the door to the development of effective strategies teachers can implement in the classroom: if young children with problem behavior are missing key social and communication skills, then a next step is to teach them those skills!

A Skill-learning Issue

Many skills are important in children's development of relationships with adults and peers. Skills help children learn self-regulation (ability to respond appropriately to anxiety, distress, or uncomfortable sensations) and how to problem solve (see "Social and Emotional Skills to Teach,"). Young children at risk for challenging behavior (children at the secondary interven-

tion level) may not be fluent in or have the ability to use these skills. The teaching pyramid model encourages early educators to teach children these skills systematically, using planned procedures within developmentally appropriate activities and with sufficient intensity to ensure that children learn the skills quickly and can use them when needed (Grisham-Brown, Hemmeter, & Pretti-Frontczak 2005).

Teaching Social Skills

In thinking about how to teach social skills systematically, teachers need to be aware of the three stages of learning (Bailey & Wolery 1992) (see "Stages of Learning"). The first stage is skill acquisition—the skill is introduced to the child; the second stage is fluency—the child has learned the skill and can use it easily; and the final stage of learning is skill maintenance and generalization—the child can use the skill over time and in new situations. In this article, we present strategies for addressing each stage of learning in the instruction of social skills.

It is important to identify the skill, demonstrate or identify when it is used, and link the idea or concept to other skills the child has.

Introducing a New Skill: Show-and-Tell

Explain the new skill. When you first teach a child a social or emotional skill, it is important to ensure that you have explained the skill in concrete terms so the child understands what the skill is and when to use it. Children who have social development challenges may find the nuances of social behavior difficult to interpret. Thus, it is important to identify the skill ("ask to take a turn"), demonstrate or identify when it is used ("Watch Emily ask to play with the water wheel"), and link the idea or concept to other skills the child has ("When you see your friends playing with a toy you want, you can watch them play, you can wait for a turn, or you can ask them for a turn").

Demonstrate it. For many children, it is helpful to provide both a positive example of someone using a skill and an example in which the skill is not used. For example, you may ask children to demonstrate the wrong way to ask for a turn and the correct way to ask for a turn. In this manner, children can practice under a teacher's guidance and receive additional information about how the skill is appropriately used.

Give positive feedback. When children first learn a new skill, they need feedback and specific encouragement on their efforts to use the skill. The importance of feedback cannot be overstated! Think, for example, about a time when you learned something new—such as a language, a sport, or a craft. The instructor most likely gave you feedback: "That's right, you did it" or "That looks good, I think you are getting it." Feedback may provide the support a child needs to persist in practicing a newly learned skill. Have you ever tried to learn a new skill and quit when you were in the early learning stages? Perhaps you did not receive encouragement or maybe those initial attempts were so uncomfortable or awkward that you decided to stop practicing.

Provide opportunities for practice. There are a variety of instructional methods for teaching new social and emotional skills (Webster-Stratton 1999; Hyson 2004; Kaiser & Rasminsky 2007). An important teaching practice at the acquisition stage of learning is providing multiple opportunities for a child to learn a skill in meaningful contexts—that is, in activities that are part of the child's natural play or routines. The more opportunities for practicing, the quicker the child will learn the skill. The box "Classroom Teaching Strategies" lists a variety of ways to teach social and emotional skills within typical classroom activities.

When a child learns a new skill, he needs to practice to build fluency in the skill.

Building Fluency: Practice Makes Perfect

When learning to play a new song on the piano, the player must practice before the song becomes easy to play. Similarly, when a child learns a new skill, he needs to practice to build fluency in the skill. When teaching social skills, teachers need to ensure that a skill is not only learned but also practiced often enough

---

Stages of Learning

Stage 1—Skill Acquisition
Show-and-Tell

The teacher introduces a new skill to a child by giving concrete examples of what the skill is and how to use it. For example, the teacher may say, "It's hard to wait until it is your turn to ride a trike. I'm going to help you learn how to wait."

Stage 2—Skill Fluency
Practice Makes Perfect

The teacher provides many opportunities to practice the skill so the child can eventually use it with ease. Practice opportunities may include prompting the child ("How can you ask to play with Brendan?"), helping the child remember to use the skill ("I know you are disappointed and you want a turn right now. What can you do instead?"), and identifying situations that call for the use of the skill ("We have three children who want to sit at the art table and only one chair. What can we do?").

Stage 3—Skill Maintenance and Generalization
"You Got It!"

The teacher continues to promote the child's use of the skill in familiar and new situations. For example, when the child uses his newly learned skill of giving compliments with his mother, the teacher says, "You gave your mom a compliment! Look, she's smiling because you said you like her haircut."

Adapted from D.B. Bailey & M. Wolery, *Teaching Infants and Preschoolers with Disabilities,* 2nd ed. (New York: Macmillan, 1992).

---

that the child becomes fluent in the skill and can easily use it. Consider the following example:

> Madison struggles when playing with peers. Recognizing that Madison needs extra help in learning how to ask others to play with toys, her teacher, Mr. Jackson, decides to read the children a story about taking turns and asking to join play during group time. On that same day, several times during center activities and outdoor play, Mr. Jackson reminds Madison to "ask to play." After that day of focused instruction on using the skill, whenever Madison tries to enter a game without asking to play, Mr. Jackson provides corrective feedback or redirection, stating, "Madison, you need to ask to play" or "Madison, you may not grab toys; ask to play." A month later, Madison still has difficulty entering play and asking to play with toys.

Why did Madison have difficulty learning the skill? Perhaps Mr. Jackson did not provide enough opportunities to practice, so

Classroom Teaching Strategies

Instruction is more effective when it is embedded in the meaningful activities and contexts that occur throughout a child's day (Katz & McClellan 1997). Here are suggestions and examples for teaching social skills within classroom activities.

Modeling. Demonstrate the skill while explaining what you are doing. As you pass a block to a child, say, "Look, I am sharing my blocks with my friend."

Modeling with puppets. Use puppets to model the skill while interacting with a child, an adult, or another puppet. A puppet can explain to the teacher and the class how she became angry and hit her brother to get a toy. You can ask the puppet to consider other solutions and then discuss what a child might do when he or she wants a toy that another child is using.

Preparing peer partners. Ask one child to show another child the skill or to help the child use the target skill. You can prompt the peer by saying, "Carmen, Justin is still learning how to wait and take turns. Since you know what to do, can you help him? Show him the line-up picture while you wait for a drink at the water fountain."

Singing. Introduce a new skill through a song. To teach children to trade toys, pass out small toys during a large group activity, then sing the following song to the tune of "Mary Had a Little Lamb" and practice trading:

I can be a problem solver, problem solver, problem solver, I can be a problem solver, let me show you how. Maybe I can trade with you, trade with you, trade with you, Maybe I can trade with you; let me show you how.

Children then practice trading toys with each other.

Doing fingerplays. Introduce the skill with a fingerplay, then follow up with a discussion or story. While showing fingers, have children recite this rhyme:

One little friend cried, "Boo-hoo"; a friend gives a hug and then there are two.
Two little friends share with me; we play together and that makes three.
Three little friends ask for more; they all say "Please," and then comes four.
Four little friends take turns down the slide; another comes to play, and that makes five.
Five little friends have fun at school, because they follow every rule.

Using a flannel board. Introduce a new skill using flannel board activities and stories. For example, to teach turn taking you could have flannel pieces for Humpty Dumpty and change the rhyme so that "All the king's horses and all the king's friends / Work as a team to put Humpty together again." As you say the rhyme, have the children take turns putting the pieces (castle, bricks, Humpty Dumpty pieces, horses, and friends) on the flannel board. When you finish the rhyme, extend the activity by talking about how Humpty felt when he sat on the wall; when he fell; and when his friends helped put him back together.

Using prompts. Give a child verbal, visual, or physical prompts to use a skill during interactions and activities. When a child who has difficulty with initiating play interactions moves toward a group playing together, you might say privately, "Remember to use your words and ask to play."

Giving encouragement. Provide specific feedback when the child uses the skill. For example, describe what the child did: "You asked Joey for a turn. I saw that you two had a good time playing together." Encouragement can be verbal or a signal (a thumbs-up or high five).

Using incidental teaching. Guide the child to use the skill during interactions and activities. Quietly say to the child, "Quan, I see that you are very angry that all the trucks are being used. What can you do when you are angry? Let's go over the steps."

Playing games. Use games to teach problem solving, words that express feelings, identification of others' feelings, friendship skills, and so on. Place photographs of each child in a bag. Have the children take turns pulling a photo out of the bag and offering a compliment to the child in the photo.

Discussing children's literature. Read books to help teach friendship skills, feeling words, problem solving, and so on. While reading a story, pause and ask the children how a character in the story might feel or ask them to suggest ideas for solving the character's problem.

Additional ideas for many of these activities may be found on the Web site of the Center on the Social and Emotional Foundations for Early Learning, at www.csefel.uiuc.edu. Under **Resources,** click on **Practical Strategies.**

Madison quickly forgot to use the new skill. Or possibly Madison had not learned when and how to use the skill: she may not have become fluent in the skill.

Teachers can offer repeated opportunities to practice the skill in familiar and new situations.

To ensure that children learn a skill to the fluency level, teachers can use several strategies. They may offer the child multiple opportunities to practice, help the child link the new concept or skill to other social skills, or remind the child in advance so he or she can use the skill or concept in new situations.

Scaffolding the use of the skill within interactions may be effective. For example, the teacher can monitor child interactions and offer a verbal bridge for problem solving when children have conflicts or face difficulties (Katz & McClellan 1997). The teacher can pose questions like "What else can you do?" to help children problem solve or "How do you think Emily felt when you said that?" to help them take the perspective of the other child. When scaffolding, the teacher need only offer as much support or guidance as the child requires to navigate the situation, and she should be cautious about becoming overly directive or controlling the situation.

Additional teaching techniques to promote fluency include reminding the child, as she goes into a situation, to use the new skill; creating opportunities to practice by staging situations that call for the skill (creating a problem-solving task or planning an activity that requires sharing or taking turns); and providing the child with peer buddies who can remind her to use the new skill.

In the fluency stage of learning, the teacher should continue to offer encouragement when the child is practicing the skill.

Promoting Maintenance and Generalization: "You Got It!"

For a child acquiring a new social skill, the final stage of learning is maintaining and generalizing the skill—learning it to the point that it becomes part of the child's social skill repertoire and he uses it in familiar and in new situations. When teaching children social skills, it is important to ensure that children reach this stage.

For many children, moving from skill acquisition to skill generalization occurs quickly and seamlessly with little teacher effort. However, for children who are at risk for social development delays or challenging behavior, a more systematic approach may be needed.

To ensure maintenance and generalization of a new skill, after introducing the skill and providing practice opportunities, teachers can offer repeated opportunities to practice the skill in familiar and new situations. At this stage of learning, children continue to need occasional encouragement to remember to use the skills, and they need feedback on the successful use of the skill in new situations. The example that follows describes how Ben's teacher supported and encouraged Ben to use his newly learned problem-solving ability in new situations.

Four-year-old Ben tends to get very frustrated when playing with his peers, especially on the playground. He screams, pushes children, and grabs toys. Ms. Mitchell, his teacher, has introduced a four-step problem-solving process to the class, using a puppet (who has a problem to solve) and picture cards depicting the problem-solving process: (1) Ask yourself, What's my problem? (2) Think, think, think of some solutions; (3) What would happen? and (4) Give it a try.

Although Ben uses the process during play times, Ms. Mitchell realizes that he needs additional prompting to problem solve in new situations. Today the class is visiting the children's museum. Before entering, Ms. Mitchell takes Ben aside and reviews the problem-solving steps.

Inside the museum, there are several magnet activity stations, all occupied. Knowing that Ben will want to play with the magnets, Ms. Mitchell moves near him to give him support. She reminds Ben about the problem-

solving steps: "Remember, think, think, think." Ben then says to a child playing with the magnets, "Can I play too?" The child hands him a magnet and they build together. Ms. Mitchell looks at Ben, winks, and smiles.

The goal at this stage of instruction is for children to use the social skills they have learned in a variety of situations, helping them build satisfying relationships with children and adults. They are then motivated by their successes and the joy they experience playing and developing relationships. As children develop new social skills and grow in their social competence, they gain access to a wider variety of play and learning opportunities; increase the duration and complexity of play interactions and engagement in social interactions; build friendships with peers; and feel good about themselves.

Conclusions

It is critically important that early educators identify children who need focused instruction—children who may be considered at risk for challenging behavior. Teachers can guide them to learn new social and emotional skills, teaching them within child-centered, developmentally appropriate activities. It is equally important to design a systematic teaching approach that allows such children to acquire and use their new skills easily, over time, and in a variety of situations.

When young children do not know how to identify emotions, handle disappointment and anger, or develop relationships with peers, a teacher's best response is to teach!

References

Bailey, D.B., & M. Wolery. 1992. *Teaching infants and preschoolers with disabilities.* 2nd ed. New York: Macmillan.

Buscemi, L., T. Bennett, D. Thomas, & D.A. Deluca. 1995. Head Start: Challenges and training needs. *Journal of Early Intervention* 20 (1): 1–13.

Fox, L., G. Dunlap, M.L. Hemmeter, G.E. Joseph, & P.S. Strain. 2003. The teaching pyramid: A model for supporting social competence and preventing challenging behavior in young children. *Young Children* 58 (4): 48–52.

Gilliam, W.S. 2005. *Prekindergarteners left behind: Expulsion rates in state prekindergarten systems.* Online: www.fcdus.org/PDFs/NationalPreKExpulsionPaper03.02_new.pdf.

Grisham-Brown, J., M.L. Hemmeter, & K. Pretti-Frontczak. 2005. *Blended practices for teaching young children in inclusive settings.* Baltimore: Brookes.

Hemmeter, M.L., R. Corso, & G. Cheatham. 2005. Issues in addressing challenging behaviors in young children: A national survey of early childhood educators. Manuscript.

Hyson, M. 2004. *The emotional development of young children: Building an emotion-centered curriculum.* 2nd ed. New York: Teachers College Press.

Joseph, G.E., & P.S. Strain. 2003. Comprehensive evidence-based social-emotional curricula for young children: An analysis of efficacious adoption potential. *Topics in Early Childhood Special Education* 23 (2): 65–76.

Kaiser, B., & J.S. Rasminsky. 2007. *Challenging behavior in young children: Understanding, preventing, and responding effectively.* 2nd ed. Boston, MA: Allyn & Bacon.

Katz, L.G., & D.E. McClellan. 1997. *Fostering children's social competence: The teacher's role.* Washington, DC: NAEYC.

Webster-Stratton, C. 1999. *How to promote children's social and emotional competence.* London: Paul Chapman.

LISE FOX, PHD, is a professor in the Department of Child and Family Studies of the Louis de la Parte Florida Mental Health Institute of the University of South Florida in Tampa. She conducts research and training and develops support programs focused on young children with challenging behavior. **ROCHELLE HARPER LENTINI,** MED, is a faculty member in the Department of Child and Family Studies of the Louis de la Parte Florida Mental Health Institute. She provides training and technical assistance to early educators and families on supporting young children with challenging behavior and promoting social and emotional competence.

Development of this article was supported by the Center for Evidence-Based Practice: Young Children with Challenging Behavior (Office of Special Education Programs, U.S. Department of Education, Cooperative Agreement #H324Z010001) and the Center on the Social and Emotional Foundations for Early Learning (Administration for Children and Families, U.S. Department of Health and Human Services, Cooperative Agreement #90YD0119/01).

Teaching Pyramid diagram adapted from L. Fox, G. Dunlap, M.L. Hemmeter, G.E. Joseph, & P.S. Strain, "The Teaching Pyramid: A Model for Supporting Social Competence and Preventing Challenging Behavior in Young Children," *Young Children* 58 (July 2003): 49.

From *Young Children,* November 2006, pp. 36–42. Copyright © 2006 by National Association for the Education of Young Children. Reprinted by permission.

The Playground as Classroom

Recess not only gives students time to socialize and exercise, but also helps them stay attentive in class.

ANNE SANTA

As I stood on the playground, 2nd graders Elena and Laura pulled hard on my sleeve. They kept pulling, pleading, "Look, look, Anne!" In their hands was a perfect oval of ice. It was flat with concentric ovals toward the middle, and the children held it reverently. Finding ice is always a treat, but this shape was exquisite, like a giant's jewel. After I shared their awe, they turned and ran back toward the playground. Recess had ended, but they weren't heading back to their classroom. They returned quickly, triumphant. Together they had decided that their precious find would melt if they took it inside. They had agreed to put it back in its home, just as they would have restored a bird's egg to its nest.

Constructing forts, collecting rocks, and digging are ways children create their own worlds and become more acquainted with the natural world. Children thrive when they have some choice in their day and time to create games and stories and to play. In addition, trying out new physical skills can be the highlight of the day. A kindergartner beams at being able to cross the monkey bars. A 3rd grader dances in celebration when he catches the football, and a 5th grader enjoys the camaraderie of a basketball game or playing gold rush with a teacher. The outdoors is a classroom of the students' own construction. The time spent in this classroom, however, is shrinking for many children.

Losing Recess

A recent U.S. Department of Education report states that 14 to 18 percent of U.S. children in grades 1–6 get 15 minutes or fewer of recess a day (National Center for Education Statistics, 2007). Forty percent of schools have reportedly eliminated some recess time to concentrate on academics (Clements, 2000). Under No Child Left Behind, preparing students for benchmark tests has become a primary goal of elementary school teachers. Life skills learned in social interactions, the health benefits of physical exercise, and exposure to the outdoors have been sidelined.

Parent groups are leading the effort to preserve recess. A campaign called Rescuing Recess (www.rescuingrecess.com) provides information on the benefits of recess and encourages children to write to local and state officials to support keeping recess. The Washington State Parent Teacher Association (2006) chose recess as one of its top five issues to address in the coming year. The American Association for the Child's Right to Play (www.ipausa.org) protects and promotes the right to play.

Benefits of Recess

Research tells us that students are more attentive and less restless after a recess break. Pellegrini and Davis (1993) found that kindergartners and 2nd and 4th graders were less attentive when there was a long period before a recess break, and the children's attention decreased as they spent more time without a break. Brain research also shows that when learning is broken up into short periods, recall improves (Dempster, 1988; Toppino, Kasserman, & Mracek, 1991). Children who are more active or struggle with attention disorders suffer when deprived of recess (Silver, 2005). These same children are often likely to lose recess because of their disruptive behavior, further exacerbating the problem.

A second reason for recess is the powerful experience it provides in social relationships. Children have freedom to practice making and keeping friends. Pellegrini, Kato, Blatchford, and Baines (2002) found that primary school children's reciprocal social play predicts their social competence one year later.

Skeptics point out that the playground can be the site of aggression, teasing, and bullying. Children often do argue about making fair teams or whether someone was "out." This give and take is part of their play and prepares them for adult negotiation. Our job as teachers is to calmly remind students to keep the conflict within bounds and find a solution everyone can agree to without resorting to aggression. Unfortunately, adults in some schools must supervise so many children on the playground at once that they can neither teach these conflict-resolution skills nor intervene to prevent disputes from escalating.

Physical health is the third reason we need recess. The U.S. Department of Health and Human Services recommends that all children over 2 years old get 60 minutes of moderate to vigorous exercise on most days of the week (Council on Physical Education for Children, 2001). The percentage of school-age children who are obese has doubled in the past 30 years (Ogden, Flegal, Carroll, & Johnson, 2002). According to the American Academy of Pediatrics, over 15 percent of children in the U.S. are overweight or obese, and 80 percent of obese youth become obese adults (Council on Sports Medicine and Fitness & Council on School Heath, 2006). The National Association for Sport and Physical Education cautions schools against allowing children to be inactive for longer than two hours (Council on Physical Education for Children, 2001).

Children thrive when they have some choice in their day.

Our children need the outdoor fun, choices, and time to invent that recess provides. Recess does not require elaborate funding, but we must support it with good supervision and a belief that the social and physical well-being of our children is worthy of our time and nurture.

References

Clements, R. L. (Ed.). (2000). *Elementary school recess: Selected readings, games, and activities for teachers and parents.* Boston: American Press.

Council on Physical Education for Children. (2001). *Recess for elementary school students.* Position paper for National Association for Sport and Physical Education, Reston, VA.

Council on Sports Medicine and Fitness & Council on School Health. (2006). Active health living: Prevention of childhood obesity through increased activity. *Pediatrics, 117*(5), 1834–1842.

Dempster, F. N. (1988). The spacing effect. *American Psychologist, 43,* 627–634.

National Center for Education Statistics. (2007). *Public-use data files and documentation: Foods and physical activity in public schools 2005.* Washington, DC: Author. Available: http://nces.ed.gov/pubsearch/pubsinfo.asp?pubid=2006106

Ogden, C. L., Flegal, K. M., Carroll, M. D., & Johnson, C. L. (2002). Prevalence and trends in overweight among U. S. children and adolescents, 1999–2000. *Journal of the American Medical Association, 288,* 1728–1732.

Pellegrini, A. D., & Davis, P. (1993). Confinement effects on playground and classroom behavior. *British Journal of Educational Psychology, 63,* 88–95.

Pellegrini, A. D., Kato, K., Blatchford, P., & Baines, E. (2002). A short-term longitudinal study of children's playground games across the first year of school: Implications for social competence and adjustment to school. *American Educational Research Journal, 39,* 991–1015.

Silver, L. (2005). No recess for recess. *Additude.* Available: www.addittudemag.com/additude.asp?DEPT_NO=303_ART1CLE_NO=15&ARCV=1

Toppino, T. C., Kasserman, J. E., & Mracek, W. A. (1991). The effect of spacing repetitions on the recognition memory of young children and adults. *Journal of Experimental Child Psychology, 51* (1), 123–138.

Washington State Parent Teacher Association. (2006). *K–12 education funding: Issue Papers 2006/7.* Tacoma, WA: Author. Available: www.wastatepta.org/leg/issue_papers07top5.pdf

ANNE SANTA is Counselor for prekindergarten through 5th grade at Catlin Gabel School, 8825 SW Barnes Rd., Portland, OR 97225; 503-297-1894, ext. 336; santaa@catlin.edu.

From *Educational Leadership,* May 2007. Copyright © 2007 by ASCD. Reprinted by permission. The Association for Supervision and Curriculum Development is a worldwide community of educators advocating sound policies and sharing best practices to achieve the success of each learner. To learn more, visit ASCD at www.ascd.org

Fostering Positive Transitions for School Success

Jayma Ferguson McGann and Patricia Clark

It is the week before school starts, and Ridgeview Elementary is holding a Popsicle Night for children entering kindergarten and their families. As families arrive in the school cafeteria, the principal and a kindergarten teacher welcome each kindergarten child with a T-shirt bearing the school name and logo.

The children excitedly greet their former preschool teachers, who also attend. With their families, the children choose from the variety of activities prepared by the preschool and kindergarten teachers. At an appointed time, the principal gathers the children and reads to them a story about going to kindergarten. Afterward, the families follow the kindergarten teachers to the children's new classrooms for a visit and short talk about kindergarten. The evening ends with Popsicles for everyone.

Why is it that fewer than 20 percent of U.S. schools have transition practices in place to support children entering kindergarten and welcome their families (Love et al. 1992)? This is an important transition for young children, and its success has a lasting effect on children's school success in later years (Alexander & Entwisle 1988; Ensminer & Slusarcick 1992; Early, Pianta, & Cox 1999; Ramey et al. 2000).

Clearly, educators, schools, and communities must work together to ensure that young children's entry into kindergarten and elementary school is a smooth passage rather than a rocky road. It seems well worth the effort to find ways to support children and families during this crucial transition.

Indiana Steps Up to the Challenge

The Indiana Department of Education, through the Ready Schools Initiative, works with 12 communities across the state to help local elementary schools support children's transitions to kindergarten. The communities range from large cities with dozens of elementary schools to small towns and rural areas with one school serving an entire county.

The guiding question has been, "What can we do—in early childhood programs, in elementary schools, with families, and in the community—to facilitate children's successful transition into kindergarten and the elementary grades?" While each community addresses the issue differently based on its resources and needs, in Indiana we have pinpointed some common concerns and found a number of ways to address the transition process.

Encouraging Successful Transitions

Activities for improving children's transitions to school fall into two broad categories: (1) improving connections between early childhood programs and elementary schools, and (2) reaching out to children and families before children enter kindergarten.

Connections Between Early Childhood Programs and Schools

Preschool programs and elementary schools need to find ways to communicate. Kindergarten teachers need to know about the early childhood programs their new kindergartners attended, and preschool teachers need to know about kindergarten teachers' expectations for the children. Here are some of the ways the Indiana Ready Schools communities encourage connections:

- Kindergarten teachers visit early childhood programs to get a better idea about the programs, their curricula, and the children.
- Preschool teachers visit kindergarten classrooms, often with the children who will be going to the kindergarten.
- Kindergarten and preschool teachers share dinner and conversation to discuss issues important to both.
- Elementary school districts incorporate procedures for obtaining records from the variety of programs children attend. Schools prepare and distribute to early childhood programs parent permission forms to allow the programs to transfer children's records to the school.
- Communities provide families with a pamphlet that they can read and complete to communicate personal information about their child. These pamphlets are distributed at community fairs, through prekindergarten programs, and

A Read-Aloud for Families

A number of principals read *The Kissing Hand,* by Audrey Penn, at family-welcoming events in Indiana. Parents with tears in their eyes have attested to the power of this story about a young raccoon preparing to go to kindergarten.

Remember, a child going off to kindergarten can be as big a step for the family as it is for the child.

at kindergarten registration, and then are returned to the kindergarten teacher.

- School districts involve early childhood teachers who work in programs outside the schools, as well as those within the schools, and kindergarten teachers in joint professional development experiences.

Connections Between Schools and Families

The extent to which families are involved in their children's education is a strong predictor of children's academic success (Henderson & Berla 1994). To facilitate family-school communication and linkages, ready schools reach out to families, establish links *before* the first day of school, and make personal contacts (Pianta & Walsh 1996). However, typical elementary school transition practices often involve experiences taking place *after* the start of school and/or making contact through flyers, brochures, and group open houses.

Here are some of the things that the Indiana Ready Schools communities do to reach out to families before kindergarten:

- Special events held before the school year begins welcome incoming kindergarten children and families. The events often happen in the evening and include a light supper, activities for children and families together, an opportunity to meet the kindergarten teachers and visit the classrooms, and the principal reading a story aloud (see "A Read-Aloud for Families").
- Elementary schools invite preschoolers and their families to Family Night during the school year before the children's kindergarten entry.
- Teachers make home visits before school begins to the families whose children will be starting kindergarten in the fall.
- Communities distribute brochures, videos, and home activity calendars to children and families at community events, through pediatricians and libraries, and with the help of community agencies that work with families (housing authority, social service agencies, etc.). The resources emphasize the importance of the early years and encourage families to contact their local elementary school before their child enters kindergarten.

Conclusion

Nearly half of all kindergarten teachers nationally report that 50 percent of children experience some degree of difficulty in the transition to formal schooling and 16 percent face serious adjustment

problems (Rimm-Kaufman, Pianta, & Cox 2000). Strategies to prepare children for change and address the challenges of adjustment can help ensure that children's transitions to school are positive.

The transition to kindergarten is a process among partners rather than an event happening to a child. According to Pianta and Kraft-Sayre, "most important for the transition process are the relationships—those between children and teachers, parents and teachers, children and their peers, and children and their parents" (1999, 52). Effective practices are planned locally, taking into consideration children's cultural backgrounds and the multiple characteristics of the community, including family income levels, cultures, physical location and resources. Using what we know about young children and transitions, teachers, schools, and communities can adapt strategies to local needs and resources to promote children's successful transition to kindergarten and school success in the years after.

References

Alexander, K., & D. Entwisle. 1988. Achievement in the first two years of school: Patterns and processes. *Monographs of the Society for Research in Child Development* 53 (1): 157.

Early, D., R. Pianta, & M. Cox. 1999. Kindergarten teachers and classrooms: A transition context. *Early Education and Development* 10 (1): 25–46.

Ensminer, M., & A. Slusarcick. 1992. Paths to high school graduation or dropout: A longitudinal study of a first-grade cohort. *Sociological Education* 65: 95–113.

Henderson, A., & N. Berla. 1994. *A new generation of evidence: The family is critical to student achievement.* Columbia, MD: National Committee for Citizens in Education.

Love, J., M.E. Logue, J.V. Trudeau, & K. Thayer. 1992. *Transitions to kindergarten in American schools.* U.S. Department of Education report. ED 344693. Hampton, NH: RMC Research Corporation.

Pianta, R., & M. Kraft-Sayre. 1999. Parents' observations about their children's transitions to kindergarten. *Young Children* 54 (3): 47–52.

Pianta, R., & D. Walsh. 1996. *High-risk children in schools: Constructing sustaining relationships.* New York: Routledge.

Ramey, C., S. Ramey, M. Phillips, R. Lanzi, C. Brezausek, C. Katholi, & S. Snyder. 2000. *Head Start children's entry into public school: A report on the National Head Start/Public School Early Childhood Transition Demonstration Study.* Washington, DC: Head Start Bureau.

Rimm-Kaufman, S., R. Pianta, & M. Cox. 2000. Teachers' judgments of problems in the transition to kindergarten. *Early Childhood Research Quarterly* 15 (2): 147–66.

Jayma Ferguson McGann is director of the Division of Prime Time in the Indiana Department of Education, where she has worked for 10 years. She is responsible for the state's early childhood pre-K to grade 3 initiatives, including Foundations for Young Children and Ready Schools, and issues related to kindergarten and early intervention. E-mail: jferguso@doe.state.in.us. **Patricia Clark**, PhD, is an associate professor in the Department of Elementary Education at Ball State University in Muncie, Indiana. She has worked for the past four years with the Indiana Department of Education on the Ready Schools Initiative and is currently researching its impact. E-mail: pclark@bsu.edu.

From *Young Children,* November 2007, pp. 77–79. Copyright © 2007 by National Association for the Education of Young Children. Reprinted by permission.

UNIT 7

Curricular Issues

Unit Selections

Key Points to Consider

- What are the steps teachers can take to plan using an emergent curriculum planning approach?

- Can teachers support prosocial development and if so, how?

- What information should teachers send parents about their children's early literacy experiences?

- What are some of the reasons picture books should be a big part of children's learning?

- How can math and science experiences be hands-on?

- Why is physical fitness so valuable in learning for young children? How can teachers foster a healthy lifestyle?

Student Web Site

www.mhcls.com/online

Internet References

Further information regarding these Web sites may be found in this book's preface or online.

Action for Healthy Kids
www.actionforhealthykids.org

Awesome Library for Teachers
http://www.neat-schoolhouse.org/teacher.html

The Educators' Network
http://www.theeducatorsnetwork.com

The Family Involvement Storybook Corner
http://www.gse.harvard.edu/hfrp/projects/fine.html

Grade Level Reading Lists
http://www.gradelevelreadinglists.org

Idea Box
http://theideabox.com

International Reading Association
http://www.reading.org

PE Central
http://www.pecentral.org

The Perpetual Preschool
http://www.ecewebguide.com

Phi Delta Kappa
http://www.pdkintl.org

Teacher Quick Source
http://www.teacherquicksource.com

Teachers Helping Teachers
http://www.pacificnet.net/~mandel/

Tech Learning
http://www.techlearning.com

Technology Help
http://www.apples4theteacher.com

Royalty-Free/Corbis

There is a major difference between eating frozen dinners every night vs. meals that have been prepared using the freshest local ingredients. The same holds true for planning curriculum. The generic one curriculum package fits all classrooms approach allows for little if any local flavor. Curriculum that is jointly developed by the teachers and students brings the best of the children's interest coupled with what is happening in their world together for meaningful, authentic learning. The first two articles in this unit, "The Plan" and "One Teacher, 20 Preschoolers, and a Goldfish", provide an excellent overview on the use of an emergent curriculum for young children. Teachers who carefully observe and listen to their children and know the events of their local community will find plenty of possibilities for topics of investigation. Young children are most interested in authentic curriculum that is meaningful to their lives. The twelve days I spent visiting schools in China in October, 2006 provided a wonderful glimpse into how emergent curriculum is in full force in many preschools and kindergartens in three of that country's largest cities. In Beijing specifically, the streets and building sites throughout the city are filled with construction cranes and cement trucks as the city prepares to host the 2008 Olympics. Inside the classrooms I saw the most extensive block structures I have ever seen. The children are living day to day with many cranes and steel girders. It is said 25% of the world's building cranes are located in China. Construction is everywhere and quite evident in the play of young Chinese children. We wouldn't want to eat frozen dinners every night for the rest of our lives; neither would we want to teach from a pre-pack-

aged curriculum. Get out there and choose some local flavor and spice up the teaching and learning in your classroom.

Increasingly preschool teachers are becoming aware of the tremendous responsibility to plan learning experiences that are aligned with standards to allow children to develop a lifelong love of learning along with the necessary skills they will need to be successful. Standards help to guide teachers as they plan appropriate activities that will allow their students to gain the necessary skills to continue to learn as they move through school. It is the responsibility of any teacher of young children to be very familiar with standards. If you are unaware of where to start, try your state Department of Education, many of which have standards for programs serving preschool children.

The "what's in it for me?" decade of the nineties has lead to the "service for others" decade as the 21st century starts. "Fostering Prosocial Behavior in Young Children" by Kathy Preusse offers the reader an overview of prosocial development along with strategies for helping children develop prosocial or altruistic behavior. Helping and caring for others are natural behaviors that can easily be modeled by supportive adults while children are young. Learning these behaviors in the early childhood years allows children to grow into adults who are caring, compassionate, and tolerant of others as they become adults.

The well respected journal *Zero to Three* is the source for "Early Literacy and Very Young Children." Author Rebecca Parlakian examines strategies to introduce young children to reading. Educating parents and teachers of infants and toddlers about the role they play in introducing children to the many aspects of learning to read is critical for future school success. Children who enter kindergarten having an understanding of the reading process have a distinct advantage over children who are not aware of the meanings of little black squiggles on the page. This article is followed by two other early literacy articles equally important. "Using Picture Books to Support Young Children's Literacy" and "The Sweet Work of Reading" provide the reader with additional information on this most important of early childhood skills. The articles include suggestions for shared book experiences, emergent writing, and conversations with children in a variety of settings.

This unit ends with three articles each addressing an important issue for teachers of young children. Healthy discussion can take place about each of the articles and the role of math and science, social studies, and physical fitness. Beginning and veteran teachers alike need to be well versed in a variety of topics affecting young children.

A number of the articles in unit 7 provide opportunities for the reader to reflect on the authentic learning experiences available for children. How can they investigate, explore, and create while studying a particular area of interest? Make children work for their learning, or as noted early childhood author Lilian Katz says, "Engage their minds". As a teacher of young children, acquaint yourself with the importance of firsthand experiences. Teachers often confuse firsthand and hands-on experiences but they are very different. Firsthand experiences are those where the children have a personal encounter with an event, place, or activity. Firsthand experiences include a visit to a firehouse, looking for life at the end of a small pond, and touring a local art gallery. After children have these firsthand experiences they are then able to incorporate them into their play, investigating

and exploring in the classroom. Hand-on experiences allow the children to actually use their hands and manipulate materials as they learn about the activity such as making a batch of play-dough, building a garage with the blocks, or investigating bubbles in the water table.

This unit is full of articles addressing different curriculum areas. Active child involvement leads to enhanced learning. Suggestions for project-based activities in literacy, movement, and technology are also included. Again, the theme runs deep. Hands on = Minds on!

Professional organizations, researchers, and educators are reaching out to teachers of young children with a clear message that what they do in classrooms with young children is extremely important for children's future development and learning capabilities. Of course the early childhood community will continue to support a hands-on experiential based learning environment, but teachers must be clear in their objectives and have standards that will lead to future school success firmly in mind. Only when we are able to effectively communicate to others the importance of what we do and receive proper recognition and support for our work, will the education of young children be held in high regard. We are working toward that goal, but need adults who care for and educate young children to view their job as building a strong foundation for children's future learning. Think of early childhood education as the extremely strong and stable foundation for a building that is expected to provide many decades of active service to thousands of people. If we view our profession in that light we can see the importance of our jobs. Bring passion and energy to what you do with young children and their families and you will be rewarded ten times over. Enjoy your work for it is so important.

The Plan

Building on Children's Interests

Hilary Jo Seitz

During outdoor playtime four-year-old Angela discovers a loose metal nut about half an inch in diameter. She shows the nut to her teacher.

> Angela: Look what I found. It looks just like the big one on our workbench.
>
> Teacher: Yes, it sure does, Angela. It's called a nut.
>
> Angela: I wonder where it came from.
>
> Teacher: Where do you think it may have come from?
>
> Angela: Well, actually it is the same as the ones in the workbench inside.
>
> Teacher: This nut looks very similar to the nuts and bolts inside. I think this nut might be bigger than the nuts and bolts we have inside.
>
> Angela: Maybe it came off of something out here.
>
> Teacher: What do you think it is from?
>
> Angela: Umm, I don't know—something out here.
>
> Teacher: Maybe you should check.
>
> Angela: Okay.

Holding the nut tight in her fist, Angela walks around, stopping to examine the play equipment, the tables, the parked trikes, and anything else she thinks might have a missing nut. She can find only bolts with nuts on the trikes. She spies a large Stop sign, puts her special treasure in her pocket so other children cannot see it, and sets up a roadblock for the busy trike riders so she can check the nuts and bolts on their trikes.

Edmund stops and asks her what she is doing, and she explains. Edmund says he needs to see the nut. When Angela shows it to him, he gets off his trike and starts helping her inspect the other trikes. They eventually find the one that is missing the nut. Other children, curious, crowd around.

While incidents such as this are common in early childhood settings, teachers may not listen for them, seize upon them, and build on them. When teachers do pay attention, these authentic events can spark emergent curriculum that builds on children's interests. This kind of curriculum is different from a preplanned, "canned" thematic curriculum model. In emergent, or negotiated, curriculum, the child's inter-

est becomes the key focus and the child has various motivations for learning (Jones & Nimmo 1994). The motivations are intrinsic, from deep within, meaningful and compelling to the child. As such, the experience is authentic and ultimately very powerful.

This article outlines a plan that teachers, children, and families can easily initiate and follow to build on children's interests. It is a process of learning about what a child or a class is interested in and then planning a positive authentic learning experience around and beyond that interest. Teachers, children, and parents alike are the researchers in this process. All continuously observe and document the process and review the documentation to construct meaning (Edwards, Gandini, & Forman 1998). Documentation is the product that is collected by the researchers. It may include work samples, children's photos, children's dialogues, and the teacher's written interpretations.

The Plan

"The Plan," as it became known in my classroom, is a simple four-step process of investigation, circular in nature and often evolving or spinning off into new investigations. (See diagram) The Plan consists of

1. **Sparks** (provocations)—Identify emerging ideas, look at children's interests, hold conversations, and provide experiences. Document the possibilities.
2. **Conversations**—Have conversations with interested participants (teachers, children, and parents), ask questions, document conversations through video recordings, tape recordings, teacher/parent dictation, or other ways. Ask "What do we already know? What do we wonder about? How can we learn more? What is the plan?"
3. **Opportunities and experiences**—Provide opportunities and experiences in both the classroom and the community for further investigation. Document those experiences.
4. **More questions and more theories**—Think further about the process. Document questions and theories.

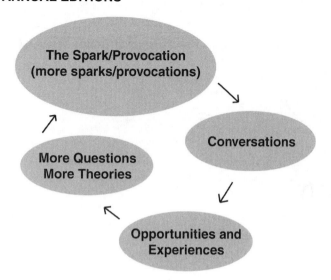

Figure 1

In other words, teachers, children, and parents identify something of interest; we discuss what we know about it or what we want to know about it; we experience it or have opportunities to learn about the idea; and then we discuss what we did and either ask more questions or make new theories. We document our understandings throughout the whole process.

The initial spark can come from anywhere or anything. For example, we might overhear children talking about the lawnmower at the park. The class, or sometimes a smaller group of children, then sits down and devises a plan with the help of interested adults.

Step 1: Sparks

Sparks can be things, phenomena, conversations—anything that provokes deeper thought. The sparks are what trigger a child (and adult) to want to know more, to investigate further. These sparks can occur at any time. They can be as simple as finding a pebble in one's shoe, grabbing an idea or story line from a book, or finding a nut on the playground. Young children have these sparks of interest all day long.

Sparks can be things, phenomena, conversations—anything that provokes deeper thought.

How Do Teachers See/Catch These Sparks?

I often hear teachers say, "How can I learn what the children are interested in?" or "How do we find out what the children want to know?" My response is always, Talk with the children, listen to them, and observe. For some teachers, it can be difficult to sit back and trust that ideas will naturally emerge. But once teachers become familiar with the process, they begin noticing how easily sparks appear.

Teachers in preschools, Head Start programs, and public school classrooms are expected to meet state standards or curriculum content goals. It is possible (although sometimes challenging) to integrate these standards and goals into emergent themes. Teachers who know and understand the "big picture" of standards and goals are more likely to *fit* a topic or emerging idea/plan into the curriculum. They document the process of The Plan (through photographs as well as descriptive narrative) to provide evidence of meeting standards and content goals.

Can We Provoke the Sparks?

Triggering sparks is sometimes helpful and can have exciting implications. Teachers can provoke children's thinking by suggesting ideas through stories, specific items, or experiences. Again, when a teacher is knowledgeable about standards and content goals, she knows when to provide appropriate sparks. For example, reading a book such as *If You Give a Moose a Muffin*, by Laura Numeroff, may trigger thinking and conversations about several different ideas (moose and what they eat and where they live, baking, puppet shows, painting, and others) as well as support literacy development. Owocki, in discussing teachable moments in literacy development, says, "Teachable moment strategies involve knowledgeably observing children and seeking out relevant opportunities to help them extend their understandings" (1999, 28).

Introducing an item into the classroom is another way of triggering sparks of thought. Watch children's eyes light up when you place a large beetle on a table or pluck an unfamiliar stringed instrument.

Finally, we can trigger sparks by offering experiences such as a neighborhood walk or a visit to the grocery store. Authentic experiences with meaningful things interest children (Fraser & Gestwicki 2001). The following is an excerpt of an observation from an early childhood classroom.

Teachers can provoke children's thinking by suggesting ideas through stories, specific items, or experiences.

A small group of four-year-olds and their teacher prepare to visit the park across the street. The teacher locks the gate and turns toward the children. She leans down and says, "Please stay on the sidewalk." Pointing to the nearby intersection, she adds, "We are going to walk over there to the crosswalk." The teacher holds hands with one child while the others pair off and walk behind her.

> Kayla: What's a crosswalk?
> José: It's over there.
> Teacher: At the corner, we are going to walk inside the lines of the crosswalk. The lines show people where to walk. That way, cars know to stop. It is safer for us to cross in the crosswalk than in the middle of the street.
> Tiana: My mom and me always cross over there by our car.
> José: That's the middle of the street.
> Michael (*motioning*): See that red sign? It says STOP, so you gotta stop at it.

As the small group negotiates the crosswalk and heads down the sidewalk on the other side of the street, José points out three more signs (a No Parking sign, a street name sign, and a Caution sign). The children are puzzled by the Caution sign and stop to try to figure it out.

The teacher documents this interest in street signs and crosswalks in writing and by drawing a sketch of the situation. Later, back in the classroom with the whole class, she brings up the subject of signs. The topic stirs interest and lots of conversation—triggering a new classroom investigation and the beginning of a new plan.

Step 2: Conversations and Writing a Plan

Formal meetings, built into the daily classroom routine, are ideal times for children, teachers, and family volunteers to have large group conversations about forming and writing a plan. In these routine meetings, children already know what to expect; they understand the process as well as the expectations. Our class meetings generally include a variety of fairly predictable experiences (reading stories, singing songs, conversations). Depending on the time of the meeting, we always discuss what has happened earlier or what is about to happen. While one teacher facilitates this meeting, another adult (teaching assistant or parent) writes down ideas, questions, and thoughts about the conversations. The adults later review this documentation to help plan and provide appropriate experiences.

Conversations also take place in settings such as activities or mealtimes. Small group conversations can be very meaningful to children and adults alike. Here is one snack time conversation:

Five girls, ages three and four, are seated at a small table, eating crackers. One child mentions going to the state fair the night before with her family. Two of the other children had been to the fair the previous week, so the teacher considers where to go with this spark of interest.

Kamie: It was cold at the fair, but the animals weren't cold 'cause they got fur on them.

Stacy: I touched the goats and the baby pig!

Kamie: Me too!

Karla: I went on a ride, but next time I'm gonna see the animals.

Teacher: Where are the animals?

Stacy: They are in this big tent, and you gotta wait real long to go inside. But you can put a penny or a dollar in the machine to get food, then you can feed the goats and pigs.

Teacher: What do they eat?

Kamie: They eats lots of stuff.

Karla: Yeah, like rice and leaves.

Stacy: The pony has big teeth and a tongue. It gets your hand sticky.

Teacher: Do all the animals eat the same food? (Kamie nods yes.) Maybe we could go to the petting zoo and feed the goats and sheep.

All the girls: Yes!

Teacher: Let's make a plan.

Karla and Stacy jump out of their seats to get a big sheet of paper and markers. Kamie reminds them to bring a clipboard too.

The teacher writes THE PLAN at the top of the paper. She prints the five girls' names under it. Then she begins writing a list, speaking the words at the same time she writes them.

1. Goats and pigs and ponies eat food.
2. What do they eat?

Karla: Where do they sleep? (The teacher makes this No. 3.)

4. Go to library to get books.
5. Go to petting zoo and talk to zoo keeper.

The Plan is set and displayed on the wall. As a form of documentation, it is revisited frequently and adjusted to meet the needs of the children (Project Zero & Reggio Children 2001). Children, teachers, and families continuously reassess The Plan to guide inquiries. Often children and teachers add revisions to the plan.

Formal Planning

Teachers should also prepare a more formal lesson plan. This planning process works best when teachers, teaching assistants, and parents have opportunities to discuss ideas together. The teacher, who usually assumes the role of facilitator, needs to be prepared. She should know and understand standards and content goals; gather documentation, including photographs, observational records, and work samples; and guide the process of creating the formal plan.

The group discusses why the emerging ideas are important and how to further the investigations. Lesson plans should include the children's questions or inquiries as well as the teacher's; both are integrated into a formal plan.

Step 3: Opportunities and Experiences

Essential in a good plan is providing, facilitating, and initiating *meaningful* and *authentic* opportunities and experiences to help children further understand ideas. The word *meaningful* is the critical element here. Significant experiences create a sense of purpose for the child. John Dewey cautioned, "Attentive care must be devoted to the conditions which give each present experience a worthwhile meaning" (1938, 49).

One way to promote meaningful experiences is to find opportunities for authentic experiences that allow young children to see, negotiate, and participate in the real world. The experiences should be based on ideas that emerge from conversations or the written plan. For example, when the children initiated the conversation about street signs, their authentic experience of seeing and learning about street signs prompted a written plan for deeper understanding. The class began to take walks to explore different signs. Several children created a map showing where the street signs were located. Another group drew all the street signs they saw. Back in the classroom, everyone shared their information. Two children created signs and posted them in the classroom. There was a Stop sign and one that looked like a stop sign but read Quiet in the Library. At the sink, a yellow sign said Wash Hands.

> **One way to promote meaningful experiences is to find opportunities for authentic experiences that allow young children to see, negotiate, and participate in the real world.**

The children also decided they needed road signs on the trike paths in the outdoor play area. Some confusion arose during this phase of the experience. Children began arguing about where signs should be placed and if they had to follow the direction on the signs. This discomfort led to the next phase of the plan (see Step 4).

Several content goals were acknowledged in the above experience. Children drew and created maps of a familiar setting; they practiced writing letters and putting together sounds; they used their knowledge of street signs to create classroom rules. In all, the children experienced authentic, meaningful learning.

Step 4: More Questions, More Theories

During this phase, the teacher carefully outlines the theories and documents new questions. As children raise new questions, they are forced to deepen their thinking about the situation. These thoughts become new sparks or provocations for future plans.

In the continuing sign investigation, the teacher called a large group meeting when the arguing about the trike signs and rules persisted. She posted a large piece of paper on the wall and said, "I noticed some confusion on the trike roads today. Jacob, tell me your plan with the signs." She was careful to focus the conversation on the plan rather than encouraging a blame game ("So-and-so went the wrong way"). Jacob expressed his concern of following the sign rules for safety. The teacher wrote on the paper, "If we follow the street signs, we will stay safe." Kayla added another theory: "People who make the signs get to

make the rules, but they have to write them out." Another child brought up additional safety issues, such as wearing helmets and keeping the trikes on the path. The children and teacher decided to post several signs on the roadway to direct traffic in a clockwise pattern.

Summary

Young children learn best through active participation and experience. When helped, allowed, and encouraged to follow an interest and construct a plan to learn more, children are empowered and become intrinsically motivated. They fully engage in the experience when it is their own (Jones & Nimmo 1994). Meaningful ideas are intrinsically motivating.

A caring, observant teacher can easily promote motivation by facilitating the planning process. As the four-step process described here becomes more familiar to children, teachers, and families, The Plan gets easier. Through collaboration, they document, reflect, and interpret ideas to form deeper meanings and foster lifelong learning.

References

Dewey, J. 1938. *Experience and education*. New York: Collier.

Edwards, C., L. Gandini, & G. Forman. 1998. *The hundred languages of children: The Reggio Emilia approach—Advanced reflections.* 2nd ed. Westport, CT: Ablex.

Fraser, S., & C. Gestwicki. 2001. *Authentic childhood: Experiencing Reggio Emilia in the classroom.* Albany, NY: Delmar.

Jones, E., & J. Nimmo. 1994. *Emergent curriculum.* Washington, DC: NAEYC.

Owocki, G. 1999. *Literacy through play.* Portsmouth, NH: Heinemann.

Project Zero & Reggio Children. 2001. *Making learning visible: Children as individual and group learners.* Reggio Emilia, Italy: Project Zero.

HILARY JO SEITZ, PhD, is an assistant professor at University of Alaska, Anchorage. She has worked in early childhood settings for the past 18 years as a teacher, administrator, and instructor.

From *Young Children*, March 2006, pp. 36–41. Copyright © 2006 by National Association for the Education of Young Children. Reprinted by permission.

One Teacher, 20 Preschoolers, and a Goldfish

Environmental Awareness, Emergent Curriculum, and Documentation

ANN LEWIN-BENHAM

Teaching preschoolers about the environment is hard. Many complex concepts are involved: the interactions among everything on the planet—air, land, water, and all living things; the systems that determine weather and climate, food supply, energy resources, and the quality of life for every plant and animal; systems operating on a planetary scale or in geologic time; the organisms living in a single water drop. Chemistry, geology, physics, and biology all intersect in discussions on the environment.

This article shares the experiences of one teacher in helping preschoolers learn about the environment. The article is based on my lifelong concerns for the environment, on my own experience helping children learn to take care of a goldfish in a preschool classroom, and on a composite of many different efforts—my own and other teachers'—helping children learn about the environment. It is also based on three of my own beliefs:

1. Most young children are eager to learn about the environment.
2. A teacher who lives an environmentally friendly life can be effective in teaching young children about the environment.
3. The emergent curriculum approach (Rinaldi 1992; Jones & Nimmo 1994), including documentation, is well suited for encouraging children to develop environmentally aware behavior.

These beliefs are reflected in this article through enthusiastic children, a teacher respectful of environmental concerns, and the success of the emergent curriculum in arousing and building on children's interests.

Social Constructivist Theory

The theoretical base for the use of an emergent curriculum is social constructivist theory. Briefly, we can infer from the theory that learning occurs when children are engaged in collaborative activity about something that deeply interests them and that the teacher's role is to collaborate with the children in their exploration so her knowledge can scaffold their understanding.

"Learning and development emerge from the dynamic interaction of social and individual factors" (John-Steiner, Panofsky, & Smith 1994, 6). Today numerous psychologists and social theorists have confirmed the idea, first proposed by Lev Vygotsky, that learning is a social process (Feuerstein, Klein, & Tannenbaum 1991; John-Steiner, Panofsky, & Smith 1994; Resnick & Hall 1998; Bronfenbrenner 2004).

Social constructivist theory is robustly practiced in the schools of Reggio Emilia, Italy. In these schools projects emerge through teacher collaboration with small groups of children. The projects are based on teachers' thoughtful listening to children's conversations to determine their deep interests and on subsequent focused talk with the children about these interests. The Reggio structure also involves a carefully designed classroom that functions as a "third teacher," and as such frees the teacher to engage in projects. Literature describing these schools and certain Web sites will acquaint those unfamiliar with the Reggio Emilia approach (see Jones & Nimmo 1994; Edwards, Gandini, & Forman 1998; Lewin-Benham 2006; visit the Web sites of NAREA and Reggio Children).

Ms. Putnam, 20 Children, and a Goldfish

Ms. Putnam, a preschool teacher, wanted to arouse children's concern for the environment and to inspire them to think and act in ecologically sound ways. An evolving chain of experiences about the environment emerged from the introduction of a goldfish to her class.

Projects are based on teachers' thoughtful listening to children's conversations to determine their deep interests and on subsequent focused talk with the children about these interests.

Emergent Curriculum

Rather than sets of lesson plans and objectives, emergent curriculum is a *process* that roughly follows these steps:

1. Select a topic that reflects interests expressed by children in their conversations or that you as their teacher suspect may be of high interest. Ms. Putnam brought a goldfish to school with the idea that the children's care of the fish might interest them in exploring environment-related subjects.
2. Brainstorm, alone or with colleagues, the many ways the experience could develop to ensure that the topic has rich "generative" (Perkins 1992, 92–95) potential. As it evolves, the project may or may not follow what you brainstormed.
3. Use something concrete—from the children, their families, or the teacher—to pique initial interest and to maintain it. The concrete "thing" may be children's own words as recorded by the teacher. Ms. Putnam used children's questions about the goldfish as the starter for many pursuits. Throughout the year she recorded, saved, and studied the children's conversations and kept using their words to arouse further interest.
4. Tape or take notes of the children's words as they react. Study their words to determine what *really* grabs their attention. You may let a day or more pass to heighten the children's anticipation and to allow yourself time to study their words.
5. Continue to bring the children's own words back to them: "On Monday you said the fish's water was really dirty. Joey said, 'It's full of poop.' Would you like to help me clean the fishbowl?"
6. Brainstorm what might happen before any new activity. Knowing she wanted to build environmental awareness, Ms. Putnam had a container available to save the dirty water. When the children asked why she was saving it, she asked, "What do you think we could do with this water?" Again she recorded and studied the children's answers, and brought back those that she had selected for their potential to spark environmental awareness.
7. Use children's words, some particular things they have made, or photo(s) taken during the process as the stimulus for the next steps.
8. Document the experience as each step happens. Record the story of the emerging project as *it emerges,* using children's words, photos of them, their drawings or other work, and a photojournalistic-type retelling. (See "Documentation.").

Documentation

Documentation is the process of recording children's thoughts and actions on a topic to maintain their focus and expand their interest. It works like this:

1. As an experience begins, create a large panel out of sturdy cardstock or illustration board. Write a question, repeat a child's comment, or make up a title as a headline for the panel. Include a photo, a drawing, or an object to show what sparked the project.
2. Continue to add information to the panel as the experience continues. Information can be key words from the teacher or children, a child's drawing, or a photo or series of photos of the children, even an object. The information should reflect a pivotal moment which led to next steps. Ms. Putnam added a photo of the full class at the first group meeting with the fishbowl in the center, one child's comment, and one question each from two other children. As the project continued, she added drawings of children's ideas for how to clean the fish bowl—one a theory, the other the process the class eventually adopted.
3. Whenever a panel is hung or words or photos are added, and before continuing the experience, gather the children who were involved, and read the panel to them (or have them "read"—retell—to you) what has happened thus far. This is called *revisiting.* Ms. Putnam and the small group revisited the panel at least once a day.
4. Add whatever photos and comments or questions bring the experience to a conclusion. In this case, Ms. Putnam added a series of photos—cleaning the fishbowl, discovering Big Eyes dead, everyone crying, and the fish's grave. At the end she added two children's questions which stimulated new projects: "What are we going to do with the dirty water?" and "What will happen to the dead fish?"

A finished documentation panel should convey what started the experience, how it developed and why, and its outcome or the open-ended questions it sparked. As children revisit panels, they begin to retell the experience to themselves, to one another, and to their parents or classroom visitors. Revisiting helps the experience move forward, keeps the children focused, and deepens their understanding of their experiences. Documentation gives parents and visitors a window into life in the classroom and builds both appreciation for and trust in the school.

In September Ms. Putnam made five commitments. During the coming year she would:

- bring into the classroom things related to the environment.
- listen closely to children's conversations and observe their activities and explorations around the items, then use the children's interests as the basis for projects.

- use related vocabulary often and read aloud books on the environment twice weekly.
- keep parents informed so they could reinforce the topic at home.
- follow an emergent curriculum approach—teaching through small group projects, documenting the projects, and revisiting the documentation.

Where do subjects for in-depth projects come from? Ms. Putnam knew that the information she needed for projects to emerge would come from a variety of sources: actively conversing with the children, listening to their conversations with each other to determine what they already knew and what else they wanted to know, and studying her notes on these conversations. Having decided to bring a goldfish to the classroom—because she believed it would be of great interest to the children—she brainstormed concepts that might emerge over time. Her list included the following areas:

- the ecosystem a goldfish requires
- energy sources for living things
- clean and unclean water
- waste disposal
- relationships between living things and the environment

The Goldfish Arrives

On the day Ms. Putnam brought the goldfish to school, Joey, the most active four-year-old in the class, spotted it immediately: "Ms. Putnam, what have we got?" She knew his enthusiasm would spread. During group time she asked Joey to describe what he had seen: "It's orange, and it's swimming, and . . ." jumping up and pointing, "it's THERE!"

Carefully, Ms. Putnam carried the bowl to the full class meeting. Immediately, an animated conversation ensued. Ms. Putnam made notes on the children's comments and, over the next few days, took photos of them observing the fish. After analyzing this information she determined which children were most interested in the goldfish. She created a documentation panel with the heading "Joey Discovered a New Fish" and two photos of children observing the fish, and she hung the panel in the classroom. Later she discussed the panel with the small group of children whom she had observed were most interested. Revisiting the panel with the children revealed more of their ideas because it sparked another conversation.

As the children and teacher discussed the panel, questions tumbled out:

- Where did the goldfish come from? The stream near the school?
- Where did you get the bowl?
- Can we feed the fish from our lunchboxes?
- How does it poop?
- Can I hold it?
- Will it have babies?
- Can I take it home?
- Will it get old and die?
- What do you do with a dead fish?

Like most children, the four-year-olds in Ms. Putnam's class are interested in everything around them. Even by age 4 they have had many experiences, and know more than adults may realize. They are naturally empathetic, know instinctively if living things feel sad or are hurt, and express their concern with words and hugs. Ms. Putnam felt certain she could focus their empathy on the environment, helping them to acquire a sense of what the environment is, an awareness of all living things'

needs, and some knowledge of how those needs relate to the environment (Gardner 1991). From the children's comments, she added this one to the documentation panel: "How can we get this poop out of the water?" She also added a photo of the fishbowl with its dirty water.

That evening Ms. Putnam matched the concepts she had originally brainstormed with the children's questions. The comparison convinced her to use the children's own questions to begin exploring environmental issues with them. She added two of their most fertile questions to the panel: "How can we clean the water?" and "What will we do with the dirty water?"

Planning for Learning

In educating children about anything, a teacher needs to determine what they already know and find the intersections between her perceptions and their interests. Teachers use this information to decide what to do next (Vecchi 1994). Through analyzing her own brainstorming list and comparing it to the interests children expressed, Ms. Putnam hypothesized that an environmental curriculum in her classroom, sparked by the children's interest in the goldfish, could cover these topics: ecosystem; land, water, and air; food and energy; pollution. The curriculum would emerge as children's investigations and activities led to the evolution of old interests and the development of new ideas. How she prepared the classroom environment and documented the children's experiences would be critical. Ms. Putnam asked herself if she could also:

- Care for an animal in addition to the plants already maintained in the classroom?
- Model environmentally conscious behaviors for the children consistently? For example, could she
  — make sure to turn out lights *whenever* the class left the classroom or sunshine provided adequate light and each time tell the children her actions were taken to save energy?
  — teach the children to conserve by running only a trickle of water then turning it off while soaping hands or brushing teeth?
  — set up a system to segregate leftover food, paper, glass, and plastic, and with the children analyze which leftovers could be reused and how? During meals, Ms. Putnam began to play a game with the children, Compost Collection, in which they discussed what leftovers would make good compost. This sparked the children's curiosity about what to do when the compost container was full, and led to a project to develop a compost pile in a remote corner of the play yard.
- Reach beyond the classroom to engage in environmentally friendly efforts? For example, she
  — toured the school with the children to detect how to save resources.
  — asked parents to send to school examples of community environmental activities. One family sent an article about the installation of energy-saving light bulbs in the local public libraries. Ms. Putnam read every item to the whole class, and discussed it in depth with those children

who were most interested. Often the children had their own theories, which Ms. Putnam recorded, studied, and later discussed with them. On subsequent days she had them draw pictures or represent their ideas in other materials, like paper, cardboard, clay, wire, or blocks.

— invited parents to help on field trips. One involved a visit to the city's waste recycling plant, another to a nearby stream to look for effects of pollution.

Using Observations and Conversations to Facilitate Learning

For several days after introducing the goldfish, Ms. Putnam left a tape recorder next to the fishbowl to capture the children's comments. As the children observed the fish, she took photos and added two to the panel. All the children visited the fishbowl at least once a day, most two or three times; five children were regulars, sometimes checking on the fish several times a day and naming it Big Eyes. Children's comments on tape ranged from how fish are born to fish weddings, death, play, and fighting. Most often the children wondered how fish get food, what happens when they poop in the water, and how to clean the water.

After observing and revisiting the panel with the children and while excitement was still high, Ms. Putnam revisited the panel again with the five most interested children and asked, "What else would you like to know about the fish?" Questions poured out. Ms. Putnam then asked another question: "How can we find out?" "These two questions are powerful and universally applicable. The first taps the wealth of experiences even very young children have already accumulated. The second stretches them to make connections from one particular bit of information to their other ideas, which adults cannot intuit" (Lewin-Benham 2006, p. 51).

From this discussion Ms. Putnam realized the children knew these things: the fish should be fed just once daily, it pooped a lot, and its water was already dirty. This bothered them, and they wanted to do something about it.

Ms. Putnam asked the five children, "Can you draw pictures showing how we could clean the bowl?" She added two of the children's drawings to the panel. Two days later, she gathered the five children again, revisited the panel, and asked them to use their drawings to describe to one another how to clean the bowl. Their ideas ranged from fantasy—using a magic vacuum that unrolled from a long tube—to reality—finding ways to clean the bowl without hurting Big Eyes, since cleaning utensils might be rough and cleansers could poison him. Danielle, one of the children, had been to a pet store where she gleaned this information, which she then shared with the others during one of their many small group discussions.

Ms. Putnam suggested that the group discuss which method would be best and then make one drawing to represent it. Several more days passed as the children debated among themselves, sometimes arguing fiercely, often joined by Ms. Putnam. They finally agreed on how to clean the bowl: Catch Big Eyes in a fish net (Danielle had seen this in the pet store also), put him quickly into a pitcher of clean water, empty the old water, carefully scour the bowl, then pour in Big Eyes,

clean water and all. The group collaborated on making one drawing of this process, which Ms. Putnam added to the panel.

Big Eyes Dies!

Because the class had not allowed the changing water to stand overnight so the chlorine could evaporate, Big Eyes did not survive the change. Ms. Putnam had not told the children this vital knowledge, something she knew but, in the excitement, had forgotten to share with them. The children were distraught. Ms. Putnam blamed herself. The children saw how sad she was.

"Hey! I know," Joey exclaimed. "Let's go to the pet store and buy a new fish!"

Teacher and children cried—all still sad about Big Eyes, Donnie and Charles in distress at Ms. Putnam's sadness, Danielle and Darrell not to be left out, Ms. Putnam upset at her omission and deeply moved by the children's compassion.

"What are we gonna do with Big Eyes?" asked Joey. Crying ceased as the children began a conversation that became animated. Many ideas later, they toured the yard and found an ideal spot to bury Big Eyes—under the pussy willow, their favorite with its soft, silky-haired blooms. Ms. Putnam added a photo of Big Eyes's grave to the documentation panel. She saw the echoes of this powerful experience in many of the projects that emerged later that year.

Emerging Projects

The experience with Big Eyes sparked a new project on the environment with these themes: What happens when dirty water is poured on the earth? What is earth? What would happen to Big Eyes in the earth? Ms. Putnam documented the earth project on a second panel. A small group went with her to the pet store to buy a new fish in response to Joey's suggestion (the subject of a third panel). The children were full of questions about how stores find fish. This led to a project on ecosystems that support different fish. By year's end the children's evolving interests led to:

- Questioning what's in water and how evaporation works.
- Reading the fish food label, which prompted a big project on food sources.
- Carefully watching the ceaseless swimming of the new fish, which led to a project on energy.
- Discussing how pollutants get into air and water.
- Studying the labels on cleansers, which resulted in a search for environmentally friendly cleaning products and replacing commercial cleansers with homemade solutions of baking soda, vinegar, and water, natural products that the children learned would not pollute.

When the children learned how dangerous plastic can be to wild animals, they organized a Plastic Patrol and involved their families in a clean-up day.

When the children learned how dangerous plastic can be to wild animals, they organized a Plastic Patrol and involved their families in a clean-up day. When they learned that fish poop makes good fertilizer, they went on a hunt for other waste to recycle, and visited their town's recycling center.

Each project involved only a small group, generally different for each project. Ms. Putnam documented every project on its own panel. Usually the entire class toured each panel, led in small groups by the children involved. With one group, Ms. Putnam wrote to parents discussing how to use the classroom's environmentally friendly practices at home. The whole class read the letter; several children added words and drawings, and everyone carried a copy home.

It was possible for Ms. Putnam to teach to a small group for two reasons. First, there were two adults in the classroom. Second, the classroom environment was richly prepared. "In practice this means . . . [the teachers] trust the environment as much as they trust one another, and create a three-member team from two teachers and an environment. Their painstaking organization results in environment-guided activity that is as valuable as teacher-guided activity" (Lewin-Benham 2006, 14–15).

A Year in Review

At the end of the year Ms. Putnam reviewed her teaching and the children's learning. Projects on a wide range of areas covered 10 different panels. She had learned to be more thoughtful about when to add her own knowledge to the children's explorations. This is the essence of emergent curriculum: the learning that results for children and teacher from the teacher's knowledge and skills through collaboration with the children. Because the teacher scaffolds the children's ability, it makes it possible for her knowledge to merge with, expand, or alter their knowledge. What the children learned was evident in their

- favorite books, like *Cactus Hotel,* about a saguaro's life cycle and relationship to other desert plants and animals;
- daily vocabulary, which now included words like *environment, relationship, impact, pollutant,* and *earth-friendly;*
- drawings, which showed increasingly thoughtful ideas about the environment;
- interest in food content, concern about clean air and water, and knowledge of the plants and animals that lived near the school;
- comments, like Joey's after burying Big Eyes: "You see, we're all connected to everything, fish to insects, insects to earth, earth to goldfish, what we eat to earth. It's all connected."

Conclusion

Ms. Putnam's experience illustrates how to raise preschool children's environmental awareness. Her approach was grounded in the social constructivist theory that we learn through relationships with others who mediate our interactions with things

around us. Her approach was influenced by Reggio Emilia school practices, especially belief in children's ability; attentive listening to children's ideas; collaborative small-group projects including the teacher; the use of a well-designed environment as a third teacher; extensive use of various materials as vehicles for children to express and reformulate ideas; and documentation.

Teachers wanting to raise children's environmental awareness can use a fish, a plant, an insect, a book, an environmentally focused local event, or many other things. Wherever they start, teachers should allow plenty of time for conversation and should use the children's own reactions, comments, and questions as the basis for what they do next.

The interconnectedness of everything on our planet dovetails with a teaching approach based on collaboration and a theory of learning based on relationships. In this case the children's interest in the life and death of a goldfish enabled the teacher to arouse their concern for the well-being of the environment and to help the children think and act in ecologically sound ways.

References

Bronfenbrenner, U. 2004. *Making human beings human.* London: Sage.

Edwards, C., L. Gandini, G. Forman, eds. 1998. *The hundred languages of children: The Reggio Emilia approach—Advanced reflections.* 2nd ed. Greenwich, CT: Ablex.

Feuerstein, R., P. Klein, A. Tannenbaum. 1991. *Mediated learning experience (MLE): Theoretical, psychosocial and learning implications.* London: Freund.

Gardner, H. 1991. *The uschooled mind.* New York: Basic Books.

John-Steiner, V., C.P. Panofsky, & L.W. Smith. 1994. *Sociocultural approaches to language and literacy.* New York: Cambridge University Press.

Jones, E., & J. Nimmo. 1994. *Emergent curriculum.* Washington, DC: NAEYC.

Lewin-Benham, A. 2006. *Possible schools: The Reggio approach to urban education.* New York: Teachers College Press.

NAREA (North American Reggio Emilia Alliance). Online: www.reggioalliance.org.

Perkins, D. 1992. *Smart schools.* New York: Free Press.

Reggio Children. Online: http://zerosei.comune.re.it/inter/reggiochildren.htm.

Resnick, L.B., & M.W. Hall. 1998. Learning organizations for sustainable education reform. *Daedalus* 127 (4): 89–118. Online: www.instituteforlearning.org/media/docs/learningorgforsustain.pdf.

Rinaldi, C. 1992. Lecture. Ida College, Newton Centre, Massachusetts, June.

Vecchi, V. 1994. Lecture/Study Seminar. "Experience of the Municipal Infant-Toddler Centers and Preprimary Schools." June. Reggio Emilia, Italy.

ANN LEWIN-BENHAM, AB, was founder/director of the Model Early Learning Center (MELC) and Capital Children's Museum in Washington, D.C. Her recent book, *Possible Schools:* The *Reggio Approach to Urban Education,* tells MELC's story. Ann writes and lectures on early education.

Further resources on environmental education—a bibliography and a listing of curriculum activities—are available through *Beyond the Journal* at www.journal.naeyc.org/btj.

From *Young Children*, March 2006, pp. 28–34. Copyright © 2006 by National Association for the Education of Young Children. Reprinted by permission.

Fostering Prosocial Behavior in Young Children

KATHY PREUSSE

According to the National Center for Education Statistics (2001), there are over 21 million children under the age of six in center-based child care programs in the United States. Programs vary in their content, but one of the aspects common to all is the social context in which learning and care occurs. All early childhood teachers have a tremendous responsibility to meet the developmental needs of the whole child, and more than that, to help children develop the prosocial skills necessary to succeed in a group setting, as well as in society.

Social Development in Young Children

From infancy, children are active participates in a complex world. Interactions with parents are the first type of social exchange infants experience. Healthy exchanges create a bond or attachment. Attachment is a sense of connection between two people that forms the foundation for a relationship (Pruitt, 1998). Exchanges such as facial expressions, movements, and verbal interactions help create an attachment or bond. Experts feel that the first year of life is a critical period for bonding. Bonds create a sense of trust that supports an infant's exploration of the world and serves as a base for future development (Raikes, 1996). "Numerous studies have shown that infants with secure attachments to their mothers and fathers are at an advantage for acquiring competencies in language and in cognitive, social, and emotional development" (Raikes, 1996, p. 59). If attachment does not occur, children may have problems later in life and may display asocial behaviors (Wardle, 2003).

Today, with an increasing number of children enrolled in center-based programs, educators and caregivers play an important role in promoting the development of prosocial skills. "The teacher-child relationship is an extension of the primary parent-child relationship, and teachers invest in building supportive relationships with families around their common interest, the child" (Edwards & Raikes, 2002, p. 12). Many programs have been designed based on the principle that attachment is vital to the social development of young children. Some centers have focused on the importance of attachment and relationships by creating small groups or 'families.' In these programs, an early childhood teacher is assigned to a group of children over an extended period of time, sometimes several years, which is called looping. Primary caregivers provide children predictability, consistency and a secure base, which helps promote the development of trust. It is from this base the child can explore his physical and social environment. According to Howes and others (cited in Raikes, 1996, p. 61) "There are multiple advantages of secure-based behavior for infants: infants explore more, have more productive play, and interact more and more resourcefully with adults in group settings when their attachments to teachers are secure." Furthermore, children with a secure teacher-child relationship tended to have more positive peer relationships (Raikes, 1996).

During the preschool years, children are developing a sense of independence and capacity for cooperation. As they become more verbal, self-aware, and able to think about another person's point of view, they become more able to interact with peers (Berk, 2002). Furthermore, children at this age move from parallel play to more advanced levels such as associative and cooperative play. It is through cooperative play that children experience play in groups in which they must set aside their needs for the good of the group (Wardle, 2003). Thus, they are developing positive social skills.

Early social development is complex and closely intertwined with other areas of development: cognitive, physical, emotional, linguistic, and aesthetic. The National Association for the Education of Young Children (NAEYC; Bredekamp & Copple, 1997) emphasizes the need for socialization and the development of social skills as a vital part of early childhood education. They advocate principles that educators should use as a guide to developmentally appropriate practices. Listed below are five of these principles. As you can see socialization is intertwined and important to each of these principles (as well as the remaining ones not listed).

- Development and learning occur in and are influenced by multiple social and cultural contexts.
- Children are active learners, drawing on direct physical and social experiences as well as culturally transmitted

knowledge to construct their own understandings of the world around them.

- Development and learning result from interaction of biological maturation and the environment, which includes both the physical and social worlds that children live in.
- Play is an important vehicle for children's social, emotional, and cognitive development as well as a reflection of their development.
- Children develop and learn best in the context of a community where they are safe and valued, their physical needs are met, and they feel psychologically secure (cited in Bredekamp & Copple, 1997, p. 10).

Prosocial behaviors are crucial to children's well being. Thus, it is our responsibility as early childhood educators to provide opportunities for the development of necessary social skills.

Play

Play is a common form of interaction between and among children. "Children do not construct their own understanding of a concept in isolation but in the course of interaction with others" (Bredekamp and Copple 1997, p. 114). Some of the social skills fostered through play are the ability to work towards a common goal, initiating and/or keeping a conversation going, and cooperating with peers. Attachments are formed with other children of similar interests and can lead to friendships. Friendship can be defined as "a mutual relationship involving companionship, sharing, understanding of thoughts and feelings, and caring for and comforting one another in times of need" (Berk, 2002, p. 377). Many of the social skills children develop at this time are listed in this definition. As social skills become more developed, friendships and interactions can become more complex.

Prosocial Skills

Prosocial behaviors allow a child to interact with adults and children in a successful and appropriate manner (Wardle, 2003). The interaction should be beneficial to one, the other, or both parties involved. An added component is the "individual's ability to perceive the situation and be aware when a particular set of behaviors will result in positive outcomes" (cited in Cartledge & Milburn, 1986, p. 7). According to this, a child needs more than specific skills. A child also needs the ability to navigate specific situations.

Prosocial behaviors can be grouped into three distinct categories: sharing (dividing up or bestowing), helping (acts of kindness, rescuing, removing distress), and cooperation (working together to reach a goal) (Marion, 2003). Other experts include showing sympathy and kindness, helping, giving, sharing, showing positive verbal and physical contact, showing concern, taking the perspective of another person, and cooperating. Kostelnik et al. (1988) placed prosocial behavior in two categories: cooperation and helpfulness. The authors defined cooperation as the act of working together for a common goal. Helpfulness was defined as the act of removing distress from another person.

Developing Prosocial Skills

Many experts have looked at the process of developing prosocial skills. A child must develop cognitive competencies, emotional competencies, and specific skills in order to develop prosocial behavior (Marion, 2003). For example, in order to share a child must have: 1) The cognitive ability to recognize him/herself as able to make things happen; 2) The emotional capacity to empathize with the other person; and 3) The ability to perform a specific skill.

It is the combination of these three elements that result in the formation of a social skill such as sharing.

Another expert, Vygotsky, viewed socialization as two fold. First, cognition is related to social engagement, and secondly, language is a critical tool for communication within a social context (cited in Berk & Winsler, 1995). Vygotsky emphasized the importance of sociodramatic play. Play is a means by which children interact, but it is also through this social interaction that cognitive development occurs. Researchers have found that preschoolers who spend more time at pretend play are more advanced in intellectual development, have a higher capacity for empathy, and are seen by teachers as more socially competent (Berk & Winsler, 1995).

The development of prosocial skills can be viewed as a three-part process. In the *recognition* step, a child must be able to determine if someone needs help. Secondly, the child must *decide* whether to help or not to act. Thirdly, a child must *act* by selecting and performing an appropriate behavior for that situation (Kostelnik et al., 1988).

Click and Dodge looked at the social problem solving aspect of social development (cited in Berk, 2002). They developed an information-processing model that looked at 1) a child's ability to engage in several information-processing activities at a time, 2) a child's mental state, and 3) peer evaluation and response. They listed the activities a child must do in order to deal with the problem and come up with a solution. They are: "Notice social cues; Interpret social cues; Formulate social goals; Generate possible problem solving strategies; Evaluate probable effectiveness of strategies; Enact response" (cited in Berk, 2002, p. 378).

In addition, the child must have knowledge of social rules, memory of past experiences, and expectations for future experiences. Lastly, peer perspectives and responses to a child's problem solving techniques greatly impact future interactions between the children involved (Berk, 2002).

The Teacher's Role

It is the teacher's role to facilitate and encourage prosocial behaviors, provide activities that foster appropriate skills, provide necessary assistance, and develop a social network that supports children in their efforts. Teachers must provide activities that help children identify various social skills and help them understand why the skill is needed (Johnson et al., 2000).

The National Association for the Education of Young Children (NAEYC) pointed out that "preschoolers are capable of engaging in truly cooperative play with their peers and forming real friendships. However, development of these important social skills is not automatic for children. They need coaching and supervision to learn and maintain appropriate behaviors with others" (cited in Bredekamp & Copple, 1997, p. 116).

How can teachers help children develop the skills and behaviors needed to act in a prosocial manner? According to NAEYC the classroom is a place to learn about human relationships. Children should have the opportunity to:

- Play and work with others
- Make choices and encounter the consequences of those choices
- Figure out how to enter play situations with others
- Negotiate social conflicts with language
- Develop other skills that characterize socially competent human beings (cited in Bredekamp & Copple, 1997, p. 118).

Facilitating Positive Interactions

Teachers can facilitate positive play interactions for children through the use of a variety of strategies. These strategies include: 1) emphasizing cooperation rather than competition, 2) teaching games that emphasize cooperation and conflict resolution, 3) setting up classroom spaces and materials to facilitate cooperative play, 4) using literature to enhance empathy and caring, and 5) encouraging social interactions between children of different abilities whether it is social, emotional, or physical (Honig & Wittmer, 1996). Research has shown children benefit greatly from effective, positive play situations. Klein, Wirth, and Linas (2003) listed several approaches for facilitating quality play situations. These approaches include: 1) Focusing on the process by asking exploratory questions; 2) Building on children's interests and elaborate on their play; 3) Labeling emotions and feelings that children are expressing through their play; 4) Providing materials that encourage and extend exploration and 5) Providing open-ended materials such as blocks or pretend props.

Howes and Stewart (cited in Honig & Wittmer, 1996) found that children who are involved in high-quality care and have supportive parents learn how to recognize and regulate emotional signals when playing with peers.

Helping Children Make Choices

Teachers should help children make choices and deal with the consequences of their decisions. The teacher's role is to plan activities that help children think through a problem. It is also necessary to repeat the learning activity or similar activity several times (Kostelnik et al. 1988). Through this repeated step-by-step process children can learn how to identify the different path choices, apply reasoning to the process, and formulate a decision.

Promoting Entry into Play Groups

Young children frequently need encouragement to enter playgroups, whether it is to enter an ongoing group, initiate a contact with a friend or being approached by others. Children enter playgroups in a variety of ways, some more successfully than others. Preschoolers tend to enter groups in one or a combination of ways: 1) approaching and watching with no verbal or non-verbal attempt to participate, 2) starting the same activity as another child and blending into the ongoing activity, 3) making social greetings or invitations, 4) offering informational statements or questions, 5) making overt requests to join, or 6) approaching and trying to control group or get attention (Ramsey, 1991).

Preschool playgroups can be fluid, with children entering and leaving quite frequently. Teachers can respond to these already formed groups to "insure the equal participation of all children, help the group work towards a desired goal, and enrich the activity so that all the children can have a meaningful role" (Ramsey, 1991, p. 120). In some instances teachers may prefer arranging playgroups. This helps reduce children's anxiety and widens their range of contacts. Again, equal and active participation by all members and a common goal are important (Ramsey, 1991).

Helping Negotiate Conflict

Teachers need to help children develop negotiating skills to handle conflict situations. Children must use social problem solving skills to resolve issues in a matter that benefits them and is acceptable to others (Berk, 2002). Marion (2003, p. 56) suggested six steps for teaching conflict resolution:

- Identify and define the conflict.
- Invite children to participate in solving the problem.
- Work together to generate possible solutions.
- Examine each idea for how well it might work.
- Help children with plans to implement the solution.
- Follow up to evaluate how well the solution worked.

Peer mediation is another strategy used by teachers to negotiate conflicts. Peer leaders are seen by other children as being credible and serve as role models (Wardle, 2003). This method is used most effectively in elementary schools because of the skills required to implement the process. The "friendship table, or talk-it-over table," is suggested for preschoolers. The teacher's role is to remove the children to a neutral site, and facilitate the conflict resolution process (Wardle, 2003, p. 393).

Promoting Self-Control

Teachers should provide as many opportunities for young children to develop other necessary skills needed to achieve social competency. Self-control is one of the skills. Harter and Shaffer (cited in Marion, 2003, p. 56) said, "Self-control is an essential part of how children learn, is important in a child's growth and development, and is fundamental in preserving social and moral order." Self-control or self-discipline refers to the ability to internally regulate one's own behavior rather than depending on others to enforce it (Kostelnik et al., 1988). Children demonstrate self-control when they 1) control their impulses, wait, and suspend action, 2) tolerate frustration, 3) postpone immediate gratification, and 4) initiate a plan and carry it out over time (Marion, 2003).

If it is an internal process, how can teachers foster the development of self-control? Kostelnik et al. (1988) suggested four strategies:

- Use direct instruction to let children know what are appropriate behaviors, inappropriate behaviors, and alternative behaviors. For example, restricting certain behaviors ("Five more minutes on the swing.") or redirecting children's behaviors ("Don't bounce that ball inside. Go outdoors instead.").
- Model right from wrong so children can learn by example. Modeling can be nonverbal (returning library books on time) or verbal ("I'm petting the kitten very gently.").
- Introduce logical consequences to influence future behavior ("Wear an apron so paint doesn't get on your shirt.").
- Integrate emotions, development, and experience to help children make an internal map. A child can use this chart to categorize past events, interpret cues, envision various responses, and then respond appropriately ("When you share the chalk with Tommy it makes him happy.").

Self-control evolves over time. Teachers should provide repeated experiences for children to practice self-control and refine their behavior.

Environment and Curriculum

The teacher's role should include preparing the classroom environment for optimal prosocial learning opportunities and providing a comprehensive curriculum that enhances the development of prosocial skills. Opportunities for prosocial skill development should be evident in all classroom areas. To illustrate, here are some examples:

- Placing marble mazes (or other exploratory activities) in the science area that can be played by two or more children. Encourage verbal discussion as well as problem solving.
- Introducing a variety of books that deal with perspective taking, feelings and emotions in the literacy corner.
- Arranging the housekeeping area to include a dollhouse with people of many cultures represented.
- Providing rainbow ribbons in the music area so children can come together in dance to express themselves.
- Placing giant floor puzzles in the manipulative area so that children can work together towards a common goal.
- Playing a parachute game where cooperation is necessary during large motor times.
- Promoting helping skills and acts of kindness by setting up opportunities in the dramatic play area such as a pet hospital.

- Preparing muffins and sharing them as a cooking experience.
- Including open-ended materials in the block area.
- Facilitating play groups for those reluctant to join in.
- Setting up bath time for baby dolls in the sensory table. Model caring and helping behaviors.
- Supplying paint, brushes and a very large piece of paper for the whole class to make a mural in the art area.
- Displaying children's work in the classroom at their level.

Teachers must also implement curriculum that emphasizes prosocial themes and concepts. Activities and experiences should focus on the development of self-worth as well as respecting others. One such curriculum is Moonie's Kindness Curriculum which is distributed by Children's Kindness Network (moozie@childrenskindnessnetworkorg). The curriculum emphasizes respect for self, family, friend, community, animals, and the environment. Activities included promote kindness, caring and sharing (Herr et al., 2004).

Conclusion

Prosocial behavior is essential to the well being of children. Children must learn to act in an appropriate manner, one that is both beneficial to them and to others. With so many children participating in group settings, positive interactions are a necessity. The development of these skills allows children to interact with others in a socially accepted manner.

The development of prosocial skills begins in infancy with the development of healthy attachments to parents and caregiver(s). The early years are the time for children to develop prosocial skills by interacting with other children. Moreover, it is the role of early childhood teachers to facilitate the development of these behaviors in young children. Positive play opportunities, modeling, coaching, optimal room environments, and carefully designed curriculums lay the foundation.

References

Berk, L. (2002). *Infants, children, and adolescents*. Boston, MA: Allyn & Bacon.

Berk, L., & Winsler, A. (1995). *Scaffolding childrens learning: Vygotsky and early childhood education*. Washington, DC: NAEYC.

Bredekamp, S., & Copple, C. (Eds.; 1997). *Developmentally appropriate practice in early childhood programs*. Washington, DC: NAEYC.

Cartledge, G., & Milburn, J. (Eds.; 1986). *Teaching social skills to children*. New York, NY: Pergamon Books, Inc.

Edwards, C., & Raikes, H. (2002). Extending the dance: Relationship-based approaches to infant/toddler care and education. *Young Children*, 57 (4), 10–17.

Herr, J., Lynch, J., Merritt, K., Preusse, K, Wurzer, R. (2004). *Moozie s Kindness Curriculum: Preschool*. Breckenridge, CO: Children's Kindness Network.

Honig, A., & Wittmer, D. (1996). Helping children become more prosocial: Ideas for classrooms, families, and communities. *Young Children*, 51 (2), 62–70.

Johnson, C., Ironsmith, M., Snow, C., & Poteat, G. (2000). Peer acceptance and social adjustment in preschool and kindergarten. *Early Childhood Education Journal*, 27 (4), 207–212.

Klein, T., Wirth, D., & Linas, K. (2003). Play: Children's context for development. *Young Children*, 58 (3), 38–45.

Kostelnik, M., Stein, L., Whiren, A., & Soderman, A. (1988). *Guiding children of social development*. Cincinnati, OH: South-Western Publishing Co.

Marion, M. (2003). *Guidance of young children*. Columbus, OH: Merrill Prentice Hall.

National Center for Education Statistics. (2001). *Table 44. Percentage distribution of preschool children under 6 years old*. Retrieved June 24, 2004, from: www.nces.ed.gov/programs/digest/d01/dt044.asp

Pruitt, D. (Ed.; 1998). *Your child: Emotional, behavioral, and cognitive development from birth through preadolescence*. New York, NY: HarperCollins.

Raikes, H. (1996). A secure base for babies: Applying attachment concepts to the infant care setting. *Young Children*, 51 (5), 59–67.

Ramsey, P. (1991). *Making friends in school: Promoting peer relationships in early childhood*. New York, NY: Teachers College Press.

Wardle, F. (2003). *Introduction to early childhood education: A multidimension al approach to child-centered care and learning*. Boston, MA: Pearson Education, Inc.

KATHY PREUSSE is the Senior Instructional Specialist and the Head Teacher for the Child and Family Study Center at the University of Wisconsin–Stout in Menomonie, WI.

From *Earlychildhood NEWS*, March/April 2005. Copyright © 2005 by Excelligence Learning Corporation. Reprinted by permission.

Early Literacy and Very Young Children

REBECCA PARLAKIAN

Early (or emergent) literacy is what children know about reading and writing before they can actually read and write. It encompasses all the experiences—good and bad—that children have had with books, language, and print from birth onward. Because these experiences unfold in the context of relationships, they are linked to and dependent on social–emotional development.

When one imagines an infant or toddler, it is often difficult to conceptualize what early literacy "looks like" for such young children. Schickedanz (1999) has identified several commonly observed early literacy behaviors for infants and toddlers that providers may use to recognize the emergence and progression of very young children's early literacy skill development. These behaviors include:

1. *Handling books:* Physically manipulating books (e.g., page turning and chewing).
2. *Looking and recognizing:* Paying attention to and interacting with pictures in books (e.g., laughing at a picture); recognizing and beginning to understand pictures in books (e.g., pointing to pictures of familiar objects).
3. *Comprehending pictures and stories:* Understanding pictures and events in a book (e.g., imitating an action seen in a picture or talking about the events told in a story.
4. *Reading stories:* Verbally interacting with books and demonstrating an increased understanding of print in books (e.g., babbling in imitation of reading or running fingers along printed words).

What does research tell us about early literacy development in the first 3 years of life? The short answer is, not enough. There are several significant gaps in our understanding of the antecedents of early literacy skills, one being the period from birth to 3. Few longitudinal studies follow children into kindergarten or elementary school to confirm the ways and extent to which early interventions, either in the home or caregiving setting, shape later competencies in reading and writing.

The National Early Literacy Panel (NELP), funded by the National Institute for Learning and administered by the National Center for Family Literacy, has been charged with synthesizing the existing research regarding the development of early literacy in children ages birth to 5. The NELP does plan to analyze preschool children separately from kindergarten children. Although the NELP's report is not yet released, researchers Strickland

At a Glance

- [F]or infants and toddlers, education and care are "two sides of the same coin."
- Instructional strategies that are most appropriate to the early years include *intentionality* and *scaffolding*.
- Intentionality means thoughtfully providing children with the experiences they need to achieve developmentally appropriate skills in early literacy.
- Scaffolding is the continuum of supportive learning experiences that more competent others (adults or peers) offer to children as they master a new strategy or skill.

and Shanahan recently shared preliminary findings highlighting the skills and abilities that "have direct links to children's eventual success in early literacy development" (2004). These skills included oral language ability, alphabetic knowledge, and print knowledge.

Oral Language Development and Literacy

Language development provides the foundation for the development of literacy skills. Speaking, reading aloud, and singing all stimulate a child's understanding and use of language. Studies linking oral language to literacy address vocabulary growth and listening comprehension. Oral language development is facilitated (a) when children have many opportunities to use language in interactions with adults, and (b) when they listen and respond to stories that are read and told to them (Strickland & Shanahan, 2004). A growing body of research affirms this link between children's early language skills and later reading abilities (Strickland & Shanahan, 2004).

Parents are essential supports of their children's language development. The more time that parents spend talking with their children, the more rapidly their children's vocabulary will grow (Hart & Risley, 1999). Listening to books being read—and having the opportunity to discuss illustrations, characters, and storylines—is also important. The experience of shared reading, whether with parents or other caring partners, is integral to language development. Research in this area finds that the repeated reading and discussion of a story enhances a child's receptive and expressive vocabulary (Senechal, 1997).

Being able to communicate and being understood by those around them is a powerful achievement for very young children.

Language development occurs gradually across the first 3 years of life, and indeed, throughout childhood. Speaking, reading, and writing are reciprocal, interactive skills, each supporting the other's development. For example, toddlers engaged in a pretend-play dramatic scenario (e.g., talking into a plastic banana "phone") possess not only the oral language skills required for this "conversation" but also the ability for symbolic thought, which is integral to understanding that letter symbols can represent sounds and vice versa.

Being able to communicate and being understood by those around them is a powerful achievement for very young children. It is also a critical social–emotional skill originating in the reflexive communication (such as crying, cooing, body and facial movements) that is apparent from birth. Intentional communication emerges as very young children are increasingly able to use gestures and words to convey needs, desires, and ideas. Most important expressive language (such as spoken speech) helps children communicate, to connect with another: to request, protest, greet or take leave of someone, respond to a comment, ask a question, solve a problem, and share their feelings and ideas (Weitzman & Greenberg, 2002). These interactions form the basis of the child's relationships with family members and the outside world.

Alphabetic Knowledge and Literacy

By listening to others and speaking themselves, children develop phonemic awareness—the insight that every spoken word can be conceived as a sequence of phonemes (Snow, Burns, & Griffin, 1998). An example of phonemic awareness is recognizing that *bug, bear,* and *button* all start with "b." Because phonemes are the units of sound that are represented by the letters of an alphabet, an awareness of phonemes is key to understanding the logic of the alphabetic principle. Learning the letters of the alphabet and recognizing the sounds within words are two skills that form the foundation for later decoding and spelling—which is linked to learning to read. Research has shown that phonemic awareness and alphabetic knowledge (an understanding of the names and shapes of the alphabet) predict whether a child will learn to read during his first 2 years of school (National Reading Panel, 2000).

Print Knowledge and Literacy

Print knowledge is a recognition of the many uses of the printed word and an understanding of how printed language works. The research base here emphasizes the importance of infusing the caregiving environment with print. For example, when children are provided literacy "props" (menus, newspapers, magazines, tablets, writing utensils, etc.), they will incorporate these items into their play (e.g., "reading" a menu and playing restaurant; Neuman & Roskos, 1992). This play offers repeated opportunities for children to practice and expand early literacy skills.

Exposure to environmental print—the print that appears on signs, labels, and products in our everyday environment—also contributes to a child's early literacy skills (Kuby, Goodstadt-Killoran, Aldridge, & Kirkland, 1999). Often, awareness of environmental print emerges organically in a child's life—for example, when a toddler learns to "read" a fast-food sign or recognizes the meaning behind a stop sign. Infant–family professionals can promote children's awareness of and facility with recognizing environmental print by pointing it out, discussing it with children, or integrating it into play activities (e.g., pointing out street signs on walks or noting labeled play spaces).

Social–Emotional Development and Literacy

For babies and toddlers, all learning happens within a relationship. The social–emotional context of a child's most important relationships—parents, family members, and infant–family professionals—directly affects young children's motivation to learn to read and write. In short, for infants and toddlers, the learning of a new skill and the emotional context in which the learning takes place are equally important (National Research Council, 2001).

Social–emotional skills are an integral part of school readiness because they give very young children the skills they need to communicate, cooperate, and cope in new environments. Over the long term, social–emotional skills contribute to a successful first year of school. For example, research has shown that the quality of children's relationships with their kindergarten teachers predicts how well those children adapt and learn, that year *and* the next (Bowman, 2001). In addition, at the end of the kindergarten year, the children who were considered to have made a positive adjustment to school also had the most friends, were able to maintain those friendships over time, and established new friendships across that first year (National Education Goals Panel, 1997). A positive adjustment to kindergarten is an important achievement: Children who are not successful in the early years of school often fall behind from the start (Peth-Pierce, 2000).

Children who are not successful in the early years of school often fall behind from the start.

School readiness means that children enter the classroom able to form relationships with teachers and peers, listen and communicate, cooperate with others, cope with challenges, persist when faced with difficult tasks, and believe in their own competence. The relationship between school readiness and social–emotional development can be summarized in five key points (adapted from Bowman, 2001):

1. Responsive, supportive relationships with parents, caregivers, and other significant adults nurture a child's desire to learn.
2. Learning requires a solid foundation of social–emotional skills.
3. The development of social–emotional skills depends on, and is responsive to, experience.
4. Children acquire new experiences within the context of relationships with the significant adults in their lives; this is why, for infants and toddlers, education and care are "two sides of the same coin."
5. Social–emotional development and academic achievement *are united priorities.* They represent a developmental continuum, a gathering-up of all the skills, abilities, and attributes that children need to succeed in school and, later, in life.

Social–emotional skills help children to adapt and be resilient, to resolve conflict, to make sense of their feelings, and to establish a new network of supportive satisfying relationships to depend on and grow within. Social–emotional skills enable children to concentrate on learning.

Cognitive Development and Literacy

Cognitive development—a crucial part of school readiness—is the natural product of warm and loving families, experienced and well-trained caregivers and enriching environments. Infants and toddlers do not need organized instruction to develop their cognitive skills. Young children's everyday activities and experiences provide ample opportunity for infusing learning into play.

It is possible to introduce cognitive skills such as literacy during the infant and toddler years. Rote learning, flash cards, and one-size-fits-all approaches, however, are developmentally inappropriate for very young children. Drill and practice may reduce children's natural curiosity and enthusiasm for the learning process and so undermine their interest in learning. Toddlers who feel pushed to read, for example, may become frustrated and fearful, and they may begin to associate those negative feelings with books. Although introducing emergent literacy skills is important, these abilities are unlikely to flourish in very young children when presented out of context as isolated skills (National Association for the Education of Young Children, 1995).

Until the body of research on the early learning skills of the birth-to-3 population becomes more robust, infant–family professionals are challenged to "translate" successful, research-based instructional strategies for older children to meet the needs of infants and toddlers. Instructional strategies that are most appropriate to the early years include *intentionality* and *scaffolding* (Collins, 2004). Rather than use a didactic approach, adults who work with infants and toddlers can creatively integrate these strategies into the day-to-day "teachable moments" that unfold during their natural interactions with very young children.

Intentionality, in this context, means thoughtfully providing children with the support and experiences they need to achieve developmentally appropriate skills in early literacy (and other domains). For example, an intentional provider may offer 14-month-olds the opportunity to pick up raisins and cereal by themselves (which builds fine motor skills critical to writing) and then later offer children crayons to experiment with (which gives them direct experience with writing and drawing). Intentionality is at play here when the provider recognizes the relationship between these experiences, offers these experiences purposefully, and understands the shared developmental goal they both support.

Infants and toddlers learn best when the adults in their lives provide opportunities for exploration and learning in their everyday routines and interactions. The concept of intentionality underscores the role that planning, knowledge, and expertise play in devising and introducing these opportunities. It is the cumulative effect of intentional teaching—the thoughtful repetition of early literacy experiences, the introduction of literacy props into play, modified teacher behavior (e.g., pointing to words on the page), and the creation of language-rich, stimulating environments—that yields the early and important learning that takes place in very young children ages birth to 3.

Scaffolding, a concept introduced by Vygotsky (1962), refers to the continuum of supportive learning experiences that more competent others (adults or other children) offer to children as they master a new strategy or skill (Kemple, Batey, & Hartie, 2004). Children need engaged, responsive adults in their lives who offer them appropriate opportunities to question and problem solve, to hypothesize and take action, to (safely) fail and try again. The richest opportunity for learning—in which children experience a challenge as they pursue a task but do not struggle so intensely as to become frustrated—is called the one of proximal development (Vygotsky, 1962). To help children perform in this zone, teachers must provide scaffolding that incorporates the development of new skills and concepts on the foundation of established ones. This scaffolding requires that teachers know each child in their care—their skills, achievements, and needs—and offer a careful balance of planned, teacher-initiated activities and child-initiated ones, as well. In working with infants and toddlers, a teacher could initiate the practice of reading to children one-on-one each day while placing books at the child's level to enable child-initiated, spontaneous exploration, as well.

The more time that parents spend talking with their children, the more rapidly their children's vocabulary will grow.

Introducing Literacy Concepts to Young Children

Teachers can introduce early literacy concepts to infants and toddlers in a variety of fun, meaningful, and developmentally appropriate ways.

Oral Language

Read to very young children: The most important thing that providers can do to support children's emerging literacy skills is read to them and discuss the stories, at the children's pace and based on their cues.

Talk to children: Children learn language when adults talk to them and with them.

Rhyme and sing: Rhyming activities such as songs and poems promote very young children's knowledge of sounds of speech.

"Narrate" the child's day: Providers can describe what happened that day, which creates opportunities to expand children's vocabulary.

Alphabetic Knowledge

Repeat letter sounds: Providers can point out and say the letters they see in signs or books.

Make a game of repetition: Children love knowing what comes next in a story and anticipating a picture or phrase.

Sing the ABC song and read alphabet books: Both verbal and visual experience with letters help children learn the alphabet.

Play with letters: Arranging and rearranging magnetic letters, alphabet blocks, and puzzles help children with letter recognition and letter sounds.

Use the child's name: Providers can teach children their own names and the sounds that make up their names.

Print Awareness

Make literacy part of playtime: Providers can stock children's play spaces with literacy "props."

Encourage children's own writing: Make paper and writing utensils (markers, crayons, fingerpaint, chalk) available to children. Let infants "write" in applesauce or yogurt.

Point out signs in your neighborhood: When taking walks, providers can look for opportunities to point out stop signs, street signs, and school crossing signs.

Show how adults use writing: Providers can encourage children to watch as they write notes to themselves or colleagues, make a shopping list, or compose the class's weekly update for parents. Providers can also give older toddlers the opportunity to "write" (dictate) notes to one another and family members.

Help children "read" their food: When preparing meals and snacks, providers should read children the words on the food labels, or ask them to "read" the labels to themselves.

Read while you're out and about: Pointing out and reading the signs that say "women" and "men," "exit" and "entrance," and "open" and "closed" are easy ways of sensitizing children to environmental print. Point to the words while reading them aloud to children.

In working with older toddlers, skilled teachers can combine a child-initiated interest that arises in the classroom—for example, a passion for castles—and create a series of teacher-initiated early literacy activities that are responsive and flexible. Using the castle example, such activities might include:

- drawing pictures of castles (which helps build fine motor skills for writing);
- reading books about castles; asking older toddlers to dictate stories to the teacher about castles; and
- making a cardboard box castle for the classroom and encouraging children to "act out" storylines using the castle prop (which creates opportunities to expand vocabulary—*moat, knight, king, queen, drawbridge,* etc.).

This "castle" project may last for several days (or weeks), depending on the children's intensity of interest. By remaining observant and responsive to the children's engagement with the topic and activities, teachers can gauge when the children's interest has shifted and when it might be time to introduce a set of early literacy-based activities around a new theme.

Supporting and nurturing early literacy and language skills in infants and toddlers is complex. These skills cannot be developed in isolation but, rather, emerge together with a child's growing competency in all domains—including the social–emotional, motor, and cognitive domains. When providers can recognize

and observe each child's current stage of development, they are better positioned to use the strategies above to appropriately extend and build upon a child's existing skills and abilities.

Parents, School Readiness, and Early Literacy

Relationships—especially those between parent and child—play a critical role in ensuring that infants and toddlers are adequately prepared for school. Parents' beliefs about the appropriate ways to express emotion, resolve conflict, persuade, and cooperate with others have a profound influence on toddlers' abilities to get along with peers, follow rules, and cooperate with adults—and ultimately, to be ready for school (Morisset, 1994). In addition, children's positive, satisfying relationships with parents set the tone for equally positive, secure relationships with preschool teachers (DeMulder, Denham, Schmidt, & Mitchell, 2000). This crucial achievement is an important predictor of a successful transition to early education environments (Bowman, 2001).

Parents are the most important people in a child's life. Parents' attitudes toward education, their aspirations for children, the language models and literacy materials they provide, and the activities they encourage all contribute to children's language development. Parental behaviors also influence children's early learning. For example, research shows that the type of at-home language environment is the most powerful influence on children's language growth (Educational Research Service, 1998). Preschool children who live in homes where literacy is supported amass 1,000 to 1,700 hours of informal reading and writing encounters before entering school, whereas children without similar family support may enter school with only about 25 hours of literacy experiences (Adams,1990). Not surprisingly, most children who have difficulties learning to read have been read to one tenth as much as those who are the most successful with acquiring this skill (Adams, 1990).

When infants and very young children receive what they need from their parents, they learn to believe that the world is a good place, that it is safe to explore, and that loving adults will provide comfort, affection, and security. Children who do not receive this loving care expend a great deal of energy trying to ensure that these needs are fulfilled by someone, sometime. How much energy do these children have left for learning and exploration—and, later, for the new concepts and challenges that are a part of going to school?

The Role of Infant–Family Professionals in Supporting Early Literacy

The adults who populate the lives of very young children (including family members and the professionals who support them) make important contributions to children's school readiness. In working with infants and toddlers, teachers and child-care providers are reminded that care and education are not separate activities. They unfold together—one leading to the other, one supporting the other.

Children begin kindergarten with 5 years of accumulated life experiences. Because each set of experiences is unique, children have different perspectives on education, different approaches to relationships with adults and peers, and different levels of competency with social–emotional and academic skills. The ability of direct-service professionals to individualize their approaches to specific children and families is crucial to ensuring that services are meaningful and effective.

Infant–family professionals can support the development of very young children's school readiness skills in several ways.

Responding to children's individual needs and temperaments. Staff members in all infant–family fields can respond to children as individuals, build on their strengths, and support their development. Staff members in infant–family programs must be excellent observers of children. Responsive staff members search for the meaning behind infants' and toddlers' gestures, gurgles, cries, and glances. They wonder why particular behaviors occur, come up with educated guesses to explain why, and interact with children to determine whether their guesses are correct.

Encouraging children's curiosity and exploration. If caregivers select all the "lessons" that are to be learned or provide an environment that is not stimulating, children will push to do activities that interest them or to create their own stimulation.

Often children are told "No," "Stop," or "Bad"—not because these children are not learning, but because they are following their own learning agenda or searching for experiences that interest them. Although setting some limits is important and helps keep children safe, it is equally important to allow children to engage in self-directed learning—that is, to follow their interests and allow them to become immersed in new ideas. This approach supports their development of persistence, motivation, critical thinking, and logical thinking skills.

Introducing early literacy and numeracy concepts in developmentally appropriate ways. A program that serves infants and toddlers can introduce literacy concepts in ways that are fun, meaningful, and developmentally appropriate for very young children (Collins, 2004).

Appreciating the magic of everyday moments. Children often develop social–emotional skills not in specially planned lessons but in the context of their daily interactions and experiences—such as napping, eating, playing, and diapering (Lerner, Dambra, & Levine, 2000). When staff members use these everyday moments to support and expand children's current repertoire of social–emotional skills, they help prepare young ones to enter the larger world with all of its demands.

To help parents do the same, staff members should emphasize the important learning that takes place in everyday interactions. For example, the give-and-take of parents imitating their babies' babbling teaches children about turn-taking and communication and, from a social–emotional perspective, that they are important, loved, and listened to. Observing this ongoing, daily learning also encourages parents' pride in and enjoyment of their children.

Establishing strong working relationships with families. When interactions between parents and staff members are open and collaborative, parents receive the support they need to learn and grow in their new roles as mothers and fathers. Parents are then better able to support their children's development with affection, responsiveness, and sensitivity. Staff members can provide parents with an outlet in which to explore the questions and challenges associated with child rearing; wonder about their children's behavior, needs, and motivations; and brainstorm about how best to respond.

Recognizing and respecting family culture. By entering a dialogue with parents about how they want their child raised and what family or cultural practices they value, staff members let families know that they are respected partners in the program. If it is difficult to incorporate families' wishes into program practices, a solid foundation of respect and openness makes negotiating these differences easier and more helpful for everyone.

Reducing parents' anxiety about school success. A newborn does not need expensive "developmental" toys or flash cards to become intellectually curious and academically successful. Staff members can help parents understand that the foundation of school readiness is in supportive, nurturing relationships that provide children with a safe "home base" from which they can explore, learn, and grow. This close parent–child bond also helps children develop the key social–emotional competencies that are necessary for a successful transition to school.

Providing anticipatory guidance. When staff members help parents anticipate their children's developmental changes, parents are better prepared to support their children's learning. Armed with accurate information, parents can respond to their children's changing developmental needs in appropriate ways. Parents' ability to meet their children's needs contributes to a greater sense of competency and confidence, which in turn strengthens the family as a whole.

> **Speaking, reading, and writing are reciprocal, interactive skills, each supporting the other's development.**

Supporting inclusive environments. Very young children with special needs may face unique challenges in achieving the skills (social–emotional or otherwise) necessary to enter school. Inclusion is an important intervention because it draws children with disabilities into the mainstream. Ongoing interactions with typically developing children may help support the development of children with disabilities. Inclusion is also important for children whose development is more typical, because diversity helps them to broaden their experiences and learning and to develop empathy.

Conclusion

Developing early literacy skills across the first 3 years of life is a critical ingredient in ensuring that children are school-ready at age 5. By using all domains of development as well as all their senses, children develop the foundational skills necessary for cultivating a lifelong love of literacy. Supported by healthy relationships formed early in life with parents and caregivers, children experience the world as both safe and exhilarating, they view new challenges as exciting, and they believe themselves to be competent learners. In short, infants and toddlers have a lust for life and learning. When we reject the notion of children as passive "sponges," we are able to truly follow in "the wake of a curious, motivated, social child who is dying to learn" (Lally, 2001).

References

Adams, M. J. (1990). *Beginning to read: Thinking and learning about print.* Cambridge, MA: MIT Press.

Bowman, B. (2001, December). *Eager to learn.* Plenary presentation at the 16th Annual National Training Institute of ZERO TO THREE, San Diego, CA.

Collins, R. (2004, April). *Early steps to language and literacy.* Workshop presented at the meeting of the National Head Start Association, Anaheim, CA.

DeMulder, E. K., Denham, S., Schmidt, M., & Mitchell, J. (2000). Q-Sort assessment of attachment security during the preschool years: Links from home to school *Developmental Psychology, 36*(2), 274–282.

Educational Research Service. (1998). *Reading aloud to children.* ERS Info-File #F1-342. Arlington, VA: Author.

Hart, B., & Risley, T. R. (1999). *The social world of children learning to talk.* Baltimore: Paul H. Brookes.

Kemple, K. M., Batey, J. J., & Hartie, L. C. (2004). Music play: Creating centers for musical play and exploration. *Young Children, 59*(4), 30–37.

Kuby, P., Goodstadt-Killoran, I., Aldridge, J., & Kirkland, L. (1999). A review of the research on environmental print. *Journal of Instructional Psychology, 26*(3), 173–183.

Lally, R. (2001, December). *School readiness.* Plenary presentation at the 6th Annual National Training Institute of ZERO TO THREE, San Diego, CA.

Lerner, C., Dombro, L., & Levine, K. (2000). *The magic of everyday moments'* [series]. Washington, DC: ZERO TO THREE.

Morisset, C. E. (1994, October). *School readiness: Parents and professionals speak on social and emotional needs of young children* [Report No. 26]. Center on Families, Communities, Schools, and Children's Learning. Retrieved January 25, 2002, from http://readyweb.crc.uiuc.edu/library/1994/cfam-sr/cfam-sr.html

National Association for the Education of Young Children. (1995). *NAEYC position statement on school readiness.* Revived January 24, 2002, from www.naeyc.org/resources/position_statements/psredy98.htm

National Education Goals Panel. (1997). *Getting a good start in school.* Retrieved January 23, 2002, from http://www.negp.gov/Reports/good-sta.htm

National Reading Panel. (2000). *Report of the National Reading Panel. Teaching children to read: An evidence-based assessment of the scientific research literature on reading and its implications for reading instruction.*

This article was adapted from *Before the ABCs: Promoting School Readiness in Infants and Toddlers,* a publication written by Rebecca Parlakian for Zero to Three's Center for Program Excellence.

From *Zero to Three,* September 2004, pp. 37–44. Copyright © 2004 by National Center for Infants, Toddlers and Families. Reprinted by permission.

Using Picture Books To Support Young Children's Literacy

JANIS STRASSER AND HOLLY SEPLOCHA

Five-year-old Levi is listening to his teacher read *Why Epossumondas Has No Hair on His Tail* (Salley, 2004). This richly woven and engaging tale includes several unfamiliar words, like "lollygagging," "skedaddle," and "persimmon." It also contains phrases that Levi has never heard before, including "my sweet little pattootie" and "no sirree." Because the art and text so beautifully express the joy of eating a persimmon, Levi asks questions about the fruit once the teacher has finished the story. The next day, the teacher brings several persimmons to class. As the children examine them, cut them, and taste them, they recall the events in the story, sing the song that is part of the story, and remember such rich descriptive terms as "powder-puff tails." Later, in the art area, Levi draws a sketch of a persimmon and tries to write the word, coming up with "PRSMN." The children ask to sing the song about persimmons for the next several days. The teacher suggests that they change the words to create their own version. She writes their version on large chart paper. In the library area, two weeks after the initial whole-group story reading, three children are making the "RRRRRR" sound of Papapossum's stomach as they point to the text in the book that matches the sound. Two of them decide to go into the art area and make puppets to act out the story. As the teacher watches them glue wiggly eyes and a tail made out of yarn onto a large oval shape they have cut out from cardboard, she asks, "What do you think are some good things about not having hair on your tail?"

This example shows the multiple ways in which a picture book can support literacy in the classroom. Literacy skills can be embedded when using an engaging children's picture book, as in the example above, instead of focusing on skills in isolation (as in "letter of the week" types of activities).

Literacy skills can be embedded when using an engaging children's picture book instead of focusing on skills in isolation.

How Do Picture Books Support Literacy?

The benefits of storybook reading are well documented (Aram & Biron, 2004; Neuman, 1999; Neuman, Copple, & Bredekamp, 2000; Strickland & Morrow, 1989). As preschoolers, children should be active participants in picture book reading—chiming in on the refrain of predictable books, dramatizing stories they love, and reciting the text of books "so familiar that they have been committed to memory" (Jalongo, 2004, p. 91).

A joint position paper issued by the National Association for the Education of Young Children and the International Reading Association (cited in Neuman, Copple, & Bredekamp, 2000) states, "The single most important activity for building . . . understandings and skills essential for reading success appears to be reading aloud to children" (p. 8). Neuman (1999) explains how storybook reading helps children gain general knowledge, practice cognitive thinking, and learn about the rhythms and conventions of written language.

Vygotskian theory supports the notion that through interaction with text (written by other authors or themselves), "children transfer the understandings and skills they have gleaned from dialogues with others to their own literacy-related discourse . . . they converse not just with themselves but also with the text narrative" (Berk & Winsler, 1995, p. 115). Creating opportunities for young children to explore literature, individually and in small groups, helps this discourse to flourish. Through such activities as looking through new books, rereading (or "pretend reading") stories that the teacher has read, imagining new endings for popular stories, or creating artistic renderings of favorite stories, young children can interact with text in meaningful ways. In considering extension activities for literature, teachers should consider whether the activity grows naturally out of the literature, encourages students to thoughtfully reexamine the book, and/or demonstrates something the reader has gained from the book (Routman, 1991, p. 87).

Definition of a Picture Book

A picture book is different from a children's book that contains illustrations. In a picture book, both the picture and text are equally important. There exists "a balance between the pictures and text . . . neither of them is completely effective without the other" (Norton, 1999, p. 214). They contain at least three elements: what is told with words, what is told through the pictures, and what is conveyed from the combination of the two (Jalongo, 2004). A fourth element is the child's personal association with the book. Anyone who has read a good picture book has experienced the unique magic and beauty of this relationship. The story line is brief (about 200 words) and straightforward, with a limited number of concepts; the text is written in a direct, simple style; illustrations complement the text; and the book is usually 32 pages long (Jalongo, 2004). Classic picture books that fit these criteria include Keats' *The Snowy Day* (1962), Numeroff's *If You Give a Mouse a Cookie* (1985), and Ringgold's *Tar Beach* (1996). They are more than "cute little books" or useful teaching tools, however; they "also exist as an art form that transcends the functions of informing, entertaining and providing emotional release" (Jalongo, 2004, p. 13). They can be fiction or nonfiction and the illustrations can be photographs as well as drawings, paintings, or collage.

Language Learning with Picture Books

Picture books not only expose young children to words and pictures, they also provide the following experiences that support the dispositions and feelings in learning how to read (Jalongo, 2004):

- Holding Attention: with powerful, vivid illustrations
- Accommodating Difference: within the developmental differences of individual children
- Giving Pleasure: within an intellectually stimulating context
- Challenging the Brain: as the brain seeks patterns out of the complexity of stimulation from text and illustrations at the same time
- Provoking Conversation: hearing stories increases children's vocabulary
- Connecting Experiences: from home and family to stories

Oral language is a key area of literacy development in early childhood. The components of language skills include: Communication, Forms and Functions, Purposeful Verbal Interactions, and Play With Language (Isenberg & Jalongo, 2001). In one classroom of 3-year-olds, the teacher has read Vera B. Williams' *"More More More" Said the Baby* (1997) to individual children and small groups many times, at their request, over a two-week period. She has documented the ways in which the children have practiced the four components of language skills as they connect with elements of the picture book (about the ways that three families show their love for the children in their family):

- Communication: The children pretend to be mommies, grandmothers, and uncles putting their babies to bed, singing to them and kissing them goodnight.
- Forms and Functions: Some children scold the "babies" when they don't go right to sleep, others sing in a gentle voice, and some pretend to laugh as they tickle the "babies."
- Purposeful Verbal Interaction: In their play, the children problem solve how to undress the "baby" and put her in the cradle quietly, as she has fallen asleep while the "grandma" sang to her. Two other children figure out what materials to use to make a blanket when they can't find the blanket that used to be in the dramatic play area.
- Play With Language. The children make up funny names for the babies (with reference in their play to one of the babies in the book who was called "Little Bird"). They call the babies "Little Quacky Duck" and "Puppy Poo Poo."

Picture books should be a part of every day in the early childhood years. Reading to children and engaging them in activities that encourage the use of expressive language, phonological awareness, and high-level thinking is critical for the development of the skills and dispositions that are necessary for reading and writing.

In another classroom, the teacher supported one child's language and cognitive development after reading Ehlert's *Eating the Alphabet* (1993). She watched the child begin to create "vegetables" by cutting orange, brown, and green pieces of foam and gluing them onto her paper. The child then said to the teacher, "When you do this, you have to use your imagination." The teacher responded, "That's very true when creating art. I like how you used the word 'imagination.' " The child then went over and brought back Sendak's *Where the Wild Things Are* (1998) and said, "This is an imagination book, because you can see in the pictures that his room changes. It's pretend." The child was clearly responding to the illustrations and text of the two books, and synthesizing the information in her conversation. The classroom environment had supported this learning through its accessible art area, rich selection of books, flexibility allowing children to bring books into the art area, and the scaffolding conversation between the child and the adult.

Rich Vocabulary

A preschool teacher is reading *Giraffes Can't Dance* (Andreae, 1999) to her class of 4-year-olds. The lavish, colorful illustrations help to illuminate the rich text describing animals dancing in a contest. Verbs like "prance" and "sway" and phrases like "buckled at the knees" and "swishing round" are new for the children. Rhyme and alliteration appear throughout the book; for example:

The warthogs started waltzing and the rhinos rock'n'rolled.

The lions danced a tango

That was elegant and bold.

When the children ask about the waltz and tango, the teacher downloads these two types of music from the computer for the children to listen to during center time. She puts the book into the music center so that the children can look at the illustrations of the warthogs, rhinos, and lions dancing as they listen to different types of music. She stays in the music center for a while so that she can explain which type of music is played for each type of dance. Her questions invite the children to compare and contrast the two different styles. They don't have to ask about "buckled at the knees." The illustration clearly shows what this means.

The fact that reading to young children supports language development is clearly evidenced in the literature (Aram & Biron, 2004; Bus, van IJzendoorn, & Pelligrini, 1995; Hargrave & Senechal, 2000; Koralek, 2003; Schickedanz, 1999). When the story reading includes explanations of particular words, dialogue about new vocabulary, high-level questions, and other active participation by children, that language development is further enhanced (Hargrave & Senechal, 2000).

Although such wordless picture books as *Good Dog, Carl* (Day, 1989) do not fit the traditional definition of a picture book, they are a wonderful way to encourage children to use expressive language, as they use visual literacy and knowledge of story sequence to become the author of the story (Owocki, 2001). Teachers can audiotape children's voices as they "read" the story to their friends and keep the tape in the listening area with the book.

Phonological and Phonemic Awareness

Phonological awareness is "the ability to hear, identify and manipulate the sounds of spoken language (hearing and repeating sounds, separating and blending sounds, identifying similar sounds in different words, hearing parts of syllables in words)" (Seplocha & Jablon, 2004, p. 2). It includes "the whole spectrum[,] from primitive awareness of speech sounds and rhythms to rhyme awareness and sound similarities and, at the highest level, awareness of syllables or phonemes" (Neuman, Copple, & Bredekamp, 2000, p. 124).

As children listen to songs, nursery rhymes, poems, and books with repetitive words and phrases, they begin to play with language. For example, when chanting alliterative phrases, such as, "Splash, splosh, splash, splosh, splash, splosh" to describe the river and "Squelch, squerch, squelch, squerch, squelch, squerch" to describe the "thick, oozy mud" in Rosen's *We're Going on a Bear Hunt* (1997), children revel in the sounds and begin to want to create their own descriptive, playful phrases. Teachers can begin by reading the book, inviting children to join in the repetitive parts with their voices while slapping their knees to the rhythm, and helping them to create their own versions of the story (hunting other animals in other environments). A perfect companion to this book is Axtell's *We're Going on a Lion Hunt* (1999). This version, situated in the jungle, also contains lots of alliteration and rhythm as the suspense builds to a crescendo. Using both books, followed by a compare and con-

trast discussion, encourages higher order thinking and promotes ample use of rich descriptive language, as well as analysis and attention to phonological awareness.

Children learn to pay attention to the sounds in spoken language through rhymes, chants, nonsense words, and poetry. Many picture books, such as the Dr. Seuss books, contain predictable rhymes, rhythms, alliteration, and a great deal of word play that invite children to complete lines, make up nonsense words, and engage in other types of phonological-based activities, when these types of activities are promoted by the teacher.

Phonemes are the building blocks of words. They are "perceivable, manipulable units of sound; they can be combined and contrasted with one another in ways that matter to language users, that is, in ways that make possible the production and perception of words" (McGee & Richgels, 2004, p. 20). The ability to hear phonemes (i.e., words that begin or end with the same sounds) is called phonemic awareness. It is more finite, more related to specific letters and sounds, and usually develops later than phonological awareness. It is a critical skill for reading and writing. It usually does not develop spontaneously, but is supported as teachers plan activities and interactions that draw attention to the phonemes in spoken words (Neuman, Copple, & Bredekamp, 2000).

As mentioned above, phonological and phonemic awareness can be supported when teachers choose books to read aloud that focus on sounds. Many picture books are based on songs that children love to sing. Among them are *Miss Polly Has a Dolly* (Edwards, 2003), *The Itsy Bitsy Spider* (Trapani, 1997), and *Miss Mary Mack* (Hoberman, 1998). Reading/singing these books, and making up new words to the familiar tunes, promote the development of phonological and phonemic awareness.

In a mixed-age class (3- to 5-year-olds), 3-year-old Jacob runs over to his teacher, bringing a piece of paper that is colored with red marks and taped to two Popsicle sticks. He says, "Look, I made a stop sign for our bus." His older friend Deshawn says, "No. You have to put S on the sign and some other letters if you want it to be a real stop sign." Deshawn shows him where and how to add the letters SDP. The teacher had read *Don't Let the Pigeon Drive the Bus* (Willems, 2003) several days earlier, and some of the children were making "things that go" in various areas of the classroom. The main character of the story, the pigeon, is just like a 3-year-old: impulsive, easily frustrated, and seeing the world only from his own perspective. The children, like the pigeon, wish they could really drive. So, they make a three-dimensional bus from a dishwasher crate that the teacher placed in the art area (after moving around some furniture), an airplane from some chairs in the dramatic play area, and a train in the block area. The teacher had suggested that 5-year-olds Rebecca and Devone write instructions for how to drive their train. They are writing on large chart paper taped to the wall in the block area. They are figuring out how to write "Don't Go Too Fast." Devone says, "Don't starts like Devone, with D." They make some other marks on the paper, followed by FS and an exclamation mark. Their teacher had pointed out the many exclamation marks contained in the book. She draws their attention to the page on which the pigeon describes the sound of the bus as "Vroom-vroom, vroomy-vroom!," and suggests they try to figure out how to write some noises that their train makes. Five-year-old Aisha decides to write "CHKU CHKU CHU! CHU!" on a separate piece of paper. The exclamation mark was used in this picture as well as on the large chart made by the children. This example shows how easily the children transfer the phonemic and phonological awareness skills linked to prior knowledge, engaging picture books, and play.

Teachers can support language development and cognitive thinking through such activities as reading multiple versions of the same folktale (e.g., a traditional version of "The Three Little Pigs," Lowell's *The Three Little Javelinas* (1992), and Scieszka's *The True Story of the Three Little Pigs!* (1989)) and asking children to compare and contrast the versions. Creating new endings to favorite stories and/or planning open-ended art projects that synthesize knowledge (e.g., a mural depicting metamorphosis, as explained in Eric Carle's *The Very Hungry Caterpillar* (1981), helps children learn to synthesize information. Assembling diverse collections of subjects of interest from particular books, such as *Bread, Bread, Bread* (1993) or *Hats, Hats, Hats* (1993), both by Ann Morris, and charting which are the favorites, help children learn to evaluate and discuss others' opinions.

Print-Rich Environments

Research has shown that when additional literacy props and tools are added to various centers in preschool classrooms, children's conversations and understanding of written language are enhanced (Neuman & Roskos, 1991; Schickedanz, 1999). Literacy props include the types of things that would naturally occur in each of the centers, such as recipe cards, coupons, cookbooks, pencils, and notepads in the kitchen area. Using picture books to support these literacy tools makes play scenarios even richer. For example, one teacher read *The Little Red Hen Makes a Pizza* (Sturges, 2002). The book contains funny and interesting ingredients from the hen's kitchen, such as pickled eggplant, anchovies, and blue cheese. The teacher saw how eager the children were to make their own shopping lists, copying words from the labels of the variety of strange and interesting items that the teacher brought into the kitchen area (marinated artichokes, hearts of palm, Kalamata olives, etc). The children and teacher ultimately made real individual pizzas, choosing their own toppings.

In order for children to extend the experiences they read about in books, they must have many other literacy tools to do so. Art areas with open-ended materials from which children can choose, writing/drawing tools and other implements, a variety of types of paper, paint, three-dimensional materials, and long periods of time to work on independent or collaborative projects are important. For example, one kindergarten teacher always finds several of her children engaged in book-making activities after she reads high-quality picture books. After reading *The Napping House* (Wood, 1994), some of the children made felt figures of the characters in the book in order to reenact the story with their flannel board. Additionally, the children made their own version of the book, called "The Kindergarten Napping House," in which each child contributed a page with various texts, according to their writing abilities and interests.

Picture books focused on writing, such as *Click, Clack, Moo: Cows That Type* (Cronin, 2000), offer a perfect vehicle through which teachers can introduce writing for a purpose. Just as the cows type their complaints to the farmer, Children can voice their opinions in print on issues related to classroom problems or concerns.

Exploring picture books and creating lists of the types of literacy tools (or making prop boxes) that would support the content of specific books is a valuable exercise. Additionally, thinking about which books should be included in *each* of the early childhood interest areas (changed regularly, to allow for changes in children's interests, themes, etc.) is important.

Teachers also should consider the needs and interests of specific children when considering which books to read to individuals. One teacher noted that Quincy was having difficulty creating rhymes. So, she read Trapani's (1998) *The Itsy Bitsy Spider* to him. Then, using a flannel board, Quincy acted out the song with a flannel spider and other props. The next day, the teacher extended this activity even further. She put other felt animals next to the flannel board and invited Quincy and Fatima to change the animals and make up a new song. Together, the two children giggled as they sang, *"The itsy bitsy kitty went up the water spout. Down came the water and cried the kitty out. Out came the sun and the kitty cried away and the itsy bitsy spider went out the day-de-day."*

Conclusions

The text and illustrations of high-quality picture books weave rich stories that can excite and surprise children, make them laugh, make them wonder, and make them think. Turning each page brings another element to the magic. Whether the pictures are photographs, black-and-white line drawings, unusual designs, paintings, woodcuts, or collage, the visual art form excites the young audience. Whether the text is factual, fictional, historical, readily identifiable to the listener, or something from another culture, the stories fill young children with a multitude of ideas, words, and questions.

Using the wealth of classic and new picture books available, adults can support literacy in ways that are engaging to children. Picture books should be a part of every day in the early childhood years. Reading to children and engaging them in activities that encourage the use of expressive language, phonological awareness, and high-level thinking is critical for the development of the skills and dispositions that are necessary for reading and writing.

In the picture book *Book!* (George, 2001), a preschool child opens a present and falls in love with his new picture book. He typifies the relationship young children can have with books when he says:

I'll take you on a wagon ride to my secret place, Where both of us can hide.
After that, we'll find an empty lap before I take my nap.
We'll read you warm and snug, Book!
I'll give you a hug, Book!
Open wide.
Look inside.
Book!

References

Andreae, G. (1999). *Giraffes can't dance*. New York: Orchard Books.

Aram, D., & Biron, S. (2004). Joint storybook reading and joint writing interventions among low SES preschoolers: Differential contributions to early literacy. *Early Childhood Research Quarterly, 19*, 588–610.

Axtell, D. (1999). *We're going on a lion hunt*. New York: Henry Holt and Company.

Berk, L. E., & Winsler, A. (1995). Scaffolding children's learning: *Vygotsky and early childhood education*. Washington, DC: National Association for the Education of Young Children.

Bosschaert, G. (2000). *Teenie bird and how she learned to fly*. New York: Harry N. Abrams, Inc.

Bus, A. G., van IJzendoorn, M. H., & Pelligrini, A. D. (1995). Joint book reading makes for success in learning to read: A meta-analysis on intergenerational transmission of literacy. *Review of Educational Research, 65*, 1–21.

Carle, E. (1981). *The very hungry caterpillar*. New York: Philomel Books.

Cronin, D. (2000). *Click, clack, moo: Cows that type:* New York: Simon & Schuster.

Day, A. (1989). *Good dog, Carl*. New York: Simon & Schuster.

Edwards, P. D. (2003). *Miss Polly has a dolly*. New York: Penguin Young Readers Group.

Ehlert, L. (1993). *Eating the alphabet*. New York: Harcourt Brace Company.

George, K. O. (2001). *Book!* New York: Clarion Books/Houghton Mifflin.

Hargrave, A. C., & Senechal, M. (2000). A book reading intervention with preschool children who have limited vocabularies: The benefits of regular reading and dialogic reading. *Early Childhood Research Quarterly, 15*, 75–90.

Hoberman, M. A. (1998). *Miss Mary Mack*. Hong Kong: Little Brown.

Isenberg, J. P., & Jalongo, M. R. (2001). *Creative expression and play in early childhood*. Upper Saddle River, NJ: Merrill.

Jalongo, M. R. (2004). *Young children and picture books* (2nd ed.). Washington, DC: National Association for the Education of Young Children.

Keats, E. J. (1962). *The snowy day*. New York: Viking Juvenile.

Koralek, D. (Ed.). (2003). *Spotlight on young children and language*. Washington, DC: National Association for the Education of Young Children.

Lowell, S. (1992). *The three little javelinas*. Flagstaff, AZ: Rising Moon.

McGee, L. M., & Richgels, D. J. (2004). *Literacy's beginnings: Supporting young readers and writers*. New York: Pearson, Allyn and Bacon.

Morris, A. (1993). *Bread, bread, bread*. New York: HarperCollins.

Morris, A. (1993). *Hats, hats, hats*. New York: William Morrow & Company.

Neuman, S. B. (1999). Books make a difference: A study of access to literacy. *Reading Research Quarterly, 34*, 286–311.

Neuman, S. B., Copple, C., & Bredekamp, S. (2000). *Learning to read and write: Developmentally appropriate practices for young children*. Washington, DC: National Association for the Education of Young Children.

Neuman, S. B., & Roskos, K. (1991). Peers as literacy informants: A description of young children's literacy conversations in play. *Early Childhood Research Quarterly, 6*, 23–248.

Norton, D. E. (1999). *Through the eyes of a child: An introduction to children's literature* (5th ed.). Columbus, OH: Merrill.

Numeroff, L. J. (1985). *If you give a mouse a cookie*. New York: HarperCollins.

Owocki, G. (2001). *Make way for literacy: Teaching the way young children learn*. Portsmouth, NH: Heinemann & Washington, DC: National Association for the Education of Young Children.

Ringgold, F. (1996). *Tar beach*. New York: Dragonfly.

Rosen, M. (1997). *We're going on a bear hunt*. New York: Simon and Schuster Children's Publishing Division.

Routman, R. (1991). *Invitations: Changing as teachers and learners K-12*. Portsmouth, NH: Heinemann.

Salley, C. (2004). *Why Epossumondas has no hair on his tail*. New York: Harcourt.

Schickedanz, J. A. (1999). *Much more than the ABC's: The early stages of reading and writing*. Washington, DC: National Association for the Education of Young Children.

Scieszka, J. (1989). *The true story of the three little pigs*. New York: Penguin Group.

Sendak, M. (1998). *Where the wild things are*. San Diego: HarperCollins.

Seplocha, H., & Jablon, J. (2004). *New Jersey early learning assessment system: Trainer's box*. Trenton, NJ: New Jersey Department of Education.

Strickland, D.S., & Morrow, L. M. (1989). *Emerging literacy: Young children learn to read and write*. Newark, DE: International Reading Association.

Sturges, P. (2002). *The little red hen makes a pizza*. New York: Puffin.

Trapani, I. (1997). *The itsy bitsy spider*. New York: Charlesbridge.

Williams, V. B. (1997). *"More more more," said the baby*. New York: HarperCollins.

Willems, M. (2003). *Don't let the pigeon drive the bus!* New York: Scholastic.

Wood, A. (1994). *The napping house*. New York: Harcourt.

JANIS STRASSER is Associate Professor of Early Childhood Education and **HOLLY SEPLOCHA** is Associate Professor of Early Childhood Education, Willam Paterson University, Wayne, New Jersey.

Thank you to Darcee Chaplick, Christina Komsa, Lisa Mufson, Joe Murray, and Sage Seaton for sharing their experiences with children.

From *Childhood Education*, Summer 2007. Copyright © 2007 by the Association for Childhood Education International. Reprinted by permission of Janis Strasser and Holly Seplocha and the Association for Childhood Education International, 17904 Georgia Avenue, Suite 215, Olney, MD 20832.

The Sweet Work of Reading

Kindergartners explore reading comprehension using a surprisingly complex array of strategies.

ANDIE CUNNINGHAM AND RUTH SHAGOURY

Andie, a kindergarten teacher, sits before her class of 5- and 6-year-olds and holds up the book *Owl Moon* (Yolen, 1987) for the students to see.

"Open up the part of your brains that's brilliant," Andie tells them. "We're learning a new strategy today. You're going to use your brains to make a picture of the book. Ready?"

Andie directs her students' attention toward the fresh piece of butcher paper on the easel. She points out the sticky notes and pens. "It's time to read *Owl Moon*," she says. "As I read, pay attention to the place in your brain that makes a picture of the part of the book that's most important to you."

She starts to read, and the class enters the hushed night of owl-calling. Faces turn to the book; from time to time, the students use their "owl voices" to hoot with the owls in the story.

When she finishes, Andie asks the students to decide on the one picture in their heads that's most important to them. "When you're ready," she says, "get your pen and paper and draw your *one* picture. Be specific and detailed."

Slowly and intentionally, Megan picks up a sticky note and pen and walks to a table to draw her picture. Austin looks up at the ceiling, smiles, picks up his pen, and settles down to work. Lacey scrunches up her face, squeezing her eyes shut. "I'm still thinkin'," she says. "I gotta choose 'cuz I got five in my head."

This kindergarten is a workshop of readers and thinkers who take seriously the work of making meaning from books. Andie has set the tone for their comprehension work through deliberate instructions and by providing her students with the tools they need. Students are writing about their reading. They use fine-line black pens to make meaningful marks on large sticky notes that serve as placeholders for their thinking.

This lesson is not reproduced from a published reading program, nor is it a yearly unit trotted out for every new group of kindergartners. This particular book choice was in response to Carrie's interest in becoming an expert in trees and Kenya's desire to learn more about big birds and where they live.

Building on Interests

As a kindergarten teacher-researcher and a university researcher, we have been investigating what is possible for young children as they acquire literacy skills. Educators concerned with kin-

dergarten curriculum are all asking the same questions: What reading comprehension skills do today's kindergartners truly require? What skills do they need to become avid learners in school and in the world, active and compassionate citizens, and their best selves?

Building on their interests helps students make authentic connections.

Contemporary researchers (Harvey & Goudvis, 2000; Keene & Zimmermann, 1997; Miller, 2002) have shown how readers can explore comprehension using a range of strategies (see "Reading Comprehension Strategies"). The students in Andie's class are teaching us that kindergartners can use these important comprehension strategies to bring their home knowledge into school. Some students realize for the first time that their understanding of a book is important. As they make text-to-self connections in books that the teacher reads to them, students learn the importance of schema—what they bring to a text in terms of their background knowledge and life experiences. As they tap into their knowledge of the world and make connections, they are more prepared to go on to other important reading comprehension skills, such as text-to-text connections, inferences, questioning, and synthesis. For example, when we read *Too Many Tamales* (Soto, 1993), with its central theme of losing an important object, the students made bridges from the book to each of their schemas. Daniel remembered misplacing a screw for a toy truck headlight; Ryan relived the memory of losing a ring in a swimming pool; Bao Jun detailed her loss of a cat in China.

Student interests create our reading curriculum. Nathaniel's interest in pumpkins led to our decision to read *Pumpkin Circle* (Levens, 1999). We read *Miss Twiggly's Treehouse* (Fox, 1966) to focus on Bianca's interest in studying friendships. Building on their interests helps students make their own authentic connections, the foundation of our work together. The lesson on making mental pictures from *Owl Moon* is not isolated from the rest of the students' lives. They paint what they know, write and tell stories, and read books that link their background knowledge to this new academic world.

Reading Comprehension Strategies

- *Making connections*—between texts, the world, and students' lives (sometimes called text-to-text, text-to-world, and text-to-self connections). Readers bring their background knowledge and experiences of life to a text.
- *Creating mental images.* These "mind pictures" help readers enter the text visually in their mind's eye.
- *Asking questions.* Readers who use this strategy actively ask questions of the text as they read.
- *Determining importance.* This strategy describes a reader's conscious and ongoing determination of what is important in a text.
- *Inferring.* When readers infer, they create new meaning on the basis of their life experiences and clues from the book.
- *Synthesizing.* Although this strategy is sometimes considered a retell, synthesizing is a way of spiraling deeper into the book. Readers might explore the text through the perspective of different characters to come to new understandings about the character's life and world.

A Community of Learners

Andie's classroom is in a K–3 school in Portland, Oregon, that has the highest number of families living in poverty in the district. Of its 540 students, more than 85 percent receive free or reduced-price breakfasts and lunches. There are six half-day kindergarten classes, each with 20–25 students. Students speak at least 13 languages other than English; the school employs two full-time, in-house translators for Spanish and Russian families.

Many languages swirl through the classroom. During daily calendar work, for example, we usually count in Russian, Spanish, and English, thanks to the help of parents who are teaching us to count in their home languages. Sharing our home languages, experiences, knowledge, and questions is an important element of becoming a community. Comprehension and community go hand in hand as the students learn to work together and do the hard work that goes along with making meaning out of difficult texts.

Bringing each student's schema to the classroom discussion is challenging. It requires thoughtful planning on the part of the teacher and ample time for learners to grapple with meaning so they can contribute their ideas to the community.

Mind Pictures

This morning, the students wrestle with important "mind pictures" that they have in their heads as a result of listening to *Owl Moon.* Lacey shows her completed picture to Ruth, a university researcher. "This is a big tree where the man was calling out," she says.

Benjamin shows his drawing to Andie. "This is the guy who is telling her to be quiet," he says, pointing to the two figures on the sticky note. Benjamin shows her the arrow between the two

figures, indicating from which direction the voice is coming. He points to two large orbs hovering over the people. "This is the owl's eyes," he says. As the students finish drawing on their sticky notes, they carry them to Andie, who records their words on the notes and sticks them on the butcher paper.

Together we look at and read the individual writing and drawing on the sticky notes, noticing first the differences. For example, Carrie has drawn a picture of an owl landing on a branch, whereas Ivan focused on one of the characters, the Grandpa. Andie reinforces the idea that although everyone is bringing a different schema to the story, they have all drawn owls, trees, and people. The chart has stimulated rich new discussions of the story. With contributions from each class member secured, conversations have a grounded place in which to flourish.

Digging Deep

Readers who care about making sense of the books they read don't give up on stories when meaning eludes them. They come back and struggle with the text until they make sense of it. There is an excitement to uncovering layers of meaning when we spiral back to difficult texts. Few kindergartners are taught how to experience this kind of "hard fun" when they read. But when we give them a chance to play with it, they rise to the challenge.

When Andie finishes reading *Almost to Freedom* (Nelson, 2003), Austin's first words are, "There were a lot of words in there!" This book is challenging. Besides having "lots of words," it tells the painful story of a young girl fleeing slavery on the Underground Railroad.

"Yeah," Nathaniel piggybacks, "like a hundred million words. I want to keep it in the room and read it the next day and the day after that and the day after that."

Nathaniel understands that the more we revisit those tough reads with millions of words, the better our chances of discovering their riches. Throughout the year, we explore such provocative books as *The Three Questions* (Muth, 2002), a retelling of a philosophical tale by Leo Tolstoy; *The Cats of Krasinsky Square* (Hesse, 2004), set in Poland during World War II; *Where Is Grandpa?* (Barron & Soentpiet, 2001), a story of one family dealing with death and loss; and *Visiting Day* (Woodson, 2002), in which a little girl tells of looking forward to her weekly visits to her dad in prison.

Kindergartners are capable of far more sophisticated reading strategies than educators often suspect. As they write, draw, paint, and move their bodies to the stories, they dig deep to make sense. Students might use clay to portray their mental images, dramatize what is important to them in a book, or paint watercolors of their inferences. With these strategies, they have a firm foundation for building reading success.

Synthesizing Meaning

Synthesizing is one of the most complex strategies that readers use to spiral into deeper layers of meaning. Readers "hold their thinking" as they progress through a book. In other words, they keep track of how their thinking is evolving, using their schemas to make inferences. They come to view the book and the world through new lenses.

This week, we dig into synthesizing with the clever picture book *No Such Thing* (Koller, 1997), in which a human child and a monster child are repeatedly assured by their mommies that the other doesn't exist—that there is "no such thing." It's a perfect book for seeing the world through another's eyes and gaining insights about perceptions other than one's own.

Early in the week, the students hold their thinking by writing and making drawings on sticky notes of what they remember from the book. When they finish, they place their notes on Andie's anchor chart. Later in the week, on the third reading of the book, Andie tells her students to use a new lens as they read the book:

> Decide who you are going to think like. The boy? His mom? The monster? Or the monster's mom? You'll be bringing your schema and using it to think like that person.

At the end of the reading, Carrie and Megan crawl under one of the tables and pretend they're lying in bed. Some boys head to the coat rack where they peer back over their shoulders. Around us, we see children pretending to be the little monster and the little boy. Bianca behaves as though she were the mother, looking in the door at her little boy.

After a few moments, the chime ringer rings the bell and the students return to the circle area. Andie tells the students that they can act out their characters for the class and that everyone will try to guess who they are.

Austin volunteers to start. He lies on the floor in the middle of the circle. It turns out he is being the monster screaming "AAAAHHHHH!" When it's his turn, José also lies in the middle of the floor, but he shakes his head no to all the guesses. He explains, "I was the boy at the end of the book when he was under the bed."

"Did that actually happen in the book?" Andie asks.

"No," José tells us. "They were just *gonna* switch when the book ends."

"José made a great inference!" Andie exclaims. "He used clues to figure out what was going to happen next—even after the book ends. Sweet work!"

As kindergartners write, draw, paint, and move their bodies to the stories, they dig deep to make sense.

The students take turns acting out different roles. Shy Bianca walks slowly to the center of the circle and hugs her arms tight around herself, rocking from side to side. We guess that she's the monster or the boy being scared.

"No," she says. "I'm huggin' the boy. I'm the mom huggin' the boy."

Bianca lived the book through the mom's eyes, sharing two different parts of the book as she moved: the mother looking at the boy through the doorway and the mother hugging her son. She spiraled deeper as she synthesized meaning.

Too many educators think that there's "no such thing" as kindergartners making sophisticated inferences that help them synthesize what they read. These students show what is possible.

A Nourishing Environment

Kindergartners face enormous challenges. Most of the students in Andie's class have little or no alphabet knowledge when they enter the classroom in the fall. English is a second or third language for many of the families in this impoverished working-class community. Instead of viewing kindergarten as a garden of children, we prefer the metaphor of a tide pool:

> Kindergartens, like tide pools, are a meeting place of two systems. The land and the sea meet at tide pools, and organisms in tide pools must adapt to adjust to the drastic changes in environment that come with the changing of the tides each day. (Barnhart & Leon, 1994, p. 7)

This image helps remind us of the way in which children must adjust to the differing environments of home and school at the cultural meeting place that is kindergarten. Kindergartners need specific learning tools. They need honor and respect to thrive. They need similar souls nearby, without the threat of predators. They need a climate that invites and supports their learning, and they need plenty of time to link literacy with their lives in the challenging world of school (Cunningham & Shagoury, 2005).

Building bridges between the books in the classroom and what students have learned in their first five years takes work. A publisher-designed curriculum might not connect to these children's lives at all. By incorporating students' interests into the curriculum, we can create a community in which we learn together. Within that community, students can learn the kind of reading comprehension skills that will help them become readers who turn to books for meaning, understanding, reflection, and pleasure.

References

Barnhart, D., & Leon, V. (1994). *Tidepools: The bright world of the rocky shoreline.* Upper Saddle River, NJ: Pearson Educational.

Cunningham, A., & Shagoury, R. (2005). *Starting with comprehension: Reading strategies for the youngest learners.* Portland, ME: Stenhouse Publishers.

Harvey, S., & Goudvis, A. (2000). *Strategies that work: Teaching comprehension to enhance understanding.* Portland, ME: Stenhouse Publishers.

Keene, E., & Zimmermann, S. (1997). *Mosaic of thought: Teaching comprehension in a reader's workshop.* Portsmouth, NH: Heinemann.

Miller, D. (2002). *Reading with meaning: Teaching comprehension in the primary grades.* Portland, ME: Stenhouse Publishers.

ANDIE CUNNINGHAM teaches kindergarten at Harold Oliver Primary School in Portland, Oregon; rupali@easystreet.com. **RUTH SHAGOURY** is Mary Stuart Rogers Professor of Education at the Graduate School of Education and Counseling, Lewis & Clark College, 0615 S. W. Palatine Hill Rd., Portland, OR 97219; shagoury@lclark.edu.

From *Educational Leadership,* October 2005. Reprinted by permission of the Association for Supervision and Curriculum Development. Copyright © 2005 by ASCD. All rights reserved. The Association for Supervision and Curriculum Development is a worldwide community of educators advocating sound policies and sharing best practices to achieve the success of each learner. To learn more, visit ASCD at www.ascd.org

Meeting the Challenge of Math and Science

BARBARA SPRUNG

Two 4-year-olds are in the block area. There are only two double-unit blocks on the shelf and the children know they need four to make a rectangular base for their structure. (Another child has used many blocks in a special building and has requested that it be left up until her dad can see it at pick-up time.) As they observe the remaining blocks in the cubby, one child says, "I have an idea." He takes the two remaining doubles and four single blocks from the shelf. He places two single blocks alongside a double and sees that they are of equal length. Both children are excited to see that the two single-unit blocks can be used in place of one double-unit block, and they can build their rectangle after all.

These children have made a math discovery that uses the skills of observation, problem-solving, creative-thinking, geometry, and fractions!

On another day, Amy and Eric are working at each side of the double easel. The paint colors of the day are blue, yellow, and white, and there is a can of plain water for cleaning the brushes. The classroom rule is not to mix paint colors in the cans. Eric is busy painting a sun on the top of his paper. Next, he plans to make a blue sky around the sun. As Eric leans around the easel to see what Amy is painting, his blue brush hits the yellow sun. Eric is surprised to see that his "sun" has turned green and he shows Amy, who begins to chant, "Eric made a green sun, Eric made a green sun." Eric says, "Look Mrs. Sumner, look what happened to my painting."

Eric and Amy have had a science experience. They have discovered that two colors can combine to make a third color. They have experienced firsthand that yellow and blue make green.

Seizing Teachable Moments

These two anecdotes tell a story: Math and science are everywhere in your classroom! The challenge is to take these wonderful "teachable moments" that happen all the time and intentionally incorporate them into the curriculum. As early childhood teachers, we need to learn to seize these teaching and learning opportunities, and to let children know that you value their discoveries and ideas by sharing them with other children and adults in the classroom. When I was teaching kindergarten, Yigal, an Israeli boy in my class, brought in a retractable measuring tape, which was obviously a treasure for him. We used it at various times during the morning to measure areas of the classroom that he designated, and we wrote a story for the class library, entitled "Yigal's Measuring Story." Yigal's interest in math was validated, all the children became interested, and Yigal gained some much-needed recognition and stature among his classmates.

Sometimes the lessons might be for an individual child or a small group, and other times the moment may turn into a lesson or book that can benefit the entire class!

Math and Science Around the Room

In addition to acting on children's discoveries, there are many ways you can promote math and science skill development in your learning centers. As children engage in the activities, you'll discover that math and science activities enhance all those other skill areas we work so hard to develop in early childhood classrooms, including literacy and language, social/emotional, physical, small- and large-motor, eye-hand coordination, and observation. Let's start by taking a look at how you can integrate math learning into your classroom centers.

Block Area Math

The unit blocks that are standard equipment in most early childhood classrooms are a multi-disciplinary curriculum in themselves. Think about the potential of this area for developing math awareness and skills. Through blocks, children gain experience with geometry, shape recognition, fractions, and counting, as well as spatial relations, creative thinking, problem-solving, and decision-making, which are essential higher-order skills. They are also fun—and enjoyment is an important component of learning.

For a change of pace, try conducting a math lesson right in the block area with small groups of children at a time. Here's what you can do:

- Ask children to sit in a semicircle.
- Place one block of each size in a row on the floor and name all the different block types with children: unit, half unit, double, quad, and wedge.
- Together, describe the shapes of the blocks, for example: rectangle, square, and triangle.
- Pose a challenge or brain teaser: "Can someone tell us one interesting thing he or she notices about the blocks?" If no one volunteers, give children a clue by placing the half-unit on the unit block. Children may notice that:
  - Two half-units equal (are the same as) one unit.
  - Two units equal one double.
  - Four units equal one quad.
- After you have thoroughly explored all the possibilities for combining the blocks on the floor, ask: "Can someone find other blocks in the cubby to match up?" If needed, give an example by putting two half-circles together to make a whole circle.
- Place the semicircle block in front of the children and ask, "Does anyone see something about this block and the way we are sitting?" Help children observe that they are sitting in a semicircle—the same shape as the block only much larger. This comparison will provide children with an early experience in scale, a concept they will learn more about in the upper elementary grades.
- As a final step, create an experience chart to document the lesson.
- Repeat the math lesson with other small groups until everyone has had a chance to participate.

During a math lesson in the block area, children are gaining many other important skills. They are building literacy skills by listening, talking about their discoveries, and using math vocabulary and word recognition, for instance: "This block is a rectangle"; "This one's a triangle"; "This one is half as big as that one"; "This one is twice as big"; "Look, Mrs. Sumner put two halves together and made a whole circle"; "This is fun."

As children engage in block-building they learn to organize their play, share materials, negotiate with others, and cooperate with their building partners. So, this one area of the classroom offers opportunities for planned lessons, experiential learning, math and science skill-building, and a host of other interdisciplinary skills.

Dramatic-Play Area

As the year progresses, the dramatic-play area might be turned into a food store or a restaurant for a week. Either scenario will provide children with math experiences, including the use and value of money for buying and selling; pricing items for sale and creating price lists or menus; and counting items to buy and sell. Children can use play money of different denominations or make their own money from construction paper. As they engage in this play, children will gain math vocabulary and additional practice in higher-order thinking skills—organizing, decision-

---

Quick-and-Easy Learning Center Ideas

These few activities are just the tip of the iceberg: You will be able to discover many other ways to highlight the math and science opportunities that abound in your classroom. Here are some other quick ideas:

- Experiment with the concepts of wet and dry using clay.
- Cut sponges into shapes for sponge painting.
- Have children sort and count Legos and other stacking toys by size and color.
- Use the water table for "sink or float" experiments. Provide a variety of objects and have a supply of pencils and picture charts nearby so children can record which items sank and which items floated.
- In the spring, blow bubbles outdoors using a variety of found materials as bubble makers—plastic strawberry containers a plastic cup with a hole in the bottom, or pipe cleaners. To make a strong bubble solution; mix a gallon of distilled water with liquid dishwashing detergent and two ounces of glycerin (available in the hand lotion section of drug-stores). Let children experiment with various bubble makers, wind direction, and their breath to make discoveries.

---

making, problem-solving—and the essential early childhood skill of cooperative play. Here's how to begin:

- Call a class meeting to talk about the idea of creating a store or restaurant.
- Let the children decide between the two ideas.
- Take a neighborhood field trip to a store or restaurant. If the choice is a restaurant, ask for a menu to take back to school. If the choice is a store, select one that doesn't sell too many items (a bodega or deli).

After the Field Trip:

- Hold a planning meeting to assign jobs.
- Make the play money.
- Set up the restaurant or shop (use play food or pictures of items cut from magazines or drawn by the children).
- Keep the restaurant or shop up for at least one week, or as long as interest lasts. Ask children to help to take the store or restaurant apart.

While the restaurant or store is active, observe and keep notes on children's discussions. You will learn about their ideas concerning the use of money and how the "real world" works. After the activity is complete:

- Call a class meeting to talk with children about the activity.
- Ask children to talk about how it felt to be a customer or a worker.
- Print children's comments on sheets of chart paper.
- Talk about observations that you made, especially about children's use of numbers and money, and about how well they cooperated.
- Relate the activity to how real stores and restaurants work.

Home-School Connection

In today's early childhood programs, there is a growing emphasis on skill-building. Families can become willing partners in providing developmentally appropriate math and science experiences at home. Here are ways to partner with families:

- Through your regular school communication channels—family letters, newsletters, online messages—share information about the math and science activities you are doing in the classroom.
- If family members work in a job related to math and science, ask them to come for a visit to talk about their work.
- Send home directions for making Oobleck, or other cooking activities, so that families can try them out with children.
- Encourage parents to take children on "Shape Hunting Walks." These can be easily done on the way to the supermarket or playground.
- Suggest that letting children help with chores—such as sorting laundry, pairing socks, putting groceries into sets, and sorting silverware—is a great way to reinforce math skills.
- If possible, arrange a school and family trip to a local children's science or discovery museum.
- Encourage families to visit their local science resources—children's museums, aquariums, parks, science museums, and botanical gardens.
- Give parents some ideas for "bathtub science"— providing measuring cups, funnels, and tubes as bathtub toys. They can also provide a variety of sink and float objects—a small rock, a plastic spoon, and other small and large plastic objects.
- Invite family members into the classroom to participate in activities where extra adults would be helpful.

Outdoor Area

Learning about shapes is a standard part of the early childhood curriculum but, too often, we begin and end with children being able to recognize and name the shapes—the square, rectangle, triangle, and circle. Think about taking the study of shapes outside the classroom and into the hallways, the gym, on a walk around the school, and, most fun of all, into the playground or park. Try a playground scavenger hunt to find shapes. To get ready:

- Make a large chart with a set of shapes you have cut from construction paper glued down the left margin.
- Gather enough pieces of stiff cardboard and small clips to make a "clipboard" for each pair of children. Tie a string around a pencil and attach it to the clip.
- Place sets of shape cutouts, drawing paper, and glue sticks on each of the work tables.

The Playground Activity:

- At class meeting time, tell children about going on a "Shapes Scavenger Hunt."
- Divide the class into pairs and ask each pair to sit at a table.
- Ask each pair to glue a row of shapes onto a piece of paper down the left side. (Be sure your sample chart is set up in a place where all the children can see it.)
- Attach the shape charts to the cardboard clipboard.
- Explain that every time someone sees a shape on the playground they should put a mark next to that shape with the pencil.

As children hunt for shapes, you may need to clue them in to shapes in different places around the playground, for instance: the frame of the slide might have triangles; the fence might have squares or diamond shapes; and the climbing equipment could be a stack of rectangles. If needed, ask some questions:

- "Does the door to the yard have a shape we know?"
- "How about the steps, are they made of shapes we know?"
- "Has anyone looked at the fence yet?"

Back in the Classroom:

- Ask children to sit at their tables with their clipboards.
- Ask them to count the number of marks they made next to each shape, and write the number on their charts.
- Circulate around the tables to help children count and write the numbers.
- Add up the cumulative numbers for each shape.
- At meeting time (it could be the next day), bring out the large shape chart you made and demonstrate how you tallied up all the shapes children found. For example, next to each construction-paper shape, draw a smaller shape representing each one found by the children. Then, count out loud: "Ricky and Sam found four rectangles. Jake and Jamala found three rectangles. Daniela and Karim also found three, and Kari and Irene found five. All together we found 15."
- Continue tallying for each shape on the chart.

Science Is Everywhere!

Important science concepts are continuously being investigated all around the classroom. In the block area, for example, children are learning by trial and error that a wide base creates a stronger building (balance); that if the building is too asymmetrical (symmetry), or if it is too high and narrow, it will fall down; and that they must be aware of themselves and others or they might bump into their own or someone else's building (spatial relations). As children are working on their buildings, you can introduce these terms. They will love the sound of these new "grown-up" words, and will begin to use them as they work together!

Block Area Science

Try a small-group "What will happen if . . . ?" lesson in the block area:

- Invite children to sit in a semicircle.
- Ask them a "What will happen if . . . ?" question. For example: "I've been wondering, what will happen if I try to build a tall building with this one unit block on the bottom?"
- Invite children to respond with their ideas and then say, "Let's experiment and see what happens." As you build together, you may want to pause and say, "Should we build it higher? What do you think will happen?"
- Depending on the result of the experiment (most likely the building will collapse), ask children why they think it happened. What was the problem? If the building does collapse, explain that many times scientists have to repeat an experiment, but they learn from their mistakes.
- Ask children if anyone has another "What will happen if . . . ?" question and continue to experiment.

From time to time, try "What will happen if . . . ?" questions in the block area with other small groups of children. The experimentation will reinforce what they are already learning through trial and error during block play.

Cook Up Some Learning!

If you cook with children, you already are doing math and science in a very "real-world" context. Following recipe charts and measuring ingredients are math activities, and as they stir, beat, and bake children are engaging in chemistry. They also are experiencing the properties of solids and liquids as they watch the batter, which is a liquid, become a solid cookie, cake, or bread.

When doing these cooking activities, let children know that cooking is a form of science, and build science words into the activity. For example, a class story about a cooking experience might say something like:

"Today, we made pancakes for lunch. We measured and mixed water and milk—which are liquids—with eggs and flour. After we stirred everything together, the mixture was like a thick liquid. When the ingredients were cooked, our pancakes turned into solids."

Art Area

Eric and Amy's discovery in the opening anecdote can be turned into a wonderful color-mixing activity. Of course, color-mixing often happens by chance as children paint or use markers, but it can so easily be turned into an intentional science experience. To prepare:

- Cover the tables with newsprint.
- Put several pieces of drawing paper on each table (one for each child in the group, plus extras).
- On one table, place small containers of red, yellow, and white paints; on another table, put containers of blue, yellow, and white; on a third table, red, blue, and white (repeat the process for each additional table).
- Put a small piece of sponge near each container. Have extra pieces on hand.
- Explain to children that in this activity they will work like scientists, experimenting with mixing different colors of paint.
- Assign children to tables and demonstrate how to dip a sponge lightly into the paint and make a print on the paper.
- Let all the children try the sponge painting, using a different sponge for each color.
- After a bit, if children haven't already done so, ask them to put one color over the other and see what happens.
- Circulate around the tables as children are working and help them notice the color changes.
- Ask some questions to spur their observations, such as, "Did anyone put white paint over the other colors? Please tell us what happened."

After about 15 minutes of experimentation, ask children at each table to talk about their discoveries. Begin by asking one child to name the colors of paint that she worked with, and then ask each child to report on one discovery. There will be repetition as the children report, but that is a way to reaffirm for everyone that blue and yellow create green, red and yellow create orange, red and blue create purple, and white makes the colors lighter. As a finale, you may want to ask: What do you think will happen if we combine all the colors together?

- Let children make guesses (they may know from experience at the easel), and then try it!
- Document the experiment on an experience chart that records each child's contribution.
- Revisit the scientific process with children around this activity.

Oodles of Oobleck

Many teachers regularly make play dough for, or with, children. This simple mixture of flour, water, and salt provides much fun, experimentation, and imaginative play. Oobleck is a wonderful variation of play dough, and provides engaging experiences with solids and liquids, since it has the properties of both. The added value of Oobleck is that it is an excellent medium for introducing the scientific process. And, because it reverts quickly to a smooth powder (once the water dries up), it appeals to children who are reluctant to touch "yucky" substances.

Oobleck consists of two parts cornstarch to one part water, with a few drops of food coloring added (optional). The water should be added to the cornstarch slowly and stirred with a popsicle stick. (You may need to add a drop or two of extra water or a sprinkle of extra cornstarch to get the right consistency.) For the whole class, two cups of cornstarch and one cup of water (to which food coloring has been added) will be enough. It's best to make it in an aluminum cake pan or a plastic deli container. The Oobleck is ready when it resists a hard smack, but a finger gently pushing against it goes right in. Once the Oobleck is made, you can:

- Gather a small group of children around the table in the art area, which has been covered with newsprint or a plastic cloth and say, "Today, we're going to do a science experiment with something new."
- Mix the Oobleck in front of the children or have a batch ready in advance.
- Give each child a small lump of Oobleck for experimentation.
- Let them make it into a ball and watch it melt through their fingers like a liquid (remind children that it's both a liquid and a solid).
- While children are playing, ask: "Does anyone want to guess what this stuff is?" "What do you observe about Oobleck?" "Can you make it into a ball?" "Then what happens?"
- Suggest putting one finger into the Oobleck. Ask what children notice when they do that.
- Try putting a penny or other small object into the Oobleck. What happens? (The object sinks out of sight.)
- When children have finished experimenting, print their discoveries on the chart paper.
- Let children know that they have been working like scientists using a special process. Make a scientific-process chart for the classroom that includes the following:
  - First we *Wondered*—What is this gooey stuff?
  - Then we *Predicted*—Guessed it might be flour or goo
  - Then we *Tried it*—Experimented
  - Then we *Found Out*—We used our senses
  - Then we *Talked About It*—Documented our discoveries

As a follow-up activity, children can make their own Oobleck. You will need a deli container for each child, popsicle sticks for stirring, scoops, small pitchers of water with the food coloring added (two to three drops is all you need). The formula is the same, two parts cornstarch to one part water, with adjustments as needed.

Library Links

At story time, read *Bartholomew and the Oobleck* by Dr. Seuss. The book is quite long, so you can plan to read it in parts.

As a follow-up to the color-mixing activity, read *Little Blue and Little Yellow* by Leo Lionni. It's a wonderful story about color-mixing and other important things!

As an early childhood teacher, you're familiar with creating a curriculum that excites young children and stimulates learning. You already do many activities that are inherently about math and science. However, it's important to label these activities as math and science experiences—for yourself and for the children in your classroom. Affirm children's discoveries as math or science, and, whenever possible, turn their discoveries into lessons for everyone. It is so important to create an attitude in children that says, "Math and science, I like them—and I can do them!"

BARBARA SPRUNG has over 40 years of experience in early childhood education. Currently, she is co-director of the Educational Equity Center at AED (Academy for Educational Development).

From *Scholastic Early Childhood Today*, January /February 2006, pp. 44–51. Copyright © 2006 by Scholastic Inc. Reprinted by permission.

Beyond Community Helpers

The Project Approach in the Early Childhood Social Studies Curriculum

My fellow teachers and I would sit down and plan out the year, starting with the theme "All About Me," moving on to "My Family," and eventually arriving at "Community Helpers," yet I sometimes asked myself, "What exactly are we learning here, and why?"

TED L. MAPLE

Traditionally, early childhood educators address the gaping hole in their planning books under the "social studies" header by teaching a smattering of thematic units. When I began teaching my kindergarten and 1st-grade classes, my approach was no exception. My fellow teachers and I would sit down and plan out the year, starting with the theme "All About Me," moving on to "My Family," and eventually arriving at "Community Helpers." Although the progression of these topics seemed to follow what I understood to be logical child development theory, I was concerned that the children and I were not making as much sense out of what we were discussing as we could have. The songs, books, poems, games, centers, and art activities I planned to accompany these units were fun, and certainly not harmful; yet I sometimes asked myself, "What exactly are we learning here, and why?"

My whole style of teaching changed when I began to study the project approach. According to Lilian Katz (1994),

> A project is an in-depth investigation of a topic worth learning more about. The investigation is usually undertaken by a small group of children within a class, sometimes by a whole class, and occasionally by an individual child. The key feature of a project is that it is a research effort deliberately focused on finding answers to questions about a topic posed either by the children, the teacher, or the teachers working with the children. The goal of a project is to learn more about the topic rather than to seek right answers to questions posed by the teacher.

After listening to Katz speak at a local professional meeting, reading *Engaging Children's Minds* by Lilian Katz and Sylvia Chard (2000), and seeing a project in action at a local elementary school, I gradually stopped being a teacher who relied heavily on pre-planned thematic units of study. I began to value children's interests and questions above what came next in the thematic teaching resource book on the shelf in our staff lounge.

My transformation in teaching style did not happen overnight, nor did I become a "projects purist"—using one way to teach everything when working with young children. But I soon found the difference between merely covering material laid out months in advance, and what Katz called "uncovering" rich, meaningful, and interesting topics with children's ideas as the driving force (personal communication, August 6, 2001).

Social Studies and the Project Approach

Most early childhood educators now know the importance of planning experiences for social studies, or any other content area, that are integrated, meaningful, and of high interest (Seefeldt, 2001). Many teaching methods use these criteria, but the project approach goes further. A project is unique because it does not simply introduce subject matter that integrates content area, it also provides a meaningful context for that subject and draws interest by connecting with children's background experiences. A project does all these things while providing an opportunity to attend to curriculum goals and standards, as well as addressing desirable dispositions (e.g., making sense of an experience, showing persistence in seeking solutions to problems, grasping the consequences of actions) as goals for learning (Helm & Katz, 2000).

The goal of social studies is to "promote civic competence"; for young children, this begins with finding their own voice (National Council for the Social Studies [NCSS], 2002). According to a position statement from NCSS called *Social Studies for Early Childhood and Elementary School Children Preparing for the 21st Century* (1988), "Children can also develop, within the context of social studies, positive attitudes toward knowledge and learning and develop a spirit of inquiry that will enhance their understanding of their world so that they will become rational, humane, participating, effective members of a democratic society." Children need opportunities to function as part of a community of learners if they are to gain the skills and dispositions that lead to civic competence, and grow into contributing members of society.

Katz and Chard (2000) point to "community ethos" as an important benefit of the project approach. They write: "Community ethos is created when all of the children are expected and encouraged to contribute to the life of the whole group, even though they may do so in different ways" (p. 9). In order to grow into positive, contributing members of a democratic society, children must learn to work together, appreciate and respect differences in others, and play a role in the common good.

Wood and Judikis (2002) identify "six essential elements" of a community: 1) common purpose or interest among the group, 2) assumption of mutual responsibility, 3) acknowledgment of interconnectedness, 4) mutual respect for individual differences, 5) mutual commitment to the well-being of each other, and 6) commitment by the members to the integrity or well-being of the group. While the phrase "classroom community" and "community of learners" are common slogans among teachers and teacher educators, do we really understand the concept of "community"? It may be beneficial for us to keep Wood and Judikis's definition in mind when striving to build community in our classrooms. Children best learn to work in a group, respect others, and work toward a common goal by experiencing these traits—and ultimately civic competence—as part of real events, much like those made available through the project approach.

Explorers' Express: A Post Office Project

My first teaching assignment was in a kindergarten/1st-grade multiage classroom at a suburban elementary school. By most standards, this was a fairly innovative school that embraced mixed-age grouping and followed a year-round calendar. The teaching staff was very dedicated to integrated thematic instruction. I knew this was not quite the same as the project approach, but it was fairly compatible with what I thought I could do. I also found that the school's philosophy and system for curriculum planning was, while somewhat shortsighted, flexible enough for me to embed project work in my own classroom.

According to the thematic instruction model, we (the teachers) were to devise a yearlong theme, and choose sub-themes or "components" within that theme to serve as guides for all our curriculum planning. Since our school calendar was divided into three trimesters, each had its own component. The primary (kindergarten and 1st-grade) team's sub-theme for the winter of 2000 was the ever-popular theme of "Community Helpers." Most early childhood teachers have used this concept in their classroom at some point in their teaching careers, to fill the social studies section of their lesson plan. This type of study often would involve a survey of all the different jobs or occupations people have in a local community. This is a fine idea, but often ends up being a very shallow endeavor in which a smattering of careers, from police officer to truck driver, are only superficially examined.

Our trimester began just this way. Children had an opportunity to share what their mothers and fathers did for a living. We had guest speakers, books, poems, songs, learning center activities, and all the necessary parts of a thematic study one could easily find in a teacher-store book. As we were making our way through the different community helpers, we came to the postal worker. I remembered the mail project I learned about three years ago when watching Lilian Katz speak and suddenly became excited. Here was a way out of the "community helpers" doldrums.

Projects begin in many different ways. Some of the best projects happen spontaneously; a teacher carefully observes children at work and play, and chooses a topic based on their questions and interests. Other times, teachers may plan a project based on curriculum goals and what they know to be an appropriate area of study. This project began the second way. I chose the topic based on what I thought would provide many opportunities for firsthand experiences and that would connect to something within most of the children's existing experiences. I decided it would be a much better use of our time if we were to look at one occupation or career in-depth, as opposed to lightly covering all the "community helpers" we could think of throughout the trimester. We had to study something the children were somewhat familiar with, which left out jobs like sailors (we lived in Indiana), soldiers, politicians, and the like. The postal worker was perfect. Also, this being my first full-fledged project, it helped to know that it had been done before by the preschool children Katz mentioned.

Getting Started

How was I to begin? I already had some books about postal workers that I had gathered for the community helpers theme. Beginning a project with a book seemed too familiar, however. I wanted to try another technique to grab the children's interests. It need not be glamorous, but should be interesting and familiar. On the first day of the project, we sat down for the morning meeting and I pulled out a box of envelopes I had "borrowed" from the school supply closet. I took one of the envelopes out and we talked about it.

Immediately, the children began talking about the mail and, more important, talking about their own mailboxes, mail carriers, and times when they had received or sent mail. Some of the children, as many children would in a similar circumstance, began playing with the envelope I had passed around and started taking it apart. I recognized that through their actions the children had asked their first questions: What is an envelope and how is it made? Questions are the main ingredient to any good project, and they are what distinguish project work from other types of instruction. I became very excited to see it actually working!

I then invited the children to explore the envelopes. They proceeded to take them apart and examine the rounded corners and the edges covered with dried glue. I gave the children a piece of plain white paper and challenged them to make their own envelopes. I wanted to see if they could discover the answer to their own questions. I was not sure how well their homemade envelopes would hold a letter, but I think this project got off to a good start and set the tone for a child-centered, question-driven investigation.

Delving Deeper

Our discussions about the mail continued as we read some informational books about postal workers and the post office. The children continued to share stories about times when they mailed a letter with their parents, or when they actually went to the post office. A class field trip to the local post office seemed the next logical step when the children began to ask questions pertaining to how the mail system works, such as, "Where do the letters go when we put them in the mailbox?"

I called the post office and set up a class trip, which would turn out to be one of the highlights of our post office project.

We prepared for the trip by reviewing some guidelines concerning safety around the machinery they might see, and compiling some questions for the postal workers. The post office manager, Mrs. Smith, was our tour guide, and the children really did an exceptional job of listening carefully to her instructions as they were shown around the lobby and "behind the scenes" at the post office. They saw the postal materials that the clerks sold at the front desk. They were able to see a customer make a purchase, and watched the clerks weigh the package and make the transaction.

Next, we entered the back room of the post office. The children gasped as they looked around the huge area, and all the things that were going on. The first area Mrs. Smith showed the children was the mail-sorting machine. She explained that the envelopes were sorted by ZIP code, and asked the technician to show the children how it worked. The children were fascinated by it all—the machine, the computers, and especially when the sorter broke down and had to be serviced right before our eyes. I took several pictures to ensure that we had it well-documented. A parent who came along for the trip videotaped the event so we could revisit what we had experienced.

Mrs. Smith introduced us to several mail carriers who were getting ready to go out on their routes. She showed the children many of the different machines that they used to help them sort and deliver the mail more efficiently, different tools the mail carriers used (such as carts, bins, and bags), and the post office boxes. The trip culminated with a walk outside to look at the inside of a mail truck, and we had a conversation with a mail carrier getting ready to go on his route. Although the tour was mostly a passive one, which I would later learn how to avoid, I believed the group gained much from the experience.

Bringing It Together

When we returned to school, the children sat down to write in their individual journals and draw pictures of the experience. The next day, I asked our school secretary to call down to our classroom when the school's mail carrier arrived to deliver the day's mail. When she did, we dropped everything and went down to see and talk with her. This was a nice way to connect our previous trip to real life. We saw a carrier in action, and she became the expert who would be able to answer any questions that were remaining from the day before.

During choice time, the children began to show what they were learning about mail and the post office in different ways. Allie drew a picture on the dry erase board of the sorting machine from the post office trip. Another group of children built mail trucks with Legos. As they pursued these activities, the children demonstrated what part of the mail process interested them the most. After much discussion, we decided as a class to make our own post office right there in the classroom. The planning began. First, we would need a name. The children came up with several ideas, but finally voted for "Explorers' Express" (the "Explorer" is the school mascot). In order to plan for the creation of Explorers' Express, the group reflected on what they had learned from the visit to the real post office.

We talked about how the postal workers all had different jobs and had to work together in order to complete the big task of delivering the U.S. mail. We also would have to work together in order to make our mail system work. After reviewing what we had learned so far from our reading, the expert's insight, and the field trip, we broke the mail process down into four basic tasks: delivering and picking up mail, sorting mail, producing stamps and envelopes, and selling stamps and envelopes. Each child chose an operation that most interested him or her. Four interest groups were formed to produce stamps and envelopes, sell the items, deliver and pick up mail, and sort the mail for delivery.

As the stamp and envelope group produced stamps (some were mass-produced, and others were "special edition" stamps made individually), the mail clerks set up a makeshift post office using our puppet stand. Some of the children wrote messages on the front, describing the price of stamps, hours of operations, etc. One child brought in a toy cash register, and soon they were ready for customers. Meanwhile the mail carriers devised mail bags made of paper and staples (which they later would find ineffective for large packages) and sat down with me to divide the school into "mail routes." There were 30 classrooms in the school, so each of the six mail carriers had five classrooms on a route. Each carrier chose a color, and we painted the mailboxes on his or her route that color to help remind them which classrooms were theirs. The color code system also helped the sorting group.

When the mail came in (either picked up by the mail carriers or brought in by "customers"), the members of the sorting group put a dot on the back of the envelope with a marker. The marker color matched the color of the mailbox to which it would be delivered. The sorting group knew what color to put on the envelope because the sender had to put the classroom number in the address area on the front of the envelope. We had devised a chart to help the sorters do their job. For example, if the envelope said, "John Doe, Rm. 16" on the front, the sorters would look for the number 16 on the chart and mark the letter with the appropriate color. They then would put the letter in the corresponding mail carrier's bin to be delivered that afternoon.

Every part of this project was planned and carried out by the children and teacher together. On most occasions, a problem was posed by the teacher to the children, and then discussed—or vice versa. On no occasion was an action taken unilaterally. Some of the children took on extraordinary roles in the Explorers' Express. David, a child advanced beyond most in reading, writing, and math, became our unofficial "Postmaster General." He helped children count money, write signage, tell time, etc. He kept us in line and on time. Another child, Jason, became so engaged in the mail project, his mother joked with me that it was bordering on obsession. He had his mother buy him a planner, and he "scheduled meetings" with various members from various groups in the Explorers' Express. He would go home at night and devise new plans for the next day, write countless letters to friends, and make new stamp designs.

The mail carriers soon became school-wide celebrities. Older children waved at them as they went down the hall. Every classroom in the school participated in the project. Children were lined up outside of our room every morning from 9 a.m. to 9:30 a.m. The post office opened and closed on time every morning, without fail. Kindergartners who had never learned how to tell time before this project were learning now because they had a purpose. In three weeks, we processed over 1,000 pieces of mail. After those three weeks, we closed the Explorers' Express mail service and celebrated our accomplishments. We made a scrapbook together that documented the experience, which each child took home. The book told the story of an unforgettable classroom project that lasted for a total of nine weeks.

The Impact of the Project Approach on Children

What is the point of spending nine weeks talking about mail? In an atmosphere of rigorous standards and academic accountability, this question is sure to be asked. The real reason I spent so much time focused on one seemingly insignificant topic is simple. The primary purpose was not to teach children about the mail system, but rather how to be empirical, strive for accuracy, and work cooperatively. It was not really terribly important to me that the children in my classroom learn about the different parts of a post office. I did want them to learn, however, how to carefully observe people, places, things, and events. My goal was for the children to become active participants in a group that had a common goal and supported each other in their search for knowledge and truth. I hoped for them to become citizens of our classroom and school community. Those are the dispositions that in-depth projects help to foster and strengthen in children, and they are crucial.

When these goals are kept in mind, a project can be a transformational experience for children and teachers. A child's background, developmental level, behavior problems, or other traits and features that typically separate the haves from the have-nots are diminished by project work because the children are allowed to pursue their own interests and be challenged at their own levels. Children often transcend their problems or differences, and come to life in the joyous exploration of a topic that has meaning and is of interest to them.

My students have been transformed by projects in many ways—both individually and as a whole. Billy, a child with behavior and emotional problems, could not sit still for more than two minutes of circle time or last for five minutes on the playground without creating a disturbance. When I brought in a collection of bike parts for the children to explore during a project on bicycles, Billy took leave of his typically destructive and distracting behavior for the day. I watched him become engrossed in figuring out how the bike parts fit together and how they work, and I observed him testing his theories for 45 minutes. For a child who has difficulty sticking with one task for more than five minutes, this was a wonderful thing to behold.

The personality of Calbert, a socially awkward kindergartner who struggled academically, also emerged during the workings of a project. He was a member of the sorting group for the post office project, whose job it was to sort the incoming mail for the mail carriers to deliver around the school. The sorting group needed a location to sort the mail and, for whatever reason, chose the loft in our classroom as the "sorting room." One day Calbert had a great idea. He decided that since the loft was up high, and the mail needed to come back down, they should have a mail chute to send the mail down to the carriers' boxes for delivery. The group loved the idea, and they got busy working together to bring Calbert's idea to fruition. They first tried to slide the envelopes and packages down the steps, but had the difficulties one might expect. They used trial and error to test several different methods, and finally were able to use long cardboard pieces to create a tunnel that would guide the mail pieces down between the wall and the steps. This was all accomplished with Calbert leading the way; from that moment on he had a new sense of pride and confidence.

Another unique attribute of projects is the opportunity they provide for service learning. Projects that offer these experiences, according to NCSS's position statement on service learning, provide: 1) relevant opportunities to connect civic life with practical community problem solving; 2) an increased awareness of children's immediate surroundings and its unmet needs (as well as opportunities to learn strategies to meet those needs); and 3) enhancement of "democratic values and attitudes" (NCSS Citizenship Select Subcommittee, 2000). The Explorers' Express gave the children all these experiences, and our classroom community grew together because of it.

Conclusion

According to NCSS, the "primary goal of public education is to prepare students to be engaged and effective citizens." To reach that goal, the NCSS position statement titled Creating Effective Citizens explains that students should participate in activities that "expand civic knowledge, develop participation skills, and support the belief that, in a democracy, the actions of each person make a difference … as they work to solve real problems" (NCSS Task Force on Revitalizing Citizenship Education, 2002).

When given the opportunity to become an active, participating member of a community of learners, a child learns to be an effective citizen. We need not lecture young children about the historical roots of our democratic republic, or go through the silly, artificial motions of participating in a mock election, in order to teach them about citizenship and democracy. What we must do is provide opportunities for children to be part of an endeavor that celebrates our ideals through cooperative group efforts, in which they strive to better themselves by developing the disposition to find things out and respect each other's individual differences and talents. That is where democracy begins for our children.

References

Helm, J. H., & Katz, L. (2000). *Young investigators: The project approach in the early years*. New York: Teachers College Press.

Katz, L. G. (1994). *The project approach*. Champaign, IL: Children's Research Center. (ERIC Document Reproduction Service No. EDO-PS-94-6)

Katz, L. G., & Chard, S. C. (2000). *Engaging children's minds: The project approach* (2nd ed.). Stamford, CT: Ablex Publishing

National Council for the Social Studies Citizenship Select Subcommittee. (2000). *Service learning: An essential component of citizenship education*. Retrieved September 3, 2004, from http://socialstudies.org.

National Council for the Social Studies Task Force on Early Childhood/Elementary Social Studies. (1988). *Social studies for early childhood and elementary school children preparing for the 21st century*. Retrieved October 28, 2003, from http://socialstudies.org.

National Council for the Social Studies Task Force on Revitalizing Citizenship Education. (2002). *Creating effective citizens*. Retrieved October 28, 2003, from http://socialstudies.org.

Seefeldt, C. (2001). *Social studies for the preschool/primary child* (6th ed.). Upper Saddle River, NJ: Merrill Prentice Hall.

Wood, G. S., & Judikis, J. C. (2002). *Conversations on community theory*. West Lafayette, IN: Purdue University Press.

TED L. MAPLE is Director, Success by Six, Indianapolis, Indiana, and former Director, St. Mary's Child Center, Indianapolis, Indiana.

From *Childhood Education*, Spring 2005. Copyright © 2005 by the Association for Childhood Education International. Reprinted by permission of Ted L. Maples and the Association for Childhood Education International.

Physical Fitness and the Early Childhood Curriculum

RAE PICA

You can hardly open the newspaper these days without reading headlines about the children's obesity crisis in the United States. The problem of overweight and obese children is growing at a faster rate than the problem of adult obesity, and the primary culprit is physical inactivity. Children today lead much more sedentary lifestyles than their predecessors, and society places less and less value on movement and recreation, as evidenced by reductions in physical education programs and recess in schools across the country.

Obese children bound for lifelong health problems, experts warn.

Children's Fitness: Whose Responsibility?

Should the physical fitness of young children be the concern of early childhood professionals? Or is it a matter for the family, and the family alone, to worry about? Consider that 40 percent of five- to eight-year-olds show at least one heart disease risk factor (Berenson 1980; Ross et al. 1987; Bar-Or et al. 1998). Heart disease is the leading killer of adults in the United States, accounting for more than half of all deaths every year (U.S. DHHS 1990). With risk factors appearing in children as young as five, cardiovascular disease may become an even greater threat in future generations. Furthermore, the Centers for Disease Control (CDC 2005) reports that from 1979 to 2000, annual hospital costs for obesity-related conditions in children ages 6 to 17 rose from $34 million to $127 million.

As early childhood professionals we have a duty to educate the whole (thinking, feeling, *moving*) child.

Given these alarming facts, the state of children's fitness is clearly the responsibility of all who are involved with children.

As early childhood professionals we have a duty to educate the whole (thinking, feeling, *moving*) child. Moreover, teachers of preschoolers can be more realistic than parents in their assessment of children's physical activity levels (Noland et al. 1990), and preschool teachers' prompting of children has a positive influence on those levels (McKenzie et al. 1997).

Also significant, inactive preschool children were almost four times more likely than their active peers to gain body fatness as they enter first grade (Moore et al. 1995). And body fatness established in childhood tends to carry over into adulthood (Bar-Or et al. 1998). So too does physical inactivity (Moore et al. 1995).

Thus, childhood fitness is an issue upon which early childhood professionals can have a significant impact. By ensuring that children stay active while in our care, we can help combat obesity and promote healthy lifestyles from the beginning.

Playing tag, marching, riding a tricycle, dancing to moderate- to fast-paced music, and jumping rope are other forms of moderate- to vigorous-intensity exercise for children.

Definitions of Physical Fitness

It's important to understand what physical fitness is and how it applies to children (as opposed to adults). The National Association for Sport and Physical Education (NASPE) describes physical fitness as

> a condition where the body is in a state of well-being and readily able to meet the physical challenges of everyday life. Most experts believe physical fitness is the result of practicing a physically active lifestyle. For young children, appropriate movement tasks and experiences can enhance overall body strength, bone density, and developmental functioning of the cardiovascular system. (NASPE 2002, 18)

Physical fitness comprises two components: health-related fitness and skill-related fitness. The latter includes balance, agility, coordination, power, speed, and reaction time. However, it is the former that is relevant to our discussion about young children. Health-related fitness incorporates cardiovascular endurance, muscular strength, muscular endurance, flexibility, and body composition.

Cardiovascular Endurance

Cardiovascular endurance is the ability of the heart and lungs to supply oxygen and nutrients to the muscles. Someone with great cardiovascular endurance has a strong heart—a heart that is larger and pumps more blood per beat than the heart of an individual who is not fit. Good cardiovascular endurance results when an individual exercises regularly. Typically, aerobic exercise improves cardiovascular fitness; but for children, we think of aerobics in a different way than we do for adults.

Young children, particularly before the age of six, are not ready for long, uninterrupted periods of strenuous activity. Expecting them to perform organized exercises for 30 continuous minutes, as an adult does, is not only unrealistic but also could be physically damaging. At the very least it can instill an intense dislike of physical activity.

Developmentally appropriate aerobic activities for children include moderate to vigorous play and movement. Moderately intense physical activity, like walking, increases the heart rate and breathing somewhat; vigorously intense movement, like pretending to be an Olympic sprinter, takes a lot more effort and results in a noticeable increase in breathing. Playing tag, marching, riding a tricycle, dancing to moderate- to fast-paced music, and jumping rope are other forms of moderate- to vigorous-intensity exercise for children.

Muscular Strength

Strong muscles are necessary not only for performing certain actions, like throwing a ball for distance, hanging and swinging, climbing, and carrying heavy books or groceries, but they also prevent injury and help us maintain proper posture. As an added bonus, increasing muscle strength increases strength in tendons, ligaments, and bones.

Strength training—also known as resistance or weight training—is the best way to build muscular strength. For adults, strength training usually means working with weights and equipment. For children, such a regimen is not appropriate. It is never a good idea to modify an adult strength-training program for use by children. Adults' bodies are fully developed; children's are still growing. Adults have long attention spans and the motivation to endure the monotony of repetitive exercises; children do not. Adults can follow specific instructions for proper form and understand the risks in handling strength-training equipment; children cannot. For these reasons the best strength training for children uses children's own weight in physical activities they typically enjoy, like jumping, playing tug-of-war, and pumping their legs to go higher on a swing.

The best strength training for children uses children's own weight in physical activities they typically enjoy, like jumping, playing tug-of-war, and pumping their legs to go higher on a swing.

Muscular Endurance

Muscular endurance, which is related to stamina, is the muscles' ability to continue contracting over an extended period of time. Children's muscular endurance is important because "a child who has good muscular endurance will enjoy and have greater success in his/her daily work activities, in play, and in sporting and athletic competitions" (Landy & Burridge 1997, 8).

Muscular endurance is tied to muscular strength, so many activities and exercises benefit both. However, muscular endurance also depends on skill level. A skilled individual can perform movements efficiently, meaning she can sustain movement for longer periods of time. This ability comes with practice and perseverance. A child, having less practice than an adult in most skills, tends to use maximum force and contract more muscles than needed to perform a movement. Therefore, he cannot sustain the movement as long as a skilled mover.

Flexibility

This fitness factor involves the range of motion around joints. People with good flexibility can bend and stretch without effort or pain, and they can take part in physical activities without fear of muscle strain, sprain, or spasm.

Most young children are flexible, and girls tend to be more flexible than boys. Boys who are inactive start to lose their flexibility at around age 10; inactive girls, at 12. However, if children are physically active, they will continue to be flexible.

Adults should encourage children to work specifically on their flexibility, using gentle, static stretches that take a muscle just beyond its usual length (without pain) and holding a stretch for at least 10 seconds. Activities such as stretching to pretend to climb a ladder, reach for something on a high shelf, shoot a basketball through a hoop, or tie shoes, pick flowers, or pet a cat—as well as hanging and swinging from monkey bars—help increase flexibility. Two cautions regarding stretching: first, children should work their own limbs through their range of motion because an adult can easily stretch a child's muscles and joints too far. Second, children should be warned against ballistic stretching—bouncing while stretching. Ballistic stretching can cause small tears in the muscle fibers, and it is not as effective as static stretching.

Body Composition

The final component of health-related fitness is the body's makeup in terms of fat, muscle, tissue, and bone, or the percentage of lean body tissue to fat.

Due to the burgeoning childhood obesity crisis, a lot of attention is focused on body weight. Weight alone, however, is not a good indicator of fitness. For example, some children are simply large-boned and thus heavier than other children. Also, muscle weighs more than fat, so two children may have the same weight but very different body composition, one having muscle and very little fat and the other having too much fat.

Physical activity, and particularly aerobic and muscle-strengthening activities, is the key to combating body fat.

Movement Suggestions

Here are some suggestions for encouraging children's active movement.

Arrange the environment to allow for movement. Is there room indoors for you and the children to dance or play Follow the Leader, to set up an obstacle course, or to twirl hoops around various body parts? Does the outdoor environment have open areas for running, jumping, rolling, and other active play and games? Is there equipment for safe climbing, hanging, and swinging?

Buy equipment and props with movement in mind. Choose items like parachutes, plastic hoops, jump ropes, juggling scarves, ribbon sticks, and balls in a variety of shapes, sizes, and textures. Purchase enough so all children have access. Invest in tricycles, scooters, and climbing equipment.

Demonstrate enthusiasm for physical activity. Children learn by watching the important adults in their lives. If you spend the majority of your time in sedentary activities, that is what the children will want to do. But if you spend time playing actively with them, the children will have a wonderful role model.

If rainy or very cold weather forces the children to stay indoors, break out the juggling scarves. Do the children need to take a break or burn some energy? Take them for a walk. With all the excitement you can muster, set off to see and hear everything you can in the block around the school or center.

Too often activities such as running laps or doing pushups are meted out as punishment, linking negative associations with physical activity in children's minds. But a teacher's playful, enthusiastic attitude toward physical activity helps children form positive associations with movement.

Help children understand why movement is important. Recognizing why physical activity is necessary promotes a positive attitude toward fitness that endures beyond childhood. All it takes is a well-placed word or two. For example, as children stretch: "It's important to stretch after exercising so your muscles don't get all bunched up." Or to stimulate children's natural curiosity: "Wow! Chasing bubbles really got my heart pumping. It's healthy to do that sometimes. Is your heart going faster too?"

Children should understand why you offer activities like chasing bubbles, dancing, and pretending to jump like rabbits and kangaroos. And they should have a voice in deciding which physical activity they take part in. Would they rather play Statues or Cooperative Musical Chairs? Choice is a necessary ingredient in fostering intrinsic motivation, and intrinsic motivation goes a long way toward ensuring lifelong fitness.

Physical Activity Recommendations

The position of the National Association for Sport and Physical Education is that "all children birth to age five should engage in daily physical activity that promotes health-related fitness and movement skills" (2002, 2). Their guidelines for physical activities for young children state that young children should not be sedentary for more than 60 minutes at a time, except when sleeping (NASPE 2002). NASPE recommends that toddlers accumulate daily at least 30 minutes of structured physical activity and at least 60 minutes (and up to several hours) of unstructured physical activity. Preschoolers should engage in the same amount of unstructured activity but accumulate at least 60 minutes daily of structured physical activity.

Physical activity, and particularly aerobic and muscle-strengthening activities, is the key to combating body fat.

The key word is *accumulate*. No longer are we told that to attain benefits, we must perform 30 minutes of uninterrupted aerobic activity. Rather, new recommendations from such groups as the Centers for Disease Control, the National Institutes of Health, NASPE, and the American Heart Association recommend 10- to 15-minute "bouts" of at least moderate-intensity physical activity, adding up to 30 minutes, on most or all days of the week.

This is good news for children, who are not equipped physically, emotionally, or cognitively to participate in strenuous, nonstop, 30-minute exercise sessions. Children are naturally intermittent movers, so the concept of physical activity in bouts is ideal for them.

When children jump like rabbits and kangaroos, they develop muscular strength and endurance and, depending on how continuously they jump, cardiovascular endurance.

Fitting Fitness into the Curriculum

Given the increasing emphasis on accountability and academics, physical activity is in danger of falling by the wayside in the early childhood curriculum. Indeed, more and more early childhood professionals say they have trouble fitting movement into the program because they're too busy preparing children for academics.

Developmentally appropriate practice dictates that we educate the whole child. Furthermore, academics and physical activity are *not* mutually exclusive. A number of researchers (Martens 1982; Hannaford 1995; Sallis et al. 1999) have found that regular physical activity contributes to improved school performance. For example, in one study, 500 Canadian students spent an extra hour a day in physical education class and performed better on tests than children who were less active (Hannaford 1995). A

Active Start—Physical Activity Guidelines for Children Birth to Five Years

National Association for Sport and Physical Education (NASPE)

The guidelines presented below support NASPE's position that all children birth to age five should engage in daily physical activity that promotes health-related fitness and movement skills.

Infants (Birth to 12 Months)

1. Infants should interact with parents and/or caregivers in daily physical activities that are dedicated to promoting the exploration of their environment.
2. Infants should be placed in safe settings that facilitate physical activity and do not restrict movement for prolonged periods of time.
3. Infants' physical activity should promote the development of movement skills.
4. Infants should have an environment that meets or exceeds recommended safety standards for performing large muscle activities.
5. Individuals responsible for the well-being of infants should be aware of the importance of physical activity and facilitate the child's movement skills.

Toddlers (12 to 36 Months)

1. Toddlers should accumulate at least 30 minutes daily of structured physical activity.
2. Toddlers should engage in at least 60 minutes and up to several hours per day of daily, unstructured physical activity and should not be sedentary for more than 60 minutes at a time except when sleeping.
3. Toddlers should develop movement skills that are building blocks for more complex movement tasks.

4. Toddlers should have indoor and outdoor areas that meet or exceed recommended safety standards for performing large muscle activities.
5. Individuals responsible for the well-being of toddlers should be aware of the importance of physical activity and facilitate the child's movement skills.

Preschoolers (3 to 5 Years)

1. Preschoolers should accumulate at least 60 minutes daily of structured physical activity.
2. Preschoolers should engage in at least 60 minutes and up to several hours per day of daily, unstructured physical activity and should not be sedentary for more than 60 minutes at a time except when sleeping.
3. Preschoolers should develop competence in movement skills that are building blocks for more complex movement tasks.
4. Preschoolers should have indoor and outdoor areas that meet or exceed recommended safety standards for performing large muscle activities.
5. Individuals responsible for the well-being of preschoolers should be aware of the importance of physical activity and facilitate the child's movement skills.

Excerpted with permission, from the National Association for Sport and Physical Education (NASPE), an association of the American Alliance for Health, Physical Education, Recreation and Dance, *Active Start: A Statement of Physical Activity Guidelines for Children Birth to Five Years* (Reston, VA: NASPE, 2002), 5–11.

neurophysiologist, Hannaford states that because movement activates the neural wiring throughout the body, the whole body, and not just the brain, is an instrument of learning.

Here are some suggestions for fitting physical activity into the schedule.

Use Movement Across the Curriculum

Young children are experiential learners, and the more senses they use in the learning process, the more they retain (Fauth 1990). Brain research has shown us that the mind and body are *not* separate entities—that the functions of the body contribute to the functions of the mind (Jensen 2000). Moreover, Gardner's recognition of the bodily/kinesthetic intelligence (1993) supports the use of the body and body parts as a way of learning and knowing.

When children have opportunities to get into high, low, wide, and narrow shapes, they increase their flexibility (one of the five fitness factors). They also learn about mathematics and art because these are quantitative ideas (math), and shape is both

an art and a mathematics concept. If they practice these shapes with partners, the concept of cooperation, a social studies skill, is added. When children jump like rabbits and kangaroos, they develop muscular strength and endurance and, depending on how continuously they jump, cardiovascular endurance. They explore the concepts of light/heavy, big/small, up/down, and high/low. These are also quantitative math concepts, but physically experiencing them enhances word comprehension, which contributes to emergent literacy.

Regardless of the content area or concept being explored, there is a way for children to experience it physically. Doing so benefits children because they learn best by doing and it promotes physical fitness.

A brain break can be any kind of physical activity that gets the blood flowing and provides a change of pace.

Take "Brain Breaks"

Research (Jarrett et al. 1998) shows that individuals—but particularly children, due to their stage of brain development—accomplish more when their efforts are distributed over time rather than concentrated. In other words, we all need the occasional break! If the break lasts at least 5 to 10 minutes and consists of moderate- to vigorous-intensity movement, it qualifies as a fitness bout.

A brain break can be any kind of physical activity that gets the blood flowing (and glucose and oxygen to the brain) and provides a change of pace. However, if you want to focus particularly on cognitive benefits, cross-lateral movements are an excellent choice, because they require the two hemispheres of the brain to communicate across the corpus callosum (the matter connecting the two hemispheres) (Hannaford 1995).

Cross-lateral movement is anything that requires the left arm and right leg, or vice versa, to move simultaneously. Walking, marching, creeping, and crawling all fit this category. You can also lead an activity that requires children to cross the midline of the body—the vertical line that runs from the top of the head to the feet and divides the body into left and right sides. For example, lead the children in reaching one arm at a time across the body, or in alternatively touching right elbow to a lifted left knee and the reverse (Dennison & Dennison 1989).

Use Transitions to Promote Fitness

Children move from one activity to another during transitions, so they may as well move in ways that are both functional and fun. Promote flexibility by challenging children to move in a tall, straight shape or a crooked shape; by tiptoeing; or on three body parts. Enhance children's muscular strength, muscular endurance, and cardiovascular endurance by challenging them to hop, skip, or jog lightly.

Teach Movement Skills!

Most people believe children automatically acquire motor skills as their bodies develop—that it is a natural, "magical" process that occurs along with maturation. The truth is that maturation influences only part of the process, allowing a child to execute most movement skills at an immature level. A child whose skill stays at the same level will lack confidence in her movement abilities and is unlikely to take part in physical activities beyond childhood. The end result is an individual who is not physically fit.

Just as other skills are taught in early childhood, so too must movement skills have a place in the curriculum. Carson (2001) tells us that engaging in unplanned, self-selected physical activities—or even a movement learning center—is not enough for young children to gain movement skills. She points out that families and teachers "would not advocate learning to read or communicate by having their children enter a 'gross cognitive area' where children could engage in self-selected 'reading play' with a variety of books" (p. 9).

Conclusion

The notion of leaving cognitive or social/emotional development to chance is ludicrous. Yet we feel no similar sense of absurdity at the idea of leaving physical development to chance—that all we need to do is let children play and they will be prepared for all the physical challenges life brings their way.

Yes, the pressure to focus on academics is fierce and, unfortunately, mounting. But as early childhood professionals who understand how young children really learn, and who keep in mind the whole child, we must withstand the pressure and do what will best prepare the children for the future—cognitively, affectively, *and* physically. Society may place less and less value on movement, but we do not have to. By helping children to be more physically active, early childhood professionals can help combat the obesity crisis and promote lifelong physical fitness.

References

Bar-Or, O., J. Foreyt, C. Bouchard, K.D. Brownell, W.H. Dietz, E. Ravussin, A.D. Salbe, S. Schwenger, S. St. Jore, & B. Torun. 1998. Physical activity, genetic, and nutritional considerations in childhood weight management. *Medicine and Science in Sports and Exercise* 30 (1): 2–10.

Berenson, G.S., ed. 1980. *Cardiovascular risk factors in children: The early natural history of atherosclerosis and essential hypertension.* New York: Oxford University Press.

Carson, L.M. 2001. The "I am learning" curriculum: Developing a movement awareness in young children. *Teaching Elementary Physical Education* 12 (5): 9–13.

Centers for Disease Control. 2005. Preventing obesity and chronic diseases through good nutrition and physical activity. Online: www.cdc.gov/nccdphp/publications/factsheets/Prevention/obesity.htm.

Dennison, P.E., & G.E. Dennison. 1989. *Brain gym.* Ventura, CA: Edu-Kinesthetics.

Fauth, B. 1990. Linking the visual arts with drama, movement, and dance for the young child. In *Moving and learning for the young child*, ed. W.J. Stinson, 159–87. Reston, VA: AAHPERD.

Gardner, H. 1993. *Frames of mind: The theory of multiple intelligences.* New York: Basic Books.

Hannaford, C. 1995. *Smart moves: Why learning is not all in your head.* Arlington, VA: Great Ocean.

Institute for Aerobic Fitness. 1987. *Get fit.* Dallas: Author.

Jarrett, O.S., D.M. Maxwell, C. Dickerson, P. Hoge, G. Davies, & A. Yetley. 1998. Impact of recess on classroom behavior: Group effects and individual differences. *Journal of Physical Education, Recreation, and Dance* 53 (3): 55–58.

Jensen, E. 2000. *Brain-based learning: The new science of teaching and training.* San Diego: The Brain Store.

Landy, J., & K. Burridge. 1997. *Fifty simple things you can do to raise a child who is physically fit.* New York: Macmillan.

Martens, F.L. 1982. Daily physical education—A boon to Canadian elementary schools. *Journal of Physical Education, Recreation, and Dance* 53 (3): 55–58.

McKenzie, T.L., J.F. Sallis, J.P. Elder, C.C. Berry, P.L. Hoy, P.R. Nader, M.M. Zive, & S.C. Broyles. 1997. Physical activity levels and prompts in young children at recess: A two-year study of a biethnic sample. *Research Quarterly for Exercise and Sport* 68 (3): 195–202.

Moore, L.L., U.D.T. Nguyen, K.J. Rothman, L.A. Cupples, & R.C. Ellison. 1995. Preschool physical activity level and change in body fatness in young children. *American Journal of Epidemiology* 142 (9): 982–88.

NASPE (National Association for Sport and Physical Education). 2002. *Active start: A statement of physical activity guidelines for children birth to five years*. Reston, VA: Author.

Noland, M., F. Danner, & K. Dewalt. 1990. The measurement of physical activity in young children. *Research Quarterly for Exercise and Sport* 61 (2): 146–53.

Ross, J.G., R.R. Pate, T.G. Lohman, & G.M. Christenson. 1987. Changes in body composition of children. *Journal of Physical Education, Recreation, and Dance* 58 (9): 74–77.

U.S. Department of Health and Human Services. 1990. Health, United States, 1989 and Prevention Profile. DHHS pub. No. (PHS) 90-1232. Washington, DC: U.S. Government Printing Office.

RAE PICA is a movement consultant and author based in Center Barnstead, New Hampshire. She speaks throughout North America and has shared her expertise with such groups as the *Sesame Street* Research Department, Gymboree, and the Head Start Bureau.

From *Young Children*, May 2006, pp. 12–19. Copyright © 2006 by National Association for the Education of Young Children. Reprinted by permission.

Test Your Knowledge Form

We encourage you to photocopy and use this page as a tool to assess how the articles in *Annual Editions* expand on the information in your textbook. By reflecting on the articles you will gain enhanced text information. You can also access this useful form on a product's book support Web site at *http://www.mhcls.com/online/*.

NAME: _____   DATE: _____

TITLE AND NUMBER OF ARTICLE: _____

BRIEFLY STATE THE MAIN IDEA OF THIS ARTICLE:

_____

LIST THREE IMPORTANT FACTS THAT THE AUTHOR USES TO SUPPORT THE MAIN IDEA:

_____

WHAT INFORMATION OR IDEAS DISCUSSED IN THIS ARTICLE ARE ALSO DISCUSSED IN YOUR TEXTBOOK OR OTHER READINGS THAT YOU HAVE DONE? LIST THE TEXTBOOK CHAPTERS AND PAGE NUMBERS:

_____

LIST ANY EXAMPLES OF BIAS OR FAULTY REASONING THAT YOU FOUND IN THE ARTICLE:

_____

LIST ANY NEW TERMS/CONCEPTS THAT WERE DISCUSSED IN THE ARTICLE, AND WRITE A SHORT DEFINITION:

We Want Your Advice

ANNUAL EDITIONS revisions depend on two major opinion sources: one is our Advisory Board, listed in the front of this volume, which works with us in scanning the thousands of articles published in the public press each year; the other is you—the person actually using the book. Please help us and the users of the next edition by completing the prepaid article rating form on this page and returning it to us. Thank you for your help!

ANNUAL EDITIONS: Early Childhood Education 08/09

ARTICLE RATING FORM

Here is an opportunity for you to have direct input into the next revision of this volume.
We would like you to rate each of the articles listed below, using the following scale:

1. **Excellent: should definitely be retained**
2. **Above average: should probably be retained**
3. **Below average: should probably be deleted**
4. **Poor: should definitely be deleted**

Your ratings will play a vital part in the next revision.
Please mail this prepaid form to us as soon as possible.
Thanks for your help!

RATING	ARTICLE
	1. The Changing Culture of Childhood
	2. The Preschool Promise
	3. Preschool Pays
	4. Accountability Comes to Preschool
	5. No Child Left Behind
	6. Preschool Comes of Age
	7. Taking a Stand
	8. Meeting of the Minds
	9. Fear and Allergies in the Lunchroom
	10. Supporting Grandparents Who Raise Grandchildren
	11. Children of Teen Parents
	12. Giving Intervention a Head Start
	13. Including Children with Disabilities in Early Childhood Education Programs
	14. Creative Play
	15. Helping Young Hispanic Learners
	16. Reading Your Baby's Mind
	17. Teaching to Temperaments
	18. Which Hand?
	19. Research 101: Tools for Reading and Interpreting Early Childhood Research
	20. What Can We Do to Prevent Childhood Obesity?
	21. Back to Basics
	22. Scripted Curriculum

RATING	ARTICLE
	23. *Rethinking* Early Childhood Practices
	24. One District's Study on the Propriety of Transition-Grade Classrooms
	25. Successful Transition to Kindergarten
	26. Making the Case for Play Policy
	27. The Looping Classroom
	28. The Case For and Against Homework
	29. Ready or Not, Here We Come
	30. Heading Off Disruptive Behavior
	31. Relationships at the Forefront of Effective Practice
	32. "You Got It!"
	33. The Playground as Classroom
	34. Fostering Positive Transitions for School Success
	35. The Plan
	36. One Teacher, 20 Preschoolers, and a Goldfish
	37. Fostering Prosocial Behavior in Young Children
	38. Early Literacy and Very Young Children
	39. Using Picture Books to Support Young Children's Literacy
	40. The Sweet Work of Reading
	41. Meeting the Challenge of Math and Science
	42. Beyond Community Helpers
	43. Physical Fitness and the Early Childhood Curriculum

BUSINESS REPLY MAIL
FIRST CLASS MAIL PERMIT NO. 551 DUBUQUE IA

POSTAGE WILL BE PAID BY ADDRESSEE

McGraw-Hill Contemporary Learning Series
501 Bell Street
Dubuque, IA 52001

NO POSTAGE
NECESSARY
IF MAILED
IN THE
UNITED STATES

ABOUT YOU

Name   Date

_____

Are you a teacher? ☐ A student? ☐
Your school's name

_____

Department

_____

Address   City   State   Zip

_____

School telephone #

_____

YOUR COMMENTS ARE IMPORTANT TO US!

Please fill in the following information:
For which course did you use this book?

_____

Did you use a text with this ANNUAL EDITION? ☐ yes ☐ no
What was the title of the text?

_____

What are your general reactions to the Annual Editions concept?

_____

Have you read any pertinent articles recently that you think should be included in the next edition? Explain.

_____

Are there any articles that you feel should be replaced in the next edition? Why?

_____

Are there any World Wide Web sites that you feel should be included in the next edition? Please annotate.

_____

May we contact you for editorial input? ☐ yes ☐ no
May we quote your comments? ☐ yes ☐ no